## What they said about *The Enemy Within*:

'Seumas Milne has subjected this story to one of the most remarkable demolition jobs ever committed to hard covers ... meticulously argued.' *Spectator*

'A real-life thriller which debunks the Robert Maxwell-organized smear against Arthur Scargill, Peter Heathfield and the miners' union.' *Evening Standard*

'Riveting. It knocks spots off the usual "whodunnit" ... It is not the role of MI5 to act as agents provocateurs, nor to plant newspaper reports ... The allegation about the use of GCHQ in the United Kingdom must be cleared up.' Merlyn Rees, former Home Secretary, *Guardian*

'Excellent ... Seumas Milne possesses reportorial skills and tenacities which ... will one day make him what he seems least to care about being – a famous and admired journalist ... an important, perhaps very important, book.' Christopher Hitchens, *London Review of Books*

'An astonishing book ... Milne's appalling story shows secret government in full and evil flower.' *The Nation* (US)

'Milne's book is a tribute to detailed journalistic investigation. It strips away the myths and lies about Scargill ... Milne rightly focuses on MI5.' *New Statesman & Society*

'When Stella Rimington was elevated to her present eminence, there were some who wondered why she had received such preferment. Now, courtesy of *The Enemy Within* ... we are beginning to have an inkling.' *Observer*

'This thriller-like book proves that, in the turmoil of conflict, lies possess more vigour than truth.' *Independent on Sunday*

'If the disturbing allegations in *The Enemy Within* ... are shown to be well-founded, Stella Rimington is not a fit person to run the security service and should be dismissed.' House of Commons motion signed by 50 MPs

'If you want to savour the tang of corruption, sense the odour of industrial decay and feel the steamy heat of class warfare, this is the book for you.' *Time Out*

'The most important exposé of contemporary political Britain I have read.' 'Journalism owes Seumas Milne a debt for elevating the craft of fine reporting ... above vicious untruth.' John Pilger, *New Statesman*

'Until Seumas Milne published this book, no one could have known the full extent of the treachery, deception and crude skulduggery that was practised by the establishment in its determination to secure the victory that it won ... Seumas Milne has written a major work ... He has told us how Britain is really governed.' Tony Benn, *Tribune*

'Seumas Milne meticulously strips away the thin veneer to reveal those who are truly unaccountable, corrupt and subversive.' Michael Mansfield QC

'If you like conspiracy theories, you'll love this book. It is on strong ground when it argues that Arthur Scargill ... was subject to a succession of smears ... in particular when he is tracing what happened to Russian donations to the miners' cause, Seumas Milne is entirely convincing.' *The Economist*

'A cracking story ... a stunning piece of work.' *Wakefield Express*

'This is a brilliant, thrilling but disturbing book ... Seumas Milne flinches at nothing. He has unravelled a spy thriller that makes Le Carré look superficial.' *Morning Star*

'This cannot be dismissed simply as the stuff of conspiracy theorists' dreams. It is indeed ... a most important exposé of contemporary political Britain.' *Gloucestershire Echo*

'Seumas Milne has produced a book to match any fictional best-seller. It has it all ... But the most disturbing aspect of *The Enemy Within* is that this is no work of fiction, but a meticulously researched piece of journalism.' *Bolton Evening News*

'*The Enemy Within* is compulsive reading and I recommend it wholeheartedly. Read it, analyse it and then tell your friends to read it.' *Camden New Journal*

'This book is a must.' *Scottish Trade Union Review*

'Dogged research and incontrovertible evidence.' *Stoke Evening Sentinel*

'Seumas Milne has written an important book, and a brave one.' *Socialist Review*

'*The Enemy Within* is a tribute to every NUM member and Women Against Pit Closures activist who has fought over the past decade to save pits and miners' jobs and to sustain mining communities.' *1995 NUM Annual Report*

'Part detective thriller and part political primer, *The Enemy Within* ... should be read by every trade unionist.' *NUCPS Journal*

'The definitive account of the strike – the best book on the Thatcher era.' Naomi Klein, author of *The Shock Doctrine*

**Seumas Milne** is a columnist and Associate Editor at the *Guardian* and the paper's former Comment Editor. He was previously the *Guardian*'s Labour Editor and a winner of the What the Papers Say Scoop of the Year Award. He studied economics and politics at Oxford and London universities and worked as a staff journalist on the *Economist*. He is the author of *The Revenge of History* and co-author of *Beyond the Casino Economy*.

# THE ENEMY WITHIN

*The Secret War Against the Miners*

◆

Fourth Edition

**SEUMAS MILNE**

**VERSO**
London • New York

This fourth edition paperback first published by Verso 2014
First published by Verso 1994
© Seumas Milne 1994, 1995, 2004, 2014

3 5 7 9 10 8 6 4 2

**Verso**
UK: 6 Meard Street, London W1F 0EG
US: 20 Jay Street, Suite 1010, Brooklyn, NY 11201
www.versobooks.com

Verso is the imprint of New Left Books

ISBN-13: 978-1-78168-342-2
eISBN-13: 978-1-78168-636-2 (UK)
eISBN-13: 978-1-78168-343-9 (US)


**British Library Cataloguing in Publication Data**
A catalogue record for this book is available from the British Library

**Library of Congress Cataloging-in-Publication Data**
A catalog record for this book is available from the Library of Congress

Typeset in Garamond by YHT Ltd., London
Printed and bound by CPI Group (UK) Ltd, Croydon, CR0 4YY

# CONTENTS

# CONTENTS

# PREFACE TO THE FOURTH EDITION

The aftershocks of the miners' strike of 1984–5 can still be felt in Britain thirty years later. The strike was without doubt a watershed in the country's postwar history. Indeed, it has had no real parallel – in size, duration and impact – anywhere in the world. It was the decisive domestic confrontation of the Thatcher years: a conflict which pitted the most powerful and politicized trade union in the country against a hard-right Conservative administration bent on class revenge and prepared to lay waste to the country's industrial heartlands and energy sector in the process, regardless of cost. It convulsed Britain, turned coalfield communities into occupied territory, and came far closer than was understood at the time to breaking the Thatcher government's onslaught on organized labour.

The year-long strike was a defensive battle to protect livelihoods and communities that the miners could not have avoided. But it was also a challenge to the destructive profit- and market-driven transformation of economic life already then in full flow. And it raised the alternative of a different kind of Britain, rooted in solidarity and collective action, against the individualism and private greed of the Thatcher years – symbolized by the wads of overtime cash her riot squads waved at the miners' picket lines.

A generation on, the market fundamentalism unleashed by Margaret Thatcher in the wake of the pit strike has had the ground cut from beneath it by the crisis of deregulated capitalism she championed – and not just in Britain, of course. For two decades after the country's miners ended their outright resistance to what became an untrammelled state assault, the legacy of Thatcher's shock therapy remained largely unchallenged at home, while the neoliberal order she trail-blazed reigned supreme across most of the world. In Britain, privatization, City and corporate deregulation, low taxes on the wealthy and labour flexibility became the order of the day – both under John Major and, with modifications, Tony Blair. With trade unions on their knees, wages stagnated and job insecurity spread, as profits and boardroom pay ballooned. Globally, the 'free market' Washington Consensus was barely contested throughout the 1990s.

The financial crash of 2008 and the epochal economic crisis it triggered discredited that orthodoxy, which was seen to have failed in the most spectacular and destructive fashion. A model of capitalism that Thatcher had borrowed from the Chilean dictator General Pinochet – and, along with Ronald Reagan, came to symbolize – was only rescued from collapse by the largest state intervention in history. That didn't stop governments across the western world, including David Cameron's Tory-led coalition in Britain, from using the crisis to try to reconstruct and entrench it further through austerity and yet more far-reaching privatization. But the neoliberal spell had been broken and the pressure for economic and social alternatives had begun in earnest.

Well before Thatcher's death, true believers were already alarmed at the collapse of their heroine's reputation. As the full costs of her financial free-for-all and industrial scorched earth policy became undeniable, the Tory London mayor Boris Johnson complained that the former prime minister's name had become a 'boo-word', a 'shorthand for selfishness and me-firstism'. Her one-time PR guru Maurice Saatchi fretted that 'her principles of capitalism are under question'. If only young people realized, the irreconcilables insisted, what a basket case Britain had been in the 1970s – the High Tory commentator Simon Heffer declared the country had felt like the Soviet bloc, as men with 'bad teeth and ill-fitting suits' (by which he meant union leaders) called the shots in public life – they would understand why millions had to lose their jobs, industries and communities had to be destroyed, and billions handed over to the wealthy. The more mainstream establishment view was that while Thatcher had taken harsh measures and 'gone too far', her medicine had been necessary to restore a sick economy to robust health.

In reality it did nothing of the sort. Average economic growth in the Thatcherite 1980s, at 2.4 per cent, was exactly the same as in the sick 1970s. It was lower again during the post-Thatcher 1990s, at 2.2 per cent, while in the corporatist 1960s it averaged over 3 per cent. Her government's savage deflation destroyed a fifth of Britain's industrial base in two years, created mass unemployment, hollowed out manufacturing, and delivered a productivity miracle that never was: productivity growth was also higher in the 1960s and went into sharp reverse under Cameron. And her deregulation of the City laid the basis for the financial crisis that engulfed us a quarter of a century later. (Even the free-market *Economist* conceded her reforms could be said to have 'sowed the seeds' of the crash.)

What she did succeed in doing was to redistribute from the poor to the rich, driving up profits and inequality, and slashing employees' share of national income through privatization, deregulation and her assault on trade unions. That's why it felt like a boom in better-off Britain, as the top rate of income tax was more than halved, while real incomes fell for the poorest 40 per cent in her first decade in power – and why the regal, state-sponsored funeral of a widely hated politician who had never won the votes of more than a third of the electorate provoked such revulsion across the country. As far as most people in Britain were concerned, polling showed, the attempt to rehabilitate her had failed.

Britain faced a structural crisis in the 1970s, but there were multiple routes out of it. Success for the miners in 1984–5 could not, of course, have turned the neoliberal tide by itself. That was a global phenomenon, which would soon afterwards engulf Soviet and East European communism, and draw hundreds of millions of educated, low-wage workers into the global capitalist market. But it would have at least seriously weakened Thatcher, reined in her government's worst excesses and put a brake on Labour's headlong rush for the 'third way' – which would eventually turn into New Labour and its embrace of the core Thatcher settlement.

In all likelihood, it would also have bolstered investment in clean coal technology. Instead, cutting edge research was abandoned, as the dispute's outcome helped shape a City and corporate-led future for the country.

Little of what was really at stake was reflected at the time in the mainstream media, which mostly portrayed the strike as an anti-democratic insurrection that defied economic logic – while the full coercive power and resources of the state were mobilized to crush the miners' defence of jobs and communities. The dispute's bitter outcome left both the National Union of Mineworkers and wider trade-union movement weakened and divided. Nevertheless, the miners continued to fight a dogged industrial rearguard action in the coalfields for the better part of the next decade. And the political establishment – from the government to the bulk of the media to Labour and union leaders who dreamed of a new era of 'social partnership' – never forgot the seriousness of the challenge posed by the NUM in both the 1970s and 1980s, nor lost an opportunity to rubbish the 1984–5 strike and its leadership. That 'received wisdom' of myths and half-truths about the strike and its supposedly inevitable defeat seeped into the thinking of many labour-movement activists in the years that followed and helped limit their sense of the possible.

But in the wake of the political crisis over Tory pit closures in 1992, there was something of a sea change in popular attitudes towards the confrontation of the mid-1980s. The realization that the Thatcher government really had been intent on the destruction of the coal industry – as the NUM President Arthur Scargill had warned to accusations of demagogic scaremongering – cast a new light on the miners' determined endurance. Films such as *Billy Elliot* and *Brassed Off* rammed home the devastation of the mining areas wrought by the politically driven closures. A new generation of anti-corporate activists was able to identify with those who had confronted a violent, militarized police invasion of their communities a decade earlier. Meanwhile, labour-movement anger at the indulgence shown by police and oil companies to the fuel-tax blockades by self-employed farmers and truckers in the autumn of 2000 (including hauliers who had once rampaged through NUM pickets) was heightened by the contrast with the treatment that had been meted out to the miners. Blair's deputy prime minister, John Prescott, reminded delegates at the Labour conference a few weeks later that the coalfield communities had been 'destroyed by the prejudice of the Thatcher regime'.

That by then reflected a dominant strain of public opinion, which had been sharply divided at the time of the strike itself. But with the emergence of a new generation of left-wing trade-union officials during Tony Blair's second term in office, the old demonology of 1984–5 returned to national politics. As a firefighters' dispute with the New Labour government came to a head in 2002, the prime minister branded their leaders 'Scargillite' and insisted, in full jaw-jutting Thatcher revivalist mode, that there would be no return to 'those days'. In reality, neither the dispute nor the firefighters' leaders bore much resemblance to the miners' strike or NUM president. But by making the link, Blair hoped to raise the spectre of a return of militant trade unionism and cast the firefighters' cause as an illegitimate throwback.

In an era of weak unions, overweening employers and rampant job insecurity, that was never likely to cut much ice. But two decades after the 1984–5 strike, the hostile propaganda and fantasy that became so familiar during the year-long confrontation came flooding back in retrospective press and television coverage. Once again, we were in a world where miners' flying pickets were 'storm troopers' and 'hit squads' and their leaders' tactics a 'blitzkrieg' (all terms used in the commentary on a Channel Four television documentary about the strike, *When Britain Went to War*, broadcast in 2004); where Arthur Scargill, not Margaret Thatcher, was to blame for the shutdown of the coal industry and the hardships of the miners (who bafflingly still elected and re-elected him); where the miners' cause was 'futile' – but would nevertheless have surely been won if only the NUM leadership had called a national ballot or strikers had not fought running battles with strikebreakers and the police. It was the same story at the time of the twenty-fifth anniversary. From Thatcher's close ally Norman Tebbit, who recalled the strike as a 'war on democracy', to the former Labour leader Neil Kinnock, who was still denouncing the miners' leaders' 'madness', to the BBC broadcaster Andrew Marr, who blamed Scargill's 'incompetence' for coal's early demise, an Alice-in-Wonderland consensus stretched across the media mainstream. The strike had caused the breakneck rundown of mining, they all agreed against the evidence, not the government that ordered it.

It is a measure of the enduring impact of the miners' sacrifice and the potential power of radical trade unionism – even in a very different industrial and economic context – that, a generation after the event, it is still felt necessary to paint the strike as a dismal morality tale and its leadership as the epitome of megalomaniacal self-delusion. In the years immediately after the dispute, when British coal continued to generate 80 per cent of the country's electricity, that determination to bury the miners' leaders' reputation once and for all was of course much sharper. This was the context of the extraordinary campaign of corruption allegations against the NUM leadership – based on the events of the strike – which first led me to write this book.

Launched by the *Daily Mirror* and the popular *Cook Report* television programme in the spring of 1990, it was a scandal that attracted intense national newspaper and broadcasting coverage for the better part of a year, led to a dozen legal actions and investigations, and cost the NUM hundreds of thousands of pounds. Partly as a result, the miners and their union were immobilized while the Conservative government prepared for the final rundown and privatization of the coal industry. For a time, speculation was rife that the NUM president, leader of Britain's most important postwar strike, would be forced out of his job or even end up in jail.

When the first set of 'revelations' was published in the *Daily Mirror* on 5 March 1990, it seemed incredible that the authors of what was billed as an exhaustive investigation, backed up by so many apparently independent witnesses, could have simply got it all wrong. But, as I reported the controversy for the *Guardian*, it became increasingly obvious that the real story was not at all what I and others had at first imagined – still less what had been printed in the *Mirror* or broadcast on Central Television. And as the allegations unravelled and the court cases and investigations collapsed, glimpses of what in fact lay behind the affair began to emerge: of dirty tricks, agents provocateurs, surveillance operations, political manipulation and diplomatic deception, and the devastating lengths to which the security services were prepared to go in the war against the NUM, both during and after the 1984–5 strike. This is the story I tried to tell in these pages.

Since the first edition of the book was published in 1994 under the title *The Enemy Within: MI5, Maxwell and the Scargill Affair* – and an accompanying documentary, *Spy in the Camp*, broadcast by Channel Four television – more has emerged about the covert methods used against the NUM and other trade unions; formerly secret cabinet papers have thrown new light on the Thatcher government's plans to break the miners' union, with troops if necessary, drawn up before and after the strike; the principal accuser of the miners' leaders in the 1990 scandal was repeatedly found by the French courts to have lied and himself signed documents he claimed were forged by Scargill (and the judgments enforced in England); the *Mirror* conceded that its original allegations had 'falsely smeared' Scargill's reputation; and fifty MPs called for a public inquiry into security service operations against the miners' union. On the basis of the allegations set out here and in the Channel Four film, the parliamentarians declared at the time, Stella Rimington should be sacked as head of MI5.

Instead, she retired two years later and glided effortlessly into a new role as a corporate non-executive director, dining off the system her organization had spent so many years working to protect – and later turning her hand to writing spy fiction. But in 2001, Rimington herself ran into trouble with the secret state for publishing a book of heavily filleted memoirs. Her successor as head of MI5, Stephen Lander, was particularly insistent on deleting passages about the 1984–5 miners' strike. She did at least publicly confirm for the first time – as earlier laid out in this book – her own role during the strike and MI5's targeting of Scargill and other NUM leaders, while attempting to pass the buck for the most controversial operations to police Special Branch. But the experience of coming into conflict with the Whitehall security machine also appeared to bring out the former spy's inner civil libertarian: she attacked New Labour for undermining civil rights, warned it was playing into the hands of terrorists by fuelling fear of a 'police state', criticized the US over torture (while insisting MI5 'doesn't do that') and called for greater oversight of the intelligence services.

Meanwhile, the MI5 whistleblower David Shayler revealed that while working for the security service he had seen part of Scargill's personal file, which made clear there had been at least one agent operating at a senior level in the NUM national office during the 1984–5 strike. Former senior police officers also claimed Special Branch had had a high-level agent in Scargill's office who helped 'beat the strike'. As the Cold War has receded into history, veterans of the secret state have been increasingly prepared to yield up a little bit more of their seedy, anti-democratic world: the mass blacklisting of activists, the use of agents and informers at all levels of the labour movement, the destabilization and undermining of strikes, and the betrayal of their members by trade-union leaders who secretly worked for the security services. A retired police Special Branch officer told the BBC *True Spies* programme in 2002 that one of his covert sources inside the miners' union during the 1970s had been none other than its then president: the bluff 'moderate' Joe Gormley.

Neither the security services nor their political masters have ever been called to account for any of these abuses of power. But given that MI5 has never even been held accountable for the fact that a faction in the agency plotted to bring down Harold Wilson's Labour government in the 1970s, perhaps that should come as no surprise. Rimington insisted when she was the security service's director general, both in public and private, that the plot against Wilson had been a figment of the former MI5 assistant director Peter Wright's imagination (the more recent MI5 authorized history does so as well). However, as Lord Hunt, the cabinet secretary during Wilson's second administration, was prepared to concede in 1996: 'There is absolutely no doubt at all that a few malcontents in MI5 . . . were spreading damaging and malicious stories about some members of that Labour government'. That was also acknowledged in private by Stephen Lander during his time as head of the security service. But no external body has ever investigated what, by any measure, was a genuinely subversive conspiracy against democratic government.

In fact, MI5 has flourished unchecked since the end of the Cold War, despite the decline of its old enemies on the left and in the unions and the impact of the peace process in Northern Ireland. From Soviet spies, the IRA and assorted 'subversives', the security service moved seamlessly on to target radical Islamist groups and, in the aftermath of the attacks on New York and Washington in 2001, to a central role in the British front of the US 'war on terror'. Far from living under the shadow of its murky past, MI5 has more than doubled in size, given a new veneer of public credibility by the sense that its agents are now working to prevent atrocities, instead of bugging political activists and infiltrating trade unions. Glamorised beyond parody in fictional portrayals such as the TV drama *Spooks*, MI5's usually unverifiable pronouncements on its own activities and supposed triumphs are routinely relayed by the media as fact.

But the scale of deception and misinformation about non-existent weapons of mass destruction provided by the intelligence services to justify the US–British invasion of Iraq in 2003 was a brutal reminder of the secret agencies' long record of unreliability and political manipulation. Both MI5 and MI6 have since played a central role in the imprisonment without trial of Islamist terror suspects, as evidence has piled up of their deep complicity in state kidnapping and outsourced torture, from Bagram to Guantánamo and Pakistan to Morocco. And despite one police and judicial inquiry after another, they have yet to be held to account for such rampant illegality and abuse of power, which itself fuels the threat they are supposed to be fighting. The system of legal and parliamentary oversight of the intelligence agencies established in the 1990s has proved to be barely cosmetic.

Meanwhile, a good part of MI5's 'counter-subversion work' – which the security service itself claims to have abandoned – has been absorbed by the police, both in the form of the Special Branch and newer outfits such as the National Domestic Extremism Unit and the National Public Order Intelligence Unit (both originally under the control of the opaque and unaccountable Association of Chief Police Officers). They have already become notorious for the infiltration of undercover agents and agents provocateurs into environmental, animal rights, anti-racist and other protest groups, as well as for disinformation campaigns, while evidence has grown of systematic Special Branch collaboration with private corporations to blacklist trade unionists.

Of course, the global blanket surveillance of mobile phone, email and internet traffic by the US National Security Agency and Britain's GCHQ – revealed by the NSA whistleblower Edward Snowden in 2013 – is on another scale entirely from the then unprecedented operations they carried out against the British miners' union and its international solidarity network in 1984–5. Both agencies were founded to spy on the rest of the world, but have ended up targeting their own people without effective restraint, hand in glove with a roll call of household-name global corporations. And by providing intelligence for drone attacks that have killed thousands of civilians in Pakistan, Afghanistan, Yemen and Somalia, the NSA and GCHQ are, like their sister spying outfits, spreading the terror they are supposed to be making war on. In reality, all these state espionage agencies are instruments of both domestic and global power, operating far beyond the world of terrorism. And despite the fig leaf of a latter-day British legal framework, parliamentary trusties' committees and ministerial rubber stamps, their effective accountability has scarcely advanced in thirty years.

In retrospect, the 1990 intelligence-inspired smear campaign against Arthur Scargill and the NUM appears almost a classic of its kind. Its pattern was uncannily echoed immediately after the Iraq war in the barrage of allegations launched against the leading anti-war Labour MP George Galloway. By chance, I had seen Galloway on the first day of the media campaign against Scargill in March 1990 and found him, unlike others on the left at the time, convinced from the start that the allegations of corruption against the miners' leaders were false. Thirteen years later, within days of the capture of Baghdad by US forces, Galloway

himself stood accused of taking £375,000 a year in secret payments from Saddam Hussein, on the basis of documents allegedly
found by a *Daily Telegraph* reporter in the burned-out shell of
the Iraqi foreign ministry building. As in the Scargill case, the
original funding claims, vociferously denied by Galloway, opened
the floodgates to a relentless media onslaught, in which it seemed
that almost any accusation, however outlandish, could be made
with impunity. The *Telegraph*, which hoped its story would help
discredit the biggest protest movement in British history, joined
the *Sun* in denouncing the left-wing MP as a traitor and even suggested the death penalty might be appropriate.

As with the NUM smear campaign, the original newspaper
charges triggered a string of other investigations, including by
the charity commission and the parliamentary commissioner for
standards, into Galloway's anti-sanctions Mariam Appeal, while
the Scottish MP was suspended, and later expelled, from the
Labour Party for the ferocity of his attacks on Bush and Blair
over the war. Following the Scargill precedent, there was even
a walk-on role for Galloway's former driver – who by his own
account attempted to defraud an insurance company over the
hire of the MP's car – to make some suitably lurid allegations. In
contrast to the 1990 case, however, Galloway sued the *Telegraph*
for libel, though initially that had little impact on the wider
campaign. What seemed to bring it to a halt was a humiliating
apology (and substantial bill for damages) from the US-owned
*Christian Science Monitor* after its own tale of multimillion Iraqi
payments to Galloway proved to have been based on forged documents. Another set of papers purporting to show Iraqi payments
to Galloway had already been exposed as forgeries by the *Mail on
Sunday*.

By the autumn of 2003, the *Telegraph* (whose former owner
Lord Conrad Black was by now being sued by his own company
for unauthorized 'executive payments') was no longer claiming
its original allegations were actually true, but simply pleading
its right to report its documents in the public interest. Roy
Greenslade, the *Mirror* editor who had published the false allegations about Arthur Scargill in 1990 and apologized to him in print

over the stories twelve years later, speculated about a common link with the intelligence services: 'The similarities between the Scargill and Galloway cases are so pronounced it's impossible not to believe that the next stage in the Galloway saga', he wrote in the *Guardian*, 'will eventually end up echoing the Scargill affair.'

The following year, Galloway duly won his libel action against the Telegraph, which was ordered by the High Court to pay £150,000 in damages and costs of close to £2 million. Soon afterwards, he took the East London seat of Bethnal Green from New Labour at the 2005 general election as leader of Respect – the first parliamentary victory for a left-of-Labour candidate in England since 1945. The same month Galloway turned the tables on a US Senate committee in Washington – which claimed he had been given 'oil allocations' by the former Iraqi government – in a performance reported by the *New York Post* as 'Brit Fries Senators in Oil'. By 2007, the former *Telegraph* owner Lord Black had been jailed for fraud (a fate that would have almost certainly befallen Robert Maxwell, the *Mirror*'s owner in 1990, if he hadn't died the following year). The case against Galloway at Westminster had meanwhile been scaled back still further to complaints that donations to his anti-sanctions campaign had come from an Arab businessman trading with the Iraqi government – though the parliamentary standards commissioner conceded there was no evidence the MP had benefited personally. And whatever damage had been done to Galloway by such a ferocious campaign, it didn't stop him winning a 2012 parliamentary by-election in Bradford with one of the largest electoral swings in British electoral history. Scepticism in the ant-war movement over the accusations against Galloway from the start perhaps partly reflected the lessons some had learned a decade earlier about how the powers-that-be seek to punish those who take their opposition beyond acceptable limits.

As for Britain's coal industry, after forty-eight years in public ownership most of what was left of it was sold in 1994 to Richard Budge, an entrepreneur identified in a confidential report to government as 'unfit to be concerned in the management of a company'. But he and other private coal-owners nevertheless still found it profitable enough to reopen more than a dozen collieries the government and British Coal had insisted were 'uneconomic'. Budge was ousted in 2001 as chief executive of what was by then UK Coal (and declared bankrupt twelve years later), the biggest player in what had become the privatized shadow of a once great industry, employing a few thousand in a handful of deep mines.

More than a decade later, coal still accounted for well over a third of Britain's electricity generation, but the bulk of that was now imported from countries such as Russia, Colombia and the US. By 2013, UK Coal – now renamed Coalfield Resources – had been reduced to a couple of pits and a property business, saved from collapse by government intervention. The argument about coal is now dominated by the threat of global warming and the need for rapid reductions in carbon emissions, rather than the small workforce still mining it in Britain. Paradoxically, the destruction of the publicly owned industry played an especially damaging role in holding back the development of clean coal technology and carbon capture and storage, in which Britain led the world until Major's government closed the Coal Research Establishment in Cheltenham at the time of privatisation. So the country has been left dependent on foreign energy imports and high-carbon-emitting power stations – many of which will be forced to close – while China and other states are at the cutting edge of green technology investment.

But the battle over coal in the 1980s was in any case about power and class, not fuel – just as the arguments about the legacy of the miners' strike are as much about the future as the past. The social scars left by the closure of the vast bulk of the industry can be seen across Britain's former mining areas, in levels of unemployment and deprivation mostly far above the national average. Estimates of the full economic cost of the war on the miners – including those of the 1984–5 strike, pit closures, redundancy payments, as well as the wider economic and welfare costs – run to more than £37 billion at 2012 prices. That war, it is now evident, was an act not only of political revenge, but also of national vandalism. A generation on, the economic and social rationality of the miners' resistance could not be clearer, while the self-serving attacks on the NUM and its leaders that became common in parts of the labour movement in the years after the dispute ring increasingly hollow. The industrial and political conditions that gave rise to the 1984–5 strike, along with the miners' victories of the early 1970s, will never recur in that particular form. But as the economic order that Thatcher helped build has foundered, the message of the miners' struggle can speak to our times – and both its lessons and example will be an inspiration long into the future.

*The Enemy Within* was first published in 1994 and has remained in print, through several editions, ever since. For this new edition I have tried to bring the original text up to date and have expanded the postscript to take account of later developments. I am indebted to a large number of people who originally agreed to talk to me and provide information – both on and off the record, directly and indirectly – in the preparation of *The Enemy Within* and since the publication of the first edition. Wherever possible, I have named sources. But clearly with a subject of this kind, some informants have to remain anonymous. There are those who regard that as an intolerable weakness. When the *Guardian* published details of the first leaks from GCHQ about operations against Scargill and the miners, Joe Haines – Harold Wilson's former press secretary and retired confidant of Robert Maxwell – denounced us for using 'unnamed intelligence sources'. The proof of the pudding, however, is in the eating. Since that time, many of the key allegations made by our informants have been corroborated. And, in the case of the intelligence services, to reject the use of unnamed sources is in practice to provide a permanent cover for the abuse of unaccountable power.

A large part of what appears here has never been published elsewhere. I have had unprecedented access to people and documents – such as those held in Tripoli, Moscow and at the International Energy and Miners' Organization in Paris – associated with these events. I have also been able to draw on discussions with many others in the course of researching and writing about the miners, the coal industry and the British and international trade-union movement. At the *Guardian*, Richard Norton-Taylor and Paul Brown played an essential role in getting this story off the ground. I also had valued help from Keith Harper, Jonathan Steele – who got hold of the Soviet Communist Party Central Committee records in Moscow – Simon Beavis, Simon Bowers, Victoria Brittain, Rob Evans, Georgina Henry, Paul Johnson, Nick Pandya, Nick Richmond, Katy Stoddard, Katharine Viner and the *Guardian* library staff.

In 1994, I benefited from collaboration with Oliver Wilson, Callum Macrae, Ray Fitzwalter and Kimi Zabihyan of Observer Films in the development and production of the Channel Four *Dispatches* programme based on the research in this book, and I have drawn on extensive interviews by Oliver Wilson and Callum Macrae. The transcripts of Lorraine Heggessey's interviews for the 1991 *Dispatches* film about the *Mirror–Cook Report* allegations also proved extremely useful: thanks to Ken Loach, Ian Pollard and Lorraine Heggessey. Ian Pollard carried out research in the summer of 1993 for Chapter 4 of *The Enemy Within*.

From the NUM, particular thanks are due to Arthur Scargill and Nell Myers, who both gave generously of their time to answer questions and provide essential information during a period when they and the union were under immense pressure as a result of the pit-closures crisis, and have continued to do so in the years since. Peter Heathfield was also very helpful, as were Margaret Fellows, Ken Hollingsworth, Tyrone O'Sullivan, Henry Richardson, Hazel Riley, Simon Pirani and Ian White. At the IEMO (or IMO, as it was), Alain Simon, Michelle Simon and Madjid Cherikh repeatedly put themselves out to deal with my queries. Former NUM employees who talked to me include Hilary Cave, Mick Clapham, Dave Feickert, Kim Howells, Stephen Hudson and Jim Parker.

Among others I spoke to, or who provided help or information, before or since the first edition of *The Enemy Within*, are Altaf Abbasi, Ray Alderson, Vic Allen, Jeff Apter, Peter Archer, Miles Barter, Tony Benn, Rodney Bickerstaffe, John Booth, Damian Brown, Doug Bulmer, Sarah Burton, Ken Cameron, Ken Capstick, Pete Carter, Tony Cooper, Tam Dalyell, Vera Derer, Vladimir Derer, Steve Dorril, Jimmy Douglas, Clive Entwistle, Kenny Farquharson, Paul Foot, George Galloway, Ken Gill,

Geoffrey Goodman, Mick Gosling, Roy Greenslade, John Hendy, Mark Hollingsworth, Jimmy Hood, Kelvin Hopkins, Gareth Howells, Eric Hunt, Salem Ibrahim, Barry Johnson, Nicholas Jones, Angela Kelly, Stephen Lander, Lawrence Lustgarten, Annie Machon, Peter McNestry, Kevin Maguire, John Maitland, Mike Marqusee, Cathy Massiter, Anatoli Mikhailyov, Alasdair Milne, Andrew Murray, Jim Neilson, Daniel Ojij, Stuart Oliver, Dave Osler, Joe Owens, Terry Pattinson, John Pilger, Alan Ramsay, Robin Ramsay, Frank Redman, Stella Rimington, Robbie Robison, Sue Rolstone, David Rosenberg, Anne Scargill, Geoff Seed, Michael Selfert, David Seymour, David Shayler, Mike Simons, Victor Shonfield, Dennis Skinner, Tom Sibley, Bill Sirs, Ken Smith, Phil Turner, Frank Watters, Granville Williams, Pete Willsman, Bob Wylie and Mustapha Zakari. Thanks also to the staff at the *Sheffield Star* library and Bathgate public library in West Lothian.

Roger Windsor was the only person who refused to be interviewed for *The Enemy Within*, or to answer written questions. I have, however, spoken to him at length on several occasions over the years. I have also been able to draw on unpublished articles he has written and the wide-ranging, largely unbroadcast, interviews he gave to Lorraine Heggessey and Callum Macrae for Channel Four in 1991 and 1994.

I have had generous legal advice and assistance, at different stages of the book's production, from Andrew Nicol; Mark Stephens, Nikki Keat and Peter Woods at Stephens Innocent; Michael Seifert; Gareth Peirce; John Hendy; Sarah Burton; Robin Lewis; and Anthony Hudson. Their help has been much appreciated.

The same goes for the support offered by the many people who have contacted me since the book was first published – and then took on a life of its own, from featuring in the BBC TV drama series *New Tricks* to providing source material for David Peace's miners' strike novel, *GB 84*. And the efforts of George Galloway, Tam Dalyell, Max Madden and others in the House of Commons to keep the issues raised in the book on the parliamentary agenda were exemplary.

Ronan Bennett, Faith Evans, Kirsty Milne, Andrew Murray, Colin Robinson and Michael Seifert read various drafts of the book and made valuable suggestions and criticisms. Thanks also to my agent, Faith Evans, for all her other efforts. At Verso, for the original hardback edition, Colin Robinson gave unstinting support throughout, and Isobel Rorison, Dusty Miller, Robin Blackburn, Perry Anderson, Lucy Heller, Anna Del Nevo and Monica Ali contributed in essential ways to making sure the book actually appeared – and was then in enough demand to be reprinted twice in as many months. I'm also grateful to Lucy Morton and Robin Gable, who copyedited the original manuscript at breakneck speed, and Leigh Priest, who prepared the original index. At Macmillan, I had great enthusiasm and practical back-up from William Armstrong, Claire Evans and Jonathan Riley for the second, paperback edition. For the third edition, published in 2004, thanks to Tariq Ali, John Pilger, Jane Hindle, Tim Clark, Andrea Woodman and Gavin Everall. For this edition, thanks to Leo Hollis, Rowan Wilson, Mark Martin, Angelica Sgouros, Jennifer Tighe and Sarah Shin. They have all been very tolerant – though not half as much as Cristina, Anna Aurora and Patch, for whom a special thanks.

*Seumas Milne*
*December 2013*

# THE SECRET WAR AGAINST THE MINERS

> Never underestimate the British establishment's ruthless
> determination to destroy its enemies. *Roy Hattersley,*
> *former Labour Party deputy leader, 1993*[1]

In the spring of 1990, Arthur Scargill received an unexpected phone call at his Sheffield headquarters. Miles Copeland, a retired senior CIA officer and latter-day intelligence pundit, was anxious to speak to the embattled miners' leader. It was only a couple of days since the launch of one of the most savage media and legal campaigns against a public figure in Britain in recent times. The National Union of Mineworkers' president, the country's best-known trade unionist and unrepentant class warrior, stood accused of flagrant embezzlement and corruption. The man described even by opponents as 'ferociously principled' was said to have lined his pockets with hardship funds intended for striking miners, and salted away millions of pounds secretly procured from the Soviet Union and Colonel Gaddafi's Libya. Peter Heathfield, the union's general secretary, faced similar charges. The allegations were becoming daily more outlandish. Scargill had demanded not only cash from Gaddafi, it was claimed, but guns. With Robert Maxwell's Daily Mirror as cheerleader, Scargill's enemies crowed for his head. Some predicted he would be in jail by Christmas. What had erupted in the tabloid press and on prime-time television was being enthusiastically seized on by hostile trade-union leaders and politicians from both Tory and Labour parties, with calls for criminal prosecutions and public inquiries. Sir Geoffrey Howe, the Deputy Prime Minister, announced in the House of Commons that the police stood ready to act.[2]

Scargill was on nodding terms with Copeland – better known to some as father of the drummer in the rock band The Police. The two men had met informally on a couple of occasions in television chat-show studios. But this time, the American dispensed with hospitality-room small talk and came brutally to the point. 'I don't like your views, Mr Scargill, and I never have,' he said, 'but I don't agree with the way you're being treated. You are being set up.' Copeland had made repeated attempts to track down the miners' leader, even calling the NUM's barrister, John Hendy QC, at his Lincoln's Inn chambers in London, to leave an urgent message. Now he explained why. The former CIA man warned Scargill and Heathfield – who listened in to the discussion on a conference phone – that he had reliable information that both the domestic security service, MI5, and the CIA had been closely involved in kick-starting the media campaign. They had, Copeland said, in different ways helped to frame the corruption allegations against the miners' leadership. However, he refused to expand on his remarks and promptly disappeared into the ether. Copeland was well known to have maintained close connections with the CIA's powerful London station after his retirement. Whether the crusty old spy was genuinely drawing on inside knowledge or instead relying on informed guesswork – or whether he simply wanted to fuel the NUM president's growing paranoia – must remain a matter for speculation. Copeland died shortly afterwards. Nonetheless, as the scandal-mongering onslaught against Scargill and Heathfield unfolded over subsequent months, and as each allegation was knocked down only to be replaced by another, evidence of the deep involvement of the intelligence services – among others – in the web of intrigue around what the *Daily Mirror* christened the 'Scargill Affair' relentlessly built up.[3]

The central allegation made by the *Daily Mirror* and Central Television's *Cook Report* against the miners' leader – that he used Libyan hardship donations to pay off his mortgage during the

1984–5 miners' strike – was in fact entirely false and demonstrated to be so within a few months. Not only did Scargill have no mortgage to pay off, but – as the evidence in this book now shows – the money identified as having been used for the phantasmic mortgage transaction never came from Libya at all. Indeed, the question of who did in fact advance that cash provides a key to explaining what lay behind the whole canard. The second main accusation, which the *Mirror* and *Cook Report* fell back on once the first had disintegrated on the most cursory examination, was that Scargill had diverted a sum amounting to between one million dollars and ten million pounds, donated by Soviet miners, to a secret trust fund to further his personal political ambitions. That claim, too, was eventually shown to be wrong in almost all its details. The story ran on regardless. Facts were never allowed to get seriously in the way of a campaign that commanded such powerful support and offered the chance to destroy once and for all the symbol of militant class trade unionism that Scargill obstinately remained.[4]

But it was not until disaffected employees at the government's GCHQ electronic spying headquarters began to leak information about intelligence and secret-service dirty-tricks operations against the NUM to the *Guardian* in the winter of 1990–1 that the full extent of the secret war against Britain's miners started to become clear. Margaret Thatcher personally authorized a 'Get Scargill' campaign both during and after the 1984–5 strike, the GCHQ whistleblowers alleged, which was coordinated and run by MI5. She had also, they said, bent her government's own rules and ordered an unprecedented mobilization of British and American electronic surveillance networks to underpin the anti-NUM operations. Our informants provided details of the large-scale misuse of GCHQ and its outstations in Britain, co-sponsored and co-financed by the US National Security Agency, to track the activities of NUM officials and the movement of the miners' funds around the European banking system. Action by the security service to discredit Scargill had, they said, led to abortive attempts to implicate him in the theft of phoney cash deposits of hundreds of thousands of pounds. The GCHQ moles also confirmed Copeland's claim that there had been a direct intelligence input into the 1990 Maxwell-funded media campaign against the miners' leadership.

Nothing like this had ever before emerged about security-service operations against domestic 'subversives' – the catch-all term still used by the British government to target those active in campaigns for radical social or political change. Gradually, one part of the GCHQ eavesdroppers' story after another was corroborated, and the pieces of a remarkable jigsaw started to fit together. There was, however, plenty more to come. In December 1991, almost exactly a year after the original GCHQ material was passed to the *Guardian*, Stella Rimington became the first director-general of MI5 whose appointment would be publicly disclosed by the most secretive government bureaucracy in the Western world. But within twenty-four hours of the announcement, as the government preened itself over its unaccustomed glasnost and equal-opportunities policies for eminent spies, less palatable aspects of the new chief state-security mandarin's career emerged.

Stella Rimington was not, it transpired, quite the 'new face of the service' portrayed in official briefings. Climbing her way up MI5's greasy promotion pole, she had headed the department in charge of 'monitoring' the trade-union movement at the time of its greatest industrial conflict with the Thatcher government. In that job, she had played the central role in MI5 operations against the 1984–5 miners' strike – which, it was already becoming clear, had been the dirtiest outside the Northern Ireland conflict since the war. A House of Commons motion calling for a statement on her activities – and linking her with David Hart, the right-wing adviser to Margaret Thatcher, Michael Portillo and Malcolm Rifkind, who helped organize the 'back-to-work movement' during the strike – was tabled by the well-connected dissenting Labour MP, Tam Dalyell. His demand was given added credibility by public support from the former Labour Home Secretary, Merlyn Rees, himself the Cabinet minister technically in charge of MI5 in the late 1970s, and the ex-Solicitor General, Peter Archer. The motion needled bureaucratic wounds, already inflamed by MI5's predatory encroachments on police territory. A few weeks later, on the basis of briefings from two separate high-level Whitehall sources, Dalyell returned to parliament with an even more startling claim. Roger Windsor – the NUM's chief executive during and after the miners' strike, and the main source for the allegations made by the *Daily Mirror* and the *Cook Report* against Scargill in 1990 – had also been 'involved' with Stella Rimington and MI5, the MP alleged on the floor of the House. Dalyell's Whitehall 'deep throats' continued to drip-feed him with further details and by the summer of 1993, Dalyell, George Galloway and a group of other Labour MPs were prepared to abandon the earlier euphemisms. Windsor was named in a Commons motion as an MI5 agent sent into the NUM by Stella Rimington to 'destabilize and sabotage' the union. The new secret-service boss had 'subverted democratic liberties', the MPs charged, and should be brought to account.[5]

Taken together with an accumulation of other evidence, allegations and persistent leaks, it has now become apparent that the 1990 attack against the miners' leaders – and Scargill in particular – was the product of the single most ambitious 'counter-subversion' operation ever mounted in Britain. This was a covert campaign which reached its apogee during the 1984–5 strike, but continued long afterwards. In its breach of what had long been seen as the established rules of the political game, it went beyond even the propaganda, policing and industrial effort openly deployed by the government to destroy the country's most powerful trade union. As far as the Thatcherite faction in the Cabinet and their supporters in the security services were concerned, the NUM under Scargill's stewardship was the most serious domestic threat to state security in modern times. And they showed themselves prepared to encourage any and every method available – from the secret financing of strikebreakers to mass electronic surveillance, from the manipulation of agents provocateurs to attempts to 'fit up' miners' officials – in order to undermine or discredit the union and its leaders. It is a record of the abuse of unaccountable power which would later return to haunt both those who pulled the strings and those who carried out the orders.

## A TWENTY-YEAR VENDETTA

The secret war against the miners was the hidden counterpart to the open struggle by successive Tory governments against the NUM, a struggle which helped shape the course of British politics over two decades. The extraordinary nature of the covert operations against the miners' leaders only makes sense when seen in the context of the long-run determination of the Tory Party – and of Margaret Thatcher above all – to avenge absolutely and unequivocally their double humiliation at the hands of the miners in the historic strikes of 1972 and 1974. The problem of how to 'deal' with the miners and their recalcitrant leadership became one of the great obsessions of Conservative political life.

Confrontations between Tory administrations and the miners, for many years the most politicized and strategically important section of the country's workforce, punctuated British twentieth-century history at its moments of greatest domestic political and industrial stress: 1926, 1972–4 and 1984–5. And just as the betrayal and defeat of the miners in 1926 remained a festering wound in mining communities for a generation or more, so in more recent times it was the shattering experience for the Tory Party of the two pit strikes of the early 1970s which laid the ground for what became a twenty-year vendetta against the miners: a single-minded and ruthless drive to destroy the NUM and, if necessary, the bulk of the British coal industry in the process.

As one labour-movement observer commented in the early stages of the 1984–5 strike, Britain's ruling class 'has its folk memories, too, and miners emerging from the bowels of the earth to demand their rights touch a raw nerve'. The visceral Tory fear of the 'black avenging host', as Émile Zola described insurgent miners in *Germinal*, proved perfectly rational. After years of suffering heavy pit closures and declining relative pay under a right-wing corporatist leadership, the miners became in the early 1970s the cutting edge of a new working-class assertiveness. The decisive battle of the 1972 strike – when miners' flying pickets led by Scargill and others, with the support of 10,000 striking engineering workers, closed the Saltley coke depot in Birmingham, and clinched the strike victory – sent panic waves throughout the political and administrative establishment. The dispute of 1974, which led to a three-day week, precipitated a general election and brought about the defeat of the Heath government, was if anything even more devastating for the Conservative Party.[6]

The NUM's dramatic successes were, of course, part of the wider conflict between the state and organized labour which came to dominate British politics from the late 1960s until well into the Thatcher years. As the British economy's relative decline progressively narrowed the scope for accommodating working-class demands, the clashes with both Tory and Labour governments became sharper: first over Barbara Castle's efforts to bring the unions to heel with her abortive 'In Place of Strife' proposals, then in the successful resistance to Edward Heath's anti-union Industrial Relations Act, then in the breakdown of Jim Callaghan's attempts to cut real wages in the 'Winter of Discontent'. The Tories returned to power in 1979 determined to break the back of the entire trade-union movement. The NUM was not the only powerful union in the establishment's sights – the giant Transport and General Workers' Union, with its hold on the docks and road transport, for example, was also singled out for special treatment during the Thatcher years. But the NUM's unique industrial position, its unmatched radicalization, and the Conservative Party's spectacular humbling at the miners' hands left little question as to which union would become the new government's most important target.

There was none more single-minded in the pursuit of political revenge against the miners than Margaret Thatcher, one of only two Cabinet ministers during the coal dispute of 1974 to oppose Heath's decision to call a general election. As her biographer, Hugo Young, puts it:

> No name was scarred more deeply on the Conservative soul than that of the NUM. For Margaret Thatcher the miners were where she came in. If they hadn't humiliated the Heath government into fighting an election which it lost, she would not now be party leader and prime minister. But this mattered less than the memory of that bloody defeat itself, and the apprehension that it might always be capable of happening again.

In 1981, a few months before Scargill was elected NUM president with a majority of more than 100,000 votes, Thatcher had herself been compelled to back down in the face of spontaneous strikes which erupted across the coalfields against the threat of large-scale pit closures. Peter Walker, Energy Secretary during the 1984–5 strike, remembered the 1981 climbdown as being 'scorched' on Thatcher's mind. But as Mick McGahey, the NUM's vice-president, predicted at the time, it was 'not so much a U-turn, more a body swerve'.[7]

Serious thinking about how to settle the coal question for good had begun during the 1973 oil crisis, at a time when the pre-1974-strike overtime ban was already in force. Wilfred Miron, a Coal Board member, prepared a secret report for Derek Ezra, then NCB chairman, arguing that the rise of the communist and Marxist left in the NUM would have to be broken by 'reinforcing union moderates', reintroducing pit and area incentive payments, which had been phased out after 1966, and promoting membership of non-NUM unions. All this was attempted or carried out in the 1970s and 1980s. 'The aims should be', Miron concluded, 'to limit the future manning of the industry to restrict, to neutralize, alien or subversive political influences' and to 'ensure that of those employed in the mining industry the maximum number should be outwith the NUM'.[8]

Five years later, while the Tories were still in opposition, Nicholas Ridley, the right-wing MP and Thatcher ally, drew up the necessary contingency plans to take the miners on. Even in such a vulnerable industry, with the likelihood of the 'full force of communist disrupters', Ridley assured his future Prime Minister that a strike could be defeated. What was needed was a build-up of coal stocks and imports, the encouragement of non-union road hauliers to move coal, the rapid introduction of dual coal-oil firing at all power stations, the withdrawal of social-security benefits from strikers' families, and the creation of a large, mobile squad of police. All these steps were in the event taken during, or in the run-up to, the 1984–5 coal strike, when Ridley was a member of the Cabinet committee in charge of the government's strike tactics. A decade on, Nigel (now Lord) Lawson, who had been intimately involved in planning for a confrontation with the miners as Energy Secretary, recalled that government preparation for the strike was 'just like re-arming to face the threat of Hitler in the late 1930s'.[9]

But the Tory commitment to solving Britain's coal problem once and for all went far beyond the tactical preparations for, and all-out resistance to, a major national strike. As one set of ministerial memoirs from the Thatcher era after another has made indisputably clear, the overriding aim of the British government's entire energy policy from 1979 onwards was to destroy for ever the power-base of the National Union of Mineworkers and exorcize the Tory nightmares of the early 1970s. The miners' industrial muscle was based on their grip on electricity supply. Throughout the 1970s and 1980s, around 80 per cent of Britain's electricity was generated from domestic coal. For the Tories, that dependence on coal had to be broken, at almost any cost. This was the principal motivation behind the government's systematic promotion of nuclear power at enormous public expense, the break-up and privatization of electricity supply, the 'dash for gas', and the long-delayed sale of the coal industry itself.[10]

The strategy began with nuclear power. The fact that the Thatcher government's enthusiastic support for a pressurized-water-reactor (PWR) programme was mainly aimed at under-cutting the NUM was first revealed in leaked Cabinet minutes during her first administration. Nigel Lawson, Energy Secretary in the early 1980s and later Chancellor, explained much later: 'The need for "diversification" of energy sources, the argument I used to justify the PWR programme, was code for freedom from NUM blackmail.' Lawson regarded Scargill as one of the two 'energy tsars' of the industrialized world – the other being Sheikh Yamani, the Saudi oil minister. Money was therefore no object. But despite the billions of pounds of subsidy poured into the nuclear industry – the nuclear-featherbedding 'fossil fuel levy' was still running at over £1.2 billion a year in 1994 (£2 billion at 2012 prices) – nuclear power never proved enough by itself to knock 'King Coal' off its throne.[11]

To hold the line, there was a determined bid to drive up coal imports by encouraging the building of new ports and terminals. When that proved insufficient, the Tories turned to denationalization and industrial break-up to achieve their perennial ambition. At the 1988 Tory Party conference in Brighton, Cecil Parkinson, then Thatcher's Energy Secretary, announced that the coal industry – the jewel in the crown of the 1945 Attlee government's public-ownership programme – would be sold off. This, he declared, would be the 'ultimate privatization'. Parkinson later explained in the privacy of his own memoirs: 'What was ultimate about the proposed privatization of coal was that it would mark the end of the political power of the National Union of Mineworkers.'

Despite the bravado, the denationalization of coal would have to be repeatedly postponed. Instead, it was the privatization of electricity supply, combined with a market rigged in favour of the nuclear and gas industries, that would finally destroy coal's historic pre-eminence and create the conditions for its replacement as the country's industrial lifeblood in the 1990s. The ministers responsible for this bizarre industrial architecture were at least frank in retrospect about what had been their intention. As Parkinson described the planned impact of electricity privatization: 'It was obvious that the reorganisation of the electricity industry, and the weakening of British Coal's monopoly as a coal supplier, would fundamentally change the shape of the [coal] industry.' Breaking the monopoly of either electricity or coal would, he argued, 'curtail the power of the miners'. Privatizing both would 'destroy' the 'political and economic power' of the NUM for good.[12]

The rigging of the market against coal was as ruthless as it was neat. By splitting the old state-owned monopoly Central Electricity Generating Board into a private duopoly of National Power and PowerGen, the government gave the newly privatized regional electricity-distribution companies a compelling interest in building their own new gas-fired power stations as a way of buying commercial independence from the two big generators. It was of little consequence to the new privateers if power generated from gas turned out to be more expensive than electricity from coal-fired stations – let alone exorbitantly subsidized nuclear power – so long as the government kept handing out gas-station licences and the industry regulator allowed costs to be passed on to consumers. Thus was the 'dash for gas' born and the NUM's grip on electricity generation finally brought to an end.[13]

When the Major government's pit-closure plans ran into an unforeseen wall of popular protest in the autumn of 1992, much public comment focused on the supposed irrationality of the relentless promotion of coal imports and expensive nuclear power and gas. But it was only irrational if judged primarily in terms of cost. Market forces, competition and costs were never the Conservative government's primary concerns when it came to dealing with the mining industry. In the words of two widely respected energy economists: 'Throughout the period [1979–92], the underlying policy objective for coal was primarily to break the power of the NUM and the perceived stranglehold of coal on the electricity supply industry.' Privatization and the devastating 1992–4 closure programme was the endgame of that strategy.[14]

But it was a process which took many years to bear fruit. As late as 1990, the year of the Scargill Affair and of Margaret Thatcher's fall from office, almost four-fifths of Britain's power supply was still being generated from domestic coal. And around the same proportion of that coal was still produced by NUM members. For all the dramatic fall in the size of the mining workforce – achieved at a cost of £8 billion in redundancy payments – Thatcher failed while in office to achieve her strategic goal of destroying the source of the NUM's strength. The massive cuts in the mining workforce in the aftermath of the 1984–5 strike were to a large extent the result of large-scale productivity gains, both from longer hours and the effects of long-term investment in new machinery. Between 1983 and 1990, output from BC pits fell from 90 to 76 million tonnes. At 16 per cent, that was a significant cut, but nothing like the dramatic 64 per cent reduction in the number of miners which slashed the corporation's industrial workforce from 181,000 to 65,000 over the same period. The number of working BC pits was cut from 170 to 73, as production was concentrated in the most productive 'big hitter' collieries.[15]

In other words, by the end of the 1980s a far smaller group of miners potentially exercised even more concentrated industrial power than before. The NUM was very far from being the busted flush of received media and labour-movement wisdom. To keep the Tories' wolf from the door, the Thatcher government was forced to rely on gigantic coal stockpiles and the careful encouragement of divisions within and between the mining and other energy unions. What ultimately held the miners back from flexing their industrial muscle were internal splits, fostered both from within and from without, and the continuing presence of the government-promoted breakaway Union of Democratic Mineworkers in the Nottinghamshire coalfield.

Michael Heseltine's politically disastrous decision in October 1992 to close thirty-one of the surviving fifty British Coal collieries at a stroke and to sack 30,000 miners was not only an inevitable result of the long-term Tory strategy to destroy the NUM. It was also clear confirmation that the government's enthusiasm for its war on the miners had by no means evaporated with Thatcher's political demise. Of course, mining jobs had been lost throughout the world, mostly as a result of higher productivity and changing energy costs. But the destruction of the British market for coal and the closure of collieries producing far below the cost of imports and other fuels was a deliberate act of policy. Even as late as the spring of 1993 domestic coal still accounted for 60 per cent of electricity generation, but that proportion would fall dramatically as British Coal's guaranteed sales to the privatized generators were cut by more than half. By that point, the torrent of redundancies had become the straightforward outcome of the calculated rundown of the industry and the ruthless displacement of coal in the newly privatized electricity market. Despite the political cost, Major's government made sure the job was finished. By the tenth anniversary of the 1984–5 strike, Heseltine's much-vaunted 'agonizing' over pit closures had miraculously subsided. The 'political power of the extremist-led union' had, he now explained, been to blame for the most drastic industrial rundown in Britain's history.[16]

## THE SCARGILL FACTOR

For the Tories and the British establishment as a whole, Arthur Scargill came to embody all that they most feared and hated about trade-union power in general and the miners in particular. Originally one of a group of charismatic militant rank-and-file union leaders thrown up by the industrial upheavals of the early 1970s, Scargill in time became 'a man apart' for the Conservatives, the living 'embodiment of the enemy within'. There was cause enough for the obsession – which was also well represented in the labour-movement hierarchy. It was Scargill who in 1972 had masterminded the single most successful mass-picketing operation of the postwar period. In 1974, he and other left-wing NUM area leaders pushed through a strike which helped bring down the government of the day. And in 1984–5, he led the longest national strike in the country's history and was the central actor in the decisive confrontation of the Thatcher decade. It can be argued that a mythology around

Scargill was encouraged on both sides of Britain's 'coal wars' – and that the origins of the Tory vendetta against the miners predate his national leadership of the NUM. But there is also no doubt that Scargill became the focus of everything it was designed to root out.[17]

In the late 1960s and early 1970s, Scargill emerged as the central figure in the left's rise to power in the Yorkshire NUM, the largest, and traditionally right-wing, coalfield. The capture of Yorkshire was in turn the key to the radicalization of the whole union. The turning point for the NUM came in October 1969, when young left-wing miners' activists – Scargill prominent amongst them – led an explosive unofficial strike. Starting in Yorkshire, action spread across the entire British coalfield, drawing in well over a hundred thousand miners. It was the first time that 'flying pickets' were used in a large-scale and highly organized way to build a strike. Squads of cars and minibuses were mobilized to ferry hundreds of miners at a time to picket outside targeted collieries. In the NUM, the strike became known as the 'October Revolution'. The tactics were repeated the following year and the ground laid for the NUM's dramatic success in the coal dispute of 1972. This was the first official national miners' strike since 1926. While the national media predicted a defeat for the miners, the stoppage spectacularly broke the Heath government's wage-restraint policy. Scargill's role in the crucial set-piece battle of the strike, at Saltley, made his name and provided a model for the use of mass picketing in other industrial disputes of the 1970s.

Scargill himself came to epitomize Britain's experience of the new industrial and political militancy then sweeping the advanced capitalist world. The 1972 strike coincided with the celebrated occupation of Upper Clyde Shipbuilders in Glasgow and growing union resistance to the government's Industrial Relations Act. The agitation against the Act culminated the same year in a group of London dockers – who became known as the Pentonville Five after they were imprisoned for contempt of court – being hurriedly released under the threat of a TUC-led general strike. Within months of the 1972 coal strike, the previously unknown pit delegate from Woolley colliery had been voted onto the NUM national executive and into a full-time union job, as Yorkshire area compensation agent. Less than a year later, Scargill was elected president of the Yorkshire miners by a landslide. More alarming still for the Tory government and media at the time was the elevation of the communist Scottish miners' leader, Mick McGahey, to the vice-presidency of the national union.[18]

Two years on, the miners repeated their victory with even more far-reaching repercussions. In spite of the government's attempt to turn the build-up to the 1974 strike into a witch-hunt against communist and other left-wing NUM leaders, miners once again delivered an overwhelming vote to take industrial action over pay. The strike, a direct challenge to the government's wage-restraint strategy, was unleashed against the background of a growing international oil crisis. Edward Heath responded by calling a general election on a 'Who Governs Britain?' ticket – and lost. These confrontations could scarcely have been more humiliating and demoralizing, not only for the Tory Party but for the whole political establishment. The miners had twice smashed the government's pay policy, the cornerstone of its entire economic programme, and precipitated the most bitter election of modern times.

Unlike the strikes of 1972 and 1974, the cataclysmic battle of 1984–5 – the 'most important industrial dispute since the General Strike of 1926' and 'one of the most significant events in Britain's postwar history', as the Thatcherite editor of the *Sunday Times* described it shortly afterwards – was essentially defensive. A detailed analysis of the strategy and tactics adopted by the NUM leadership is beyond the scope of this book. But some corrective to current received wisdom on the 1984–5 strike is necessary to make sense of the wider picture. The standard fairy tale, still routinely recycled by media and politicians alike, has it that Scargill 'called' the action in the spring – in a classic example of his poor generalship and tactical sense – at a time when coal stocks were at an all-time high and just as the arrival of warmer weather was cutting back demand for power. The dispute in fact began with a highly effective over-time ban in the autumn of 1983. And while both the union and the government had been preparing for the inevitable collision since Thatcher's climbdown of 1981, the timing of the final all-out confrontation was clearly that of the Coal Board and the government.[19]

In the wake of her 1983 general-election victory, Thatcher appointed Peter Walker Energy Secretary with the words: 'We are going to have a miners' strike.' It would, she told him, be a political assault orchestrated by Scargill and aimed at achieving his 'Marxist objectives'. The decision to recruit as Coal Board chairman the union-busting American industrialist Ian Mac-Gregor – fresh from subjecting the British steel industry to his tender mercies – was an unmistakable signal that the government intended to cut coal down to size and subject the industry to narrowly defined, job-destroying commercial criteria. On the union side, the NUM leadership was equally determined to resist. The overtime ban imposed at the end of October 1983 over pay and closures was manifestly designed to shrink coal stockpiles in preparation for the widely expected showdown.[20]

However, it was the Board's decision to, in MacGregor's words, 'pre-empt' the union – first by announcing it would close a Yorkshire pit, Cortonwood, on purely financial grounds and without consultation, and then six days later giving deliber-ately provocative notice of the closure of a further twenty pits and 20,000 more redundancies – that triggered the eruption of the strike. The Central Electricity Generating Board had pri-vately told the government in the run-up to the Cortonwood announcement, it emerged years later, that the overtime ban was biting deep into power-station coal stocks. If it was allowed to continue until the autumn, managers warned, a twelve-week strike would be enough to put the country's lights out. Even before the Cortonwood announcement, pit-level management provocations and local disputes were spreading – notably at Polmaise colliery in Scotland, which was already out on strike against the threat of closure. Against such a background, any attempt by the union leadership to postpone action in March would have been interpreted as a sign of weakness, encouraged a further acceleration of closures, and very likely led to a battle in still more unfavourable circumstances.[21]

As in 1969, 1970 and 1981, there was a domino effect as activists spread the action from area to area through mass picketing. Within a fortnight, 80 per cent of Britain's miners had stopped work and most would remain on strike for twelve months. Once most miners had joined the rolling dispute, there was never any serious question of calling it off or holding a national ballot – as opposed to voting at area or branch level – on whether or not to strike. The decision not to hold a national ballot would dog the NUM's efforts to win support for the strike, even though it essentially repeated the tactics of 1969–70 and 1981 on a larger scale. So far as the union's leadership and activists were concerned, to ballot after the strike had already drawn in the overwhelming majority would have been seen as a 'get-out' and have invited a 'no' vote. Jack Taylor, then the Yorkshire miners' leader and well to the right of Scargill, reflected a widespread view when he said his members would 'murder' him if he asked them to vote on what they were already doing.

The 1984–5 dispute, unlike the strikes of the early 1970s, was not in any case primarily about pay and conditions which affected all miners across the board, but about pit closures, unemployment and the survival of mining communities under widely varying degrees of threat. As Peter Heathfield – elected NUM general secretary just before the 1984–5 strike began – commented a couple of months into the full-blown dispute, a national ballot was in effect being promoted as a 'veto to prevent people in other areas defending their jobs'. The division between what appeared at the time to be pits and coalfields guaranteed a long-term future – notably Nottinghamshire, where most miners carried on working during 1984–5 – and the rest had been deliberately nurtured by the Coal Board's reintroduction of incentive payments favouring miners at higher productivity pits. In an ironic mirror image of the ballot arguments of 1984–5, the incentive scheme had been rejected by miners in a national ballot in 1977 and then introduced regardless through local deals, area by area. At that time, the old Nottinghamshire NUM, which in 1984–5 cried foul at the absence of a ballot and went on to form the core of the Union of Democratic Mineworkers, ignored both the union conference and the ballot result and went away to negotiate its own incentive scheme.[22]

The 1984–5 strike was a last-ditch fight to defend jobs, mining communities and the NUM itself against a government prepared to bring into play unlimited resources and its entire panoply of coercive powers as and where necessary to break the union and its backbone of support. It was also a challenge to the 'logic of capital', to the savage, job-devouring 'restructuring' of industry on the basis of narrow profit-and-loss criteria, rather than broader social and economic costs and benefits. The strike was, of course, a gamble: but not, as is often implied, in the sense of throwing away the opportunity of a gentle and humane decline in exchange for the chance of all-out political and industrial victory. Rather, it gambled the certainty of acceler-ated rundown and Thatcherization of the coal industry against the chance of stopping that assault in its tracks. The only two periods when pit closures were temporarily suspended were the years of resistance: 1984–85 and 1992–93. Otherwise, the rate of closures ran at about the same level – between ten and twenty collieries a year – both before and after the strike.[23]

There is no evidence whatever for the widespread assumption that more accommodating NUM tactics during or after the 1984–5 strike – or any of the settlements actually on offer – would have significantly slowed the rundown of the British coal industry. The experience of steel demonstrated that there were few prizes for traditional give-and-take trade unionism in Thatcher's Britain. Despite studied moderation, the steel unions were forced to acquiesce in the industry's dramatic job-shedding contraction in the wake of their 1980 pay strike. As for the NUM, the later cauterization of those areas of the union – such as Scotland, South Wales and Derbyshire – which tried to come to an accommodation with the Coal Board in the wake of the

1984–5 strike and suffered, if anything, more rapid closures than elsewhere, makes the same point. For the miners, the die had been cast before Scargill became NUM president. But what he, Heathfield and McGahey – the troika who led the 1984–5 strike – ensured was that the national union was mobilized without reserve behind miners who were prepared to resist the closure programme. None of the three was prepared to hide behind a phoney compromise deal which might briefly postpone the day of reckoning to even less propitious circumstances. On the government side, Thatcher and her shadowy acolytes made certain that nothing else was available.[24]

## A THREAT TO LIBERTY

Thatcher's hand was, however, nothing like as strong as has generally been supposed. It only gradually become apparent during the 1990s, as memoirs were published and participants felt able to speak more freely, how near the government came to defeat at the hands of the striking miners in 1984. Norman Tebbit, Thatcher ally and member of the Cabinet committee charged with beating the NUM, remarked in the wake of the 1992 pit-closures crisis that the strike had been a 'close-run thing' – and eighteen months earlier the NUM would have almost certainly triumphed. The period during which the miners came closest to victory and the Thatcher government to falling was in fact in the autumn of 1984, when most pundits had already written the strike off.[25]

Two factors came together to put the government in serious danger. The first was the rundown and blockading of power-station coal stocks. The CEGB, which ran a brilliant logistical operation to keep the lights on, had only planned for a six-month strike. And it was unable to move stockpiles at some power stations because of effective picketing and solidarity action. Ten years on, Frank Ledger, the CEGB's operations director, recalled the situation as having been verging on the 'catastrophic'. Throughout the autumn months, there was a serious risk of power cuts. Secret internal forecasts predicted that – in the words of Lord Marshall, then CEGB chairman – 'Scargill would win in the autumn or certainly before Christmas'. In a tense meeting, a 'wobbly' Margaret Thatcher told him she would have to send troops in to move the coal. If that had happened, Marshall believed the power workers 'would have gone on strike immediately and the lights would have gone out within a week'. Thatcher was persuaded to hold off, while CEGB managers set to work with their chequebooks, successfully bribing groups of workers to move the vital coal supplies.[26]

The strikers' parallel near-breakthrough that autumn came when Ian MacGregor stumbled into a dispute with NACODS – the pit deputies' union responsible for safety underground – by ordering its members to cross picket lines at strike-bound collieries. They refused, balloted to join the NUM's stoppage and won an 83 per cent vote for action. A strike was called to begin on 25 October 1984. By law, work could only carry on at a mine in the presence of a pit deputy. If the NACODS strike had gone ahead, the working pits in Nottinghamshire – Thatcher's lifeline – would have had to stop production and the government back down in a matter of weeks. Thatcher recalled in her memoirs that Whitehall was awash with fears that 'a bandwagon might begin to roll in Mr Scargill's favour'. The fate of both the government and the miners hung by a thread. As the former Prime Minister described the crisis on television nine years after the strike:

> We had got so far and we were in danger of losing everything because of a silly mistake. We had to make it quite clear that if that was not cured immediately, then the actual management of the Coal Board could indeed have brought down the government. The future of the government at that moment was in their hands and they had to remedy their terrible mistake.

On Thatcher's instructions, MacGregor offered NACODS a sop – a mildly souped-up closure review procedure – which bought off most of the deputies' leaders. The strike was called off with twenty-four hours to go, and the threat to the government was averted. But in the decade that followed, the new review procedure didn't save a single coal mine.[27]

The 1984–5 miners' strike is an episode which demands a 'revisionist' reassessment. For the Tories, most of the media and for the Labour and TUC leaders who left the NUM to fight alone, the strike was a regrettable saga of picket-line violence, undemocratic manoeuvring, ranting obscurantist dogmatism and inevitable defeat: the tragic product of one man's overweening political and personal ambitions. For those who actively took part, along with millions of their supporters in Britain and abroad, it was a principled – even heroic – stand, which directly confronted the Thatcher administration and its battery of anti-democratic trade-union legislation in a way that no other force in the country was prepared or able to do. Peter Heathfield was speaking for many beyond the shrinking mining communities when at his retirement he described the strike as 'the most courageous and principled struggle in British trade-union history'.[28] It was also a campaign which transformed people's lives and view of the world, drew hundreds of thousands from outside the mining communities into active solidarity, and threw up new forms of organization – notably the Women Against Pit Closures support groups – utterly at odds with the textbook caricature of the dispute. As one highly critical account of the strike concedes of the miners who took part: 'Many said they would do it all again and many had clearly enjoyed the experience: they had lived at a pitch, physically, intellectually, morally even, which they could not expect to again, and which most who have not undergone war would never emulate.'[29]

As Scargill's Cassandra-like warnings of what lay in store for the miners were eerily borne out by the flood of job losses and pit closures after 1985, the wider popular perception of the strike in retrospect began to change. The image of striking miners as the protagonists of picket-line violence was also dented by later revelations and events. There was, for example, the decision by South Yorkshire police in 1991 to pay half a million pounds in damages to thirty-nine miners arrested on 18 June 1984 at Orgreave coking plant, the single most dramatic and violent physical confrontation of postwar industrial relations. The miners had sued the police for assault, wrongful arrest, malicious prosecution and false imprisonment after their original trial for riot had collapsed ignominiously in 1985. As the civil-rights organization Liberty remarked of the battle of Orgreave – where 8,000 riot police staged medieval-style mounted charges of unprecedented ferocity: 'There was a riot. But it was a police riot.'[30]

It is of course scarcely surprising that the Thatcher administration became fixated with Scargill in its determination to break the miners. Not only did he head the country's most powerful union in full frontal conflict with the state in a way not seen for at least sixty years, but his personality and politics made him a uniquely dangerous figure in the eyes of the British government. Scargill never played by the rules of the British trade-union game and despised the routine deal-making and bureaucratic compromises accepted as inevitable and necessary by more orthodox trade-union leaders. To many union officials, that made him a poor trade unionist and a lousy negotiator. To the Coal Board and the government, it made him alarmingly impervious to the usual accommodations. For his supporters, it was a unique advantage: here, in Scargill's description of himself, was the 'union leader that doesn't sell out'.[31]

Scargill also stood apart from other left-wingers, both in his attitudes and his style of leadership. Even during his years in the communist movement in the 1950s and early 1960s, Scargill resolutely ploughed his own political furrow. He was always, as he acknowledges, a loner. In the words of Nell Myers, his long-time assistant and closest political collaborator, Scargill's is a 'conflagrationary personality', arousing both absolute loyalty and consuming hatreds. His syndicalist-flavoured Marxism never had much in common with the more homely, house-trained version favoured by union leaders like Hugh Scanlon of the engineering union – and even Scanlon was heavily targeted by the security services. Scargill's open espousal of revolutionary class politics, his much-publicized friendship with Fidel Castro, and his avowed solidarity with left-wing regimes around the world were more than enough to give the NUM demonic status with a political establishment badly scarred by its battering at the hands of the miners' union. As Geoffrey Goodman, the *Daily Mirror* industrial editor sacked by Robert Maxwell, has put it:

> Primary responsibility for the conflict [the 1984–5 strike] has to be attributed to the government. It wanted a showdown because it had become convinced that this was the only way to destroy Arthur Scargill and 'Scargillism' – and through that route to administer a severe blow to active trade unionism.[32]

The virulence of the denunciations of Scargill and the miners during and long after the 1984–5 strike went far beyond the established boundaries of modern-day mainstream British politics. It reached a peak in the summer of 1984, when the Prime Minister compared the struggle with the miners to the war against the Argentine junta over the Falklands/Malvinas islands two years earlier. 'We had to fight an enemy without in the Falklands,' she declared at a gathering of Conservative backbench MPs. Now the war had to be taken to 'the enemy within, which is much more difficult to fight and more dangerous to liberty'. A few months later, Margaret Thatcher would return to her theme in the Carlton Club, the clubland temple of High Toryism:

> At one end of the spectrum are, the terrorist gangs within our borders and the terrorist states which finance and arm them. At the other are the hard left, operating inside our system, conspiring to use union power ... to break, defy and subvert the laws.

Her senior ministers were no less extreme. Thus Leon Brittan, the Home Secretary responsible during the strike for overseeing Britain's largest and longest-running police mobilization ever, fulminated:

Mr Scargill does not just hate our free and democratic system and seek to do everything he can to discredit and damage it; he also feels equal hatred and contempt for those miners whose servant he is meant to be but whose tyrant he has become.

The message conveyed by these remarks by Thatcher and Brittan was unmistakable, down to the use of the words 'conspiring' and 'subvert': this false prophet and his bands of untamed red guards and coalfield sans-culottes should be treated as outlaws. They were enemies of the state. By branding the miners 'the enemy within', the Prime Minister was giving a calculated signal of unambiguous clarity to all government agencies that the gloves should come off in the war with the NUM.[33]

The private instructions were inevitably more explicit. One police chief constable recalls being formally warned by a senior Home Office official early on in the dispute of the Prime Minister's frustrations at what she saw as official pussyfooting in the coalfields. She was, he was told, 'convinced that a secret communist cell around Scargill was orchestrating the strike in order to bring down the country', and that infiltration and intelligence-gathering needed to be sharply stepped up to prove the conspiracy. The NUM found itself facing the concentrated power of the state in an unprecedented form. And the much-reported nationwide police deployment, the 11,000 arrests, the roadblocks and large-scale use of force by the police were only the public face of the covert campaign – which increasingly came to guide and dominate the tactics used to try and break the miners' resistance.[34]

## THE BEAST IS NOT SLAIN

The end of the strike did not end the war. That the British government was not finished with Scargill and the miners was made abundantly clear by Sir Geoffrey Howe a few months after the return to work. 'For the first time in British post-war history, we have seen a major trade union leader openly in league with countries which threaten our security,' the habitually phlegmatic Foreign Secretary thundered, 'openly taking his storm troopers abroad for training in how to subvert our democratic, legal and economic systems, and less openly, importuning some of the least democratic governments in the world for financial contributions to his campaign against the British people.' This, from a man famously compared in the House of Commons to a dead sheep, was strong meat indeed and reflected the government's unexpected dissatisfaction at the way the strike had been wound up.[35]

As far as the Tories were concerned, there would continue to be unfinished business until Scargill and the miners' union – and indeed the coal industry in any recognizable form – were consigned to the recesses of history. But, gallingly for the government, the NUM did not accept defeat. The union had been stampeded into returning to work, divided and without a settlement, but it had not been broken. Despite being severely weakened and permanently tied up in legal action and internal battles; despite the remorseless attrition of the Coal Board, the Nottinghamshire-based breakaway outfit, the rundown of the coalfields and the dismal aftermath of the country's most intense industrial confrontation since 1926, the NUM leaders did not accept the role allotted to them. Scargill did not go the way of his hero, Arthur Cook, the syndicalist miners' leader at the time of the 1926 General Strike, who would eventually lose heart, move to the right and die a broken man. Barely four months after the miners returned to work, Scargill was telling NUM conference delegates that the union had 'challenged the very heart of the capitalist system ... we are involved in a class war ... you have written history. The only way is to fight again with the same determination, the same pride.'[36]

While the Labour Party and TUC hierarchies seized the opportunity to reap the political rewards of the strike's outcome by turning their fire on the left, the government realized that the NUM remained a potentially powerful force so long as the miners maintained their control of the country's power supply.

The Energy Secretary, Peter Walker, in particular, 'followed Scargill's post-strike manoeuvrings as closely as he had watched the strike strategy'. The union was, of course, enfeebled – not only by the exhaustion and the indebtedness of the miners, but by growing internal disputes, financial and legal problems on a gargantuan scale, and the threat posed by the Union of Democratic Mineworkers. Scargill, Heathfield and McGahey, in particular, were ensnared in a maze of litigation arising from the sequestration of the NUM's funds and the formal takeover of the union by a court-appointed receiver.[37]

But the widespread view that the miners' return to work in March 1985 marked the end of the NUM's industrial power was not shared by the government. In a backhanded recognition of the force of the union's resistance, redundancy payments aimed at convincing miners to go quietly reached levels unmatched anywhere else in industry – in the years immediately after the strike, the longest-serving miners were entitled to a package worth around £80,000 (well over £200,000 at 2012 prices). The Scargill factor was still ever-present in the Prime Minister's calculations. As she remarked in her autobiography: 'We never forgot the possibility of a second strike after the present one was finished.' When Cecil Parkinson was brought back into the Cabinet as Energy Secretary after the 1987 general election – a time when the miners' union and its leader had already been written off by most pundits as a busted flush – Thatcher urged her close ally to be vigilant.[38] 'Keep a careful eye on Arthur Scargill,' she warned him, allotting the NUM leader his accustomed role as the wicked wolf in the fairy story. Above all, Parkinson should 'make sure that coal stocks were maintained at a high enough level to see off the National Union of Mineworkers if he brought them out on strike again. She was sure that he would try.' And indeed, within a few months, the miners had voted by a huge majority to take industrial action over a new disciplinary code – though the divided NUM executive failed to press home its advantage. Local, unofficial strikes continued throughout the late 1980s as the Coal Board – renamed British Coal – waged a war of attrition against the union at pit level. Industry managers still remained, as *The Times* put it, 'half-thrilled and half-frightened' by Scargill.[39]

By the end of the decade, the NUM's membership had been drastically reduced by mine closures and mass redundancies. The union leadership was becoming increasingly isolated as the political centre of gravity in the labour movement continued to move relentlessly to the right. But largely unnoticed outside the energy sector, the industrial potential of the surviving workforce was, if anything, greater than ever. For all the government's best efforts, the proportion of electricity generated from coal actually reached a historic peak in 1989–90. Even in her last month in office, Thatcher was warning John Wakeham, her last Energy Secretary, to protect the position of the breakaway UDM. The fading premier was never sure when she might need them again. 'I knew', she explained in retrospect, 'we might have to face another strike.' Just as disturbingly for both the Tories and the Labour Party leadership, there seemed every sign that a planned merger with the country's largest union, the Transport and General Workers, could give the NUM and its larger-than-life president a new lease of political and industrial life.[40]

It was against this background that Margaret Thatcher authorized 'special measures' by the security services against Scargill, Heathfield and their core supporters towards the end of the 1980s, and that the media and legal barrage was launched in March 1990. There was much speculation in the early stages of the Scargill Affair as to why so much attention was being focused on a broken union, whose leader was a 'dead duck politically', a man who had 'slid to the very periphery of events'. In reality, there was more than a little wishful thinking in such triumphalist claims. Not only was the miners' underlying industrial clout far less affected by their decline in numbers than generally understood. But, for the Tory Prime Minister in particular, the survival of 'King Arthur' – albeit scarred, bloodied and presiding over a much-diminished kingdom – was a permanent affront and a constant reminder of a job uncompleted.[41]

The Scargill myth remained as stubbornly strong as ever, despite the decimation of the NUM leader's industrial and political base. He was far and away Britain's best-known union leader, both at home and abroad: the trade-union movement's one and only celebrity. It is hard to imagine the then South African president and African National Congress leader Nelson Mandela, for example, talking about any other British union official as a 'workers' hero, respected by progressives of all continents'. Scargill's popularity among trade-union and Labour Party activists remained high and his power to sway labour-movement audiences unchallenged. As one exponent of 1980s-style 'new realist' business unionism wrote in the wake of the collapse of the 1990 campaign: 'Few people could have survived the pounding that Mr Scargill has taken ... Mr Scargill is not only surviving, but thriving ... By any logical standards, he is a busted flush. However, such is his extraordinary nature that such standards barely apply.'[42]

Thatcher's worries over the continuing dangers posed by the miners and their president were later richly borne out at her successor's expense during the October 1992 pit-closures crisis. To the astonishment of most miners themselves, Middle England rose momentarily as one against the vandalization of the country's coal industry. In the *Guardian*'s formulation at the time: 'The most astonishing thing is that the forward march of Thatcherism should be halted in the coalfields, of all places ... The unique moral status of the miners in British life has reasserted itself.' The NUM president was transmogrified overnight from 'most hated man in Britain' into vindicated folk hero. Remarkably, in view of his media portrayal as a political dinosaur living in a class-war time-warp, Scargill was singled out by teenagers and young people as one of their foremost heroes in a 1993 poll because of what they saw as his principled stand against the government. In an exhaustive survey of the attitudes of 11- to 24-year-olds, the NUM president was ranked alongside Martin Luther King and John Kennedy.[43] Even Chief Superintendent John Nesbit, who had arrested Scargill at Orgreave in 1984, was forced to change his tune: 'Arthur was right ... I hope he wins this time.' And the *Daily Mirror*, admittedly under new management, ran a full front-page colour picture of the three men it had most savagely vilified two years earlier – Scargill, Heathfield and the International Miners' Organization official Alain Simon – clutching bouquets of flowers and grinning happily under the benign gaze of a police superintendent as they led the biggest demonstration in London for a decade. 'Cor!', the banner legend ran, 'Look What Major's Done for Old Arthur ... Yesterday, Arthur Scargill was a hero to both rich and poor.'[44]

Needless to say, the new-found media love affair was not to last. And the government had no intention of allowing its quarry to get away. The Cabinet minister given the job of negotiating the government's way around the public outcry against pit closures – the appropriately unelected Lord Wakeham – made sure there would be no tampering with the privatized structure he had himself put in place as Energy Secretary. The war on the miners and their union would be seen through to the finish. The squeeze on coal would continue. And in the process, the world's most advanced mining industry, billions of pounds of investment, and one of the country's most skilled and adaptable workforces would be sacrificed in the service of the Tory vendetta. When British Coal was finally sold off in December 1994, only 8,000 miners remained on its books at sixteen deep-mine collieries, in an industry which employed well over a million men at the time of the 1926 General Strike. As another former Energy Secretary, Tony Benn, described the frantic forced closure of twenty-one publicly owned collieries in a couple of months during the early summer of 1993: 'This is a search and destroy mission against the National Union of Mineworkers.'[45]

## UNHOLY ALLIANCE

Yet, for all its determined role in the cauterization of the nationalized coal industry, the Conservative government was not the only power in the land anxious to see the back of the miners' union and its leadership. And likewise, the secret services were only one element of the tacit coalition that turned the 1990 Maxwell-funded campaign of corruption allegations against Scargill and Peter Heathfield into a sustained political and legal attack – an onslaught that would have destroyed almost any other public figure and could well have put the miners' leaders behind bars. The Scargill Affair depended on a coincidence of purpose between an exotic array of interests, foremost among which were the Thatcher administration and the Labour leadership. The government was determined to privatize the coal industry and continued to regard Scargill – acknowledged in the City of London to be a significant turn-off for potential buyers – as a malign influence from the past. Neil Kinnock, who later described how he had felt impotent and humiliated during the 1984–5 strike, saw the miners' leader and all he represented as a deeply unwelcome presence in the new-model Labour Party he was trying to create. Robert Maxwell, the slippery-fingered media baron, was, as ever, happy to do favours for both of them.[46]

The hares set off by Maxwell's *Daily Mirror* and the *Cook Report* in 1990 were subsequently chased with great relish by the rest of the media, Tory and Labour MPs, Scargill's opponents inside the NUM, the Fraud Squad, the courts, the government-appointed Certification Officer and Commissioner for Trade Union Rights, the UDM and the maverick right-wing electricians' union, Cabinet ministers, the TUC, an eccentric alliance of Soviet trade-union bureaucrats and dissident union breakaway outfits, the Inland Revenue, even Colonel Gaddafi, as well as a vast array of accountants and lawyers – who, needless to say, made a fortune out of the affair. All had their own special axe to grind and took every opportunity of the open season on the NUM and its leaders. For six months, while the threat of accelerated closures and privatization hung over the miners, the Scargill Affair circus moved from Sheffield to London to Paris to Budapest and Moscow. Teams of NUM officials, solicitors and financial advisers searched across Europe for the miners' 'lost treasure', and official investigations and legal actions were launched with wild abandon.

The campaign was a bizarre, almost surreal, episode which revealed much about the way British public life works: its double standards and workaday corruption; the myriad ties and connections which allow different parts of the establishment to move in tandem as soon as the need arises; the comfortable relationship between sections of the Labour hierarchy and the government and security apparatus; the way politicians, government and its various agencies, newspapers, broadcasters and professionals feed off the same political menu as if to order. It also served to highlight, in exemplary fashion, the political venality and pliability of the bulk of the British media.

Just as the government and intelligence services abandoned normal restraints when it came to the NUM, so did the media. It was a habit which had taken root well before the 1984–5 strike. By the time the *Mirror* and the *Cook Report* unleashed their stream of allegations against Scargill in 1990, they were able to do so with barely a nod in the direction of routine journalistic standards. Such niceties were scarcely required when it came to targets designated by the Prime Minister, no less, as the 'Enemy Within'. It is difficult to imagine such a cavalier approach to the facts – which changed in almost every successive *Mirror* exclusive – being applied to the coverage of almost anyone else in public life, let alone a government minister or senior opposition politician. Each time one story was shot down, another was conjured up to replace it. Reporting which questioned or undermined the original *Mirror* and *Cook Report* claims was either ignored, dismissed as the special pleading of Scargill 'apologists' and 'sycophants', or treated with amused indifference. When the central allegations were disproved or discredited, and when one investigation or prosecution after another was abandoned or collapsed, there was barely a ripple of interest from the same newspapers and broadcasters that had lapped up the original allegations with such a voracious appetite.[47]

In the event, the campaign to discredit the miners' leader was itself discredited. But while the claims of embezzlement and megalomaniacal double-dealing came to carry little weight with most labour-movement activists and those who follow every twist and turn of current affairs, there is no doubt that among the public at large some of the mud stuck and the months of high-profile character assassination took their toll. In a later 'unauthorized' biography of Scargill, the former *Times* labour editor Paul Routledge felt able to rehearse the original *Mirror-Cook Report* allegations in detail, while ignoring much of the available counter evidence. Long after the campaign of allegations had fizzled out, a caller to a BBC radio programme was asked to identify a particular public figure – the subject of a 'mystery voice' commentary – who had gone to prison for fiddling the books. 'Arthur Scargill?' she suggested. Rather than slapping down the implication that the miners' leader had been involved in book-fiddling, the presenter replied with some embarrassment: 'No, Arthur Scargill didn't go to prison.' Such incidents testify both to the impact of the attacks and the scale of the Major government's later bungle in turning round the NUM leader's semi-disgraced scallywag reputation in the pit-closures crisis of October 1992. Within a few months, the miners' president had far outstripped the Prime Minister in opinion-poll ratings and won a national NUM strike ballot against pit closures for the first time in the union's history.[48]

## CONSPIRACIES AND COCK-UPS

The aim of this book is to tell the real story of the Scargill Affair: to get at the truth behind the original allegations; to discover how and why such a powerful range of interests encouraged and fed the 1990 campaign; and to expose the nature and scale of the covert operations run by the security services against the miners' union, which the unravelling of the allegations started to reveal. The standard alibi for those who are determined – for whatever reasons – to reject evidence of malpractice, dirty tricks and provocation by the secret services is that such material is the product of the fevered imaginations of 'conspiracy theorists'. No doubt similar accusations will continue to be made about the arguments and allegations set out here. Indeed, they started being made by some of those with an interest in the affair – apparently as a sort of immunization or insurance policy – even before this book was finished.[49]

When the *Guardian* first published details of large-scale counter-subversion operations against the NUM and an account of some of the political undercurrents behind the Scargill Affair, the *Daily Mirror*'s immediate response was to cry: 'Conspiracy theory!' In two full-page tirades, the *Guardian* was accused of stringing together 'an unlikely chain of people who, it implies, took part in a great conspiracy: the KGB, CIA, Margaret Thatcher, MI6, Mikhail Gorbachev, and the *Mirror* – and all of them out to get poor old Arthur'. The *Guardian*'s purpose, it was said, was to prove the NUM president to be a 'maliciously maligned hero of the working class'. In fact, the stringing together was done by the *Mirror* itself.

But as far as the journalists then working for the Maxwell-owned tabloid were concerned, just a whiff of conspiracy theory was enough to discredit the *Guardian*'s revelations. Sometimes, resistance to any attempt to cast light on the machinations of the 'secret state' and its various outposts can verge on the hysterical. Joe Haines, for example – Harold Wilson's one-time Downing Street press secretary and later a *Daily Mirror* leader-writer and confidant of Robert Maxwell – took enormous pains to rubbish the evidence of MI5 treason against his own former boss's government. The allegations by Peter Wright, former MI5 assistant director, about a plot against Wilson were nothing but the 'ramblings of a sick old man', he fulminated at the height of the *Spycatcher* affair, and a 'mountain of lies'. Haines adopted a similar tone towards the *Guardian*'s reports about the security services and the miners.[50]

In a resolutely empiricist culture like Britain's – where 'practical men' prefer to shun the bigger picture and eminent historians can take delight in claiming that world wars break out because of the requirements of railway timetables – it is hardly surprising perhaps that many people feel unhappy with any suggestion of behind-the-scenes collusion and manipulation of events. To suggest anything else is regarded as somehow naive and insufficiently worldly. Among journalists in particular, it is an article of faith to insist on the 'cock-up theory' rather than the 'conspiracy theory' of history. Real life is, of course, a mixture of the two. One side effect of this dogmatic insistence that events are largely the product of an arbitrary and contingent muddle has been the chronic refusal over the years by the mainstream media in Britain – and most opposition politicians – to probe or question the hidden agendas and unaccountable, secret power structures at the heart of government. This is in striking contrast to North American journalism, which, for all its failings – especially over the establishment policy consensus – does at least maintain some tradition of investigation and scepticism about the activities of its country's rulers. As Stephen Dorril and Robin Ramsay, two authors who have attempted to unearth some of Whitehall's dirtier secrets, have commented: 'For the most part the areas which the British state does not want examined are still left alone by our serious papers.'[51]

The result is that an entire dimension of politics and the exercise of power in Britain is usually left out of standard reporting and analysis. And by refusing to acknowledge that dimension, it is often impossible to make proper sense of what is actually going on. Worse, it lets off the hook those whose abuse of state authority is most flagrant. The security services in Britain, as elsewhere, exercise unaccountable power through the control and manipulation of privileged information. It is a world of what one American writer describes as 'parapolitics': of 'the conduct of public affairs not by rational debate and responsible decision-making but by indirection, collusion and deceit ... the political exploitation of irresponsible agencies or parastructures, such as intelligence agencies'. With the special exception of Britain's corrosive 'security' role in the north of Ireland, there have been no clearer cases of such covert action, of such comprehensive mobilization of the normally submerged power centres of the Whitehall empire, than in the history of the secret war against the miners.[52]

No doubt some will take the view that the NUM and its leaders deserved everything that happened to them. Did they not abuse industrial power for political ends, as Cecil Parkinson grumbled when genteel Cheltenham marched for the miners in 1992? Did they not launch an unashamed challenge to the constitutional power of the land, flout the law and consort with dangerous foreigners? Bernard Ingham, Margaret Thatcher's former powerful press secretary, declared in retirement that security-service action against Scargill had been entirely justified because 'since 1972, to my certain knowledge, he's been trying to overthrow the elected government'.[53] There is no evidence, however, that such attitudes are typical of the majority of the general public. Throughout the dispute of 1984–5, in the face of a wall of hostile propaganda and nightly scenes of violence played out on television, rarely less than a third of the adult population – representing around 15 million people – supported the NUM and the strike: a strike for jobs and the defence of mining communities, but also a strike for social solidarity and a different kind of Britain. During the pit-closures crisis of 1992–3, more than 90 per cent of adults consistently backed the miners against the government – reflecting in many cases, perhaps, a sense of guilt that they failed to give them more support eight years earlier. The NUM was an independent, democratic trade union operating in a vital and dangerous industry. Scargill was elected and re-elected in secret ballots with 70 and 54 per cent of the vote. Even among those critical or hostile towards the union and its leaders, it is difficult to believe that anything other than a small minority could be content with what, it has since become clear, actually went on behind the scenes – if indeed they were ever deemed trustworthy enough to be told what was done in their name.[54]

The use of informers, infiltrators and provocateurs; premeditated police violence; attempted frame-ups; bugging and surveillance on a heroic scale; the spending of billions of pounds on facing down the strike and then on forcing through large-scale pit closures: none of this commanded any public consensus. But, of course, the maintenance of absolute secrecy around such activities in the interests of 'national security' prevents any testing of opinion or accountability of those responsible. It may be no surprise that the Tory government and its footsoldiers used any and every means to break the miners' union – the only serious force to stand in the way of the Thatcherite 'counter-revolution'. But such an assault had nothing whatever to do with the defence of democracy. Indeed, it represented the very opposite.

# CHAPTER ONE

# OPERATION CYCLOPS

Our press, which you appear to regard as being free ... is the most enslaved
and the vilest thing. *William Cobbett, 1830*[1]

The story that Robert Maxwell called the 'Scoop of the Decade'
was launched with all the razzmatazz and hype of a major
national event. The first signal of what would turn into an
unrestrained media, legal and political barrage against the leaders of the most important industrial dispute since the 1920s
came at 6 p.m. on Friday, 2 March 1990, almost exactly five
years to the day after the end of the strike. One of the most
popular television programmes in the country, the travel show
*Wish You Were Here*, was to be ditched the following Monday,
Central Television announced. In its place there would be a
special edition of the investigative *Cook Report*. It was to be
entitled: 'The Miners' Strike – Where Did the Money Go?'

The programme was primed to run as a joint exposé with
Robert Maxwell's *Daily Mirror*, and ITV's last-minute sche-
duling switch followed intense haggling by Central's director of
broadcasting, Andy Allan, to secure a peak-viewing-time slot. It
had been common knowledge for months in Fleet Street that
the *Mirror* was sharpening its knives for a major hatchet-job on
Arthur Scargill. Several disgruntled former NUM employees
had been touting their wares around the media, and it was well
known that Roger Windsor, the NUM's former chief executive,
and Jim Parker, Scargill's ex-driver, had signed up with Maxwell. But Windsor was holed up in Southwest France and
Parker was under the *Mirror*'s 'protection'. Reporters working
for Maxwell's competitors chased around the country trying to

inveigle the *Mirror*'s witnesses. At the NUM's grandiose new headquarters opposite Sheffield City Hall, tension was close to breaking point. Scargill cancelled a planned trip to Australia while his inner circle attempted to second-guess the direction of the coming media offensive.

Slavering to beat its arch-rival to the kill, the *Sun* – with the *Daily Star* in hot pursuit – launched an immediate front-page 'spoiler' in response to Central's rescheduling announcement. 'Scargill Union in £1m Scandal', the Murdoch tabloid screamed, correctly predicting that the *Cook Report* would claim that up to £1 million had been sent by Soviet miners to NUM strike funds, and at least £150,000 from Libya. 'The programme is dynamite. The allegations are sensational', the *Sun* enthused. The 'harlot of Fleet Street', as the *Mirror* liked to refer to the country's biggest-selling daily, also latched on to police investigations into 'Scargill's former right hand man,' Roger Windsor. An unfortunate *Star* reporter managed to buttonhole Windsor at his new home in Cognac, but was sent packing in short order. 'The only guidance I will give you,' Windsor told him, 'is how to get back to the airport.' A former NUM employee, the *Sun* predicted, would make 'very serious allegations' about the use of the Libyan money. But, for all its inventiveness, the Rottweiler of daily journalism was unable to establish exactly what these allegations might be.[2]

Nevertheless, the fear that the prize revelations his minions had been toiling over for the previous eight months, at a cost of hundreds of thousands of pounds, were being lost to his enemies sent the *Mirror*'s proprietor into a tailspin. His most recent acquisition as *Daily Mirror* editor, Roy Greenslade, was summoned and ordered to arrange for the Mirror Group's Sunday title to run a 'taster' of the following week's poison fare, trailed as the 'full and shocking truth'. That would turn out to be a remorseless seven days of bewildering allegations against the NUM leadership in the daily paper most widely read by British miners and Labour-supporting trade unionists. In the week between 4 and 10 March 1990, the *Sunday* and *Daily Mirror* – each with a circulation of getting on for four million copies –

would between them publish twenty-five pages of reports and commentary about Scargill and the 'dishonour' he had brought on the miners' union.[3]

The taster chosen for the *Sunday Mirror* was a suitably titillating morsel about missing 'Moscow Gold'. In December 1984, at Mikhail Gorbachev's first meeting with Margaret Thatcher at Chequers, the paper revealed, the British Prime Minister had taken the future Soviet leader aside after lunch to express her 'great displeasure' about Soviet 'meddling' in the miners' strike, then in its ninth month. 'We believe that people in the Soviet Union ... are helping to prolong the strike', Thatcher told him. Gorbachev insisted that the strike was an internal British affair, and that as far as he was aware 'no money has been transferred from the Soviet Union'. The Prime Minister 'did not push the matter further' and later that day declared: 'This is a man we can do business with.'

But, the *Sunday Mirror* declared triumphantly, the NUM 'did receive Soviet cash' and the paper produced what it called 'documentary proof': a copy of a letter written in November 1984 by Peter Heathfield to the Soviet president, Konstantin Chernenko, and subsequently 'removed' from NUM files. Heathfield was quoted expressing gratitude for the solidarity of the Soviet trade unions, including 'financial assistance to relieve the hardship of our members'. The article quoted the Soviet miners' leader Mikhail Srebny as saying that 2.3 million roubles – equivalent to £2 million – had been collected for the NUM, including £1 million of hard currency in 'golden roubles'. Soviet miners had given up two days' pay for their British comrades, so it was said. 'The figures', the *Sunday Mirror* explained triumphantly, 'show a discrepancy of around £1 million. No one is saying what happened to the missing money.' The story was written by Alastair Campbell – then Neil Kinnock's closest friend and ally in Fleet Street, later Tony Blair's press secretary – while the main source for the British end of the tale was transparently Margaret Thatcher's devoted spin-doctor, Bernard Ingham. But, like John the Baptist, this was only a harbinger of greater things to come. The next day, the Sunday paper promised its readers, Maxwell's daily would treat them to the 'authentic inside story' of how Scargill also took Libyan money – and 'how he used some of it for personal transactions'.[4]

## 'THE FACTS'

On Monday, 5 March, the campaign began in earnest. 'Scargill and the Libyan Money: The Facts', the legend on the *Daily Mirror*'s front page proclaimed. The *Mirror*'s 'splash' headline – in two-inch-high letters – would later come to attract much ridicule and notoriety, but it was treated with the utmost seriousness at the time. Across the top of the page, next to the mandatory 'exclusive' tag, the principal charge was set out: 'Miners' leaders paid personal debts with Gaddafi cash.' The following five pages were given over to the first set of 'authentic' revelations, under the joint byline of Terry Pattinson, the paper's industrial editor, Frank Thorne and Ted Oliver. The most dramatic and damaging claim – and the one that Scargill later remembered 'caused me real pain, real distress' – was that the NUM president had used £25,000 of Libyan money donated for striking miners to pay off his own mortgage. As it turned out, the long-awaited Libyan connection merely added spice to the central 'revelation': the entirely unexpected accusation of embezzlement.[5]

Leaning heavily on the testimony of Roger Windsor, NUM chief executive officer from 1983 to 1989, the paper alleged:

Miners' leader Arthur Scargill got £163,000 in strike support from Libya – and used a large chunk of it to pay personal debts. While miners were losing their homes at the height of the bitter 1984–5 strike, Scargill counted out more than £70,000 from a huge pile of cash strewn over an office table. He ordered that it should be used to pay back to the NUM his mortgage and the home loans of his two top officials.

These were Peter Heathfield, the union's elected general secretary, and Windsor himself. The *Mirror* traced the story back to the controversy during the strike over Windsor's dramatically publicized trip to Libya for the NUM, when he was filmed meeting Colonel Gaddafi. Scargill had always denied taking money from the Libyan regime, but here was Roger Windsor himself now revealing the 'incredible cloak-and-dagger operation to bring a secret hoard of Libyan money into Britain'. The cash had been ferried over from Tripoli in suitcases, it was said, on three separate trips by the man first revealed as a Libyan go-between in 1984. This was Altaf Abbasi, a 'mysterious Pakistani businessman . . . [who] had been jailed for terrorism in Pakistan'. Windsor was then supposed to have collected the money from Abbasi on three separate occasions in Sheffield and Rotherham in November 1984. Finally, Windsor had – according to the *Mirror* – brought the total of £163,000 (more than £443,000 at 2012 prices) into Scargill's office on 4 December 1984 on the NUM leader's instructions. Scargill explained he was anxious to see the union's accounts 'cleaned' in readiness for the imminent takeover by a court-appointed receiver. He was worried in case the 'receiver or sequestrator would find them to be . . . "not entirely one hundred per cent"'. The NUM president had then counted out three heaps of banknotes, the former chief executive alleged, to settle the three officials' outstanding 'home loans': £25,000 to clear his own mortgage, 'around £17,000' for Heathfield's 'home improvements', and £29,500 to clear Windsor's own bridging loan advanced earlier in the year. A further £10,000 was also set aside to pay off legal expenses run up by the union's Nottinghamshire area.

It was a devastating series of allegations, which seemed to be thoroughly corroborated by other witnesses: Steve Hudson, the NUM's finance officer during the 1984–5 strike, who remembered being called to Scargill's office to pick up the cash for the repayments and provide receipts; Jim Parker, Scargill's estranged driver and minder, who confirmed taking Windsor to meet the Pakistani middleman for at least two of the cash 'pick-ups';

Abbasi himself, who described three trips to Libya to collect the money from 'Mr Bashir', head of the Libyan trade unions, and his subsequent deliveries to the NUM chief executive; Windsor's wife Angie, who remembered the Libyan cash being stored in the family house; and Abdul Ghani, who said he had acted as a witness at two of the cash handovers for his friend Abbasi.

The story could scarcely have looked more damning. The problem was not so much the confirmation that the NUM had secretly taken donations from the Soviet Union and Libya. For all the huffing and puffing, such funding had been widely assumed, despite the NUM leadership's denials. And in the case of the Soviet Union, the 'troika' of strike leaders – Scargill, Heathfield and McGahey – had all openly pressed for cash support in 1984. But the revelation that two of the miners' strike troika had apparently had their hands in the till was something else entirely. This was a real scoop. However much his critics disliked his politics and his leadership style, nobody imagined Scargill was personally corrupt. The same was true of the widely respected Heathfield. But now it seemed that the Robespierre of the British labour movement, the sea-green incorruptible, the trade-union leader that 'doesn't sell out', had been exposed as a grubby, silver-fingered union boss lining his pockets at his members' expense.

On 'Day One' of the *Mirror* campaign, the flagship of the Maxwell empire carried a special editorial, personally signed by 'Robert Maxwell, Publisher'. With the imprimatur of the great man himself and headlined 'Scargill's Waterloo', the *Mirror* conceded that the paper had never in fact supported the 1984–5 miners' strike. 'But there is no gloating on our part in exposing how hollow it was ... the hypocrisy of the NUM's disastrous leadership' was only now revealed. 'Some shady manoeuvres', the man once described by government inspectors as unfit to run a public company went on, 'were probably inevitable'. But unions had to be 'open and honest, both with their members and with the public'. The *Mirror*'s revelations about the NUM 'show that it was neither'.[6]

That night, the miners' leaders' pain was piled on in spadefuls as the *Cook Report* went into action before an even bigger audience. The saga of the Libyan money, home loans and Altaf Abbasi's international courier service was rehearsed in loving detail. As Roger Cook – the man who had unmasked a thousand small-time swindlers and petty crooks – described the scene in the programme's voice-over: 'It's December 1984, halfway through the strike, and the three men who run the NUM are counting out the cash to pay off their personal loans when many striking miners were losing their houses.' But the *Cook Report* took things a stage further, wildly upping the ante on the size of the supposed Libyan slush fund. The Libyans had not only donated £163,000, the programme declared. According to Altaf Abbasi, they had also come up with an extra $9 million – something he had apparently not thought fit to mention to the *Daily Mirror*. This huge sum had been made available, he said, for 'hardship purposes only'. Most of the money had then been returned during the previous three months after an unexplained 'official inquiry'.

There was more. At a secret meeting with Abbasi in Roger Windsor's house, it was said, Scargill had asked the Libyans to provide guns for his personal use. The former chief executive recalled: 'He wanted ... a revolver for himself, a little ladies' revolver that he could keep in the car and a pump action shotgun.' The viewer was then informed by Cook that 'Mr Scargill apparently asked other people for guns too' – we were not told who – 'but in Altaf Abbasi's case settled for the money instead.' The programme also made hay in passing with a Soviet strike donation of one million dollars – or pounds, it was not entirely clear which – that Windsor claimed had been paid into a Warsaw bank account with Scargill and Heathfield as sole signatories. Cook explained that the money had earlier appeared in an NUM account in Switzerland but been returned on Scargill's instructions, 'officially to keep it out of the hands of the sequestrators'. The clear implication was that the cash was diverted to finance Scargill's own private pet projects.

Stories were recounted of the sinister rewriting of NUM executive minutes, 'strange transactions', dodgy bank accounts, and the misuse of the International Miners' Organization for Scargill's 'Machiavellian machinations'. Jim Parker, lifelong communist, Scargill bodyguard, driver and buddy, appeared on screen to insist that the widely reported police assault on Scargill at Orgreave in the summer of 1984 had been a propaganda fraud. 'If the truth were known ... he actually slipped down a bank.' When he had been told about Scargill's mortgage scam, Parker declared, it was the last straw. 'That's something I shall never forgive him for.'[7]

The *Mirror*, it has to be said, did at least print edited highlights of the NUM's denials, if only to insist that the paper was able to 'expose the big lie'. Roger Cook relied instead on the 'doorstepping' technique which made the heavyweight New Zealander's name. 'Did you or did you not', he demanded of the miners' president as Scargill drove off from his bungalow outside Worsbrough Dale near Barnsley, count out 'bundles of cash for you, for Peter Heathfield and for Roger Windsor on your office desk?' In the view of Roy Greenslade, the *Mirror*'s editor, the scene of Scargill repeating mechanically through his car window 'If you've got any questions ... put them in writing, send them to me and I'll make inquiries' was more incriminating for the viewer than any number of detailed allegations. The phrase had in fact been insisted on by the NUM's lawyers. But it was a gift to the *Cook Report*. The programme was, in the words of the following morning's *Daily Express* banner headline, truly a 'TV trial'.[8]

Scargill and Heathfield had been well aware for months that both Windsor and Parker had taken Maxwell's shilling, and had been bracing themselves for the onslaught. But the reality turned out to be far worse than anything the two men had imagined. In the last week of February, calls to the NUM came thick and fast from current or former employees, friends and fellow trade unionists about the increasingly aggressive approaches from the *Daily Mirror* and the *Cook Report*. Nell Myers, Scargill's personal assistant and NUM press officer, kept a record. Monday, 26 February: Steve Hudson rang to say two *Mirror* reporters had come to his house with Jim Parker asking about loans and Libya ... Tuesday, 27 February: Ken Cameron, the firefighters' leader, reported that Central Television had been on to him about NUM money; Betty Heathfield (separated from Peter) called to say that the *Mirror* team had been round asking: 'Did she know her extension had been paid for with Gaddafi money?'

On Wednesday, 28 February both the *Mirror* and the *Cook Report* finally contacted the miners' leaders direct. They would be running a sixty-minute documentary and a series of articles on money from Libya and the Soviet Union. Would the NUM comment? The *Cook Report* producer, Clive Entwistle, suggested Scargill meet him 'in the presence of your lawyers' to answer questions. When the NUM president asked that they be put in writing, Central TV faxed back a note saying the questions were too 'sensitive' to commit to paper or 'public fax lines'. Roy Greenslade despatched four questions – all about Libya, nothing about mortgages. Scargill faxed back his response: the union had neither sought nor received cash from Libya during or after the strike. The following day, the NUM executive was warned what to expect.[9]

By the weekend, the media pack scented blood and were camped out in force around Scargill's house and the NUM headquarters in Sheffield. The stakeout would continue for the best part of two weeks, while Anne Scargill – the NUM leader's wife and Women Against Pit Closures activist – barricaded herself in the kitchen with the curtains drawn. At the NUM, the protective inner circle around the two union leaders huddled together ever more tightly. On the eve of the *Mirror* and *Cook Report* revelations, Nell Myers waited at King's Cross Station in London to collect the first editions of the next day's papers. The gory details were then faxed up to Scargill and Margaret Fellows, the NUM's head of administration, waiting in the NUM office. The three of them worked through the night – Myers at the union's flat in the City of London Barbican estate – to draft a first detailed defence for the lawyers to clear the following morning. Headed 'Scargill and the Libyan Money: The Lies', the statement was issued at 1.30 p.m. on Monday, 5 March, the first day of the campaign. Had the *Mirror* put its allegations to the NUM, it said, 'all of the facts ... would have been made available and this smear story would have been destroyed before publication'. In the light of the paper's failure to do so, 'one can only conclude that the *Mirror*'s primary purpose was to mount a malicious character assassination on the NUM's national officials'. The substance of the NUM officials' rebuttal was ignored in the *Cook Report*, broadcast that night. Nell Myers rang Anne Scargill, Margaret Fellows and Frank Watters, Scargill's veteran communist mentor from the 1950s and 1960s, after a 'very ugly' show. 'We all felt sick,' she wrote the same night. Scargill, looking shattered, began an exhaustive – and hostile – series of television and radio interviews in an attempt to rebut the allegations.[10]

The rest of the week was a true grotesquerie of the British media. The *Mirror* revelled in the melodrama of its daily claims of Scargillite skulduggery. Windsor had, it alleged ever more feverishly, adopted codewords to arrange the handover of the Libyan cash: Scargill was the 'patient', Abbasi the 'doctor', and the money referred to as 'X-rays'. Gaddafi's cash had been stored in biscuit tins in the Windsors' larder. Abbasi claimed to have flounced through customs at Heathrow Airport after showing officers £50,000 in cash in his briefcase. 'Windsor the Whistleblower' was reported to be living in fear of a Gaddafi hit-squad in his French mansion because of his failure to repay the funds used to settle his bridging loan. The elderly left-wing barrister John Platts-Mills had admitted asking Gaddafi for a 'substantial sum' for the miners. Faithful Jim Parker, Scargill's pal 'for 34 years', described ferrying around hundreds of thousands of pounds in cardboard boxes during the strike – and how Scargill used lacquer to hide his baldness.[11]

Maxwell was in his element, repeatedly appearing on television with Greenslade to promote himself and his 'classic piece of investigative journalism'. Complaining that Scargill's denial was 'convoluted', he insisted: 'We stand by the *Daily Mirror* story totally.' And in a refrain which would eventually become the *Mirror*'s only defence, Maxwell went on: 'If we are wrong, we challenge him to sue us.' Privacy was one thing for an ordinary, straightforward person. 'But if like Mr Scargill you have tried to bring down an elected constitutional government of the country and if, like Mr Scargill, you have led the Guards division of the trade-union movement to defeat, your conduct is ... of the greatest importance.' The rest of the media enthusiastically leaped aboard the bandwagon, reporting every twist and turn of the revelations – and, with varying degrees of fastidiousness, the miners' leaders' denials. The *Sun* found itself in a particularly tricky position, alternately throwing its weight behind the Maxwell exposé with headlines such as 'Sinister Secret of Red Cash', and then rubbishing its main competitor with the legend, 'It's All Lies', backed up by reports that Windsor was wanted for questioning by British police. Finally, it settled for turning its fire on Heathfield, who, it wrongly claimed, had moved into a house once owned by the village squire of North Anston.[12]

For most of the press, at both ends of the market, the truth or otherwise of the allegations proved to be of less interest than the opportunity once again to thunder against the union which had launched, as the *Express* put it, a 'futile and misguided attempt to bring down a democratically-elected government'. The *Independent* denounced as 'shameful' the disclosure that large sums of money had been 'shuffled' about in suitcases and cardboard boxes to escape the long arm of the law. *Today* declared that 'everything Mr Scargill stands for is fit for history's dustbin'. The *Times* took the view that 'donkey' was 'altogether too benign a word to apply to the miners' leaders'. Even the left-of-centre *New Statesman* managed to compare the NUM president to the 'oppressive regimes' then falling like dominoes in Eastern Europe.[13]

While Scargill and Heathfield denied the charges and called an emergency NUM executive for the Friday, their opponents inside and outside the union stoked up the political pressure. The former NUM receiver Michael Arnold weighed in to declare the NUM leaders' actions at least a breach of trust, at worst 'a criminal act'. The Labour leader, Neil Kinnock, was joined by Norman Willis, the TUC general secretary, in demanding a full public inquiry into the 'extremely serious' allegations. Kinnock's two closest parliamentary lieutenants with mining connections – Labour coal spokesman, Kevin Barron, and unofficial speech-writer and adviser, Kim Howells – had both appeared on the *Cook Report*, and energetically took up the leader's cue. 'There are tears in the valleys of Wales,' Howells told Maxwell's daily, 'but the *Mirror* has done the union a great service.' Tory MPs pressed for the NUM leaders to be prosecuted, and Sir Geoffrey Howe – then Leader of the Commons – said that all the evidence should be turned over to the police, who were 'very ready' to act. Ministers were reported to be anxious to use the affair to divert attention from their own difficulties. *The Times* speculated that both NUM leaders could expect a ten-year jail sentence.[14]

## COUNTDOWN

The origins of the *Mirror* and *Cook Report* stories lay in the extraordinary lengths to which the miners' leaders went to keep the NUM afloat during the 1984–5 strike, at a time when it had effectively been commandeered by the courts. From 25 October 1984, when the union's assets were 'sequestrated' – frozen and subject to seizure – not a penny could be spent from or paid into NUM accounts. From 30 November 1984, the union itself, as a legal entity, passed under the control of an official court-appointed receiver, and remained so until 27 June 1986. The union had only two options: to submit to the courts and repudiate the strike itself, or defy what it saw as anti-democratic rulings and operate entirely in cash. Not surprisingly, the NUM took the second route. Cash donations to separate accounts were stumped up by unions and sympathizers in Britain and abroad. Wages, rent, electricity, printing and picketing costs: all were paid in cash. Hundreds of thousands of pounds were carried around the country in boxes and carrier bags. Around £3 million in banknotes was processed through

the Sheffield office alone. But what made the system effective –
secrecy and trust – also made it vulnerable to those insiders who
turned, for whatever reason, against the union and its leadership.

A second vital ingredient that helped create the conditions
for the 1990 campaign was the disaffection, demoralization and
political infighting inside the NUM following the strike. With
the return to work, the tensions built up like a pressure cooker,
and opposition to Scargill's leadership solidified within and
without. As the accelerated pit-closure programme cut swathes
through the membership and led to union office closures and
job cuts, the dissension grew more bitter. Scargill's opponents
gelled around the 'Eurocommunist' wing of the Communist
Party, based in the fast-shrinking coalfields of South Wales and
Scotland. Half a century of mining-union history was turned on
its head as the traditionally most leftwing areas made common
cause with the right. The Labour Party leadership gave active
behind-the-scenes support to the internal NUM opposition.
And as the union became politically more isolated – and previously secure labour-movement career structures looked
increasingly shaky – some NUM head-office staff began to link
up with the union president's most implacable critics.[15]

One of those who turned violently against Scargill and ended
up carting a filing-cabinetful of NUM documents round Fleet
Street was Maurice Jones, editor of the union's journal *The
Miner*. Jones was an eccentric former communist with an unusual past. As a young man, he had lived in Israel and liked to
boast how he had fled the country to avoid being drafted into
the army. Like Roger Windsor, Jones achieved sudden media
notoriety with an exotic overseas trip. In the summer of 1977,
Jones was editing the *Yorkshire Miner* for Scargill, then Yorkshire area president. He was arrested, along with Scargill,
during a mass picket outside Grunwick photographic laboratory
in North London, where a group of mainly Asian women
workers were striking for union recognition. Charged with
threatening behaviour and released on bail, Jones promptly
vanished and failed to appear for his court case. He resurfaced a

few days later in East Germany with his Finnish wife and young daughter, asking for political asylum. Jones claimed that while he was being held at Wembley police station after the Grunwick clashes, unidentified plainclothes officials had produced a thick file on him and threatened his wife and child in time-honoured style: 'You have a delightful daughter, Mr Jones, and the roads become very busy at this time of the year.' The police story was that the *Yorkshire Miner* editor had 'gone grey' when they tried to take his fingerprints, supposedly fearful that they would connect him with attacks on the Manchester office of the fascist National Front. Eventually, Scargill and the NUM Yorkshire area secretary Owen Briscoe flew to East Berlin to rescue the terrified Jones and persuade him to return to Britain and answer his Grunwick charge. At Heathrow Airport, Jones was arrested again during scuffles with police and was later convicted and fined. Temporarily becalmed, he carried on with his job at the Yorkshire NUM until Scargill took over as NUM president, when he was brought over to edit the national union paper.[16]

But in the aftermath of the strike, Jones's relations with Scargill cooled rapidly. Part of the problem was political. Jones became a supporter of the Eurocommunist wing of the Communist Party, which played a key role in calling off the dispute and was increasingly hostile to the miners' president. But there were other inflammatory factors. Even before the 1984–5 dispute, Jones had become gripped by the idea that Nell Myers, among others, was a CIA plant and was manipulating the NUM leader. The main evidence appeared to be that Myers – a women's-movement activist whose father had been an East Coast seafarers' union leader and victim of the 1950s US McCarthyite witch-hunt – was American. But the accusation, spread liberally in and around the NUM, was also influenced by office jealousies. Myers had been with the national union on a part-time basis since the early 1970s. But unlike Jones, she was never part of Scargill's Yorkshire coterie and only began working full-time for him after he became national president. From the start, Jones objected to Myers being deputy editor of

*The Miner* as well as Scargill's assistant. His unhappiness increased during the strike, when Nell Myers was asked to produce an issue of the paper while he was away. Widely seen in the head office as the closest of the staff to the NUM president, she became the target of an ugly whispering campaign.

As time wore on, the 'zany and excitable' Jones moved ever further from Scargill politically and repeatedly clashed with his boss over editorial policy. He would privately brief journalists, including the *Daily Mirror's* industrial editor, Terry Pattinson, against the NUM leadership. By 1989, Jones was ready to quit and, in his own words, 'do Scargill'. On the day before he left the union, he self-consciously warned the NUM president: 'Watch your back, there are people out to get you.' In fact, Jones was one of them. He had already passed a photocopied International Miners' Organization bank statement to Pattinson in a frenzied clandestine encounter at St Pancras Station in London a month earlier. Jones was also in cahoots with Scargill's former driver, Jim Parker – who had fallen out with the NUM leader for his own reasons and taken voluntary redundancy shortly before Jones left.[17]

Parker had known Scargill on and off since they were both in the Young Communist League in the 1950s and early 1960s, and had also been his bodyguard during the strike. The miners' leader had twice helped Parker get a job at his own pit, Woolley. After ten years or so out of contact, the friendship resumed and Arthur and Anne Scargill began to see the Parkers socially again in 1978. Parker went to work for the Yorkshire NUM; and when Scargill became NUM president, Parker went with him. Scargill and those around him were to be devastated by Parker's betrayal: 'Big Jim', life-long communist, salt-of-the-earth ex-miner, the ultimate loyalist. Frank Watters, who had been the Communist Party's South Yorkshire secretary when Parker and Scargill joined the YCL, was especially shocked. Nell Myers described Parker's performance on the *Cook Report* in 1990 as 'distressing' and 'full of hate'.

Though lacking much substance, his testimony gave the media attack vital extra credibility. As Roy Greenslade put it,

Parker was 'so obviously a plain man and so eaten up with hate for Arthur'. The *New Statesman* concentrated on Parker's apostasy in a savage editorial on the *Mirror-Cook Report* allegations: 'Parker, who has known the president since the mid-fifties, deserts him now ... What is it that Jim Parker knows that we do not?' Terry Pattinson believed Parker's decision to go over to Maxwell was clinched when the *Mirror* reporters told him Roger Windsor's story about Scargill having paid off his mortgage with Libyan cash. But there was more to it than that. Parker had been collecting documents at the NUM for some time before he went, with an eye to selling his story. Well before he left the union, Parker told Sarah Burton, one of the union's solicitors, that he had been having 'long talks' with Windsor, who was widely 'misunderstood'. At the same time, all three of them had publicly pledged their loyalty to Scargill's and Heathfield's leadership at the end of the strike and all three voted for Scargill's re-election in January 1988.[18]

Parker bore a number of grudges. One was that he resented what he saw as the downgrading of his job. With a shrinking union and fewer calls for an NUM driver, Scargill and Heathfield suggested he look after the new head-office boiler as well, for extra money. Parker – who had chaired Scargill's YCL branch in Barnsley 35 years earlier – was having none of it. He took a lump sum of £27,177 and his pension instead. Shortly afterwards a story appeared in the *Mirror* headlined: 'Scargill axes minder pal'. Frank Watters was despatched to enlist Parker's help in a legal action over the piece, but quickly realized that – despite Parker's protestations of everlasting loyalty – something serious was brewing. Jim Parker's consuming hostility towards his former boss may well have another explanation. Before he left the NUM in early 1989, Parker was told that his wife, Elaine, had had an affair with Scargill in the late 1970s – the subject of much gossip in South Yorkshire NUM circles. Perhaps significantly, after the appearance of the first *Mirror* stories, Parker made a point of regaling journalists with tales of the NUM leader's alleged sexual exploits, and was despatched by the *Mirror* to try and stand up some of his stories.[19]

At all events, by the summer of 1989, Parker and Jones had hired a lawyer at considerable expense to help sell their story. But if Parker's material was a little thin, Jones's was even thinner, mainly consisting of angry memoranda from the NUM president about the contents of *The Miner*. Negotiations had nevertheless begun in earnest with the *Mirror* when relations between Jones and Parker unexpectedly soured. Parker became convinced Jones was trying to do a separate deal, though he now says: 'Maurice Jones veered off, not me. He was going to do his bit, but then he backed out.' Both Parker and Jones subsequently retired to sulk in their tents. In Jones's case, the tent was a local South Yorkshire paper, the *Rotherham Advertiser*. He later went to live in Cyprus, initially covering the Middle East as a news-agency reporter. But for all Parker's colourful tales, stacks of NUM documents and useful bits of corroboration, both he and Jones were in the end little more than bit-part players. It was Roger Windsor who was the pivot of the whole campaign.[20]

A cold, fussy man, who had spent most of his adult life doing routine office work in the suburbia of the South East, Windsor cut a bizarre figure helping to run Britain's most important strike since the 1920s. He had come to the NUM, with impressive left-wing references, to oversee the finance department about a year before the strike, but was soon afterwards promoted to chief executive officer. This was the NUM's senior nonelected position, a job which gave him knowledge of – and influence over – some of the union's most sensitive manoeuvres during and after the year-long confrontation of 1984–5. Windsor was a key player in several of the strike's more controversial episodes: notably, his own highly publicized trip to Libya, when he was filmed embracing Colonel Gaddafi six months after the killing of a British policewoman outside the Libyan Embassy in London. But in the wake of the Libyan affair and progressively thereafter, Windsor's relations with Scargill and Heathfield deteriorated. Never popular with other NUM staff or the national executive, Windsor was increasingly held responsible for the union's internal difficulties. In the late 1980s, Windsor had become involved with the internal opposition to Scargill's leadership. By the time he announced his decision to resign and move to France in July 1989, his relationship with both the national officials – who were preparing disciplinary action against him – was close to breakdown.[21]

Shortly before his sudden and mysterious departure, Windsor called the *Mirror*'s Terry Pattinson at his home in Staines, West London, and told him he was prepared to talk. Like Jones and Parker, he came armed with a dowry of internal NUM documents. Reams of confidential papers had in fact disappeared from the union's Sheffield headquarters at the beginning of July, during the 1989 annual conference in Scarborough – which Windsor had missed because his wife was ill. The approach to the *Mirror* was Windsor's shrewdest move. By selling his story to a nominally 'Labour paper', his attack on Scargill attracted credibility it would never have had if he had gone to, say, the avowedly anti-union press owned by Rupert Murdoch. It gave his denunciations the appearance of being almost an internal labour-movement affair. The *Mirror* was also the daily paper read most widely by British miners. Pattinson, who had been personally appointed industrial editor by Robert Maxwell, was, in the words of his own editor, 'motivated by an overwhelming personal animosity: he was obsessed with getting Arthur'. He had been sniffing excitedly around the NUM ever since a Soviet miners' delegate at the union's 1988 annual conference in Great Yarmouth confirmed longstanding rumours that Soviet money had indeed been sent to support the British miners' strike. But his inquiries got him nowhere and Parker had slipped through his fingers.

Now, here was Scargill's right-hand man – who had intimate knowledge of NUM affairs that Parker could never have had – knocking at his door, bearing gifts of bucketfuls of dirt. The first interviews were held at the Windsor family home in Kenbourne Road, Sheffield. Later, Windsor would stay at Pattinson's house, plotting Scargill's downfall across the kitchen table. The former NUM bureaucrat behaved, Pattinson recalls, as if he were at the dentist. He was particularly embarrassed and reluctant to discuss his own £29,500 NUM bridging loan, which he claimed had been paid off with Libyan cash. Windsor was a great deal keener to discuss his fee. Later, he would insist he 'certainly never went to the *Daily Mirror* for gain'. But in the summer of 1989, Windsor was not slow to come to the point. His original asking price, according to Pattinson, was £125,000, and he demanded a legal indemnity to protect him from libel actions and to ensure that nothing would be written without a firm contract. The final deal was not struck until the autumn. But so far as the *Mirror* was concerned, Windsor was already in the bag before he left for France with his family that August.[22]

With the NUM's former chief executive as good as signed up, the *Mirror* went back to net Parker. Scargill's ex-driver, who still likes to describe himself as a socialist, was 'uneasy' about taking money from Maxwell. 'Get wise', his wife Elaine chided him, and when he realized Windsor was being handsomely rewarded, Parker 'broke'. Both Windsor and Parker took large sums for their exclusive stories, although the *Daily Mirror* never saw fit to inform its readers that their key witnesses were hired – let alone the size of their bounties. In fact, Jim Parker got £50,000 and Roger Windsor was paid £80,000. Greenslade, the editor at the time the payments were made, insists that Windsor was given the extra £30,000 to repay his bridging loan, though Pattinson denies it. Either way, almost a quarter of a century later, Windsor's solemn pledge given in the *Daily Mirror* to repay the money either to the Libyans or to the Miners' Solidarity Fund remained unfulfilled.[23]

The NUM leadership got wind of what Windsor and Parker were up to fairly soon after the chief executive's hasty departure from England, and took pre-emptive action. Peter Heathfield signed a front-page story for *The Miner* in the autumn of 1989 revealing that Maxwell was planning a 'smear campaign' against the NUM. 'Something rather sinister is going on,' *The Miner* reported. During the union's annual conference, entire files had been stolen from the office of Scargill's secretary. Pattinson, the piece said, had got hold of bank-account details and was charging around like James Bond.

The warnings had been building up. The IMO bank statement taken from NUM headquarters and originally offered to the Mirror by Maurice Jones finally surfaced in the *Mail on Sunday* in mid July. Rumours filtered back to the NUM leaders. In October, Scargill and Heathfield met an ex-member of staff who had been named by Windsor in connection with a long-standing libel case against the NUM leaders. The former chief executive, they declared, was 'singing like a canary to Maxwell'. A few days earlier, Scargill had gone to the police with evidence, held back for three months on legal advice, of 'serious matters involving a former employee of the NUM'. This included a letter forged in the name of a UDM official, David Prendergast – the man behind the libel action – thefts of documents from NUM head-quarters, and the loss of money from a 'front' company Windsor had controlled called Oakedge. Police-inspired press reports on the NUM president's approach to them were the first public sign of the battle royal ahead.[24]

Inside the *Mirror*, the great Scargill investigation was given the codename 'Operation Cyclops', after the one-eyed giant of ancient Greek mythology, and treated with the utmost secrecy. Indeed, the *Mirror* management was so determined to protect its scoop from prying eyes and wagging tongues – a vain endeav-our, as things turned out – that a special computer was set aside for all work associated with the story, separate from the ordi-nary office mainframe machine. The *Mirror's* proprietor was duly informed of the scandal his footsoldiers had uncovered, and Pattinson was summoned to Maxwell's presence at the TUC congress in Blackpool in early September. The corrupt press baron told him to give a brief outline of the information he had so far uncovered. 'Are you sure it's right?', Pattinson recalls Maxwell demanding. Yes, he replied, he was quite certain. 'Do it', the tycoon ordered. At the *Mirror*, however, there was growing concern as to whether their man was entirely up to the job. Richard Stott, Maxwell's editor of the moment, had a particularly low opinion of Pattinson. So two other reporters –

Frank Thorne and Ted Oliver – were swiftly brought in to provide the paper's industrial editor with some investigative ballast. But Scott continued to be unhappy with the work in progress and repeatedly sent the reporters back to check their facts. Pattinson insisted later that the story could have been run without difficulty in the autumn of 1989. 'But Stott just sat on it,' he grumbled. 'He was a stickler for accuracy.'[25]

In some desperation, Thorne hired a private detective and security agency, Magnum Investigators International, to burrow into Scargill's holy of holies and crack the NUM leaders' complex financial dealings. Magnum was the kind of outfit that boasted in its promotional material of specialized 'surveillance and security services', debugging and 'undercover assignments'. Among other tasks, Magnum was instructed by the *Mirror* team to trace the various secret bank accounts in Britain and Europe that Scargill and Heathfield had used to hide the miners' cash from the sequestrators and receiver. One account the firm did manage to dig up was in the name of Jean McCrindle, friend of the NUM president and leading light of the women's support groups. The main private eye on the job would later complain bitterly about the 'spin' the *Mirror* put on his work, and Magnum itself went bust in 1993.[26]

Pattinson himself did not take kindly to his two journalistic minders, nor to the use of private detectives, and the quarrels over the Cyclops investigation between him, Thorne and Oliver became legendary in the *Mirror*'s high-rise headquarters at Holborn Circus. 'There were terrible rows between them,' Greenslade recalls. 'Pattinson told Roger Windsor not to talk to Thorne and Oliver, who were pushier about getting him to retell his story. I had to lecture them on acting like men rather than children.' Greenslade's industrial editor was, in particular, 'unable to keep his mouth shut'.[27]

For all the *Mirror*'s elaborate precautions, it wasn't long before every labour and industrial correspondent in the country knew the *Mirror* was cooking up a wicked brew of the financial secrets of the miners' strike. Rival journalists made frantic efforts to discover exactly what the *Mirror* had on Scargill.

When Jim Parker finally succumbed to Maxwell's chequebook in the autumn of 1989, the *Mirror* team booked their trophy into the Waterton Hall Hotel near Wakefield for a 'debriefing' in the grandest Fleet Street style. Maxwell's investigators had registered under their own names, and word quickly spread among local reporters and tipsters that the *Mirror*'s Scargill hit-men were there in force. Pattinson – who, like Roger Windsor, wears glasses and is often bearded – was spotted dodging through the hotel by a photographer, and the cry went up: 'There's Windsor!' The former NUM chief executive was meanwhile a thousand miles away in the South of France. But the appetites of the dozens of reporters and photographers camped in the lobby had been whetted. The *Mirror* team's predicament was made worse by the fact that the hotel is sur-rounded by a lake and has only one entrance across a footbridge.

Parker was plied with drink in a hotel bedroom, while Pattinson ran across the bridge with his anorak hood up mut-tering in an imaginary foreign language. 'Is that French, Mr Windsor?' one reporter called out. Parker himself was finally smuggled out once the journalists' pack had retired to the bar. But the story was put about by the *Mirror* team that Windsor had had to be rowed away to safety under cover of darkness. This was a wheeze which had seriously been considered to protect Parker from the danger of any contact with tabloid competitors, but was dropped during a moment of collective lucidity. The story nevertheless later appeared as fact in the *Sunday Times*. Pattinson blames his fellow sleuths for the whole fiasco. 'It is an open secret what I think of those two wallies.'[28]

Yet the Waterton Hall episode was not the end of the threesome's bungling. The process by which Maxwell's *Mirror* and Central Television's *Cook Report* came to pool their inves-tigations was portrayed at the time of the scoop as an innovative multimedia collaboration. In real life, it had more in common with a shotgun wedding. When the story first broke, the official line was that the two groups of reporters had decided to cooperate after they kept coming across each others' tracks and realized they were chasing the same quarry. But one former *Cook*

*Report* researcher who worked on the Scargill programme describes this as a sanitized version, strictly for public consumption. What had actually happened, he says, was that Clive Entwistle, Cook's producer, had got hold of the *Mirror* exclusive during an extended drinking session with Pattinson. Maxwell's industrial editor had started bragging about his forthcoming scoop. Entwistle, who had at one time worked on the *Mirror*, then kept dashing to the gents to make notes – and later briefed *Cook Report* researchers from pieces of toilet paper.[29]

Not so, says Pattinson. He accepts there were some heavy sessions with Entwistle at the London Press Club, but insists: 'I tried to con Entwistle. I told him a fib, which was that the story was about Russia.' But Entwistle, who had once had his own little scoop in the field, interviewing Gaddafi at the time of Roger Windsor's visit to Tripoli during the miners' strike, had checked up and found it was really about Libya. The *Cook Report* paid a '*Mirror* mole' for tip-offs on the investigation, Pattinson claims, and 'tried to bribe me'. But he goes on to concede, referring to a *Mirror* journalists' favoured drinking club: 'One or two bits had leaked out in Vagabonds. Thorne and Oliver were indiscreet.' Entwistle denies there was a paid mole at the *Mirror* or that there was any attempt at bribery. 'It's true I made the odd note in the loo,' the *Cook Report* producer admits, but adds that by then he already knew the outlines of the *Mirror*'s story. 'Terry was the mole, if the truth be known.'[30]

Having caught their prey, the Cook team suggested working together. Pattinson refused. Entwistle then went over his head to the *Mirror* editor Richard Stott, who also turned them down. Stott was sacked and replaced by Roy Greenslade, who once again rebuffed the pooling plan. But only Entwistle proved able to convince Altaf Abbasi – the Pakistani exile who had acted as Windsor's middleman with the Libyans during and after the 1984–5 strike – to cooperate. When the *Mirror*'s three musketeers had first tracked him down, under Windsor's guidance, Abbasi took one look at their official-looking black limousine, jumped over the garden wall and fled. Entwistle's insurance salesman's manner, however, turned out to be altogether more reassuring. He and Abbasi met in a Nottingham church hall where a Pakistani opposition politician was addressing the local community. 'We pretended we knew more about it than we actually did', Entwistle guffaws. 'We're the best conmen in the business.' There and then, Abbasi confirmed Windsor's claims about Libyan cash while the cameras rolled. The Cook producer then took Ernie Burrington, the Mirror Group's managing director, to lunch and pressed him for cooperation over the Scargill investigation. 'Leave it with me,' Burrington told him. With the added threat that the *Cook Report* would 'screw' the *Mirror* and blow their story, the *Mirror* cracked. Burrington had fixed it with Maxwell – who, it was later revealed, had been electronically bugging Burrington's office. Maxwell liked the idea of collaboration with Central Television, Greenslade says, partly because he knew he would get publicity on air for exposing the miners' leader and partly because he wouldn't be taking on Scargill alone.[31]

There was another, more delicate, factor. Maxwell also owned 20 per cent of Central Television's shares, which must have been a welcome added bonus. With the deal in the bag, money was by all accounts now spent with wild abandon as the new joint Central–*Mirror* investigation careered around Britain and a variety of suitable foreign locations: France, Australia, the Soviet Union. In Moscow, the Cook operation hired a cousin of Mikhail Gorbachev, then still the country's president, to pin down the tale of the Soviet millions. In France, the Central–Maxwell investigating team found themselves in mortal danger when, in the middle of a hurricane, the intrepid Roger Cook insisted on taking the controls of a light aircraft they had chartered. Back in Britain, researchers were pulled in from other programmes in an effort to harden up the evidence.[32]

By the time Greenslade arrived from the *Sunday Times* at the beginning of February, Maxwell had already proudly informed his new editor of the secret scoop he would be given the privilege of publishing. Greenslade discovered that a wide assortment of journalists at the *Mirror*, and at other papers, were also in the know about Operation Cyclops. The *Cook Report* – as well as Pattinson's two minders, Thorne and Oliver – warned him that his industrial editor was 'talking his head off'. Greenslade realized he had to move fast. The existing version of the story, which he found unintelligible, was entirely rewritten – it looked, he recalls, 'like a kind of tawdry local paper, in which no one was quite sure what was going on'. He then decided to run the revised package immediately – without consulting Maxwell about the date. The *Mirror*'s proprietor was 'apoplectic' when he discovered that Greenslade had pressed ahead 'without discussing it in detail with me first'. But the timing depended on synchronization with Central and there was no going back.[33]


## CRACKS IN THE EDIFICE

Hardly had the Maxwell campaign been launched on an unsuspecting world, however, than giant cracks immediately started to appear in the elaborate edifice his 'Mirrormen' had spent so many months constructing. Within a few hours of the story's publication, evidence had already been produced to show that by far the most serious allegation – that Scargill had paid off his mortgage with Libyan-supplied hardship funds – was at complete variance with the available facts. Other gaping holes in the case against the miners' leaders quickly became obvious. If testing the story against the evidence had been the main determinant of its survival, by the end of the first week of the Scargill Affair the condition of Operation Cyclops would have already been verging on the terminal.

The *Mirror* and *Cook Report* had only themselves to blame, since they had deliberately avoided putting the specific central allegation directly to either Scargill or Heathfield. 'We didn't want to alert him and give him a chance to cover up,' Greenslade explains in retrospect. ' "Fronting-up" is a very dangerous moment in a story like that.' The four questions that the *Mirror* did fax over to the NUM headquarters – all variants on the theme 'Did you seek or receive money from Libya?' – were only included at all to draw the miners' leader out. The *Mirror* was terrified that the NUM would succeed in getting a court order to stop the allegations running. 'We were deficient in documents,' Greenslade admits. 'Otherwise, we could have argued our way out of an injunction.'[34]

From the *Mirror*'s point of view, its lack of documents was probably just as well, because its most sensational claim would not have stood up to even the skimpiest of documentary examinations. Scargill couldn't have paid off his mortgage with Libyan money because he didn't have a mortgage. He had in fact repaid it with his own money months before Roger Windsor ever set foot in Libya. Heathfield couldn't have paid off his 'home loan' with Libyan money because he didn't own his home. It belonged to the Derbyshire area of the NUM. As the NUM's official statement, issued at lunchtime on 5 March 1990, put it: 'Neither the National President nor the General Secretary had a mortgage or loan, so no question of payment could have been perceived.' The only person who could have had – and in fact did have – a loan on his house paid off with the money Windsor claimed was brought from Libya was the person making the allegation. And Windsor had indeed offloaded his £29,500 NUM bridging-loan debt with the mysterious cash.

Scargill duly appeared on television the first night of the *Mirror*'s campaign waving a 1984 book of cheque stubs. These recorded that he had paid off his mortgage to the union on 8 August 1984, almost four months before Windsor said he brought Libyan money into the union's Sheffield headquarters. Windsor had also got the size of the mortgage wrong. By the time Scargill repaid it, the amount outstanding from what had originally been a £25,000 mortgage was down to £22,255.45. The repayment was made using two cheques. One was drawn on the NUM president's own account with the Co-operative Bank in Barnsley for £5,255.45 and another £17,000 was paid out of his Bradford & Bingley Building-Society account and endorsed on the back to the NUM. The full amount was deposited in the NUM's account on 14 August 1984. The cheque stubs have been examined by the author. Cork Gully, the accountancy firm, crawled all over Scargill's accounts and confirmed that the repayment was made with his own savings built up over years.[35]

But as with all effective smear stories, the mortgage allegation was constructed out of real events and real transactions. Windsor *had* brought large sums of money into Scargill's office in the wake of his trip to Libya; Scargill *had* divided up piles of cash on his desk; and he *had* used it to repay the NUM for sums of money spent on his and Heathfield's homes. But there the relation between reality and the *Mirror*–Cook tale ends. The amounts of money cited by Windsor were wildly wrong; they were not loans; and the nature of the 'repayments' was entirely different from that claimed by the *Mirror* and *Cook Report*.

Under NUM rules and longstanding contractual arrangements, the union provided homes for its national officials at a peppercorn rent. In Scargill's case, he had owned his house at 2B Yews Lane, Worsbrough, since 1967. When he became Yorkshire NUM president in 1973, he was offered by the area trustees, and accepted, a £3,000 mortgage on the house at 2½ per cent interest. Eight years later, the mortgage facility was increased to £25,000 to pay for an extension. In March 1984, just as the year-long strike was beginning, the NUM executive unanimously decided that the national union should buy both Scargill's house – something that had been agreed two years earlier, but postponed because of the move to Sheffield – and Heathfield's house, which was owned by the NUM's Derbyshire area. This arrangement was in line with union practice, had applied to all previous national officials, and was included in the two men's contracts of employment. As part of the process, Scargill's mortgage with the Yorkshire area was transferred to the national union in the same month. The plan was for the NUM then to pay off Scargill's mortgage so that the national union would own the house outright and charge him rent.

However, the strike intervened and in anticipation of the threat of sequestration, Roger Windsor recommended, on legal advice, that both the national officials' houses be transferred to a trust (the 'Mineworkers' Trust') under the NUM's control to protect them from seizure by the courts. The legal process for the transfer to the trust was started in March, but never completed. By the middle of the strike, the fate of the two officials' homes was effectively in a state of limbo. Since there was no authorization for a continuing mortgage with the national union, Scargill paid it off with his own money in August 1984 until such time as the union's purchase of his house could be completed.

Meanwhile, repairs and improvements to both houses had been carried out. In Scargill's case, the work was started at the end of 1983 and completed in March 1984. The bill for a little over £6,000 was paid by the NUM on the assumption that the house was being bought by the union. In Heathfield's case, the work on his Derbyshire NUM-owned house, which included rebuilding a tilting garage wall and a kitchen extension, was carried out in the early autumn. A large part of the cost was met directly by Heathfield. The repairs were to be paid by the NUM, since the national union was in the process of buying the house from the Derbyshire area.[36]

But once the High Court had ordered the sequestration of NUM assets on 25 October, there was increasing concern at the union headquarters that the officials' homes would be seized if it could be shown that they were NUM properties or that the union had spent money with the intention of buying them. The sequestrators tried almost immediately to take possession of the NUM flat in the Barbican in London, and only abandoned the attempt when they discovered it was rented in Scargill's name, rather than the union's. The same threat potentially hung over Roger Windsor's home because of the £29,500 bridging loan he owed to the NUM. Scargill and Heathfield had meanwhile set up an ad hoc trust fund, called the Miners' Action Committee Fund (MACF) – separate from the union and operated entirely in cash – to keep the NUM afloat and its money out of the clutches of the courts. It was therefore decided – according to Scargill and Heathfield, on Windsor's insistent advice – to 'repay' the national union with money from this fund.

On a disputed date some time after 25 October it is common ground that Roger Windsor brought a large quantity of cash into the NUM head office. Windsor told the *Mirror* and *Cook Report* that this was 'the Libyan money', but half a dozen people – including one of the *Mirror*'s star witnesses, the NUM's finance officer Steve Hudson – say Windsor told them at the time it came from the French communist-led CGT trade-union confederation. From the end of October onwards, the arrival of wads of banknotes became an almost daily occurrence. Cash donations and union loans of hundreds of thousands of pounds were regularly brought to Scargill's house and the union's Sheffield headquarters from all over the world. £225,000 was handed over in the month following the sequestration order alone. All deliveries were duly noted in the MACF records.

On this particular occasion, out of Windsor's pile of money, Scargill counted out £6,860.58 to cover bills the NUM had paid for his house; £13,511.21 for the work on Heathfield's house, then still owned by the Derbyshire NUM; and £29,000 for Windsor's bridging loan – the remaining £500 was repaid later. Steve Hudson was then called down to collect the cash and pay it over to the NUM's own account. Hudson later provided receipts and the balance of the cash went back into the MACF fund. Within four days, Scargill repaid from his own savings the £6,860.58 spent on his house – witnessed by Nell Myers – to ensure that there could be no argument that he owed money to the union. On a later date, Scargill handed £12,000 from the same Windsor cash source to the Nottinghamshire miners' leader Henry Richardson to cover striking miners' legal bills.[37]

This was the basis of the entire Scargill 'embezzlement' story. Every figure given by Windsor as being paid off on the disputed day – £25,000 for Scargill's 'mortgage', £17,500 for Heathfield's 'extension', £10,000 for the Nottinghamshire miners, and £29,500 for Windsor's bridging loan – was wrong. In the case of Scargill's house, the figure was more than £18,000 out. More importantly, they were not loan repayments but 'paper refinancing transactions', in the formulation of Gavin Lightman, then a QC. Quite simply, money which had been spent, or would have been spent, by the NUM was paid or repaid by the cash trust fund. In Heathfield's case, the cash was spent on a union property of which he was a tenant. As for Scargill, far from deriving financial benefit from the comings and goings over 2B Yews Lane, he lost a highly advantageous 2½ per cent mortgage. He also personally repaid £6,860 which the *Mirror*'s 'clinching' witness, Stephen Hudson, says he was 'not certain . . . ever had to be repaid anyhow' – because the union was supposed to be buying the property. Indeed, Hudson wrote at the time that the union would pay back the £6,680 on top of the value of the house once the sale was completed – which, in the event, it never was.[38]

Stephen Hudson's subsequent dismissal of the principal charge at the heart of the *Mirror–Cook Report* campaign was, to put it mildly, something of a blow to its credibility. Roy Greenslade describes him as the 'crucial' witness in his decision to publish Windsor's story. Hudson was present when the controversial 'repayments' were made. He had taken the money away and put it in the finance-department safe. If anyone knew the truth of what took place, he did. And he was independent. He had left the NUM in the late 1980s to work for the Coal Industry Social Welfare Organization, a huge network of facilities for working and retired miners and their families, built up since nationalization. So keen was the *Mirror* team to get Hudson to talk, they turned up on his doorstep before running the story to warn him that unless he cooperated 'it could look very bad', in Frank Thorne's words. 'We told him there would be some very irate miners thinking he was one of the guilty parties who colluded with Arthur Scargill.' Hudson, Thorne recalled, 'was crapping himself'. A former colleague of Hudson says he was 'traumatized' by the *Mirror*'s treatment.

The unfortunate former NUM finance officer travelled down to London next morning to give an interview to Terry Pattinson. 'I said to him: why not just ask me nicely?', Hudson recalls. The *Mirror* took his statement – Hudson insists it was not an affidavit, as was claimed later – to be essential corroboration. But Hudson says it was no different to his subsequent evidence

to the NUM's own inquiry, rejecting Windsor's main allegations. As he wrote to Scargill a couple of years after the original
*Mirror* allegations were published: 'As far as your mortgage is
concerned, I am staggered this old chestnut has raised its head
again ... Your mortgage was redeemed by you out of your
personal funds.'[39]

But Hudson was not the only problem. Even as the charge of
corruption – the hook on which the entire campaign was based
– started to disintegrate on its first contact with daylight, other
glaring errors, misrepresentations and almost comical inconsistencies became evident in the *Mirror-Cook Report* coverage.
The supposed 'Orwellian' rewriting of national-executive minutes described by Roger Cook was based on an episode in 1983,
when Scargill had been in the thick of controversy about Polish
Solidarnosc, a speech he had made in Moscow and the shooting
down of a South Korean airliner by the Soviet air force. The
NUM executive decided to support a complaint by Scargill to
the Press Council about wildly inaccurate newspaper reports of
its debate on the subject. To make sure there was no argument
about what had taken place, all executive members were asked
to check the note-taker's record of their own contribution before
the whole transcript of the executive meeting was sent off to the
Press Council. Several executive members made minor amendments. The complaint was upheld. And thus was a *Cook Report*
legend born.

Then there was Jim Parker's claim that his former boss had
really slipped down a bank – rather than been hit by a
policeman – when he was knocked unconscious during the mass
picketing of Orgreave coking plant in June 1984. This was a
particularly curious allegation for the *Mirror* to print, as it had
thoroughly investigated the incident at the time and come to
the opposite conclusion. The paper had even published a photograph of Scargill just after he was knocked out as supporting
evidence. As Paul Foot was able eventually to write of Parker's
new version of events in his *Mirror* column: 'I was amazed to
hear it. In 1984, I went to Yorkshire and interviewed six witnesses who saw Arthur Scargill being hit over the head by a

policeman's shield.'[40]

The main *Mirror–Cook Report* story itself proved remarkably flexible. The amount of money allegedly provided by the Libyans changed almost daily, as did the supposed size of the Soviet contribution. On 5 March 1990, the *Mirror* reported Windsor as having brought £163,000 of Libyan cash into Scargill's office on 4 December 1984. The same evening, the *Cook Report* quoted him as saying it was £150,000. The next day, the *Mirror* printed a transcript of a telephone conversation between Windsor and Steve Hudson, in which Windsor says he brought in 'about £50,000'. That would not of course have been enough to meet all the debts he claimed had been paid off, which came to more than £70,000, even without the Nottinghamshire bills. But it would have been just sufficient to cover the sums that were actually paid that day. When challenged about the £50,000 months later, Windsor suggested the tape must have been 'faulty'.[41]

The MACF cash-book in fact recorded a £100,000 donation from the CGT on 25 October 1984 – acknowledged by Scargill and Heathfield to have been backdated – and another CGT 'international collection' of £50,000 on 4 December 1984. The first is the cash out of which the home 'repayments' were made; the combined £150,000 appears to be the money Windsor later said came from Libya. The *Mirror*'s dates were hopelessly confused and contradictory. Windsor had supposedly kept all the Libyan money collected from Altaf Abbasi in biscuit tins in his larder until 4 December. But his wife Angie was quoted as saying that their bridging loan was paid off with Libyan money ten days before. In fact, the date when the cash was 'divvied up' must have been earlier still, because according to Windsor's own evidence the Libyan money was used to pay the Nottinghamshire miners' bills. Henry Richardson, the Nottinghamshire official who collected that cash, subsequently confirmed that the date on his receipt – 18 November 1984 – was genuine. Other evidence suggests Windsor produced the first £100,000 well before 18 November. The importance of these dates will become apparent later.[42]

Throughout an avalanche of coverage, the *Mirror* never found space to inform its readers that its two principal witnesses, Windsor and Parker, had been paid £130,000 for their evidence. Nor did it see fit to mention for several days that its main informant on the Libyan connection, middleman Altaf Abbasi, had something of an unusual past, including a conviction in Pakistan on a bombing conspiracy charge; nor that another of its witnesses, Abdul Ghani, had been jailed for fraud. The *Cook Report* – which managed to muddle up the TUC and Labour Party conferences – apparently also felt these details were of no interest to its viewers. By any token, such a disastrous series of mistakes, omissions and misrepresentations as those endorsed by the *Mirror* and *Cook Report* might have been thought certain to cast serious doubt on anything further they had to say on the subject. But the *Mirror* – and in due course, the *Cook Report* – ploughed on regardless, ridiculing the denials issued by the miners' leaders as nothing but lies. Windsor was quoted declaring: 'Once Arthur has created a story, that becomes the truth and the truth then becomes the lie.'[43]

It was not until the fourth day of the campaign that a major labour-movement figure spoke out in defence of Scargill and Heathfield. With the *Mirror* turning its fire on the secret financial support given to the miners' strike by other unions, both Ron Todd, general secretary of the Transport and General Workers' Union, and Ken Cameron of the Fire Brigades' Union weighed in to denounce the tabloid campaign against the miners' leaders. It was, Todd said, a 'trial by media smear' and an 'affront to natural justice'. But they were isolated voices. Despite the evidence already available that the central allegation was false, embarrassed silence reigned even among sections of the left. Only a handful of small-circulation left-wing papers made any real effort to challenge the mass-media assault.[44]

The NUM leaders' position was made more vulnerable as it quickly became obvious that suing for libel was out of the question. Maxwell and the *Mirror* palpably salivated at the prospect of making Scargill sing for his supper in the High Court. By the same token, the union's legal advisers warned that a libel action against Maxwell would be won at a very heavy price. That would doubtless include a forensic re-examination of the events of the 1984–5 miners' strike, of picketing tactics, links with other unions, and cash provided to keep the NUM afloat, not to mention days of personal and political invective against Scargill under cross-examination. The opportunities for muddying the waters around the methods the miners' leaders had used to beat sequestration and receivership – in other words, deliberate defiance of the law – would be played to the full. Despite the overwhelming evidence disproving the corruption allegations, someone of Scargill's reputation – the 'Enemy Within' incarnate, a man singled out by the Prime Minister of the day as a mortal enemy of the British way of life – clearly stood a less than sporting chance of a fair trial in a London courtroom. Scargill was nevertheless prepared to go ahead. But to do so, he needed cash and political support from the union. And the NUM president's internal enemies made it abundantly clear that they would fight tooth and nail against any cash backing for a libel case. Kevin Barron, Neil Kinnock's closest ally on the executive, wanted an inquiry under Labour Party and TUC control. Almost the entire executive opposed funding a libel action. 'You're on your own, Scargill,' the nominally communist Scottish miners' leader, George Bolton, hissed – to the *Mirror*'s delight.[45]

In the event, disposing of the embezzlement allegation was comparatively straightforward. But, with the libel route effectively closed, Maxwell was under no pressure to back down. It was open season on the NUM. The charge of personal corruption had provided the lever to prise open Scargill's box of tricks. In order to clear their names, he and Peter Heathfield found themselves forced to reveal some of the most important international and domestic cash lifelines – along with the networks of secret accounts – that had kept the NUM functioning and independent during and after the 1984–5 strike. And although the claim that they had their fingers in the till was the only accusation which, if true, was guaranteed to bring the NUM leaders down, the follow-up allegations would prove so complex, far-reaching and ripe for legal mischief-making that the sound and fury was guaranteed to continue for months and years to come.

As an emergency NUM executive gathered 'like a Star Chamber in judgement on its own leader' at the end of the first week of the Maxwell campaign, Scargill was said to look 'under great strain'. He and Heathfield disclosed for the first time the existence of fourteen different independent trust accounts set up to maintain the union when its official funds had been seized by the courts and a receiver given legal control of the organization itself. They denied any knowledge of Libyan cash deliveries. 'If Roger Windsor took delivery of money from such sources,' their report stated, 'he either lied about it when he brought the money into the NUM or he never brought the money in at all.' The national officials also revealed for the first time that the Soviet Union had sent $1 million, but had refused to donate it to the NUM or the various separate accounts. Instead, they said, it had been channelled through the Eastern-bloc-based Miners' Trade Union International to a trust fund for international solidarity after the strike.[46]

The evidence presented to the executive quietened some of Scargill's most vociferous critics – though the *Mirror* and *Cook Report* continued to refuse to withdraw a single claim. The meeting was reminded that, far from lining their pockets at the union's expense, the two national officials had drawn no salary for twenty months during and after the 1984–5 strike. With little enthusiasm for the cost and prospects of the libel courts, the executive voted to back a proposal from the national officials to set up an independent inquiry into the *Mirror–Cook Report* allegations, to be presided over by an eminent barrister. It was agreed to approach the Haldane Society of socialist lawyers to help pick a 'suitable QC'.

The *Mirror* and its retinue of camp followers insisted they detected a 'whitewash' and refused to participate. Jim Parker, Maxwell's hired witness and a life-long Communist Party member, complained: 'I am worried because the Haldane Society is a left-wing organisation.' The paper wanted no part in a 'hole-in-the-corner exercise', its editor, Roy Greenslade, thundered, demanding instead that Scargill take his medicine in court without further delay. When the NUM executive's five-man subcommittee charged with overseeing the inquiry — it later became a 'four-man team' after the Yorkshire NUM president, Jack Taylor, retired — selected Gavin Lightman QC, the predictions of a snow-job were increasingly more confident. Lightman had worked for the NUM in connection with the receiver's breach-of-trust action against Scargill, Heathfield and McGahey. And he immediately decided that his inquiry would be in private and would take confidential evidence from anonymous witnesses. But as Lightman pressed ahead with his new assignment, it became ever clearer that the whitewash predictions were very far off the mark indeed.[47]

Lightman's agreed terms of reference were: first, to establish whether or not money had been received from Libya or the USSR and, if so, what had been done with it; and second, to determine whether Scargill, Heathfield and Windsor had used strike funds to pay off their home loans. But by the time the QC returned to the NUM's four-man team at the beginning of June to ask for his terms of reference to be widened, it had become obvious that there had been miscalculations on both sides. Lightman wanted the green light to rule on another issue altogether: whether or not there had been 'breaches of duty' and 'misapplications of funds' in connection with the NUM's financial arrangements during and after the 1984–5 miners' strike. He got it and, by doing so, laid the ground for a quite different and far more sweeping report. For the *Mirror* and *Cook Report*, the main target had been Scargill, Heathfield and their respective housing arrangements, with the mysteries of Muscovite and North African gold thrown in for added glamour. Now the entire funding operation behind the 1984–5 miners' strike would be brought into the frame — and with it, the legitimacy of the strike itself.[48]

# CHAPTER TWO

# A HIDDEN HAND

Every individual ... is in this, as in many other cases, led by an invisible hand.
*Adam Smith*, WEALTH OF NATIONS, *1776*[1]

If Maxwell's 'spring offensive' had been gruelling enough for the miners' leaders, the torrent of press abuse, legal actions and official investigations unleashed by the publication of the Lightman Report four months later was to prove a veritable immolation. For ten relentless weeks from the beginning of July, the flagging media campaign of the previous March revived with a vengeance. And in the rear came a whole retinue of litigants, lawyers, accountants, state officials, Labour apparatchiks, policemen, freelance spies and Cold War professionals determined to play their part in a final settling of accounts with the insurrectionary impudence of the 1984–5 strike.

Gavin Lightman seemed a most unlikely candidate to become another Scargill tormentor. In 1990, he was a commercial barrister and part-time north-country circuit judge who, as a sideline, wielded the disciplinary rod in professional snooker – on one occasion fining Alex 'Hurricane' Higgins £12,000 for head-butting an official. But he also had a reputation as a liberal figure who had worked for the NUM during its period in receivership, advising the miners' leaders on the receiver's potentially disastrous breach-of-trust action. A religious Jew who was active in community causes such as the Anti-Defamation League, Lightman was scarcely a natural member of the right-wing – and often anti-Semitic – legal establishment. One friend has described him as 'a bit of an anarchist'.[2]

Despite a longstanding ambition to be a fully fledged judge, he was exceptionally proud of his relationship with the NUM president, whom he had invited to his birthday party and photographed with his children. Scargill even agreed on one occasion to speak at his son's school. A measure of Lightman's feelings about the most vilified public figure in Britain is revealed in the dedication he inscribed at the top of a learned legal paper he wrote about sequestration and receivership: 'To Arthur'. Lightman recorded in 1987: 'It was a trial in more ways than one – but we were, both in good days and bad, undivided.' Such a blissful state of unity would not survive the QC's entanglement with Operation Cyclops. Between mid April, when he shared a genial cup of tea with Peter Heathfield in Sheffield, and the completion of his report a couple of months later, Lightman's attitude changed dramatically. Whether as a result of what he learned about what actually took place, or because of what he was told privately – or for some other reason entirely – Scargill's bewigged admirer turned bitterly on the miners' leader. His report, based on confidential evidence from both named and anonymous witnesses – as well as on a compendious financial analysis by the accountancy firm Cork Gully – was handed to the NUM executive and released to the press on 3 July 1990. In place of the measured adjudication that might have been expected was a sustained polemic, thinly veiled in legal niceties.[3]

Lightman cleared Scargill and Heathfield of personal corruption, the blue touch-paper of the whole Scargill Affair. 'Mr Windsor's allegation that the cash he had brought in was used to repay Mr Scargill's mortgage of £25,000 is entirely untrue', Lightman found. The claim made by the *Mirror* and *Cook Report* about the repayments – which, regardless of the evidence, they clung to like limpets for years – was 'quite incorrect', he concluded. 'No such monies were used to repay any home loan of Mr Scargill or Mr Heathfield. Mr Heathfield never had a home loan until much later and Mr Scargill had some time before repaid his home loan out of his own monies.' That disposed of the original and most serious accusation. As to secret international funding, Lightman could reach no firm conclusion on whether or not the £150,000 Windsor was recorded as having turned up with in late 1984 did in fact originate from Libya. It might have, he thought. But then again, it might not. Without the cooperation of Windsor, Abbasi, the *Mirror*, the *Cook Report* and the Libyan government, he declared himself at something of a loss.

From there on in, the report took on an entirely unexpected ferocity. Despite a parallel absence of any 'direct' or overt response from the Soviet miners' union, Lightman had no doubts about the Soviet cash and what the Soviet donors had meant to be done with it. The barrister concluded that Scargill had, without authority, 'diverted' £1.4 million of Soviet and East European donations sent to the NUM in 1985 to a secret trust fund in Dublin, originally known as 'Midaf' and later by the acronym 'Mireds': the 'Miners' International Research, Education, Defence and Support' trust. The Dublin trust – which Lightman described as a 'sham' – had been set up as a solidarity fund under the auspices of the Warsaw-based Miners' Trade Union International (MTUI). After the MTUI was dissolved, the trust was amended to bring it under the wing of the new International Miners' Organization (IMO), the East-West alliance of mining unions created on the initiative of the NUM and the French CGT. Lightman contemptuously rejected the claim by Scargill and Alain Simon, the IMO's general secretary, that the Soviet and East European miners' unions had insisted their money be used for wider 'international purposes' – including the needs of the British NUM. His clear inference was that Scargill had, in cahoots with ambitious CGT leaders, diverted the cash to build up his pet international political project, the then embryonic IMO.

Such behaviour constituted a 'misapplication' of the Soviet cash and a legal breach of duty 'of the most serious character'. Lightman recommended that the NUM consider taking legal action for the 'return' of the money from the Mireds trust. Even more savage was the barrister's damnation of the entire system of secret accounts used by Scargill and Heathfield to pay the union's bills after the judicial takeover of the official NUM structures. Scargill and Heathfield gave Lightman details of seventeen accounts. In the NUM leaders' words, they were 'in all honesty designed to confuse and for secrecy', to protect whatever precious funds they could lay their hands on from seizure by the sequestrators or receiver.[4]

As far as Gavin Lightman, commercial lawyer and QC, was concerned, this was dangerous heresy. In a report originally commissioned to investigate Soviet and Libyan money and alleged embezzlement of hardship funds, a total of 41 out of 133 pages were devoted to those topics. The rest was a barely restrained tirade against the 'unofficial' secret accounts, their illegality, their continued use after the end of receivership, their 'non-disclosure' to the NUM executive, their insufficient supervision by lawyers and accountants, and their 'inter-mingling' with IMO money. Similar cash loans and donations had in fact been made to officials of NUM area organizations who were subject to their own court orders. But these were passed over in the report. Mick McGahey, the Scottish NUM vice-president, Lightman insisted, 'did not play any part in the financial arrangements'. In fact, McGahey and the NUM Scottish area played a key role in 're-routing' trade-union loans to the secret accounts – including the MACF cash fund – and issuing receipts for them. Scargill and Heathfield, however, were singled out. They were guilty, Lightman charged, of impropriety and a multiplicity of breaches of duty and mis-applications of funds over their handling of the unofficial accounts since 1984.

Lightman's conclusions amounted to an invitation to all and sundry to take legal action. The NUM leaders had quite transparently established their secret trusts and 'unofficial' accounts as independent and separate from the NUM in order to protect them from seizure. But almost Lightman's entire case against them hinged on a particular interpretation of the law: namely, that any donation to such a trust for the general benefit of the NUM became by the same token the property of the NUM. This claim was, in his own words, 'fundamental' to his report. It was the reason for his request for new terms of reference. And from it flowed many of his sharpest attacks. If the accounts were really NUM accounts, all the money in them should first of all have been paid to the sequestrator and receiver – in which case, that was the last that would have been seen of it, at least for some years. Second, the accounts should have been disclosed to the union's executive – and whatever donations and loans passed through them should have been sanctioned by and repaid to the NUM, rather than to the unions that contributed the cash.[5]

The special treatment Lightman reserved for the NUM president was striking. Roger Windsor's inconsistencies and 'mistakes' were handled with indulgence and understanding. 'Anyone's memory is likely to confuse details over that length of time', Lightman commented about Windsor's notably contradictory evidence at one point. The miners' leader was permitted no such indulgence: 'I regret', Lightman remarked witheringly, 'that it has been my strong impression that Mr Scargill's story on a number of points has changed as it suits him throughout the conduct of this inquiry.'

At times, evidence was simply left behind in the sweep of the QC's condemnation. For example, Lightman quoted an NUM switchboard operator who said she remembered putting calls from Altaf Abbasi through to Scargill in the summer of 1984 – contradicting Scargill's insistence that he had had no contact with Abbasi until several months later. Lightman recorded ominously: 'The book that logged such incoming calls at the time has been lost or destroyed.' In fact, a parallel log was kept by Yvonne Fenn, then the NUM president's secretary, which she duly reported to the Lightman Inquiry. It recorded no calls from Abbasi, but Lightman did not see fit even to mention this piece of counterevidence. In another instance, when discussing the repayment of Scargill's home expenses, Lightman asserted that the miners' leader 'knew that his house had not been conveyed and therefore that the union should be repaid their money'. But Lightman and Cork Gully had a note in their possession, sent to Scargill by the NUM's finance officer in the summer of 1984, about his tax affairs, which stated that his house had been 'bought by the union'. It was ignored.[6]

While Lightman's pedantry and barristerial manner were widely taken as signs of 'meticulousness' and 'punctiliousness' at the time, his report was in fact littered with errors. The QC also adopted at times a highly political tone. Lightman singled out for attack the then six-million-strong International Miners' Organization and its French general secretary, Alain Simon. He excoriated the IMO for secretiveness and lack of accountability. There was a clear conflict of interest, Lightman insisted, between Scargill's leadership of the NUM and his presidency of the IMO – ignoring the fact that presidents of trade-union internationals are, almost without exception, full-time officials of national affiliates. The IMO's finances were, Lightman complained, 'practically impenetrable'. And he made short shrift of Simon's and Scargill's argument that secrecy was essential because of the repressive conditions under which many of the IMO's affiliated unions had to operate. This was, of course, an organization which the NUM had played a central role in setting up and which had taken the lead in breaking the Cold War mould of international trade unionism. But Lightman had his own ideas. The union should, he recommended, 'give very serious thought' to breaking its IMO affiliation.[7]

## THE JULY MAELSTROM

The release of such an unexpectedly hostile report brought an avalanche of renewed political and media attacks. There were immediate anonymous calls by right-wing NUM executive members for the police to be called in and for Scargill to resign. One commented: 'If I had been criticized like that I'd want to chuck myself out of a window.' The ex-communist leader of the dissident South Wales area George Rees said he was 'shocked and saddened' by the report and predicted that Scargill would face legal action. 'Scargill is unfit to lead the union,' the *Independent* newspaper editorialized. 'It is difficult to think of any holder of public office, anywhere in Britain, who could have read a Lightman report on his behaviour ... and sought to stay in office,' the *Guardian* mused. David Hart, Margaret Thatcher's confidant and organizer of the 'National Working Miners' Committee' during the 1984–5 strike, was wheeled out to warn of the need for vigilance against the ever-present threat of 'unrepentant, hard-line Marxists' like Scargill rising from the lower recesses of British society.[8]

For the *Mirror* and *Cook Report*, this was Christmas all over again. Inside Maxwell's flagship, there was naturally private dismay that the *Mirror*'s main allegation had been dismissed. Terry Pattinson says he was 'surprised' to find his principal charge had been 'blown out'. 'We were astonished by Lightman,' Roy Greenslade recalls. But there was also huge relief that so much other ammunition had been helpfully made available to provide cover for any strategic retreat that might prove necessary. Indeed, the *Mirror* was so excited about the 'missing' Russian money that it had some difficulty making up its mind as to the sum involved. On 5 July 1990, it was £3.6 million; £1 million on 4 and 10 July; 'as much as £1.8 million' on 11 July; £1.4 million on 20 July; and on 12 July, £2 million 'including food'. Lightman's dismissal of the original embezzlement charge was given at best perfunctory treatment by most newspapers. So too were the protestations from Scargill and Heathfield that all donations had been accounted for and that every loan had been repaid in full. No Maxwellian retreat was required after all. The QC had digested a mountain of evidence handed over by the miners' leaders to prove their innocence and served it up in handy gobbets for hostile media regurgitation. And whereas in the initial phase of the scandal, the Maxwell press had led the field, it was now a free-for-all.[9]

The *Cook Report* immediately launched itself into a second Scargill programme with gusto, gratefully seizing on the new material provided by Lightman and the disclosures made by the NUM leaders themselves to clear their names. Far from pulling in its horns after the programme's main original allegation had been so comprehensively discredited, the *Cook Report*'s second effort was if anything more unrelentingly poisonous – and politically loaded – than the first. Indeed, while the new edition acknowledged that the Lightman Report had found Windsor's description of the mortgage and homeloan repayments 'mistaken', the claims were repeated. The viewer was left with the clear impression that Lightman had been hoodwinked by the miners' leaders.

Michael Arnold, the City of London receiver who had complete legal control of the NUM from 1984 to 1986, told Cook he thought the goings-on uncovered by Lightman were so serious that the report should in the normal run of things be handed over to the Serious Fraud Office. 'One detects a tangled web – tangled webs I was always taught were set up to deceive,' he explained. The programme dismissed the IMO – the largest grouping of miners' unions in the world – as an organization whose 'main purpose seems to be the furthering of Scargill's political ambitions'. Kim Howells and Kevin Barron, two of Neil Kinnock's closest allies in parliament, were conjured up to reinforce the political message. The IMO, Howells insisted, had been a 'total failure . . . a Mickey Mouse organization . . . a kind of piggy bank for Scargill and this unreconstructed Stalinist Alain Simon . . . for their ideas about some kind of revolution which the miners would head . . . it's just a nonsense.'[10]

But the weighty TV investigator had more than just political abuse to throw at the NUM. A document submitted by Scargill and Heathfield to the Lightman Inquiry had been forged, the *Cook Report* and *Daily Mirror* charged. Although not explained on the programme, this was a land registry form assigning Windsor's bridging loan, which the union's former chief executive said had been paid off with Libyan money, to the IMO. Windsor had told the first Cook programme that he felt guilty about the loan. He had assured the *Mirror* that he was anxious to pay it back to the Libyans or the miners' solidarity fund. Four months later, he had still not done so. He conceded there had been discussions at NUM headquarters about paying the debt to the IMO, but denied he had ever signed such a document. And indeed, the signatures of his wife Angie and his two witnesses, Meryl and Roy Hyde, were patently not genuine and appeared to have been faked by the same person. The Hydes' address was crudely falsified. 'Forgery!' roared the *Daily Mirror*'s front page, reasonably enough. Readers and viewers were left in no doubt as to the culprit: this was Scargill up to his tricks again. The true identity and motives of the forger would only emerge much later.[11]

The second *Cook Report's coup de grâce*, however, was a real Scargill home loan – as opposed to the phantom mortgage supposedly paid off with Gaddafi cash. The arrangement had been disclosed to Lightman by the NUM president, and the QC's report described it as 'disturbing'. Here seemed to be something the media campaign could really get its teeth into. Six months after the end of the miners' strike, in the autumn of 1985, Scargill had bought a new house. This was Treelands, a £125,000 double bungalow his mother had much admired in the 1950s, just outside the family's home village of Worsbrough Dale. And the £100,000 cash the NUM president had privately borrowed to buy the house – now hard up against the M1 motorway – had been drawn from the same MTUI Dublin trust fund into which the contested Soviet money was then in the process of being deposited.

One of several drawbacks with the story was that Scargill had repaid all the money with interest within three years. Half was paid back with an ordinary mortgage from the Co-operative Bank in 1987, once the threat of the receiver's breach-of-trust action had been withdrawn. The rest was settled out of the proceeds of the sale of his old home in the same village. Lightman's overriding concern was that the money originally came from the Dublin trust, 'Mireds' as it came to be known. But the bridging loan was in fact made by the MTUI – an organization to which the NUM was not affiliated. It was the MTUI which decided to withdraw the cash from the trust fund for ease of access – and the money was replaced from another account shortly afterwards. A TGWU official had helped ferry the cash over from Ireland. The terms were £50,000 at 12 per cent and £50,000 at 2½ per cent, in line with standard

NUM arrangements for its officials. The composite interest rate was 7¼ per cent – 16 per cent if Scargill's post-strike unpaid salary were taken into account. And the MTUI loan was reported to the accountants Peat Marwick and the Inland Revenue years before it was revealed in the Lightman Report.

At the time he borrowed the cash, Scargill had had no salary for seventeen months, the Bank of England had an outstanding instruction to all banks and financial institutions to report every detail of his personal finances, the receiver was in the process of bringing potentially bankrupting litigation against him and the other NUM leaders, and he had little prospect of obtaining an ordinary mortgage or loan. When he was finally able to arrange a Co-op mortgage nearly two years later, it still took six months to be approved. Lightman described Scargill's MTUI loan from the trust fund, which subsequently came under the auspices of the IMO after the MTUI was dissolved, as 'obviously wrong'. Heathfield, who borrowed money from the IMO when his marriage broke up and repaid it all with 10 per cent interest, was similarly castigated. Lightman's view hinged on his insistence that the Mireds trust was an invalid sham and that the money in the Dublin account belonged by rights to the NUM. Ironically, Lightman had himself advised Scargill in 1985 on how to buy Treelands and protect it from risk of seizure in the breach-of-trust action then being brought by the receiver, but for some reason he failed to refer to the exchange in his report.

The *Cook Report* and the *Mirror* were more concerned to make capital out of the fact that the NUM leader had bought a new house at all – at a time when miners were still up to their necks in debt from the strike. Indeed, once the original embezzlement allegation was disposed of, this was probably the only disclosure that caused significant resentment among some rank-and-file miners. One underground worker at Grimethorpe colliery in South Yorkshire – which closed in 1993 – told a *Guardian* reporter at the height of the media's 1990 summer offensive: 'To use money for buying a house at a time when people were struggling – that is wrong.' Another, half-jokingly pointing out the pit medical centre, warned the same reporter: 'This is

Scargill country – you might need treatment if you're from the newspapers.'[12]

Yet buying a house with a bridging loan from an organization with no formal links to the NUM had clearly got nothing in common with pocketing hardship funds to pay off a mortgage. It was increasingly apparent to anyone able and prepared to examine the facts that – whatever fast financial footwork there had been to keep the NUM afloat, and whatever questions the affair raised about problems of maintaining accountability in an all-out confrontation of the type the union had faced during and after the 1984–5 strike – there had been no sleaze and no fingers in the till. Nor was there any money 'missing' from the seventeen independent accounts used to protect funds from seizure by the courts. But the reaction of the NUM's core activists to such a double dose of media venom in four months was still uncertain. The first test would come at the NUM annual conference in Durham, which opened at the North East miners' magnificent headquarters at Red Hill in a state of high tension on 9 July.

Scargill describes his presidential address on the first morning of the conference as the most difficult speech of his life. He was fighting to defend not just his record, but his job. 'I apologise to no one,' he told the assembled pit delegates, 'for the role I have played during a period which has been tantamount to a state of war against everything we represent.' Receivership had led the NUM 'just like Startrek, into areas where no union has ever gone before ... I am proud to have set up a maze of accounts to confuse the sequestrators and camouflage funds and prevent them being seized by the state.' He and Heathfield, Scargill went on, turning to the phalanx of cameras and reporters in the gallery, had 'been subjected to an unprecedented trial by media', and he called on the membership to 'reject the character assassination of those who have traditionally been our enemies'. To the astonishment of many outsiders, the conference rose to give the NUM president a thunderous standing ovation. One emotional delegate even compared the NUM president to 'Jesus on the cross'.[13]

This was not what had been anticipated at all. The stark failure of the conference to turn against Scargill was greeted with dismay by the NUM leaders' enemies. Within the space of a few days, a string of investigations and legal actions had been unleashed – almost as if guided, like Adam Smith's market economy, by an unseen hand. First, the Labour leader's camp followers moved quickly to try and repair the damage and get back on top of the situation. 'It's like a football manager who always receives a vote of confidence before he gets the sack,' Kevin Barron – a member of the NUM executive and that year's chair of the miners' group of MPs – explained hopefully to reporters after Scargill's unexpected reception in Durham. Kim Howells, his fellow Kinnock lieutenant, went one further, demanding in the House of Commons that the Fraud Squad be called in forthwith to investigate the 'sordid affair'. Scargill would never be forgiven in the valleys of South Wales, Howells declared from the green leather benches, for bringing the NUM into disgrace. David Blunkett – another rising Labour star and trustee of the Miners' Solidarity Fund, set up to provide hardship relief during the strike – was quick to get in on the act as well. The Soviet money should have gone to his fund, he insisted, urging NUM members to disentangle commitment to their cause from 'commitment to Arthur Scargill'. Even Norman Willis, the TUC's bumbling general secretary and ineffectual mediator during the miners' strike, lurched back on the scene again demanding to know whether Scargill had deceived him in 1984 over assurances that the NUM had had no Libyan money.[14]

But these were just the warm-up acts. On 10 July, Geoffrey Howe, Deputy Prime Minister, said in parliament that he hoped 'the appropriate authorities' would investigate 'these gravely disquieting allegations'. South Yorkshire police told reporters they were waiting for the 'right trigger' to move. A couple of days later, the Employment Secretary, Michael Howard, announced he was considering tightening legal controls on trade-union finances in view of the Lightman Report's revelations about the secret accounts used during and after the

1984–5 strike. Fraud Squad officers arrived at the NUM head-quarters in Sheffield to interview members of the NUM finance department. Officials from the Certification Office – a hitherto anodyne and humdrum government agency in charge of super-vising union affairs – launched an unprecedented investigation of the NUM's financial returns and told the union's accountants that they were planning a criminal prosecution of the miners' leaders.[15]

Meanwhile, the man who had set the detonator for this shower of political and legal debris travelled to Ireland in search of a piece of the action. On 11 July, Roger Windsor – who had been advised by lawyers not to set foot in Britain – was given leave in the High Court in Dublin to sue Arthur Scargill, the *Sunday Times* and *Daily Express*, for libel in two separate actions over articles that had appeared the previous October. These were reports of Scargill's visit to South Yorkshire police with allega-tions of fraud, forgery and theft of documents. Two days after Windsor set in train his Irish cases, the Inland Revenue's Special Office opened its own inquiry into the NUM's financial affairs and the secret accounts denounced so vociferously by Lightman. Almost simultaneously, Ted McKay, a right-wing former secre-tary of the union's North Wales area, approached Gill Rowlands, the Warrington-based 'Commissioner for the Rights of Trade Union Members' – appointed by the government and strongly opposed by the TUC – for financial backing to prosecute Scargill and Heathfield. In London, Scotland Yard announced it was looking into the Scargill Affair. And in Paris, the French police were reported to be investigating the allegations against the IMO. Media speculation resurfaced that Scargill would end up in jail. The *Mirror*'s Terry Pattinson and the NUM defectors Jim Parker and Maurice Jones all predicted that the miners' leader would be behind bars by Christmas.[16]

Another libel action was suddenly reactivated. This had first been brought in 1985 by David Prendergast, one of the founders of the Union of Democratic Mineworkers, against Scargill, Heathfield, the NUM and two Nottinghamshire NUM officials, Henry Richardson and Jimmy Hood (who later became a Labour MP).

After years of sluggish progress, the case was unexpectedly taken in hand by Peter Carter-Ruck, the renowned and prohibitively expensive London libel lawyer. Payment for his exclusive services in the Prendergast case would from now on be provided by the right-wing Goldsmith Foundation. This was the body set up by the Anglo-French multimillionaire financier, publisher and Cold Warrior, Sir James Goldsmith. Its purpose was to fund like-minded litigants – such as the CIA 'consultant' and Cold War propagandist Brian Crozier, whom Goldsmith subsidized with hundreds of thousands of pounds – in their war of attrition against the left.[17]

Taken as a whole, this was, by any reckoning, a remarkably wide-ranging assault. Seven legal actions, prosecutions and state-backed investigations were launched or revived against Scargill, Heathfield and the NUM within one fortnight in July. Every public and government agency with any conceivable interest in the miners' affairs – backed by a supporting cast with a variety of axes to grind against the NUM leadership – took the Lightman Report as the green light to 'have a go'. The story that had set the whole affair running – Scargill's mortgage and the Libyan money – was long since forgotten. Now the target was Russian money and the Mireds fund, all of which Lightman claimed belonged to the NUM. For Scargill and Heathfield, the bitterest pill would be forced down their throats by their own national executive, under the attentive 'guidance' of lawyers. The meeting on 3 July, at which the Lightman Report had been produced by the QC's assistant barrister, Elizabeth Jones, had been grim enough. Executive members had not had the chance to read the dense 133-page document – or its 140 pages of annexes – in advance. But Scargill's opponents seized the opportunity to go on the offensive and a decision was taken there and then to accept Lightman's recommendations in principle.

In the wake of the Durham conference – which agreed that an autumn delegate conference would decide on any action over the report – Lightman met the executive's four-man inquiry team at his Lincoln's Inn chambers and outlined his plan of attack. 'If you don't get serious with these people,' the QC told them, 'they'll run you around.' There were 'individuals' in the union, he warned them, waiting in the wings to go to court if they refused. Two of the four – George Rees and Gordon Butler – were anti-Scargill men. The others – Henry Richardson and Idwal Morgan – were regarded as supporters. But all gave their consent. A couple of days later, on 19 July, the full NUM executive gathered in Sheffield. The 'four-man team' presented a legal opinion drawn up by Lightman, arguing that the union should immediately begin proceedings against its own president and general secretary. What was more, Scargill and Heathfield would have to leave the room immediately – and all communication with them over the affair would be banned. The executive acquiesced.[18]

As soon as Scargill and Heathfield had been hustled out of the meeting, Elizabeth Jones appeared on behalf of Lightman to inform NEC members that, as custodians of the union, they could themselves be personally liable for breach of trust if they voted against suing the national officials. Only three members – from Yorkshire and the North East – initially voted to resist the lawyers' demands, and even they eventually wilted in the face of such a legal barrage. Jones handed out Lightman's detailed advice: the 'further opinion'. Action must begin immediately for the recovery of the £1.4 million of Soviet and East European money, plus interest, 'diverted' to the Mireds trust fund – part of which had been moved from Dublin to a higher-interest account in Vienna. More bizarrely, Lightman also wanted the 'return' of £580,000 of British trade-union cash loans, which had at one point been held in the same account but had later been repaid to the unions concerned.

The IMO's Alain Simon and the Labour European parliament member Norman West – the two Mireds trustees – should also be sued for damages, along with Scargill and Heathfield. As his 'further opinion' unfolded, Lightman was almost palpably warming to his work. 'In view, in particular, of the attitude taken by Mr Simon,' he cautioned, with evident distaste for the recalcitrant Frenchman, there was a 'real risk' that the money would be spirited away. So immediate action would need to be taken to freeze all relevant accounts. And Lightman was already reconsidering some of the judgements made in his report as too lenient. Fortunately, the QC knew a 'competent' solicitor to take this difficult job in hand. He recommended that the NUM hire an upmarket legal firm, Frere Chomeley of Lincoln's Inn Fields. Bruce Brodie, the senior partner and chairman, had promised 'he would personally take charge of the matter'.[19]

With the threat of personal liability dangling over them, the coalfield leaders obediently followed Lightman's lead. According to papers that have since come to light, it appears that their decision was little more than a formality. Brodie, an old friend of Lightman, had actually begun acting on the NUM's behalf even before the executive voted to employ him. At 3 a.m. on the morning of 19 July, Brodie was already busy faxing out letters to a legal firm in Austria – where some of the Mireds funds were held – to take the first steps in the proceedings against the NUM and IMO leaders. And in another example of the extraordinary steps they took to assist the action against the miners' leaders, both Gavin Lightman and the accountants Cork Gully handed over Scargill's private papers and financial records, submitted in confidence to the Lightman Inquiry, to Frere Chomeley without obtaining the NUM leader's agreement. In both cases, letters were sent to the union headquarters giving him a brief opportunity to object, but Scargill was anyway out of the country. Lightman then passed over the documentation immediately; Cork Gully followed suit a few weeks later.[20]

Scargill described the NEC's decision to sue as 'crackers' and rejected out of hand calls for his resignation. Heathfield, on whom the pulverizing attacks of the previous four months were taking an even heavier personal toll, called it 'diabolical'. It was a move which had no precedent in trade-union history and would later be described by David Guy, leader of the North East miners, as one 'that will haunt this union for the rest of its days'. But the legal wheels turned swiftly. Writs were issued in the High Court in London within hours of the NUM executive's decision, and injunctions freezing the IMO trust accounts were granted in Dublin and Vienna. A private surveillance firm was employed to make sure that both Scargill and Heathfield would be at work the next morning to endure the calculated humiliation of having writs from their own union served on them in person at the NUM headquarters in Sheffield.[21]

## SOVIET AGENTS

The focus of the drama now switched to the trail of the Soviet money. The problem was now no longer that the cash was missing, but rather who owned it. Scargill and Alain Simon maintained that the Russians had insisted at the time it was originally sent that the aid go to an international miners' solidarity fund. Lightman – and his enthusiastic chorus of supporters in the media, Labour Party and police – were determined to prove it had been earmarked for the NUM alone and should therefore be prised from the control of the IMO. Meanwhile, the people who everyone assumed had been the original donors, the Soviet miners' union, had begun to issue wildly contradictory statements.

In Moscow, on 11 July, an ITN reporter cornered Vladimir Louniov, the newly elected president of the Soviet Coal Employees' Union (CEU), who confirmed that more than two million roubles had been raised from his members during 1984–5 to support the British miners. But that money had been spent on food shipments and five hundred holidays for strikers. There had, he said, been 'no currency remittances from the union of Soviet mineworkers ... not from the miners, maybe from other sources'. This directly contradicted Lightman's conclusion that the CEU had sent around £1 million for the NUM. But just as Scargill was claiming Louniov's statement as a vindication of his own longstanding position, Louniov's predecessor stepped back into the limelight. This was Mikhail Srebny, who had been ousted as the Soviet miners' president the previous March in the wave of perestroika-inspired political change then sweeping the USSR. Srebny, who had cooperated with the *Cook Report* just before he was drummed out of office, had also been the IMO's vice-president and a member of the organization's 'inner group' from its foundation.[22]

On the same day that the NUM's litigation against Scargill and Simon kicked off in three countries, Srebny gave his own interview to ITN and repeated even more forcefully his earlier claim that £1 million had been sent to the NUM alone. The sacked apparatchik, who appeared to have been told that Scargill had pocketed the Soviet money to buy his new house, declared himself thoroughly indignant. The cash had only been intended for striking miners, he insisted. More equivocally, Srebny added that until Scargill's theft was proven, he could not 'suspect him of touching that million'. And surprisingly, given his apparent certainty about where the Soviet donation had been sent, the discarded official declared himself at the same time entirely ignorant about when and how it was actually transferred. Back in Sheffield, the NUM president could only shrug off the latest broadside from his former ally. Scargill described Srebny's remarks as 'a remarkable change of mind', but said he would be delighted to see the cash come to Britain if the Soviet coal union would formally confirm that it had been intended for the NUM after all.[23]

At which point, enter on cue, stage right, anti-communist Soviet miners demanding their money back. On the eve of the NUM Durham conference, Yuri Butchenko, a twice-imprisoned dissident from the tiny Siberia-based Kuzbass Union of Workers, was paraded before the press in the National Liberal Club in London by Roy Lynk, leader of the breakaway Union of Democratic Mineworkers. Butchenko claimed that Soviet miners had donated a day's wages – between 10 and 30 roubles, or £10–£30 at the official 1984 exchange rate – to the British strike, along with clothes and other goods. As much as £10 million had gone missing, he calculated. He blamed both Scargill and the 'official' Soviet miners' union (the CEU), whose role in this 'dirty affair' should be exposed. The issue would be raised by supportive deputies in the Russian Supreme Soviet, he promised.[24]

Butchenko's visit, it soon transpired, was organized and paid for by an anti-Soviet Russian émigré newsletter, *Soviet Labour Review*. So was the timely press conference on the 'missing' Soviet money. Since 1983, the 'review' had been lavishly financed by the US government's National Endowment for Democracy (NED). This was a Reaganite quango set up to provide a more acceptable conduit than the CIA for US funding of right-wing, pro-Western groupings around the world. In 1984–5 alone, the NED channelled $129,000 into the *Soviet Labour Review* and its activities. The review's editor, a bearded 'translator' named George Miller, doubled up as the British representative of an extreme anti-Soviet clandestine organization, NTS – the 'People's Labour Alliance', sometimes known by the more cumbersome title of the Popular Labour Alliance of Russian Solidarists. The NTS had a colourful history. It collaborated enthusiastically with the Nazis during the Second World War and was a playground for Western intelligence organizations for more than half a century. Kim Philby, the Soviet agent who became one of MI6's most senior officers before defecting to Moscow in 1963, described in his memoirs how he handed over control of NTS to the CIA in the 1950s. But he added teasingly that, even after formally relinquishing control, MI6 was 'not above playing around with the Alliance under the counter'. Some would have preferred even closer links. Brian Crozier, who worked for British intelligence and the CIA as an 'alongsider', in the jargon of the secret services, would later complain bitterly to MI6 officers about their standoffish attitude to NTS. They should 'resume relations' with this heavily penetrated outfit, he argued, 'as indeed had happened between the NTS and the CIA'.[25]

Miller, some of whose undercover schemes are known to have been directly funded by the CIA during the 1980s, was busy all through the summer of 1990 stoking up the anti-Scargill campaign. A few weeks before he appeared with Yuri Butchenko at the Liberal Club, the NTS's London man had brought over a couple of other anti-communist activists from the Russian coalfields to get to work on the Scargill Affair. The pair,

Sergei Massalovitch and Nikolai Terokin, were whisked down to Weymouth to address the UDM's annual conference. Next day, the front page of the *Daily Mirror* triumphantly reported that these Soviet 'miners' leaders' had confirmed its allegations about the Soviet money. In fact, they were in no position to do any such thing. Massalovitch and Terokin were neither leaders of the official nor of the 'independent' Soviet miners' unions. But they were both members of NTS. While in London, Miller took the two men round to see his old friend Brian Crozier, to brief him about what Crozier described as 'this particular "Active Measure"'. Before they flew back to the Soviet Union, Massalovitch and Butchenko also took the opportunity to appear on the second *Cook Report* programme on the Scargill Affair. Butchenko knew not a word of English, but was nevertheless shown self-consciously studying the Lightman Report. 'I'm disgusted,' he said of what he hadn't read. 'I will be very annoyed if Scargill is not brought to account for this criminal act.'[26]

The NUM executive's legal action against Scargill, Heath-field, Simon and West ground on. But already there were the first stirrings of a coalfield revolt, as activists kicked against what they saw as the commandeering of the NUM's affairs by a posse of interlopers in wigs and gowns. The Yorkshire area council, representing more than a third of the union's membership, voted for immediate negotiations with the IMO over the Soviet cash. The North East area executive denounced the decision to go to law against the union's elected leaders. In an attempt to find a solution, Scargill flew to Paris for a council of war with IMO leaders. Since the NUM leader's efforts at travelling incognito on the outward flight came to nought, and with swarms of tabloid reporters attempting to track his and Alain Simon's every movement – Simon was in fact on holiday in the South of France – it would prove impossible to use the IMO's own headquarters in Bobigny. Scargill stayed instead at Simon's home in the Paris suburbs, from where he accepted Bruce Brodie's suggestion of a hurriedly arranged IMO-NUM meeting in the French capital for the following week.

The full-blown talks on the Soviet money were held at the Sofitel Hotel, just outside the Charles de Gaulle Airport at Roissy, on 24 July in an atmosphere of surreal hysteria. The NUM's four-man team, Scargill and Heathfield, Simon and Norman West MEP – the two Mireds trustees – were all there, along with French and British lawyers, advisers and translators. A complete Fleet Street media troupe descended in force, with a car-full of reporters (the author included) tailing Scargill and Heathfield around the Paris ring road as they were driven from the IMO offices to the meeting. The Sofitel's manageress, who had booked the conference suite in the name of a Jean-Philippe Berthet, one of Frere Chomeley's smart Parisian lawyers, was horrified by the unexpected invasion of coal miners' leaders and British journalists. Alain Simon, whose English is better than he likes to let on, delivered an uncompromising line in a Peter Sellers-style French accent. The Soviet and East European cash belonged to the IMO, he declared. 'There is no reason to give it back ... and our comrades in the NUM will understand that.' Simon accused the British government, media and Labour leadership of running a campaign of vilification against Scargill that had nothing to do with NUM or IMO finances. 'This affair is not about money,' he told a battery of cameras. 'It is about Scargill's head on a plate.'[27]

Inside the cramped negotiating room, where Bruce Brodie and the four-man team pressed Simon to open the IMO's books, the French side was unyielding. Roland Weyl, the IMO's veteran communist lawyer, dismissed the Lightman Report with contempt. 'This is nothing but a police report,' he growled, tossing it onto the table. But after seven hours of direct talks and four hours huddled with legal advisers, the two sides – with Scargill and Heathfield perched precariously between them – announced to the attendant media circus that an 'accord' had finally been reached to settle their differences. The NUM would suspend its court action while efforts were made to establish the donors' true intentions in the mid 1980s and the rightful ownership of the disputed funds. These amounted to a total of £3 million, it was now revealed, including the Soviet and East European money, £580,000 of trade-union loans temporarily lodged in the Mireds account, plus five years' interest. In return, Simon had agreed not to move the cash and would provide detailed information about the whereabouts and size of the various accounts.[28]

The High Court gave its seal of approval for a three-month suspension of the legal action the following day. The worst of the storm appeared to have passed. Henry Richardson, the Nottinghamshire NUM leader and spokesman for the executive's four wise men, said they hoped there would be no return to court, now that there was full IMO cooperation. But hardly had the miners' leaders left the courtroom and just as a settlement seemed in prospect, Scotland Yard's Serious Fraud Office threw itself into the public fray. There was to be a full investigation into Scargill's handling of the NUM's finances. This was, the police announced, in response to two formal complaints of theft, forgery and false accounting. The allegations had been passed to Alan Fry, head of the Metropolitan Police Fraud Squad. 'Scargill: Fraud Squad Cops Go In!' the *Daily Mirror's* jubilant headline proclaimed.[29]

One of the complainants turned out to be none other than Sergei Massalovitch, the 32-year-old Russian NTS miner who had been fêted around Britain by the UDM and its US-funded Russian émigré friends the month before. Massalovitch had returned home on 14 July and news of the investigation had been delayed for a suitably theatrical moment. His CIA-cosseted minder, George Miller, said Massalovitch had decided to go to the police after reading the Lightman Report. Naturally, he had 'acted totally independently'. The second complaint was anonymous. It was reported at the time to have been made by a 'former senior employee of the NUM'. This was in fact Jim Parker, Scargill's disgruntled former driver, with £50,000 of Robert Maxwell's money in his back pocket. Detectives were told that at least six others were standing ready to lay their own complaints against the NUM president. Scargill remarks in retrospect: 'Parker would not have had the nous to approach the greengrocer, let alone the Fraud Squad. So who was pushing him?'[30]

As the Fraud Squad's Chief Superintendent Tony McStravik went about his business, Cabinet sources let it be known that the government's law officers had been preparing to refer the Lightman Report to the Director of Public Prosecutions if the NUM had failed to take legal action itself. The *Daily Telegraph* reported that ministers were 'shocked' by Lightman's findings about the secret accounts. They were particularly alarmed by the fact that 'such large sums of cash were ... available to Mr Scargill' during the 1984–5 strike and 'could have affected its outcome'. This, of course – rather than arcane points of trust law or a concern that Russian miners' donations had failed to reach British strikers – was the real basis of the attack on the Mireds fund and the other accounts and trusts.[31]

Throughout the summer, the media revelled in the rich opportunities for Scargill-baiting. The pundits had their say, with a level of vituperation verging on the unhinged. Edward Pearce in the *Guardian* described Scargill as a 'despicable braggart who has squeezed the miners dry'. Neil Lyndon, renowned for his diatribes against feminism, called the NUM leader 'grimly unbenevolent' in the *Independent*. In the *New Statesman*, R.W. Johnson, the maverick South-African-born historian, derided the IMO's resistance to the demands of British lawyers as 'classical Comintern stuff'. The *Spectator*, intellectual hothouse organ of high Thatcherism, complained that the suspension of the NUM's legal action was a 'shabby compromise' and accused Scargill of a record of 'unmitigated disaster' and 'dictatorial tendencies'. In the *Observer*, Paul Routledge and John Sweeney both compared the NUM president to Nicolae Ceauşescu, the autocratic Romanian communist leader who had died in a hail of bullets a few months before.[32]

However, by the beginning of August, the campaign against the NUM leader appeared to be in danger of running out of steam. Several dozen Labour MPs, headed by the left-winger and former miner Dennis Skinner, backed a Commons motion – almost entirely ignored by the mainstream media – supporting Scargill and Heathfield. The motion denounced the 'personal attacks, smears and allegations against national officials of the NUM by unscrupulous elements of the media and two former employees of the union'. The coalfield backlash was also growing apace, as miners grumbled that their union was being taken for a ride by legal fat cats. Stan Crawford, then president of the Nottinghamshire area, demanded an immediate national delegate conference to settle the dispute: 'It's the solicitors that are costing the money. Miners are paid by the day; solicitors by the minute.'[33]

Rupert Murdoch's *Sunday Times* came to the rescue, armed with an exclusive interview with Colonel Gaddafi. From his tent inside the walls of the Aziziya barracks in Tripoli, the Libyan leader had finally spoken out on the controversy that began six years earlier with his meeting with the NUM's chief executive. The headline promised a remarkable transaction: 'Gaddafi: How I Handed Over the Libyan Cash to Arthur Scargill'. Naturally enough, that wasn't quite what the colonel said. 'Scargill's deputy came here', he was in fact reported as telling the paper's Middle East correspondent, Marie Colvin. 'I asked the General Producers' Union of Libyan Workers to provide some help to the miners. I do not know the details of the agreement between them, or how much money was given.' Gaddafi remembered Roger Windsor telling him that striking miners were unable to pay for the burial of their dead children. The Libyan leader added that he was not questioning the honesty of the NUM president, who he described as a 'very well known trade unionist'.

Colvin obtained more details from Muhammad Abdallah Ali al-Khalandi, a Libyan union official, who confirmed that a draft cheque for $200,000 – about £163,000 at late 1984 exchange rates – was handed over and cashed. But he knew nothing about how the funds were delivered. He described it as a 'lot of money for our trade union'. The suggestion that the NUM had cashed a cheque in the autumn of 1984, however, at a time when all its bank accounts had been frozen by the sequestrators, scarcely made sense. And in response to the *Sunday Times* story and a subsequent Gaddafi television interview, Scargill once again denied he knew of any money from Libya; Windsor had, he said, been sent to Libya principally to lobby against rising oil exports to Britain. But it was food and drink to his internal opponents, who had feared that the balance of NUM opinion on the controversy was moving against them. 'This could put the last nail in Scargill's coffin,' Jim Dowling, right-wing leader of the NUM's power group, said hopefully. Des Dutfield, president of the once militant South Wales area, sneered: 'Anyone with a shred of integrity would step down, but we are not dealing with men of integrity.' The story fell strangely flat, however. When Peter Heathfield was told Gaddafi had confirmed that money had been sent after all, he commented: 'It's taken him a long time to remember.'[34]

## JOURNALISM OF THE MEANEST KIND

The point at which the whole campaign palpably started to unravel was the publication of the demented *Daily Mirror* banner headline: 'Gaddafi to sue Scargill'. Fired up by Marie Colvin's exclusive, the *Mirror* despatched Frank Thorne and Ted Oliver, the two more hard-nosed of the Scargill sleuths, to Libya to get their own Gaddafi story. But the two got stuck in Malta. From Valletta, they filed a report claiming to have spoken to a 'senior Libyan official'. This character had apparently told them of Gaddafi's deep concern over what he had read in the *Mirror* about the Scargill Affair: he had, it was said, referred the allegations to his 'Attorney General'. As a result, Libyan lawyers were 'standing by', ready to sue Scargill and Heathfield – presumably in the London High Court. Terry Pattinson contributed to this creative effort but, needless to say, blames his fellow reporters for the outcome. 'The story was totally and absolutely ludicrous,' he admits. It is not for nothing that the *Mirror*'s local pub, the White Hart, was known to regulars as the Stab in the Back.[35]

The media campaign would rage throughout the summer 'silly season', legal actions and investigations would grind on, accusation and counteraccusation would continue to divide and weaken the miners' union. But the sheer absurdity of the 'Gaddafi to sue' claim splashed across the front page of Britain's second-largest-selling daily notably undermined the credibility of the whole *Mirror*-driven exercise, revealing it as more of a pantomime than a serious investigation. Officials at both the Libyan interest section of the Saudi Embassy in London and the Libyan news agency Jana were, not surprisingly, mystified by the story.[36]

Scargill and Heathfield had by this time won the necessary local agreement to take their case to most mining areas with a programme of public and internal union meetings. 'It is sure getting Arthur Scargill time,' the NUM leader said as their coalfield tour built up steam. But he would, he vowed, 'fight like hell' to defend his and Heathfield's record. 'I know that what we did is worthy of congratulation, not criticism.' In dissident NUM areas like Derbyshire, Scotland and South Wales, the two leaders' requests to address executives and councils were ignored and local supporters were compelled to organize unofficial events. Heathfield, in particular, had originally been despondent about the prospects of fighting off the remorseless personal and political attacks. But as the response to their question-and-answer rallies grew more enthusiastic, so the miners' leaders' spirits lifted. From his French retreat, Roger Windsor derided it as the 'rhetoric roadshow', but the tide was beginning to turn. A breakthrough came on 6 August, when the two leaders addressed the NUM's middle-of-the-road Midlands area council in Stafford and were given a unanimous vote of confidence. With backing already secured from Yorkshire and the North East, the two now had support from areas which represented a clear majority of the union's 60,000 members. As he left the meeting, Joe Wills, the Midlands area secretary, declared that miners were 'fed up and sick to death with the character assassination' of their national leaders.

To coincide with the speaking tour, Scargill wrote a 24-page counterattack on Lightman, distributed as a pamphlet by Women Against Pit Closures, the national organization of autonomous miners' support groups which grew out of the 1984–5 strike and played a central role in organizing the campaign in defence of Scargill and Heathfield. Within a couple of months it had sold 10,000 copies. Messages and resolutions of solidarity built up from trade unions, local Labour parties and other left groups. Hundreds of union branches and individuals signed and paid for newspaper advertisements defending the miners' leaders against 'attempts to smear them in the press'. Support from the mainstream of the labour movement still remained lukewarm at best, but even convinced political opponents of Scargill and Heathfield found it hard to believe the NUM leaders had been corrupt. Ken Hollingsworth, one of Scargill's strongest critics on the NUM executive, remarked: 'Arthur's not the sort of character to pinch money – he'd pinch men's souls, mind you.' Geoffrey Goodman, Terry Pattinson's predecessor as *Daily Mirror* industrial editor, took a similar view: 'The one single thing I would never have considered would have been personal dishonesty on their part, and frankly, I still wouldn't.'[37]

The countercampaign reached its climax on a stifling August night in Sheffield City Hall, where eight hundred people turned out to hear the leaders of the longest national strike in British history defend themselves and their record. Dennis Skinner and Paul Foot, then one of the *Daily Mirror's* star columnists, made up the rest of the platform. 'We have done nothing wrong, we have not pinched a penny-piece, we have misappropriated nothing,' Peter Heathfield told the audience, comparing the attacks on himself and Scargill to the vilification of the miners' leader A. J. Cook in the aftermath of the 1926 General Strike. Foot was on holiday in Ireland at the time and flew from Knock airport to attend the rally. 'That was the most important meeting I've ever spoken at,' Foot says. He took a calculated risk with his job that night to condemn what his own paper had done. The *Mirror's* 'scoop', he charged, was 'cheque-book journalism of the meanest kind'. Scargill, who put on a vintage performance of his own – complete with a music-hall-style re-enactment of his cross-examination by Gavin Lightman – was buoyed up by the enthusiastic response.[38]

In the dog days of August, the NUM's four-man team headed for Eastern Europe – where the old communist leaderships had disintegrated or been ousted – in an attempt to discover what the former trade-union hierarchies' most secret intentions had been five years earlier. That had already become another age. New leaders were working to very different agendas. Under the tutelage of Lightman's friend Bruce Brodie, the four NUM executive members travelled first to Paris, where Alain Simon duly produced details of the accounts where the disputed money was held. But his request to accompany the NUM group to the Soviet Union was rejected. As George Rees – with a lawyer at his elbow – told Simon, they wanted to investigate who the Soviet money had been originally earmarked for 'without any influence from anybody'. So Brodie and the four-man team flew on alone to Moscow, where the final battle between different factions of the Communist Party was coming to a head and the Soviet miners' union line over the 'missing million' had hardened over the summer.

Vladimir Louniov, who had backed Scargill's version of events barely a month before, had now miraculously switched sides and 'reinterpreted' his earlier remarks. It was true, he explained to his British visitors, that the Soviet miners had never sent cash to the NUM. The money had been sent by an 'intermediary'. Both he and Mikhail Srebny – representing the new and old miners' leaderships – now insisted this aid had always been meant for the British miners and no one else. Given their apparent certainty on the issue, the Moscow men were curiously fuzzy on the details – insisting, for example, that $1.4 million had been sent, when the actual figure was later shown to have been some $263,000 less than that. Perhaps they confused it with the figure published in the *Daily Mirror*. Certainly, Srebny knew nothing of how the money had been transferred. The nuts and bolts, he said, had been left to the Soviet Peace Fund.

The waters were further muddied when the four-man team arrived in Budapest, where the new right-wing miners' leaders produced detailed accounts of the Hungarian trade-union contributions to the 1984–5 British miners' strike. To Brodie's evident consternation, they insisted that a 200,000-Swiss-franc Hungarian donation to the Mireds international miners' aid fund in 1985 – then still called 'Midaf' – had indeed been earmarked for 'international purposes' and not the NUM alone. This directly contradicted Lightman's view and the NUM's legal claim. Back in Britain, the four-man team – three of whom became convinced that Srebny was lying to some degree – leaked to the press like a sieve. Their accounts of the Moscow talks made it abundantly clear that elements in the Soviet trade-union apparatus were intent on discrediting Scargill and the IMO. The Paris-based organization had been accused of having a work style 'characteristic of the stagnation period' – the standard propaganda term used under Gorbachev to describe the Brezhnev years. The Russians had even criticized Scargill for being 'too Marxist'.[39]

With Louniov's about-turn, however, the media smelled blood again and the fallout from the Scargill Affair hung like a cloud over the TUC conference in Blackpool that September. Six months of unrelenting attack did not appear to have done much harm to the NUM president's popularity with ordinary delegates, many of whom gave him a standing ovation. But the labour-movement hierarchy was determined to have its pound of flesh. In an unprecedented breach of platform protocol, Norman Willis heckled Scargill as he branded the TUC's retreat from its earlier commitment to the repeal of anti-union legislation a 'betrayal of principle'. And the Labour leader Neil Kinnock – most of whose finest hours with the media consisted of outbursts against his own side – took the opportunity of his congress address to join the general excoriation of the embattled miners' leader. 'No favours,' Kinnock warned the NUM president. There was, indeed, little danger of that.[40]

Away from the conference floor, the BBC's Nick Jones repeatedly pressed the miners' leader to comment on media speculation that he would end up in gaol for 'misappropriating' NUM funds. The *Mirror's* Terry Pattinson was so convinced of his prediction that Scargill would be behind bars by Christmas that he laid a bet on it. And as if he had not been pilloried enough in the editorial columns, the NUM president was now fair game for advertising copywriters as well. National newspapers ran full-page spreads, throughout the week of the TUC conference, heralding a new Revlon deodorant. Below a mugshot of Scargill ran the slogan: 'For when you're really sweating'. Leagas Delaney, the agency responsible, admitted it had not bothered to ask Scargill's permission. Neil Greatrex, the UDM president, said he thought it 'appropriate – the investigation really does smell dodgy'. But a miner from Scargill's old pit, Woolley, remarked: 'They're trying to make him look stupid. They want Arthur out of the way.' The Advertising Standards Authority later upheld a complaint about the advertisement, describing it as 'highly distasteful'.[41]

Gavin Lightman also seemed to have decided that the usual formalities were unnecessary when dealing with the miners' union and its shop-soiled leadership. The QC had originally proposed that his report be circulated throughout the union and released to the media – which was done. Lightman himself privately fed journalists with titbits about the inquiry both before and after its publication. At the same time, he specified in the introduction: 'The decision whether to publish my report is a matter for the National Executive Committee.' But what applied in July clearly no longer applied in October. In spite of unequivocal written objections from the union, the Lightman Report and its 'startling conclusions' were rushed out in a special paperback edition by Penguin Books. The views of the organization which had paid for and owned the report were contemptuously ignored.[42]

There was one more throw of the dice. On the day the TUC delegates packed up to go home, Matthew Wake, the Certification Officer for Trade Unions – the government's traditionally toothless 'trade-union watchdog' – finally announced that he would indeed be prosecuting Scargill, Heathfield and the NUM for wilfully failing to keep and submit proper accounts. The nine criminal charges, based directly on Lightman's findings, were transparently aimed at closing the financial loopholes used to protect the union from the worst effects of sequestration and receivership during and after the 1984–5 strike. They were also the first ever to be made by this Employment Department appointee since the post was established by the Labour government in 1976. Together, the charges carried a relatively modest maximum fine of £3,600. But if the prosecution stuck, it had the potential to unleash far more damaging legal retribution.[43]

It would in fact be the last gasp of the campaign. The NUM executive's case against the miners' leaders was starting to fall apart. On 10 September, the four-man team flew to Paris with Scargill and Heathfield to settle the Soviet cash dispute with the IMO. The lawyers and accountants were by now pressing for between £1.8 and £2 million to be 'returned' to the NUM. Scargill's opponents on the executive were threatening a return to the High Court unless Simon stood and delivered. The crucial meeting was to be held on this occasion at the IMO's headquarters in Bobigny, in the 'red belt' of the Paris suburbs. The night before the meeting, the media gathered as before at the Sofitel, scene of the July negotiations. Terry Pattinson stood in the bar, confidently dishing out copies of Frere Chomeley's and Cork Gully's latest confidential reports to all comers. The *Mirror's* industrial editor had even convinced himself he had found another 'missing million'. This was apparently based on a misreading of the accountants' report, but stories nevertheless appeared in the final editions of the *Daily Mirror* and *The Times* next morning claiming just that.

The media were to be disappointed. After five hours of rancorous political and legal discussion in Bobigny, the two sides – with Scargill and Heathfield now sitting with the NUM group – were getting nowhere. The IMO had fielded a carefully chosen team, including the French miners' leader Augustin Dufresne and a former Soviet MTUI apparatchik, Valery Shestakov. Both had been directly involved in the negotiations for cash aid with the Russians in 1984–5. At one point the stocky Dufresne, better known as 'Tin-Tin', exploded with rage at the

South Wales miners' secretary, George Rees. 'You haven't the faintest idea what you're talking about,' Dufresne roared. 'It was I who organized this money, not Scargill or Simon.' The problem they had, Rees retorted doggedly, was that there was no contemporaneous documentation which could settle the argument. In a well-prepared *coup de théatre*, Alain Simon suddenly produced a copy of the original Soviet bank document of February 1985, transferring $1,137,000 to the MTUI in Warsaw. Written in Russian, but using Latin letters, the deposit slip – which the author has examined – states the purpose of the transfer. 'Dlia peredachi fond solidarnosti', it reads: 'for transfer to the solidarity fund'. The document was, in Scargill's estimation, a 'torpedo'. Here was an explicit five-year-old instruction from the Soviet bank earmarking the cash for a fund that the Soviet miners' officials had told the NUM's four-man team only three weeks earlier they knew nothing whatever about.

Rees and other Scargill opponents would later claim that this instruction to the MTUI's bank in Warsaw could have referred to the Sheffield-based hardship trust, the Miners' Solidarity Fund. That was always implausible, given the circumstances of the transfer. Evidence from the Soviet archives shows it to be impossible. In Paris, the response was more straightforward. 'That's fucked it,' the Derbyshire miners' leader, Gordon Butler, muttered. The four-man team and their lawyers were understandably anxious to get their hands on the 1985 deposit slip, which Simon had only days earlier succeeded in having faxed over by the Narodowy Bank in Warsaw. Simon refused. 'You can see it in court,' he told them, triumphantly brandishing his fax. Simon also had a letter from the former East German miners' president, insisting – like the Hungarians – that their 1985 donation to the Dublin trust fund had also been for international aid. An adjournment was hastily agreed.

With Scargill and Heathfield shuttling between the two sides, Butler suggested that the IMO make a donation of £1 million to the NUM from the Mireds money, particularly in view of the massive legal bills the British union had incurred over the dispute. Dufresne and Simon were both adamant that the NUM had got itself into a mess and that the IMO was under no obligation to help it out. John Maitland, the Australian IMO vice-president, suggested a compromise. £742,000 could be paid as a donation to help the NUM out of the contested funds; and in return, the NUM would drop all legal actions against the IMO and waive any further claims on the IMO, its officials or the international solidarity fund. The £742,000 figure was an arbitrary sum. It was simply the amount left in the original Mireds bank account in Dublin and was seized on because of a mistranslation of one of Simon's answers. The rest of the Mireds money – more than £1 million – had been transferred to a Viennese bank a year earlier to earn a better rate of interest.

Maitland said it had long been intended that victimized British miners would receive around £750,000 in instalments from the Mireds fund over the following four years, and so British miners would simply be getting an up-front lump sum from money they would eventually have had anyway. Simon and Dufresne were pacified and the deal was struck. Cost, uncertainty and the political damage of continuing litigation were all factors in the decision to settle – as, apparently, was the Moscow trade union leaders' warning to the four-man team that they had broken Soviet law in 1985 to have the cash sent. When the Australian announced the agreement to waiting journalists on the steps of the IMO headquarters, Terry Pattinson looked thunderstruck. 'Don't think this is the end of it,' he assured anyone who would listen in the bar across the road.[44]

Back in Sheffield, the full NUM executive voted to accept the Paris agreement, with one abstention. The NUM leadership's opponents, both inside and outside the union, were clearly distressed by the loosening of the legal vice and the growing prospect that their prey would escape yet again. George Rees explained that the deal had been necessary because of 'conflicting evidence'. Butler said more bluntly: 'I do not think the NUM would have come out of a court action favourably.' Kevin Barron, Neil Kinnock's ally and Labour's coal spokesman, demanded that Scargill resign and stand for re-election 'in view of the situation he has brought the union into'. But by now, such attacks were becoming counterproductive and Barron was in turn accused by Henry Richardson of 'abusing his position' as an ex-officio member of the NUM executive. A week later, the IMO executive met at the CGT headquarters in Paris to endorse the deal. After seeing the 1985 bank transfer document and bank statements, Nikolai Chebyshev, the Soviet miners' new general secretary – who had come intending to oppose the IMO across the board – abstained on the £742,000 payout and, to the astonishment of the other IMO leaders, backed a vote of confidence in Scargill, Simon and Heathfield.[45]

Events were now flowing in a very different direction. On 10 October 1990, NUM delegates from all over the British coalfield gathered in Sheffield for a special conference on the Lightman Report. Normally a man of robust health, Scargill had been taken seriously ill the week before at a boarding house in Blackpool, where he was staying for the week of the Labour Party's annual conference. Transferred to hospital, he was diagnosed as having a rare strain of pneumonia usually contracted as a result of prolonged contact with caged birds. The miners' leader had had no contact with birds of any kind, caged or otherwise. He nevertheless attended and chaired the NUM special conference against doctors' advice. For the leadership, the day was an unqualified – if not entirely unexpected – triumph. All the frustration that had built up in the union's core areas while lawyers had led the executive's four-man team a costly jig through the courts and capitals of Europe burst into the open. 'As far as we are concerned, it is a class question,' Bob Anderson, the delegate from Trentham colliery in Staffordshire, told the conference. 'Kevin Barron said we have to make a decision. Yes, and the decision is whether we support two of the finest class fighters we have had this century at least, or whether we effectively side with Maxwell and his class.' David Guy, the North East area president, lashed out at Lightman's 'inconsistency', his 'bias', his reliance on hearsay and anonymous witnesses, and his failure to grasp the 'extreme circumstances' of the 1984–5 strike and its aftermath.

The critics also had their say. Des Dutfield from South Wales argued that there had been no justification for continued secrecy around the 'unofficial' accounts after the end of receivership. That was 'autocracy and not democracy'. The right-wing Derbyshire officials got into a wrangle with Heathfield over the new kitchen Heathfield had had installed in his NUM-owned house in Chesterfield. But their attacks had little resonance away from the protective embrace of the television cameras. Both national officials relished the chance to hit back at their accusers and they took full advantage of it. It would have been ridiculous, the pneumonia-afflicted NUM president said when he finally took to his feet, if accounts which had been deliberately established as independent and separate from the NUM to beat sequestration and receivership had later been declared to the executive as NUM accounts. Such a move would have endangered the future use of such loopholes, he said, both for the NUM and other trade unions. 'Think back to the days when this took place, not to a cosy atmosphere in Lincoln's Inn in 1990, but to a period when we were involved in a class war against an enemy absolutely intent on destroying us,' Scargill declared. 'We have been subjected to smears, vilification and character assassination on a scale that has been unprecedented.' The officials had done nothing wrong, he concluded, and were entitled to support.

The pit delegates then passed a vote of confidence in the NUM's leaders by a three-to-one majority and threw out by an even larger margin a call from South Wales for the national officials to resign and seek re-election. They voted overwhelmingly to endorse all financial dealings since 1984 aimed at defending the union against sequestration and receivership and repaying trade-union strike loans. The conference also ratified the deal with the IMO and supported continued IMO affiliation by a large majority. And delegates voted to condemn Kim Howells and Kevin Barron – the latter spoke in the debate – for their public role in the six-month controversy. An attempt to have the union formally accept the Lightman Report was defeated and, with studied disdain, the barrister's findings were merely 'noted'. Even more galling for the 'eminent QC', the conference attacked the decision by Lightman and Penguin Books to publish the Lightman Report without the NUM's agreement as a 'violation' of his undertakings to the union, and instructed the national executive to seek advice on possible legal action.[46]

As soon as it was clear that there was no more mileage in trying to turn the NUM against its own leaders, the six-month campaign evaporated almost as suddenly as it had begun. The media lost interest overnight once the Sheffield conference had given Scargill and Heathfield such a decisive stamp of official union approval. Two weeks later, the five-year-old libel case brought by the UDM's David Prendergast against Scargill, Heathfield, the NUM and two Nottinghamshire area officials was settled out of court. The union was forced to pay out nearly £200,000 in costs and damages in a case which only came to life after the Goldsmith Foundation and Peter Carter-Ruck became involved in the wake of the Lightman Report. The action had originally been brought over a politically embarrassing letter, forged in Prendergast's name in the early stages of the Nottinghamshire-based UDM breakaway and unwittingly circulated by NUM loyalists in the rebel county. Scargill had taken evidence about the forgery to the police in the wake of Windsor's resignation the year before. But significantly, Prendergast's lawyers were obliged to accept in court that neither Scargill nor Heathfield – who had clearly been the real targets of the libel action – had had anything to do with the letter, and no apology or payment was made on their behalf. In fact, a settlement was only reached after the two NUM leaders were dropped from the case.

Finally, in mid December, a couple of weeks after Margaret Thatcher was forced out of office, the Serious Fraud Office suddenly announced that its inquiry into the handling of miners' strike funds was being abandoned. This most implausible of investigations had been triggered by the synchronized summertime complaints about 'missing' Soviet money. A variety of explanations were now given for dropping it. Scotland

Yard Fraud Squad detectives had failed to find suitable evidence; there were problems of jurisdiction; they had discovered the case did not fall within SFO criteria; and there had been no formal complaint from the union. In reality, the investigation was dropped because there was no case. Added to that was the risk of what else might be exposed if it had ever come to court. What had looked like a good idea in the heat of July no longer seemed so sensible after all. Within hours of the Fraud Squad statement, the *Guardian* was put in touch with a group of GCHQ employees, who claimed that the decision was linked to the role of the intelligence services and a dispute over the surveillance of NUM and IMO bank accounts. They also said they had themselves taken part in surveillance operations against Scargill and the NUM and alleged that the security services had been directly involved in the media and legal campaign of the previous six months.[47]

## THE BEAST BITES BACK

However, the miners' leaders still faced a criminal prosecution by the government's Trade Union Certification Officer. And with Scargill and the NUM executive now fighting in the same corner, defence preparations quickly ran into a wall of administrative resistance from the orchestrators of the previous year's legal confrontation between the union and its officials. In early February 1991, Mark Stephens of Stephens Innocent, the union's new solicitor, applied in the normal way to Frere Chomeley for the paperwork connected with the Lightman Report and the NUM's subsequent High Court action – which were, of course, directly related to the Certification Officer's prosecution. Such handovers of documents between lawyers are the daily routine of legal life and normally pass off without event. It quickly became apparent, however, that Bruce Brodie, Frere Chomeley's chairman, was extremely loath to part with his hoard of NUM papers. Weeks of letters, telephone calls and pressure from the four-man team were necessary before Brodie could be convinced to disgorge – in dribs and drabs – the NUM's own records. Even then, papers were held back.

The correspondence began by politely referring to a 'misunderstanding' over the documentation required. But by the second half of February, Stephens was becoming increasingly exasperated with Brodie, complaining about 'editing' of the files. It was a 'quite exceptional' practice, he said. 'For reasons which remain unclear, this handover is proving to be most difficult.' The solicitors' spat grew more bad-tempered, with Brodie adopting a wounded tone: 'I take serious exception to your suggestion that our misunderstanding ... was not genuine.' By the end of February, vital files had still not been delivered and repeated calls from Stephens Innocent were not being returned. Threats to involve the Law Society oiled the wheels and Frere Chomeley finally delivered the remaining papers almost a month after the firm was first approached. One of the last to be released was a fax from Kevin Barron to Gavin Lightman about the NUM's planned legal action against the QC.

The union's lawyers then found themselves jumping through the same hoops with Cork Gully, the accountants used in the Lightman Inquiry and the 1990 High Court action against Scargill and Heathfield. The firm refused point blank to release some of its NUM files – in marked contrast to its willingness to hand over Scargill's papers to Frere Chomeley the previous summer. Gavin Lightman, who had been summoned to appear in the Certification Officer case, adopted a similar approach. Under the terms of his original agreement to undertake the Lightman Inquiry, he said, his documentation was to be secret and it would continue to be held by him. So far as the union was concerned, Lightman had already broken the terms of the agreement by breaching confidence over publication. The disputed papers – including anonymous interviews with MPs and others – nevertheless stayed firmly under Lightman's lock and key.[48]

Among the documents that did arrive from Frere Chomeley was the bill for the NUM's legal action against its own national officials, launched under the guidance of Lightman and Brodie the previous summer. To the miners' leaders' astonishment, this included a £27,000 invoice for a surveillance report on Alain Simon, commissioned by Frere Chomeley in July 1990 from a private detective agency, Network Security Management. Challenged about the purpose of its private espionage, Frere Chomeley protested that surveillance had been essential to make sure the court bailiff was able to serve the NUM's writ on the IMO leader. Bruce Brodie had apparently been fearful that the slippery Frenchman would fail to turn up at the Sofitel at the appointed hour, despite categorical assurances from Scargill. This was clearly a part of the assignment – but only part. Network's report referred to 'a covert observation' carried out on the IMO's headquarters in Bobigny on 22 and 23 July 1990 and efforts to trace Simon's holiday address in Nice. These had, it was recorded, been abandoned once Simon announced on television that he would indeed be turning up for the Paris talks. Even then, Brodie was suspicious that Simon might stage a sudden getaway from the hotel. So Network kept a team on standby: 'to follow him wherever he went, whether on foot or by vehicle'. The drama and expense proved unnecessary, as Simon accepted his writ without a murmur. But the agency continued its work after the Sofitel negotiations were over.[49]

The Network report – headed 'private and confidential to Mr Bruce Brodie' – makes clear that smoothing the path of the writ-server had only been one of the tasks in their undercover brief. At 6.20 p.m. on 20 July – the day after Lightman and Brodie had convinced the NUM executive to sue Scargill, Heathfield and Simon – Network was hired by Frere Chomeley to 'investigate the background of Mr Alain Simon ... and his associations with political organizations in France, the USSR and Libya'. Claiming police and security-service contacts, Network's 'initial report' said it was 'very probable' that Simon had 'close connections' with the KGB and 'substantial Libyan connections'. The agency also speculated feverishly that Simon 'may have an intimate relationship' with his interpreter, Claire Seleskovitch. There were references in the report to 'security sources in France and the United Kingdom', with the added rider: 'no further enquiries will be made to obtain information from these sources unless specifically instructed'. A police investigation was also mentioned as 'being arranged', with the comment: 'The product of these meetings should be passed verbally to the client.'

Most of Network's allegations were laughable and transparently based on the flimsiest evidence. Reading the report – which describes members of the 'Network team associating themselves with the press corps' in the Sofitel bar after the NUM-IMO talks broke up at around one in the morning – I realized that the 'press corps' the private eyes were referring to was in fact myself. I had indeed chatted with these characters. One was a suave upmarket, middle-aged figure with greying hair, the other a yuppie-type in his twenties. They claimed to be working for a business newsletter. A page and a half of Network's report and its imaginative ideas about Simon's love life were apparently based on nothing more than half an hour's small talk with Claire Seleskovitch herself. She had talked about working as an interpreter at conferences in Libya and mentioned that she was, like Simon, a member of the French Communist Party. This became, in Network's version: 'she claims to be a militant left-wing socialist who is a strong supporter of Gaddafi'. It also seemed to allow them to conclude that Simon 'or his close associates' had strong Libyan connections.

Similarly, Network's suspicions about Simon's supposed KGB contacts appear to have been derived from his remark that he had longstanding relations with the Soviet trade unions. This was hardly a revelation, as Simon had for several years been general secretary of the Warsaw-based Miners' Trade Union International and the MTUI's largest affiliate was the Soviet miners' union. The agency still felt able to conclude: 'This being so, it is very probable that he also has close connections within the Soviet security services.' Nevertheless, Network's claims of well-placed security and police sources were doubtless well-founded. It was then one of the largest of the British private detective agencies, a multinational, multi-million-pound operation, noted in the business for the large number of ex-Guards officers on its staff. It was also owned by Hambros, a bank traditionally known for its close links with the intelligence services, particularly MI6.

When Network's highly priced 'research' arrived in Sheffield, the NUM executive expressed unanimous horror at what had been done to a fellow miners' union leader in their name. The four-man team declared themselves 'absolutely flabbergasted'. They insisted they had never authorized any spying operations against Simon and the union resolutely refused to pick up Network's bill. Brodie suggested a discount – the cost was 'higher than anticipated', he explained – but still got no joy. A plaintive correspondence continued for a full nine months over the unpaid bill. Brodie was 'reluctant' to pursue it through the courts, he assured the union. Frere Chomeley finally went to ground on the subject in the autumn of 1991 and settled the problem directly with their friends in Network. The NUM never paid a penny.[50]

But by this time, the boot was on the other foot. In the run-up to the Certification Office prosecution in June 1991, the *Guardian* and Channel Four Television's *Dispatches* programme ran a joint investigation into the *Mirror–Cook Report* campaign and the involvement of the security services. 'The Arthur Legend' was directed by the socialist film-maker Ken Loach – creator of social-realist masterpieces such as *Kes* and *Cathy Come Home* – and broadcast on 22 May 1991. For the orchestrators of the Scargill Affair, it proved to be a painful experience. Their story 'just didn't stand up', the programme concluded. Why had neither the *Cook Report* nor the *Mirror* checked their main allegation and asked Scargill when and how he had paid off his mortgage? Why had they relied so heavily on the evidence of Roger Windsor, when he was 'involved centre-stage in the allegations he makes' – and when, time after time, Windsor had 'played a crucial role in events that have subsequently been used to discredit Arthur Scargill'? Why did they accept the word of witnesses paid thousands of pounds for their stories and fail to disentangle the political background to the Russian money?

Why had Special Branch allowed the European representative of a paramilitary group backed by Libya to bring large sums of money into the country when they had just been told he was involved in a plot to kill the former Libyan Prime Minister? And what role did the intelligence services play?

Subjecting the journalism behind the affair to forensic examination, the programme suggested some of its own brutal answers. Windsor himself conceded: 'I'm not saying that everything the *Mirror* published was totally correct. They didn't see their function to have every dot and comma correct – that's unfortunate.' Neither the *Mirror* nor the *Cook Report* would allow their reporters to be interviewed – in Cook's case, on the pretext that they had to know the time and date of the programme's transmission in advance. So both Terry Pattinson of the *Mirror* and Roger Cook – as the *Cook Report*'s presenter, a man better used to a tabloid image as the avenging angel of the airwaves – were treated to a taste of their own medicine. A startled Pattinson took the appearance of television cameras on his doorstep in good heart. 'As Mr Scargill would say', he beamed, 'it's been an honour and a privilege.' But he failed to answer the questions and retreated under the protection of the *Mirror*'s increasingly threadbare alibi: 'Why doesn't he sue us, then?'

Cook was less sanguine about his ritual humiliation. The sixteen-stone television frontman, who made his name door-stepping a thousand petty fraudsters, thrashed around like a beached whale as he found himself trapped behind his breakfast table in a Birmingham hotel. 'We are here in the interests of fairness to put some questions to you,' Lorraine Heggessey, the diminutive *Dispatches* producer, began as she advanced on the tongue-tied crusader. 'If you give us a time for your transmission ...', Cook countered helplessly. As the *Sunday Telegraph* remarked of the incident: 'They can dish it out, but they can't always take it.' Heggessey had brought along Loach, two camera teams and Ken Capstick, the Yorkshire miners' vice-president, to witness the scene. 'Answer the question, Mr Cook,' Capstick insisted quietly. 'Why didn't you find out that Mr Scargill didn't have a mortgage, or did you think your viewers didn't have a right to know that? Why didn't you tell your viewers the truth? Why did you try to discredit the National Union of Mineworkers?' Cook looked miserable. Heggessey recalled another edition of the *Cook Report*, when Cook had used eye-drops to make it appear that a Brazilian mother was crying after seeing her adopted baby for the first time for two years. 'This has got absolutely nothing to do with this programme,' Cook exploded. 'How often do you fabricate evidence in your pro-grammes, Mr Cook?' Heggessey pressed on. 'Is that the standard of journalism you used in your Arthur Scargill pro-grammes?' Pleading an 8.30 a.m. appointment, Cook made his excuses and retreated down the street to the safety of Central Television's Birmingham headquarters, his back to the pursuing cameras.

The doorstepping of Roger Cook caused much merriment in the television business, where the presenter had made his share of enemies. But it did nothing to stop Fleet Street's incestuous grandees from bestowing the British Press Awards' 'Reporter of the Year' award the following month on Terry Pattinson and his fellow *Mirror* reporters for their now-discredited Scargill 'scoop'. A 'classic of serious popular journalism', they called it. And in case anyone should imagine that the Labour hierarchy was at all concerned that the allegations it had thrown its weight behind had now proven to be false, Neil Kinnock was there to present the prizes.[51]

## AN ERROR OF JUDGEMENT

The criminal prosecution of Scargill, Heathfield and the NUM by the Certification Officer over the handling of funds for a strike that had ended more than six years earlier finally came to Sheffield magistrates' court on 17 June 1991. The miners' lea-ders were taking no chances – and nor were some of the legal profession's outstanding progressive figures. Mark Stephens was there for the union. The solicitor representing Scargill and

Heathfield was Gareth Peirce, who played a central role in overturning the IRA bombing convictions against the Birmingham Six and Guildford Four. Before the case opened, she had insisted that nothing of the defence tactics or line-up should be given away in advance, either to the media or to the other side. When Ian Crompton, the stipendiary magistrate assigned to the case, walked into his courtroom on the first day of the trial, no less than four QCs acting for the NUM and its officials – Michael Mansfield, Geoffrey Robertson, John Hendy and Kevin Garnett – rose to pay their respects. Several of the union side's lawyers had agreed to donate their fees to the miners. Roger Ter Haar, the unfortunate wispy-haired barrister employed by the prosecution, was to prove no match for such a formidable team.

All three defendants – the two national officials and the union itself – denied the string of charges that they had 'wilfully neglected' to maintain and submit proper accounts. From the first morning, the case took on all the hallmarks of a political circus. More than thirty journalists, clutching their Penguin paperback copies of the Lightman Report, jammed the press benches. The prosecution, Ter Haar told the court, had been 'prompted' by the Lightman Report, but was not concerned with Russian or Libyan money. Nor was there any suggestion of dishonesty or personal gain on the part of Scargill or Heathfield, he added – to the audible incredulity of some present. 'What the hell are we here for, then?' one pressman bellowed in frustrated bewilderment. What was at stake, Ter Haar explained, were the seventeen secret bank accounts and trusts used to evade sequestration and receivership. They had been nothing, he insisted, but a 'façade' for maintaining the NUM while bypassing the union's normal accounting system.

But the case fell at the NUM leaders' first line of defence. One after another, their counsel savaged both Lightman and the use of his report for a trial by a state agency. The original *Mirror* claims of personal corruption against the miners' leaders, Geoffrey Robertson began, 'had been made in a national newspaper as a result of very extensive bribes not disclosed to the readers. The union could have laughed off this exercise in chequebook journalism.' But instead it had taken 'exceptional and expensive steps to comply with its obligations . . . in a quite spectacular fashion'. The corruption allegations had been comprehensively rejected by the report, Robertson reminded the court. But now the Certification Officer was 'attempting to put a policeman's helmet on Lightman's brief and turn him into a general state inquisitor, without any of the safeguards'.

Michael Mansfield took up the theme. Lightman had compiled hearsay upon hearsay, he charged. The court was being misused 'to investigate the possibility of offences'. Referring to the publication of the report, Mansfield accused Lightman of having 'seduced people into the closet of his room in order to gain an approximation of the truth on the understanding that it was confidential and has breached that confidentiality'. A letter from Lightman to Peter Heathfield was then read out in which the barrister admitted that his decision to publish might indeed have been an 'error of judgement'. There was no contest. The magistrate swiftly conceded the defence argument that evidence provided to the Lightman Inquiry, which had technically been a legal opinion, was protected by 'legal privilege' and therefore inadmissible in court. Lightman himself could not testify, he ruled, because of the privileged lawyer-client relationship. It would be 'manifestly and blatantly unfair', said Crompton – a deputy judge with a reputation as a right-winger, but also a stickler for the finer points of law – to use evidence provided in confidence and without proper protection.

In the more relaxed political atmosphere of 1991, the NUM leaders' elaborately prepared second-line defence – based on trust law and evidence of the high-level political inspiration behind the prosecution – proved entirely unnecessary. Without access to Lightman's homework, Ter Haar was left toothless. He could offer no further evidence. After only three days, the magistrate threw out all the charges, dismissed the case and awarded costs to the defence. Months of preparation by the Certification Office, the Department of Employment and the Treasury Solicitor had come to nought and the government was left with a bill for more than £150,000. Crompton also refused an application for judicial review of his decisions; and Matthew Wake, the Certification Officer, later dropped an attempt to launch an appeal. The entire legal basis of the case had been destroyed. What had happened, Geoffrey Robertson mocked, was that the 'Treasury Solicitors, hot from their attempts to ban *Spycatcher* around the world, have come to Sheffield to get Mr Scargill'. They had failed – in this, the twentieth court case to embroil the NUM and its officials since the 1984–5 strike. The *Financial Times* commented: 'Mr Scargill's endurance in the face of so much hostility is a remarkable episode in union history.'[52]

As the miners' leaders walked free from the court, Gareth Peirce told reporters that the prosecution had been 'brought for political motives ... in the context of attacks coming on the union from all directions last summer'. Her remarks were based on a great deal more than rhetoric or common sense. A senior partner in an international accountancy firm involved in the preparation of the prosecution case had given an affidavit to the NUM's lawyers describing a conversation he had had in 1990 with Graham Osborne, the number two in the Certification Office. There was a 'terrific flap on upstairs', Osborne had told the man. Pressure was being put on the Certification Office, which is sponsored by the Department of Employment, to 'do something' about the NUM. Action was partly needed, it had been said, to draw attention away from the negative political impact of the Guinness fraud scandal, then at its height. The clear inference was that the impetus had come from Michael Howard, the Employment Secretary, and the Prime Minister herself. The accountant had agreed to repeat his story in court and had been standing by when the case collapsed.

Both Matthew Wake and Sir Patrick Mayhew, the then Attorney General, insisted there had been no interference whatsoever. The decision to launch the prosecution, the first ever brought against a trade union by the Certification Officer, had been Wake's alone, they both declared. This stretched the credulity of those who knew Whitehall's employment outposts well. Jim Mortimer – Labour's former general secretary who chaired the Certification Office's funding body, the conciliation service ACAS, when the union watchdog outfit was set up in the 1970s – was one. 'I believe there was pressure from the highest level of the government, probably Mrs Thatcher, that they should catch the NUM out on its financial returns,' he said. 'Over the years, the Certification Office has acted sensibly to improve the standards of trade-union accountability and financial records by persuasion. Then it suddenly jumped on the NUM. It wasn't consistent with what had gone on before.' That impression was strengthened when, on the second day of the trial, the Employment Secretary Michael Howard announced he would be including draconian new powers for the Certification Office over union finances and office-holders in a forthcoming green paper – powers which eventually became law.[53]

In the wake of the collapse of the Certification Office prosecution, NUM loyalists took their revenge for the indignities of the previous year. Two days after the end of the Sheffield trial, writs were served by the NUM against Gavin Lightman and Penguin Books for breach of confidence, fiduciary duty, contract and copyright in publishing the Lightman Report without authorization. Disciplinary action was launched against Kevin Barron – the *Mirror* campaign's chief Labour Party cheerleader and an NUM-sponsored MP – for passing details of the litigation plans to Lightman's office. Barron was finally expelled from the union over the issue the following year.

Roger Windsor had meanwhile been forced to abandon the two libel actions he had brought against Scargill in Dublin at the height of the 1990 scandal. With no case offered, all the NUM's costs were awarded against its former chief executive officer. When Windsor refused to pay up, the union won a court order docking the money from his pension. The NUM and IMO were already pursuing Windsor through the French courts for the recovery of his £29,500 NUM bridging loan, plus interest. This was the debt paid off with what Windsor claimed to be Libyan money and later assigned to the IMO in a document he refused to recognize as genuine. In due course, the outcome of the French case would prove far more damaging for Windsor than his expensive legal fiasco in Ireland.[54]

But the miners' leaders' most spectacular vindication would come from the most unlikely of sources. After an exhaustive twenty-month-long investigation, the Inland Revenue gave Scargill and Heathfield a clean bill of health over their handling of the NUM's financial affairs. It also signed a legally binding agreement accepting that none of the seventeen 'secret accounts' set up to beat sequestration and receivership belonged to the NUM, contrary to the claim by Gavin Lightman. By making its ruling, the Revenue effectively cleared the NUM officials of all the charges of misapplication of funds and breaches of duty which had littered the Lightman Report. The original decision by the tax authorities to crawl over the 1984–5 strike fund records had been set in train by the findings of the Lightman Report. But on 14 May 1992, the Inland Revenue's special investigating office accepted in full the diametrically opposite conclusions reached by the accountancy firm KPMG and a battery of trust lawyers.

The KPMG report did at least agree with Lightman about the original *Mirror–Cook* tales of personal corruption. 'These allegations and inferences were simply sensationalized reporting and wrong', it concluded. KPMG also found that all the money funnelled through the various 'unofficial' funds and trusts was accounted for and that all loans had been repaid. Unlike Lightman, the report accepted that the Mireds solidarity fund, where the Soviet and East European cash was held, was a valid trust and separate from the NUM. The same went for almost all the other independent accounts. Only two of the trusts were invalid, according to KPMG, because they were 'multi-purpose'. These were the MACF cash fund, into which the supposed Libyan donation was paid, and the Sheffield Women's Action Group account, used to pay hundreds of union bills during and after the strike. But if the trusts were invalid, KPMG pointed out, the 'money belonged to the donors', who were mostly British trade unions. Lightman's claim that these accounts belonged in law to the NUM was rejected categorically. 'His views are all the more surprising,' the report commented, 'as he, in fact, provided advice to the NUM about the creation of such trusts.' KPMG's assessment was backed up by a legal opinion from one of the country's top QCs specializing in trust law and was agreed by the tax authorities.

The immediate effect of the Inland Revenue's ruling was that the unions which had originally made loans to the independent accounts and funds were suddenly faced with a large tax bill on notional interest from two of the trust accounts. Seven years after the strike, as a direct result of the false allegations made by the *Mirror* and the *Cook Report*, the Transport and General Workers' Union, the National Union of Public Employees – now part of Unison – and the Fire Brigades' Union became liable to pay £150,000 tax between them. With some difficulty, arrangements were eventually made for the tax to be paid by or on behalf of the three unions.

But, far more significant from the point of view of the 1990 campaign, the Inland Revenue agreement completely invalidated the main basis of Gavin Lightman's sharpest attacks on the NUM leadership. Lightman had argued that any money loaned or donated to a third party to 'maintain the fabric of the union ... became the property of the NUM'. This was, he said, 'fundamental to this enquiry, and particularly to the change in my terms of reference'. From this interpretation of the law flowed the larger part of his report, most of his charges of breach of duty and misapplication of funds, his complaints about the 'intermingling' of NUM and IMO money and his damnation of the failure to declare the accounts to the NUM executive. And so far as the Inland Revenue and the trust law experts were concerned, Lightman was entirely wrong.[55]

Quite why Gavin Lightman turned on Scargill and Heathfield with such force, produced a report marked by such manifest lack of balance and accuracy, and proceeded to publish it without the union's agreement remains something of a mystery. Sarah Burton, a friend of Lightman and former NUM lawyer who went on to work for the environmental campaigners Greenpeace, says the QC felt he had been deceived by Scargill and Heathfield. He had acted for the NUM over its receivership imbroglio and then discovered in 1990 that he had not been told what was going on behind the scenes. 'He got the wrong end of the stick. He was fond of Arthur, he liked all of them, but he felt betrayed and it made him act irrationally.'

Both Scargill and Heathfield think that Lightman was privately fed choice morsels of disinformation by his nameless informants, which shaped the nature of the report. 'I always wonder in inquiries of this sort whether the establishment gets to these people,' Heathfield mused in the final stages of the 1990 campaign. As time wore on, he became less philosophical about the matter. 'I have nothing but contempt for Gavin Lightman,' he said later. 'That man preferred the evidence of faceless people, who we can't yet identify, rather than the hundredweight of documentary evidence that we compiled.' Scargill now believes there was an intelligence input. 'I am convinced that the security services supplied Lightman with so-called "evidence", either directly or indirectly via a third party,' he says. It is also possible that documents or briefings were provided by the Soviet Embassy – particularly as it later emerged that selected secret Soviet state papers were sent anonymously to members of the NUM executive during 1990.[56]

Sarah Burton, who describes Lightman's report as 'vicious', says that his 'terrible error of judgement' over its publication by Penguin was made in 'the heat of the moment'. If so, it was one he would come to regret. In December 1993, Lightman and Penguin Books agreed to an out-of-court settlement of the NUM's claim for breach of copyright, confidence, contract and fiduciary duty. The terms were kept confidential between the two sides, but court documents obtained by the author show that Lightman and Penguin agreed to pay both damages and costs, estimated to run into six figures. Under the settlement, Lightman and Penguin made a £5,000 payment to the union, agreed to pay the NUM's full costs and delivered all 2,000-odd remaining copies of the offending paperback to the NUM in Sheffield. Both publisher and barrister also put on record Lightman's letter in which he acknowledged that the report's publication might have been an 'error of judgement'. It had, both sides agreed, been a 'matter for the NUM'. There had clearly been some urgency about the settlement. In May 1994, Lightman achieved his longstanding ambition to be appointed a High Court judge, and a few days later Buckingham Palace announced he was to be made a knight of the realm.[57]

The settlement with the Inland Revenue, however, brought to an end the last official investigation into the union arising out of the 1990 media campaign. By any reckoning, it was a startling litany. Of the legal actions, prosecutions and investigations launched in July 1990, all were abandoned, dismissed or found in favour of the miners' leaders. The NUM case against Scargill, Heathfield, Simon and West was discontinued, with costs paid by the union and a legal agreement signed accepting that the NUM had no claim on any funds held in the name of the IMO or its officials. All charges brought in the Certification Office prosecution were dismissed, with costs paid by the government. Roger Windsor's libel actions were abandoned, with costs paid by Windsor. The Fraud Squad investigation was dropped; the Commissioner for Trade Unions' investigation never got anywhere and the Inland Revenue found unequivocally in the NUM leaders' favour.

For Peter Heathfield, who had assured union activists that they wouldn't see his heels for dust as soon as his name was cleared, this was the signal he had been waiting for. In an emotional retirement speech to the union's 1992 NUM annual conference, the NUM's general secretary poured out his bitterness at the treatment that had been meted out to the union's leaders two years earlier. The trial by media had, he said, taken 'more out of me than the twelve months of the strike. I've aged fifteen years in the last five. Every agency of the state was directed against Arthur Scargill and myself . . . and every allegation has been found groundless.'

But his greatest rage was reserved for those inside the union who had turned on the leadership in the summer of 1990.

I had no difficulty coming to terms with the attacks of the Max-
wells and the tabloid media – my class awareness and the
knowledge that it was a load of codswallop meant I was able to
come to terms with that. But I have to say to you, comrades, I have
not come to terms with being sued by colleagues on the national
executive committee . . . I'm sure in the course of the next few years
you will learn in some detail how Arthur Scargill, Peter Heathfield
and the NUM were stitched up.

In response to these words, Idwal Morgan, the cokemen's leader
and a member of the disbanded four-man team, came to the
rostrum and broke down as he asked for the retiring leader's
understanding. 'That decision wasn't easy for us . . . it was
something that we were probably, looking back, railroaded into
. . . Peter, I'll tell you this now. If you can find it in your heart
somehow to forgive us . . . I'll never get over it.'[58]

It was a vivid reminder of the damage that the Scargill Affair
had inflicted on an already beleaguered organization. The legal
and media assault of 1990 had failed to dislodge Arthur Scargill
from the leadership of the miners' union. But the huge effort
required to fight off the attacks had tied up the union and
absorbed the energies of its leaders at a crucial period, as the
government prepared the final savage phase of its pit-closure
programme in the run-up to privatization. It had fatally delayed
and undermined an attempt to merge the vulnerable NUM
with the country's then largest union, the Transport and General Workers' Union. It had seriously tarnished the reputation
of Britain's best-known trade-union leader, both among his own
members and large sections of the public. And for £742,000 of
international trust-fund money British miners were expected to
have had anyway, more than £750,000 had been drained from
the NUM in legal bills, and £150,000 of taxes had had to be
paid by or on behalf of three other unions. By any reckoning,
the Scargill Affair had cost the British trade-union movement
close to £1 million.

# CHAPTER THREE

# DANGEROUS LIAISONS

There are not only people who are agents out of cowardice; there are, much more dangerously, those ... taken by the idea of danger, intrigue, conspiracy, a complicated game in which they can make fools of everyone.
*Victor Serge, 1926*[1]

Roger Windsor's introduction to the British public, on peak-viewing-time television news, was as bizarre as it was dramatic. In a blurred film clip picked up from a Libyan broadcast, the bespectacled and bearded NUM chief executive officer was revealed to all, locked in an embrace with the 'mad dog of Tripoli', Colonel Gaddafi. It was 28 October 1984, nearly eight months into the year-long miners' strike and three days after a High Court judge in London had ordered the seizure of the NUM's assets. The same morning, the *Sunday Times* – closest of all the Tory newspapers to the government's strikebreaking strategists – had run an exclusive front-page exposé, recounting in extraordinary detail Windsor's furtive trip to the Libyan capital a week before in the company of Altaf Abbasi, the 'European representative of a Libyan-backed Pakistani terrorist group'. The cash-hungry NUM, it appeared, had been caught with its trousers down.

For the union, it was the worst single propaganda blow of the strike, coming only six months after the shooting of a British policewoman, Yvonne Fletcher, outside the Libyan Embassy in London. The British government had ritually expelled all Libyan government representatives and broken off diplomatic relations with the Gaddafi regime – while at the same time secretly stepping up imports of Libyan oil to help break the coal strike. Whether some kind of secret deal was struck by the

Foreign Office with the Libyans over the settlement of the Embassy crisis remains unclear. Alan Clark, the former Thatcherite Defence Minister, remarked years later of the incident that 'more lay below the surface than appears to view'. But that was a matter for the professionals. Nothing could be better calculated to work the tabloid press into a lather of righteous indignation than the revelation of independent contacts between the outlaw union and the pariah state. Here was the Enemy Within paying homage at the court of the Enemy Without.[2]

Political and media reaction reached a crescendo of hysteria over Windsor's visit to Tripoli, unmatched during the rest of the dispute. The Libyan escapade caused the NUM serious damage, heightening internal tensions, slashing cash support and tipping the balance for some miners on the verge of breaking the strike. By any reckoning, the Gaddafi kiss was a public-relations disaster for the NUM – even if in retrospect the affair has a touch of the storm in a teacup about it. In the longer run, the Libyan link would cruelly return to haunt the miners' leaders, laying the ground for Windsor's far more devastating 'whistle blowing' of 1990. Without the Tripoli connection, there could have been no credible accusations of suitcasefuls of Libyan money or stories about requests for arms supplies or allegations of embezzled secret foreign strike funds. Windsor himself traces his alienation from the NUM leadership to his Libyan mission and Scargill's behaviour on his return, complaining that the publicity around the contacts made it almost impossible to get a mainstream job outside the union. They were 'at Scargill's mercy', as Angie Windsor put it. But Libya also gave Windsor a powerful weapon, which he wielded to pulverizing effect – twice over.[3]

## A CORNER-SHOP TERRORIST

The NUM's Libyan connection has been long buried in a morass of claim and counterclaim, lies and disinformation. At the centre of the affair is Mohammed Altaf Abbasi, a Kashmiri political exile and small-time businessman who came from Pakistan to live in Britain in the mid 1960s. At the time of the 1984–5 coal strike, Abbasi – a British citizen – was living a sort of double life in the style of Superman's Clark Kent. Ostensibly, he was a respectable Asian shopkeeper, running a small grocery store with his family in the mining town of Doncaster in South Yorkshire. But in his spare time, Abbasi was the freewheeling 'European representative' of a Pakistani paramilitary opposition group, backed at different times by the Libyan and Syrian governments. This was al-Zulfikar, meaning 'the sword': an underground outfit working to overthrow the pro-American military regime of General Zia ul-Haq. Its leader was Murtaza Bhutto, committed to avenging Zia's execution of his father, Zulfikar Ali Bhutto, former Prime Minister and leader of the Pakistan People's Party (PPP).

The al-Zulfikar organization is widely acknowledged in Pakistan to have been heavily infiltrated by the Islamabad authorities. Some of its most spectacular bombing and hijacking operations have been attributed to infiltrators on the payroll of Zia and his fellow generals. These provocations are assumed to have been aimed at discrediting Murtaza Bhutto's sister, Benazir, leader of the PPP and twice Pakistan's Prime Minister during the 1980s and 1990s. The hapless Abbasi had been in Pakistan shortly after Zulfikar Ali Bhutto's hanging. He was arrested and accused of plotting with a Libyan diplomat to blow up a Shi'ite mosque in Lahore. Abbasi, a Shi'ite Muslim himself, was brutally treated and – according to his own account – only narrowly survived being thrown down a well by his captors. Later charged with treason, he was sentenced to twenty-five years' imprisonment. Abbasi says the whole affair was a 'fit-up against the opposition. It was a fantasy. I've never even been to Lahore.'[4]

Abbasi's wife Zora lobbied her local MP and Douglas Hurd, then a junior minister at the Foreign Office, and made representations to the Pakistani government, who initially denied any knowledge of Abbasi. In March 1981, al-Zulfikar carried out its most spectacular operation, hijacking a Pakistan Airlines flight and diverting it to the Afghan capital, Kabul. Demanding the release of Pakistani political prisoners, the hijackers eventually killed one hostage, a Pakistani diplomat, before flying on to Damascus. After thirteen days, General Zia released fifty-four prisoners, who were exchanged in Damascus for the remaining hostages. Altaf Abbasi, a British citizen, was one of them. But his selection for release also appears to have been partly the result of Foreign Office pressure. Physically and psychologically scarred by the experience, Abbasi – whose paternal grandmother was Libyan – was given medical treatment in Tripoli.

Back in England, Abbasi became an executive member of the Standing Conference of Pakistani Organizations and cultivated links with a variety of leftist, Irish republican and Sikh nationalist groups. His approach was described by another Pakistani exile as follows: 'He goes to any political meeting which has something unusual about it ... at the end, he comes up and offers his services.' Abbasi was regarded by many of those active in Pakistani opposition politics in Britain as an agent of the Islamabad government or of British intelligence long before his involvement with Roger Windsor. The right-wing British Sikh leader Jagjit Singh was among those who claimed to have been offered Libyan money and arms by Abbasi. Singh refused, but the story that he was going to Tripoli to forge links with Gaddafi was damagingly leaked to an Indian newspaper. Singh blamed Abbasi for the leak. The Pakistani exile claimed the Sikh leader had invented the story for the sake of publicity.[5]

Exactly when and if Abbasi made the initial approach to the NUM, offering himself as a Libyan middleman, is a matter of dispute. But there is no argument that, from the start, Windsor was the union official in charge of the relationship. The former NUM chief executive told the *Mirror* and Central Television's *Cook Report* that the contact was first made when Scargill asked him to follow up a letter from Abbasi in August or September 1984. Windsor claimed he set up a meeting with the Doncaster shopkeeper for the first time in Sheffield a few days later. Abbasi has a different story. He says Windsor approached him as a result of discussions he had had with local NUM activists. According to Abbasi's account, a strike organizer in Doncaster – aware of his Libyan links – had asked him if there was any chance of raising 'money from the Middle East'. Abbasi had put the idea to a Libyan trade-union leader in Tripoli and reported back a positive response to his Doncaster contact. This unidentified NUM man had in turn supposedly passed on the information to Windsor, who met Abbasi a few days later. In Windsor's version of the encounter, Abbasi boasted that he had direct access to Gaddafi, that the Libyans were anxious to help bring down the Thatcher government, and that cash support for the miners could be forthcoming.[6]

The following month, the miners' leaders were being fêted by delegates to the Labour Party conference in Blackpool. It was there that Windsor chose to introduce Abbasi to Scargill, fresh from a tumultuous five-minute standing ovation, in the Planet Tearoom at the Blackpool Winter Gardens. Under the arc lights of a dozen television cameras, it was scarcely the place for a secret liaison, if that was what was intended. Abbasi asked the NUM president if Libyan trade-union representatives could have a session with him the following week. Scargill said he would be in Paris for a meeting at the headquarters of the largest French trade-union confederation, the CGT. The NUM president was in fact going to France to finalize arrangements for a 45-juggernaut CGT food convoy – and, more importantly, to make contact with a senior Soviet diplomat in the hope of securing large-scale financial support for the strike. It was agreed that the Libyans could make contact at the CGT miners' federation offices.

So it was that on Monday, 8 October 1984, at the huge modernist CGT building in Montreuil, on the east side of the French capital, Scargill and Windsor met Salem Ibrahim, Colonel Gaddafi's roving envoy, with Abbasi in attendance. The short private meeting took place in the late morning, after the main business with French, Russian and Hungarian trade-union officials and diplomats had been finished. Alain Simon, then secretary of the Miners' Trade Union International, Augustin Dufresne, the French miners' leader, and Jeff Apter, a freelance journalist who acted as interpreter, all withdrew for the meeting with Ibrahim, which was held in another part of the building, in the miners' offices on floor 3B. Ibrahim and Abbasi had both been tailed by intelligence agents from the moment they arrived in the French capital. Abbasi had travelled on the boat train via Dieppe and stayed at a hotel next to the Gard du Nord. On the morning of 8 October, he had picked Ibrahim up at the Hilton Hotel near the Eiffel Tower, where staff had been told to give the Libyan VIP status and pass the bill on to the Bangladeshi Embassy.

Ibrahim, who had been arrested outside the Libyan 'People's Bureau' in London shortly before the shooting of Yvonne Fletcher and subsequently deported, was later variously described in the British press as Colonel Gaddafi's 'paymaster' and 'bagman', a 'senior Libyan intelligence officer' and the official in charge of the British desk of Libya's powerful revolutionary committees. The sources for these various accolades were admitted to have been one or other country's intelligence services or the Libyan opposition in exile. That he was a powerful figure in Libya, enjoying close relations with Gaddafi, is not in doubt. At the Montreuil meeting, Ibrahim told Scargill and Windsor that the Libyans supported the miners' struggle and were anxious to help. Would the miners' leader go to Tripoli to 'explain the NUM's position'?[7]

Scargill refused, saying if Libya wanted to help British miners, it should suspend strikebreaking sales of oil to the United Kingdom. But when Ibrahim suggested Windsor as a substitute, the NUM chief executive officer 'declared himself more than willing to go along', according to Scargill, who agreed the visit. Windsor says he was 'volunteered in the way the army volunteers people'. After the meeting, the four who had taken part, along with Simon, Apter and the CGT leader Augustin Dufresne, went to lunch in a nearby restaurant. Two weeks later, on 22 October 1984, the NUM's chief administrator set out on his ill-fated trip. Windsor travelled first to Frankfurt, where he met up with Abbasi. The Pakistani exile had been fixing up Libyan visas in West Germany, as the London embassy had been closed since the April siege. Together the pair then flew on to Tripoli, where Abbasi's contact was Bashir Howij, head of the General Producers' Union. Since 1990, Windsor has insisted that he was sent to Libya exclusively to meet Colonel Gaddafi with the single and explicit purpose of unlocking the oil-rich regime's treasure chests. While he was hanging around a Tripoli seafront hotel waiting for his audience with 'the leader', he says, he asked to see trade unionists to pass the time.[8]

Scargill and Abbasi disagree. They both say that before Windsor arrived in Libya, the sole intention had been that he would meet 'Libyan trade unionists'. The idea of his meeting Gaddafi had not, they say, been discussed at the Paris talks. Gavin Lightman, who was happy to give Windsor the benefit of the doubt over other issues, concluded that the NUM's chief executive 'probably' did not expect to meet the Libyan president when he went to Libya. Alain Simon, who became the IMO general secretary, says he was told several years after the event by Libyan trade-union leaders that Windsor had specifically asked to see Gaddafi. Abbasi, who was with Windsor at the same hotel throughout his time in Tripoli, also recalls that the audience with the Libyan leader was at Windsor's personal request.[9]

## JUDAS KISS

Either way, on 25 October – the day sequestrators were appointed by the High Court in London to seize the NUM's assets – the man from Hounslow came face-to-face with Libya's outcast president in his Bedouin tent, which Windsor described as 'the size of a garden-party marquee'. He kissed Gaddafi on both cheeks – as, he says, he had carefully rehearsed with Salem Ibrahim beforehand – and launched into his prepared pitch. Graphically describing the plight of striking British miners,

Windsor asked for 'sympathetic consideration for funds. I didn't mention a figure because I was told that was a matter for the leader.' Gaddafi gave him three copies of his 'Green Book', the Libyan equivalent of Mao Zedong's 'Little Red Book'. Windsor admits he agreed to be filmed, but claims to have had no idea that the meeting would be relayed to the world in loving detail through the good offices of Libyan television.[10]

Altaf Abbasi remembers things rather differently. Windsor asked him how he should greet Gaddafi and it was he, Abbasi says, not Salem Ibrahim, who showed Windsor the traditional Arab embrace. And not only was Windsor anxious to meet the Libyan leader in person, Abbasi says, but he also told officials in the hotel the previous day that he was more than happy for his audience with the president to be broadcast on television. 'The Libyan authorities were keen to keep it quiet, but Windsor was in favour of the broadcast. "I am not ashamed to be here," he said. Those were Windsor's precise words,' Abbasi recalls.[11]

In the months after his return, the NUM chief executive often regaled those in and around the union with yet another version of his five minutes of fame. Peter McNestry, general secretary of the pit deputies' union NACODS, remembers Windsor buttonholing him on the King's Cross to Doncaster train long after the furore had died down and telling him, unprompted, how he had gone to Libya to address a trade-union meeting, which had carried on longer than expected. As he left the meeting, he had found his car surrounded by military jeeps and was told by officials that Colonel Gaddafi wanted to meet him. He had remonstrated with his minders, but was told he had no choice but to go. He was then driven through the desert, past fortifications and rocket launchers into a fort. Eventually he was shown into Gaddafi's tent, where he had been totally unaware that there were any television cameras present, let alone that he was being filmed.[12]

The anecdote of how his Gaddafi audience had been sprung on him was recounted to others, including NUM legal advisers Mike Seifert and Sarah Burton, and Rodney Bickerstaffe, then general secretary of the National Union of Public Employees.

'He kept telling the same story over and over again,' Sarah Burton says, 'as if he'd learned it off by heart.' Lightman believed the version Windsor offered to McNestry had the 'ring of truth about it ... I can think of no reason why Mr Windsor should have told Mr McNestry an elaborate lie (if his current story is true) some months after the affair when there was no media attention on it.' McNestry puts it more bluntly: 'Either Roger Windsor was lying to me at that time or he's lying now. Whichever way you look at it, he's lied on one occasion.'[13]

Windsor flew back to Manchester and an explosion of hostile media coverage, triggered by the sensationalized coverage of his trip in the *Sunday Times*. Andrew Neil, the paper's editor, hailed the exposé as the 'scoop of the decade' – just as Robert Maxwell would describe the *Daily Mirror*'s 'revelations', based on the same events, five years later. The Libyan news agency Jana had in fact reported Windsor's meeting with Gaddafi a couple of days before, and a few Saturday papers had given it low-key, 'news-in-brief' coverage. But the *Sunday Times* exposé was another kettle of fish entirely, providing the minutest details of the movements, flights and hotel arrangements of the three protagonists – Ibrahim, Windsor and Abbasi – right down to the telephone numbers Ibrahim called from his room in the Paris Hilton. The paper's investigative 'Insight' team even had Windsor and Abbasi under surveillance on their return from Tripoli to Frankfurt airport. The overall impression given by Rupert Murdoch's British Sunday flagship was of a desperate undercover mission revealed to the world by plucky sleuthing reporters.[14]

Nell Myers, the NUM press officer, called it 'the *Sunday Times*'s Le Carré number', and the story certainly had intelligence fingerprints all over it. Indeed, the main reporter on the exclusive – Jon Swain, who had been the *Sunday Times* Paris correspondent – boasted of French intelligence sources in his opening paragraph. It was a Paris-based security official, apparently from the French counterintelligence outfit, the DST, who had told him Ibrahim was the man responsible for distributing Libyan largesse to the IRA and the Italian Red

Brigades. Swain later said the exposé had come about as a result of a tip-off from an acquaintance working at the communist-led CGT. He had cultivated the contact in the early 1980s, when there were four Communist Party ministers in Mitterrand's first government. According to Swain, the CGT 'acquaintance' rang him in London to offer him 'exclusive information' about the British miners on 19 October, eleven days after Windsor and Scargill had met Ibrahim at Montreuil. Swain flew next morning to Paris, where the CGT contact told him about the NUM's talks with the Libyan official. In 1984, the CGT was embattled, highly politicized and tightly controlled. The chances that an ordinary CGT employee or official was feeding damaging information to a right-wing British newspaper are close to zero. Asked about his contact's motives for informing on the NUM – the CGT's closest trade-union ally in Britain – Swain says: 'I didn't ask.'

It is, of course, possible that the putative contact was an intelligence plant. Indeed, the CGT leadership came to believe, on the basis of various pieces of evidence, that the national headquarters was successfully infiltrated during the 1980s. Swain now says that his French intelligence source also fed him other surveillance titbits for his story, including the fact that Ibrahim had stayed at the Hilton. As for the rest, Swain and others who worked on the story say that cajolery and petty bribery were used to extract the flight and hotel details. But there is more to it than that. While each piece of the jigsaw could theoretically have been the product of painstaking investigation, the timing, character and quantity of the material point strongly to, at the very least, an additional British security-service leg-up.

Roger Windsor himself says he has long been convinced that MI5 tipped off the press about his Libyan trip. The *Sunday Times* often had privileged access to official information during the miners' strike. Its then newly appointed editor, Andrew Neil, had at one time worked for Peter Walker, the Energy Secretary. The revelations won Swain the 1984 British Press Awards accolade of 'Reporter of the Year' – the same prize that would be jointly collected by the *Daily Mirror*'s intrepid threesome for their Scargill Affair stories six years later. Peter Gillman, who worked for the *Sunday Times* Insight team before the miners' strike, remarked of its NUM–Libya scoop: 'Some reporters remained uneasy at the extent to which their story had used intelligence sources and suited the political agenda of the British government.' So far as the then Insight editor, Paul Eddy, was concerned, however, the important thing was 'not where the information came from but whether it was true'.[15]

The political impact of Windsor's North African jamboree was incendiary, particularly after the film of Windsor and Gaddafi embracing was broadcast on the Sunday-evening national news. 'Outrageous!' the front page of the high-Tory *Daily Mail* bellowed to order. The *Daily Mirror*, under its new proprietor Robert Maxwell, called the Windsor–Gaddafi encounter a 'poisonous embrace. The miners' cause may never recover from it.' The paper later described it as a 'Judas kiss'. The Prime Minister was reported to be 'incredulous' at the NUM's 'calamitous own goal'. Whitehall officials rubbed their hands with glee at the anticipated alienation of the miners' supporters and hailed Windsor's North African adventure as the beginning of the end of the strike.

The Labour Party and TUC hierarchies tripped over each other to denounce any association with the 'odious tyranny' in Tripoli. Neil Kinnock, the Labour leader, declared: 'The Gaddafi regime is vile. Any offers from them would be an insult to everything the British labour movement stands for.' Norman Willis, TUC general secretary, weighed in, denouncing the NUM leadership for its willingness to 'consort' with a 'government which is heavily implicated in terrorist campaigns outside its own borders'. Remarkably, in view of later events, one of the few Labour politicians to defend the NUM's contacts with Libya was Kevin Barron. The *Daily Mail* claimed that a 'wave of revulsion' was sweeping the land. David Steel, the Liberal leader, said that Scargill's 'whole leadership of the NUM is motivated by a desire to extend the Marxist empire ... the strike is nakedly exposed as political, not industrial'. The same wild McCarthyite tone was seized on by his Alliance partner and Social Democratic Party leader, Dr David Owen: 'We too easily forget that he was an active member of the Communist Party: for him still today, the end justifies the means.'[16]

Gaddafi was at this time close to the pinnacle of his demonization by Western leaders and media. Within eighteen months, the United States would launch a lethal bombing raid on Tripoli from British military bases. Set against the special British interest in Libyan arms supplies to the IRA and the killing of the London policewoman, any hint of association with the Libyan regime was primed to bring forth a torrent of hysterical condemnation. The doubling of Libyan oil exports to Britain during the strike as oil-fired power stations were mobilized to offset the loss of coal output; the Tory government's own recent and enthusiastic promotion of trade with Libya; the Coal Board's longstanding trade and training links with Libya – all these uncomfortable facts were largely ignored in the media's enthusiasm at having caught the NUM leadership off-balance. Given the fact that oil was far more important than the working miners in keeping the lights on during the strike, perhaps that is hardly surprising.[17]

Those who had been directly involved refused at first to respond to questions about the Libyan contacts. Windsor threatened to call the police when confronted at his Sheffield home by *Sunday Times* reporters. Dogged by another pressman, the NUM president walked thirty yards in silence, together with Mick McGahey, who then told a bodyguard: 'Throw this man off the road.' Ibrahim and Abbasi – who had been boasting of organizing Libyan funding for the NUM at a Pakistan People's Party meeting in Peterborough well before news of Windsor's trip was published – denied any knowledge of the affair. However, once the story was out, Scargill was up and running on television and radio, insisting that no cash support had been sought or received from the Libyan government and that Windsor had simply gone to put the miners' case – like dozens of other NUM emissaries around the world. He added that he would, however, 'welcome financial assistance from trade unions anywhere'. Norman Willis demanded, and was given, an assurance by the miners' leader that the NUM would not accept donations from the Libyan regime.[18]

Back at the NUM headquarters, Scargill and Heathfield held a council of war at which they carpeted their errant chief executive officer. Windsor would later say that they concocted a cover story. Scargill 'promised to stand by me, as if what had happened had not been at his behest', Windsor told the *Mirror*. 'Scargill was distancing himself from events.' Both McGahey and Heathfield were furious about the Tripoli connection. Heathfield had been in Prague earlier in the week lobbying the Soviet miners' union for cash support, and complained he had not been given details of the Libyan trip in advance. Scargill insisted he had been told, and Nell Myers says she was present during the discussion. But unlike Scargill, the NUM general secretary had no public misgivings about taking Libyan cash. 'When Windsor came back,' Scargill recalls, 'Heathfield yelled at him: "What the bloody hell do you think you were doing kissing Gaddafi on TV? I'm surprised he didn't bite thee."' The now famed chief executive officer was mocked mercilessly by some of the less kindly members of staff and developed an acute case of shingles – a stress-related illness – in the aftermath of the affair.[19]

Fortunately for the union and to the fury of the Tory Cabinet, the great propaganda coup against the miners was partly squandered by the ineptitude of Ian MacGregor, the Coal Board chairman, and the gathering legal onslaught against the NUM. MacGregor flew in from Boston as the British media were in full Scargill-baiting flood over Libya and ordered the immediate cancellation of a string of planned press briefings by his newly appointed head of communications, Michael Eaton. MacGregor's idea was to leave the field 'clear for the media to exploit the Libyan story to its fullest'. The tactic backfired and news of the NCB chairman's 'gagging' of Eaton knocked the Gaddafi meeting off the front pages. In retaliation, Geoff Kirk, the Coal Board's head of information, was sent on 'indefinite leave'. Eaton later became a private coalowner in South Wales.

Kirk decamped to the Scottish islands to write a book about the strike and died soon afterwards.[20]

There were those who were naturally distressed to see the Libyan story wasted. Three weeks after Windsor's visit to Tripoli, two British businessmen were arrested in Cairo for their alleged part in a Tripoli-backed assassination attempt on a former Libyan Prime Minister. The 'assassination' was revealed in Cairo a couple of days later to have been staged by the Egyptian intelligence service, apparently to head off a genuine murder plot. The businessmen had supposedly been paid by the Libyans to arrange the assassination and had then hired contract killers – who were in fact undercover Egyptian security agents. Faked pictures of the blood-spattered body of the ex-Libyan premier, Abd el-Hamid Bakoush, were secretly passed to the Gaddafi regime, which announced his execution by revolutionary forces as a 'stray dog'. The Egyptian government then revealed its 'sting' to the world.

Exciting enough though this tale was, the British tabloid press had fish of its own to fry. The *Daily Express*, in a lurid front-page story on the Bakoush affair, triumphantly claimed contacts between Altaf Abbasi and the 'Libyan death squad'. Under the headline, 'Scargill linked with Libya "death plot Briton"', the paper reported that Bakoush's supposed would-be killers – the two arrested businessmen and their Maltese accomplices – had been led by a 'veteran terrorist' named Anthony William Gill. According to the Egyptian Foreign Minister, Gill had admitted to contacts in Tripoli with both Carlos, the legendary South American hitman, and 'Mohammed Abbas', who had 'connections with Arthur Scargill' and had been involved in arranging funding for the British 'opposition movement'.[21]

Abbasi had indeed met Gill at a Tripoli hotel on one of his many Libyan trips – 'we were both long-staying passengers', as Abbasi puts it coyly – and was later questioned by British police about the contact. Gill seemed to be a rather pathetic figure, who confessed that working for the Libyans had made him feel like James Bond. He was, surprisingly, never charged by the Egyptians. After five months in a Cairo jail, Gill was instead deported to Britain and released on bail. A year later, he was tried and convicted of helping a distant relative of Colonel Gaddafi to escape from the United Kingdom to avoid facing trial on drugs charges. He was sentenced to five years in prison for conspiring to pervert the course of justice. One of those Gill approached to help with Libyan operations against political exiles turned out to be a positively vetted SAS reservist, who was employed by a private security firm and had worked on foreign contracts with the 'unofficial blessing' of the Ministry of Defence. The involvement led to press speculation that Gill's activities had been at least 'monitored' by the British security services.[22]

## THE PHANTOM COURIER

At almost exactly the same time as the story about contacts between Altaf Abbasi and Gill's unlikely 'Libyan death squad' was running on the front page of a mass-circulation British tabloid newspaper, Abbasi claimed that he calmly strolled through customs at Heathrow Airport – the most closely monitored entry-point in Britain – on three separate occasions carrying briefcases full of Libyan cash for the miners. It was £50,000 the first two times, he said, and £63,000 on the last trip – collected directly from Bashir Howij in Tripoli. 'It was in sterling, £20 notes,' Abbasi told the *Mirror*. In fact, he even re-enacted the scene for the opening sequences of the first *Cook Report* programme on the Scargill Affair, broadcast on 5 March 1990.

The film has a customs officer asking the Pakistani-born activist to step to one side and open his briefcase. Abbasi obliges, the customs officer glances at the packets of £20 notes and says respectfully: 'Right sir, that seems to be in order. Thank you very much.' He then waves Abbasi through. This is the treatment supposed to have been given in November 1984 to an Asian political exile, convicted of plotting a bomb attack in Pakistan, named the previous month on the front page of almost every British newspaper as the middleman in contacts between the NUM and Colonel Gaddafi at the height of the miners' strike, cited during the same month in a topselling British tabloid as linked to a Libyan death squad. The claim stretches credulity to breaking point.

Even the *Daily Mirror* felt the need to explain why Abbasi was supposedly able to carry a Libyan cash hoard through London's main international airport under the benign gaze of British customs, immigration and Special Branch police officers without even the gentlest questioning. 'There are no British exchange controls,' the paper pointed out at the height of its March 1990 campaign. 'Travellers can bring in and take out as much cash as they want without having to declare it.' This is true so far as it goes. Carrying suitcases full of Libyan-supplied banknotes in and out of Britain is not in itself illegal. However, customs officials say that anyone carrying more than £10,000 in cash would be expected to account for its origin and purpose. At Heathrow, senior customs sources confirm that Special Branch would certainly be alerted if someone with Abbasi's record was discovered carrying large sums of money. Early in November 1984, the *Sunday Times* reported that Abbasi was already 'well known' to South Yorkshire Special Branch officers, who would routinely visit him on his return from foreign trips. If Abbasi had indeed carried the cash unhindered through Heathrow, he would have done so with the knowledge and connivance of Special Branch.[23]

According to both Abbasi and Windsor, the Pakistani exile passed the Libyan cash to Windsor at three separate rendezvous – one in Sheffield, two in Rotherham – in November 1984. For a couple of the pick-ups, Jim Parker was said to have driven Windsor to the meeting place in Scargill's car. Parker claimed to the *Mirror* that he was 'told that we were picking up money from Libya' – though Dave Feickert, former head of NUM research, remembers Parker telling him at the time that 'he didn't know where it had come from'. Two of the handovers were witnessed by a friend of Abbasi, Abdul Ghani, modestly described by the *Daily Mirror* in March 1990 as a 'builder'. 'I saw that man Windsor come in and Altaf gave him the money,' Ghani reminisced to the *Mirror*. 'The suitcase was packed with bundles of big notes. Windsor counted it out carefully and I think he signed a paper, like a receipt.' Abbasi also remembers the NUM chief executive counting the money out repeatedly – he would have therefore known the exact sum – but Windsor denies it: 'He must be mistaken.' The *Mirror* never bothered to mention the fact that Ghani, the independent witness at the cash drops, had been jailed for eighteen months in 1987 for running a massive housing-improvement-grants fraud. After a nine-week trial, Ghani was found guilty of eight offences involving deception, using false estimates and giving false information.[24]

The total Libyan donation – £150,000 according to Windsor's account in the *Cook Report*; £163,000 in the *Daily Mirror*'s version – was then supposedly stored in biscuit tins in the larder of the Windsors' Sheffield house. The terrifying notion of North African cash lurking in a respectable English biscuit tin was played for all it was worth across the centre pages of the *Mirror*. 'Biscuit tins crammed with bank notes shared the shelves with baked beans and salad cream', the paper reported. The top shelf of the larder was, said Windsor, the 'only place my wife and I could think to put it'. Angie Windsor had the sequence of events as follows:

> Roger came back one day with a suitcase. He said Arthur didn't want the money in the office and he stashed it in the larder. He told me our loan had been paid back with Libyan money. I told him it was no more than he deserved.

The *Mirror*'s account went on: 'The cash remained in the pantry of the Windsors' Sheffield home for ten days until Scargill asked for delivery at his office on December 4, 1984.'

Windsor subsequently claimed that he took the cash into the union's headquarters at 9.30 in the morning that day and gave it to Scargill, who then used it for the celebrated 'divvying up' on his office table. In fact, the NUM president was at a strike rally at Goldthorpe colliery in South Yorkshire all morning on 4 December 1984. Film of him speaking at Goldthorpe was broadcast that night on television news and a picture of him at the pit printed in the next day's *Times*, among other papers. So Windsor's timing is impossible. There are other obvious contradictions in the Windsor–*Mirror* version of the clandestine Libyan funding. If Angie Windsor's reported comments are taken at face value, Windsor's bridging loan was paid off with Libyan money before he brought the leftover cash home. If that was the case, it clearly could not have been paid off again ten days later when he took it back to NUM headquarters to hand over to Scargill on 4 December. Yet that is the day when Windsor has always insisted Scargill's 'mortgage', Heathfield's 'home loan' and his own bridging loan were all paid back with Libyan money. And he has clung to that claim through thick and thin.[25]

Everyone else associated with this much-rehearsed event remembers it differently. Both Scargill and Heathfield are adamant that the money used for refinancing the various debts and payments on the officials' homes was brought in by Windsor at the end of October or the beginning of November. As discussed above, £100,000 was recorded as having been paid into the 'MACF' cash trust fund on 25 October 1984. But this was acknowledged to have been backdated because of the threat from the sequestrators. And the records giving the real dates – kept by Scargill's secretary, Yvonne Fenn – were stolen from the NUM offices. Scargill, Heathfield, Nell Myers and Steve Hudson, the NUM's finance officer, who were present in Scargill's office on the disputed day, all claim Windsor said at the time that the cash was from the French CGT miners' union. Strike funds were coming through regularly from the CGT during the autumn – including money collected from third countries – and it was one source guaranteed not to arouse suspicion. It is also common ground that Windsor produced some cash on 4 December, though it was certainly not in the morning. And while Windsor claims he arrived with £150,000 or £163,000 that day, the MACF records show it to have been £50,000 – interestingly, the figure Windsor mentioned in 1989 in a recorded telephone conversation with Hudson and reproduced in the *Mirror*. In the accounts of the MACF, into which the money was paid, it was described as an 'international collection via CGT'.[26]

There can be no serious doubt that Windsor did press the Libyans for financial support or that the Libyan trade unions sent money which they intended should go to support the miners' strike. The record of Windsor's audience with Gaddafi made by Libyan television and Jana, the Libyan news agency, has Windsor requesting – and Gaddafi promising – financial support from the Libyan trade-union movement. And in 1990, Gaddafi spoke publicly about Libya's aid, both in press interviews and on television. He remembered meeting Windsor and asking the General Producers' Union of Libyan Workers to 'provide some help'. Libyan trade-union leaders confirmed that a draft cheque for $200,000 had been issued from union accounts, but were unsure how the money had been delivered.[27] But how far Windsor was acting on his own initiative in his contacts with the Libyans and to what extent he kept Scargill informed is another question. The possibility of large-scale Libyan support for the miners' strike had been floated quite early on in the dispute. In the summer of 1984, Tom Sibley, the British representative of the Prague-based World Federation of Trade Unions, came to Sheffield with Denys Bonvalot, a CGT man based at the WFTU headquarters, who later worked for Laurent Fabius, the French Prime Minister. Sibley says Bonvalot met Peter Heathfield and told him that the Libyan unions were prepared to make substantial funding available on certain unspecified conditions, but that Heathfield regarded the political risks as too great. Ten years later, Heathfield – as well as Jeff Apter, who was acting as Bonvalot's interpreter – had no recollection of any such offer but said, if it had been made, he would certainly not have turned it down.[28]

Several pro-NUM MPs and strike sympathizers had unofficially explored the possibility of Libyan backing for the miners in the summer and autumn of 1984. They included people like Ron Brown, the maverick left-wing Labour MP for Leith; Mick Welch, MP for Doncaster North and an NUM trustee; Alan Meale, who then worked for the left-wing Campaign Group of Labour MPs and later became an MP and junior minister; as well as the veteran radical and internationally connected lawyer, John Platts-Mills. But it was not until the *Mirror*'s investigation was well in hand more than five years later that Meale told Scargill and Heathfield what had been going on behind the scenes. He had, he said, approached the Saudi Embassy – then representing Libyan interests in Britain – in the summer of 1984 with Ron Brown to sound out the possibility of Libyan financial support. He had also been in contact with Roger Windsor about Libya during the same period and had stayed at the Windsors' Sheffield home. Scargill and Heathfield both insist they knew nothing about these approaches at the time and only got to hear about Meale's role after they were tipped off in late 1989 that he had given an interview about it to the *Cook Report*.[29]

Windsor continued to maintain contact with Abbasi and the Libyans after the strike – he says at Scargill's insistence – and the repeated meetings would provide a rich source of outlandish allegations when the NUM's chief executive officer hurriedly resigned and took his tale to Robert Maxwell. The miners' leaders were anxious that the well-endowed Libyan energy unions affiliate to the new IMO; and, in the spring of 1985, Windsor went with Peter Heathfield and Alain Simon to meet Salem Ibrahim and Abbasi in Normandy to press their case. Heathfield says the possibility of cash support for sacked miners was also discussed, but nothing came of it. According to Windsor's version, they went to demand £2 million.

At the Labour Party conference in Bournemouth the same year, Scargill had a five-minute discussion with Abbasi in his car to find out why the affiliations had still not come through. In the *Mirror* and *Cook Report* version, this became a 'highly dangerous secret trip to meet the Libyans', with Jim Parker checking the area for MI5 tails. Another encounter was engineered between the NUM leader and Abbasi at Windsor's house. Scargill says he had arranged to pick up some papers from his chief executive on the way back from a rally in Nottinghamshire with his wife Anne. To his surprise, Abbasi was at the house when he arrived. According to one of the Windsors' former babysitters, Abbasi – or someone who looked very like him – was often at their home. But it was during this meeting that Windsor claimed Scargill asked the Doncaster shopkeeper if he could arrange supplies of guns. 'He wanted personal firearms,' Windsor told the *Cook Report*, 'a revolver for himself ... and a pump action shotgun'. Abbasi today describes the weapons story as entirely without foundation. 'If there had been any mention of guns, I would have remembered it. That would have been extraordinary.'[30]

Yet, by far the wildest story to arise out of Windsor's ongoing dealings with Abbasi was the allegation that as much as $9 million had been 'made available' to the NUM by the Libyans – on top of the £150,000 or £163,000 delivered in November and December 1984. The exact sum fluctuated even during the course of the *Cook Report* television programme where the claim was first made. At one point in the show it was £5 million; at another, £5–£7 million; another still, $9 million. The latter was Abbasi's favoured figure. The middleman explained that the 'money was transferred to Europe and it was made available for the trade-union movement or NUM to use as and when they found it necessary'. Roger Cook triumphantly described it as 'the biggest foreign donation ... also the most controversial: so controversial in fact that for five years Arthur Scargill has consistently denied that it was ever given or even offered'.

This tale was eagerly taken up by Windsor – though he preferred a figure of $7 million – and promoted by him long after the Lightman Report had discredited his central allegations of embezzlement. Windsor was apparently convinced that the real fruits of Gaddafi's largesse had gone into a secret account in Malta. In early 1985, Dave Feickert, the NUM's head of research, flew to Malta to see whether an independent account could be opened there as part of the effort to keep the union going under receivership. The suggestion had come directly from Dom Mintoff, the Maltese Prime Minister. In an attempt to avoid telephone taps, all contact between Scargill and Mintoff's office was made from a dentist's house in Sheffield. In the event, it soon became clear that too many people knew about the idea and no account was ever opened. But Windsor was not the only one to show an interest in exploring the Maltese connection, which looked more interesting than it was because of the island's close relationship with Libya. Abbasi told the *Mirror*'s Terry Pattinson that he had met an NUM official 'with a German-sounding name' in Malta. Feickert says he is baffled by the claim: 'He was nowhere to be seen when I was in Malta.'[31]

By the time the *Cook Report* went to work on Scargill the second time around, in July 1990, Abbasi's story about the missing $9 million had had to be modified. 'Altaf Abbasi', Roger Cook explained, 'says the Libyans gave over £5 million but have now demanded and got most of it back because it didn't reach Britain.' In reality, this vast Libyan treasure-trove was even more of a phantasm than the ludicrous 'secret service estimates' – supplied to the British government and then leaked to suitable journalists – that the Soviet Union had funded the miners' strike to the tune of £7 million. The only source for the story, Altaf Abbasi, has now said he 'just heard about it ... I didn't see the actual transfer in front of me.' How the '$9 million' was made available was 'something between Roger [Windsor] and the trade-union movement in Tripoli'. Windsor himself in turn admits that he only heard about the supposed multi-million-dollar Libyan donation from the *Cook Report* team and, although they provided him with no evidence, he had 'no reason to disbelieve it'. Most recently, Abbasi has claimed that part of the money had begun to be transferred to Europe, but was siphoned off in a scam operated by employees at the Bank of Credit and Commerce International – BCCI – which was closed down by the Bank of England in 1991 for fraudulent dealing. And although no such sum was ever sent or received, there is indeed a basis in fact for Abbasi's erratic stories.[32]

## THE TRIPOLI PAPERS

For all the column inches and lawyers' fees devoted to the Scargill Affair, the exact nature of the NUM's Libyan connection has remained obscured for a decade by a cacophony of unsubstantiated claims and innuendo, with almost nothing in the way of hard evidence to go by. While it was obvious to anyone prepared to consider the facts that Libyan money had not been used to pay off Scargill's nonexistent mortgage, it was generally assumed that the union's officials must at least have got their hands on some Libyan cash. Lightman had left open the question of whether the £150,000 recorded as having been brought into the NUM in the October–December 1984 period came from Libya or not. There was a 'real possibility', he said, that it came from Libya; there was also a 'real possibility' that it came from elsewhere. Scargill stuck doggedly to his line that he knew of no money 'emanating' from Libya and that 'if Mr Windsor ever took delivery of money from Libyan sources, he either lied about the sources when he brought the money into the NUM, or he never brought the money into the NUM at all'. Few, however, believed Scargill could not have had a good idea of what Windsor was up to at a time when they were still apparently such close allies.[33]

It took a string of entirely unexpected developments in the summer and autumn of 1993 to explode the myth of the Libyan money and throw a dramatic new light on the roles played by Windsor and Abbasi. It began, appropriately enough, at a seaside conference in North Africa. On 8 May, Arthur Scargill was in Algiers for the four-yearly congress of the International Miners' Organization. It was the Saturday before formal business began. Without any prior warning, Scargill was asked by Alain Simon – the IMO's general secretary and one of those who had been present at the fateful Paris rendezvous with the Libyans nine years earlier – to meet a 'Libyan representative' in a hotel in central Algiers. Scargill was, as he put it later, more than a little 'reluctant to go because of my past experiences with Libyan representatives'. But Simon was equally anxious that the

IMO-affiliated Libyan unions cough up their subscription fees. In the taxi to the meeting, the British miners' leader told Simon he had no intention of observing diplomatic niceties over the Libyans' behaviour and their 'failure to criticize Roger Windsor and Altaf Abbasi for the untrue allegations' they had made.

Scargill described the encounter:

> At approximately 11.35 a.m. we entered Room 818 in the hotel to be met by none other than Salem Ibrahim. After a brief discussion between Ibrahim and Alain Simon, I began to express my anger about the events of 1990, in particular the *Daily Mirror* and Central Television's *Cook Report* stories, all of which were built on patent untruths.

The meeting with Gaddafi's envoy – the first time Scargill had seen him since the miners' strike – lasted for an hour and a half. Scargill retraced the history of the NUM's contacts with Abbasi and Ibrahim, Windsor's 1984 trip to Libya, and the subsequent scandals. He recalled with some bitterness that he had agreed to his chief executive going to Tripoli 'on the understanding that he was going to meet Libyan trade-union leaders', and that he had had 'no idea that Roger Windsor was going to meet the leader of the Libyan government'. If the money which Windsor later turned up with had indeed been Libyan money, it was without the NUM leaders' knowledge. In any case, the money was all accounted for. The 'entire episode had caused a great deal of distress to a number of people, in particular Peter Heathfield and myself'.

According to Scargill's and Simon's account of the meeting, Ibrahim apologized for what had happened and said the Libyans were well aware that neither the NUM president nor Peter Heathfield had taken money, as Windsor had alleged. He told them that Gaddafi had given his 1990 television interview about cash aid for the British miners under 'immense pressure' and against Ibrahim's advice. Abbasi was not, Ibrahim said, a Libyan representative. But he had approached the Libyans in 1984 with a recommendation that they give financial backing to the British miners. Windsor had indeed been invited to Libya to see the trade unions, but while in Tripoli it had been suggested he could meet the Libyan leader, as was common in such cases. Windsor had readily agreed.

Ibrahim confirmed that the Libyan trade unions had issued a draft cheque for $200,000. But the elaborate reconstruction of the handover of the Libyan cash in the *Cook Report* – the trips back and forth to Tripoli, the briefcases full of money, the miraculous airport encounters with customs officers – had, Ibrahim said, been a complete fabrication. The cash had in fact gone via the Libyan People's Bureau in Frankfurt and had been deposited in a British bank, from where it had been withdrawn. Part of the money then appeared to have been siphoned off. Ibrahim declared that he knew nothing of Abbasi's claims about a Libyan donation of $8 million or $9 million. Perhaps this had been part of a 'dirty tricks' strategy to destabilize the NUM and IMO. The Libyans had indeed sent a further $500,000, but the money had never come anywhere near Britain and had in fact 'gone missing'. He said that Windsor had been involved in some way, but it appeared that the money had all been spent by one of the People's Bureaux. At all events, it was a matter for Libya to deal with. Finally, Ibrahim said that the Libyans were now convinced that the British security services had been directly involved in their 1984 contacts with the NUM.[34]

Such a startling series of allegations stood to turn upside down the entire elaborate structure of testimony which had been built up by Windsor and Abbasi and which provided the foundation for the *Mirror* and *Cook Report* 'revelations'. Ibrahim was, after all, the man at the heart of the Libyan connection. Throughout the 1990 campaign, he refused to speak to journalists or comment publicly on the allegations against Scargill and Heathfield or his role in the affair. This was in spite of determined efforts by British reporters to get him to talk, including the 'doorstepping' of his Tripoli office. Now, it appeared, either the drip-drip effect of claims about Roger Windsor's real allegiances or the Byzantine politics of the Tripoli regime were smoking him out. But why, if Windsor's and Abbasi's story about the cash handovers was a fiction, had the Libyans not seen fit to mention the matter before? Certainly, if the Libyan money had simply been sent through the banking system, as Ibrahim claimed, that disposed of the apparent puzzle of how the convicted bombing conspirator Abbasi had managed to carry it through Heathrow Airport. But why should Abbasi have lied about the transfer and claimed to have made three trips to Libya to pick the cash up? In any event, allegations were one thing, proof another. That would, in due course, be forthcoming.

At the Algiers meeting, Ibrahim told Scargill and Simon that records of the 1984 contacts and cash transfer, originally supplied by Abbasi, were held in Tripoli. After protracted negotiations, a file of documents – including bank statements, deposit slips, cash receipts and papers signed by Roger Windsor – was made available to the author. The Tripoli documents tell a completely different and far more extraordinary story than the fairy tale peddled to 15 million *Cook Report* viewers and *Mirror* readers in the spring and summer of 1990. The sequence begins with a note signed by Roger Windsor and dated 19 November 1984 – just three weeks after the dramatic exposure of his trip to Libya. 'To Mr M. Abbasi', it reads. 'Please transfer the sum of $198,005 in sterling to Sheffield and pay cash.' Windsor had clearly been told by this stage exactly how much money to expect – though $1,995 appears to have been deducted from the $200,000 released in Tripoli, perhaps partly accounted for by bank charges.

Within a week, the money had been collected from the People's Bureau in Frankfurt and $198,000 deposited at a branch of Lloyds Bank International in Guernsey. From there it was transferred to Geneva and held in a dollar account in Abbasi's name, at the LBI branch in Place Bel Air. Among the Libyan-held documents is a bank statement issued on 26 November 1984 by Lloyds Bank International, Geneva, recording that $198,000 was still sitting in the account of Mr Mohammed Mumtaz Abbasi, 133 Bennetthorpe, Doncaster at that date. Already, the bank documents show Windsor's and

Abbasi's stories to be impossible in every detail. According to Abbasi, by this stage in his courier service, he was already supposed to have made three journeys back and forth to Tripoli to pick up the money. According to Windsor, by 26 November he had already carried out three Libyan cash pick-ups from Abbasi in Sheffield and Rotherham and all the money was safely in biscuit tins in his larder. In fact, it was all still in a Swiss bank account.[35]

The following day, Abbasi wrote to the LBI Geneva branch asking for $197,000 to be transferred to another dollar account in his name in Britain, specifying that he wanted the money to be available by Sunday, 2 December 1984. A Mrs Cvorovic was the account manageress in charge of the arrangements. On 29 November, the money was withdrawn from his Geneva account and routed through Lloyds Bank in Eastcheap, London – where Lloyds UK international operations were based at that time – ending up a couple of days later in Abbasi's dollar account at Lloyds High Street branch in Doncaster. As Ibrahim had insisted, Abbasi's trips through airports with phantom brief-cases packed with crisp £20 notes from Tripoli never took place. Nor, by the beginning of December, had the Libyan trade-union funds seen the inside of Roger Windsor's larder – or been picked up in three different clandestine cash drops, with or without Jim Parker. On Monday, 3 December – in flat con-tradiction of the elaborate tale spun for the *Mirror* and *Cook Report* – the Libyan money was still in dollars and still in the banking system.[36]

On 4 December 1984 – the day Roger Windsor consistently claimed he brought the Libyan cash into the NUM headquarters and Scargill used it to pay off his mortgage – the money was changed from dollars into sterling and £163,701.36 was deposited at a Lloyds branch into another account. Among the papers in the Tripoli file is a Lloyds paying-in slip, stamped and signed for that amount. The first four and only readable digits of the sort code on the slip point to the deposit having been made in Doncaster. At the close of business on 3 December 1984, the exchange rate was $1.197 dollars to the pound, which works out at £164,578 for $197,000. Allowing for bank margins and commissions, the fit is exact. In other words, on the day Windsor and Abbasi claim the Libyan money was finally handed over to the NUM leadership for all manner of dodgy dealings – and long after it was supposed to have been passed to Windsor in cash on three separate occasions – documentary evidence demonstrates it had still not left the banking system. On the contrary, that was the day it is recorded as having been paid into a new sterling account.[37]

But after 4 December, when the £163,701.36 deposit was made, the trail left by the official bank documentation runs cold. Among the Libyan-held papers, however, are two other notes which suggest the deception was even more far-reaching. They are two Lloyds Bank credit slips, signed with Roger Windsor's initials, REW, in his characteristic swirl. In one, the figure of £113,500 has been written into the 'total' box; in the other, the sum of £50,000 – together, the two amounts making £163,500. In the 'paid in by' space are the words: 'Abbasi – for TINTIN'. This was the nickname of Augustin Dufresne, leader of the French CGT miners' federation, and appears to provide for the first time a link with the claim by four witnesses that Windsor told them the cash he brought into the NUM came from the CGT.

The implication of the two initialled slips is that the money was being redirected to the CGT official most involved in raising international cash support for the coal strike – or, at least, that was how Windsor and Abbasi wanted to make it appear. The slips are undated, but evidently must have been written and initialled on or after 4 December 1984, since the money had already been changed into sterling (and £201.36 deducted). The style of initialling on the second slip, for £50,000, seems to have been deliberately varied. In an interview with Lorraine Heggessey for Channel Four television in April 1991, Windsor mentioned that he had signed some 'pieces of paper' for Abbasi when the money was handed over.[38]

The Tripoli papers reveal the claims made by Windsor and Abbasi about how and when the Libyan money was brought to

Britain and what they did with it to be completely untrue. But the documents also demonstrate that the £163,000 from Libya could not possibly have been, as Windsor alleged, the money which was used to protect the NUM leaders' homes from the sequestrators and which later formed the basis of the false embezzlement allegations in the *Mirror* and *Cook Report*. To see why, it is necessary to establish, at least roughly, when the 'paper refinancings', as Gavin Lightman called them, actually took place. The dates are crucial. The MACF cash fund accounts, as already mentioned, have £100,000 being paid in on 25 October 1984 and another £50,000 on 4 December, though the first entry was backdated. Both sums were recorded as coming from the CGT. On the day Windsor produced the money, a total of just under £50,000 was counted out in Scargill's office and used to 'repay' to the NUM the various sums spent on the officials' homes, as well as Windsor's own bridging loan. At a later date, £12,000 was taken from the same pile of cash and passed to the Nottinghamshire NUM miners' secretary, Henry Richardson, to pay striking miners' legal costs.

To disguise what had been done, back- and forward-dated letters of receipt were provided by Stephen Hudson, the NUM's finance officer, which makes it difficult to pinpoint when the money was in fact brought in and the payments made. But other evidence can be used to narrow down the options and show that the payments were made well before 4 December. During November and December, a series of secret meetings with left-leaning trade-union leaders led to a steady supply of cash loans and donations to help the NUM survive the tightening grip of the courts. One of the first to deliver was Jimmy Knapp, general secretary of what was then the National Union of Railwaymen and now the leader of the Rail, Maritime and Transport Union. Knapp sent £100,000 in cash for the newly-established MACF fund on 28 November 1984. The money was taken up to Sheffield by Austin Fairest of the Derbyshire NUM and booked in to MACF on the same day. The NUR's payment slip was mistakenly made out to the NUM rather than MACF and the money therefore had to be transferred into official union funds. As a result – and because of the number of different records of the donation – there was no possibility of backdating the NUR money or moving the entry.[39]

Common sense suggests that if by 28 November Scargill and Heathfield had still not dealt with the potential threat to their homes from the sequestrators, they would have used the NUR money for the 'paper refinancing', rather than wait another six days, when Windsor claims he handed over the Libyan money. In fact, there was other ready cash available before the NUR money arrived. For example, £58,000 had been paid into the NUM's own cash fund from the Transport and General Workers' Union between 7 and 20 November. Even more striking, though, is the clear evidence that the money for the Nottinghamshire legal bills was given to Henry Richardson more than two weeks before 4 December. Windsor always insisted the cash for the Nottinghamshire miners came out of his briefcase of 'Libyan money'; and Scargill and Heathfield agreed it had come from Windsor's first delivery of £100,000.

But the receipt for the money, signed by Richardson, is dated 18 November 1984 and there was no reason whatever in this case to backdate the paperwork. The money was needed not because of problems over sequestration, but because the new anti-strike Nottinghamshire executive refused to back local NUM members arrested on picket lines. Richardson is absolutely certain that he picked the money up from Scargill at the NUM headquarters that day – a Sunday – before the two men drove to Leeds for a meeting of the union's national left caucus. During his 1990 inquiry, Gavin Lightman queried the date with Richardson, saying it was an 'important factor'. The Nottinghamshire NUM leader wrote back insisting: 'The receipt for the £12,000 that I signed on 18 November is the correct date.'[40]

In fact, the date of the 'divvying up' of Windsor's money on Scargill's office table was almost certainly some time earlier still. Everyone involved agrees that Scargill, Heathfield, Hudson and Windsor were all present when the money was produced out of Windsor's safe and the home 'repayments' made. But an examination of diaries and expense claims for the weeks before 18 November – as well as for the period up until 4 December – shows that very few windows of opportunity existed when all four men were in the Sheffield office. It was a period of frenetic activity, with Scargill and Heathfield often speaking at public meetings in different parts of the country, and Windsor and Hudson in Dublin, Paris and Luxembourg at different times. There are a couple of days when all four were in the office in early November, but the presence of Mick McGahey or CGT leaders effectively rules them out. Working backwards, the first plausible date which fits the agreed circumstances is Monday, 29 October – interestingly, one day after the *Sunday Times* exposure of Windsor's trip to Libya.[41]

Other factors point to 29 October. It was the day the court sequestration writ arrived at NUM headquarters and so makes sense as the point at which the miners' leaders would want to deal with the threat to their homes. The first builder's receipt for the extension and improvements on Peter Heathfield's Derbyshire NUM-owned house, 'refinanced' with Windsor's cash, is dated 29 October 1984; the second, 12 November. Heathfield remembers taking the cash for the first invoice for £5,750 from Steve Hudson – on the same day Windsor had produced his £100,000 – to pay the contractor, who was threatening action over the bill. There was no conceivable reason for either receipt date to be falsified. And since the Lightman Report was published, a formal receipt for the £6,860 'repayment' on Scargill's house has come to light – made out independently of Hudson's backdated letter of receipt and held since 1984 by the accountants Peat Marwick in Leeds for Scargill's tax returns – which is also dated 29 October 1984. All the evidence suggests that was the day when the cash 'repayments' described in the *Cook Report* and *Daily Mirror* were in fact made.[42]

## AUTUMN RESHUFFLE

It is self-evident that the Libyan money, still in dollars in Lloyds Bank on 3 December and deposited into a sterling account on 4 December, cannot have been the money Windsor produced from his safe on 29 October, some five weeks earlier. It cannot have been the money brought through customs by Altaf Abbasi – if indeed that ever happened. It cannot have been the money picked up by Windsor in Sheffield and Rotherham and stored in his larder for ten days in late November. And it cannot have been the money used to 'repay' the repairs on the NUM officials' homes and Roger Windsor's bridging loan. Nor is there the slightest possibility that, having deposited £163,000 in a Lloyds Bank account on 4 December, Abbasi could have withdrawn the same money immediately and rushed it over to Sheffield for Windsor to pass on £50,000 to Scargill. Not only would such a bizarre sequence of events fly in the face of common sense and banking practice – withdrawals of that size require at least 24 hours' notice – but it is flatly contradicted by the evidence that the 'repayments' were made more than a month earlier. It would also leave no time whatever for the various cash pick-ups around South Yorkshire – something the like of which do appear to have happened – let alone for the money to soil the Windsor family's biscuit tins.

The only rational explanation for what took place in the light of the new documentary evidence is that there must have been *two* sets of money: the Libyan union donation and cash from another unidentified source. And the money that Windsor fetched from his safe for the various home 'repayments' and the Nottinghamshire miners' legal bills must have come from this other donor. With two separate sets of money, otherwise baffling pieces of evidence slot into place. If the £100,000 used for the repayments at the end of October had nothing to do with the $198,000 Libyan donation working its way through the Swiss banking system at the end of November, then it is quite possible that Windsor did arrange three pick-ups from Abbasi at some point and that he did store cash in his house. And if the

£12,000 donation paid to the Nottinghamshire NUM leader on 18 November was drawn not from the Libyan money but from some other source of funds altogether, the date presents no problems at all.

But if the cash produced by Windsor did not come from Libya, where did it come from? One possible inference from the Tripoli file would be that the money was in fact provided by the CGT as part of a laundering operation. Theoretically, the CGT could have advanced £150,000 as a way of protecting the NUM leadership from any direct funding relationship with Libya in the wake of the scandal surrounding Windsor's adventures in Tripoli. When the Libyan money finally arrived in Britain in early December, the CGT advance could then have been repaid – though, for the figures to add up, someone would have had to have pocketed £13,701.36 along the way. The theory would obviously explain why four witnesses remember Windsor saying the cash came from the CGT – and why the 'paid in by' space on the credit slips initialled by Windsor reads: 'Abbasi, for TINTIN'.

The CGT, however, vehemently denies any involvement. Augustin Dufresne – the 'Tin-Tin' referred to in the mysterious credit slips – died of a stroke while fishing in 1991. But Alain Simon, who worked more closely with Dufresne than any other union official both during and after the 1984–5 period, insists he would certainly have known of any such arrangement and none was made. From Scargill's point of view, the CGT explanation would at least give credence to his longstanding claim that Windsor told him his cash pile came from the French trade union and at the same time confirm that the NUM leadership never received any Libyan cash. And it would present no very great problems for the CGT, which maintains friendly relations with the Libyan unions.

But Simon insists: 'It is absolutely excluded.' There is no record of any such payment in the CGT accounts, and, in any case, it would have been impossible for the CGT to arrange an advance in the time available. Windsor, it should be remembered, has stoutly maintained that his £150,000 or £163,000 came direct from Libya via Abbasi. He has never even hinted that the money was routed through the CGT – let alone that it was actually CGT cash. If the CGT theory were true, it would not only completely contradict Windsor's own version of events: it would also show that he had actively intended to set up his former boss in his 'revelations' to the *Mirror*. But most tellingly, if that were what had happened, it would have been just as good a story for Windsor to sell to Robert Maxwell. In fact, 'Scargill pays off mortgage with laundered Libyan cash' would, if anything, have been even better than what the *Mirror* actually ran. The CGT theory makes no sense.[43]

The strong likelihood must be that the first briefcase of cash, produced by Windsor for the home 'repayments', came from another source altogether. One possibility is that it was supplied either directly or indirectly by the security services or another government proxy. In the light of claims made by GCHQ staff to the *Guardian* that the security services tried to make a phoney deposit in a Scargill-linked account several years after the strike, it hardly seems a fanciful suggestion. From the security services' point of view, there was good reason to be pulling out every stop to discredit the NUM leadership in October 1984. It was the crucial month of the strike and the point at which Margaret Thatcher admitted in retrospect that her government came close to defeat.

Throughout the autumn, available coal supplies were running dangerously low and there was a serious risk of power cuts. Secret forecasts showed, in the words of Lord Marshall, chairman of the Central Electricity Generating Board, that 'Scargill would win in the autumn'. Thatcher was contemplating sending in troops to move coal. At the same time, the dispute with the pit deputies' union NACODS was coming to a head, threatening to close the working Nottinghamshire pits – Thatcher's lifeline. On 29 September, NACODS announced an 83 per cent vote for a strike. The walkout was called for 25 October 1984. This was exactly the period when Windsor and Abbasi were busy setting up the NUM's Libyan connection. If the NACODS strike had gone ahead – rather than being called off on the eve of the stoppage – catching Scargill red-handed with a pot of 'Libyan' gold would have been most convenient. Since there was evidently doubt about whether or when any real Libyan donation would come through, it might well have seemed only prudent to put some cash up front in case it was needed in a hurry. But that must remain in the realm of speculation.[44]

What is not now open to dispute is that the story peddled by Windsor and Abbasi about the Libyan money has no credibility whatever. Given the evidence now available, there are no escape routes. It might be thought, for example, that there could have been two Libyan cash donations of similar size, one of which arrived at the end of October and the other which came through at the beginning of December. But no one involved – Windsor, Abbasi, Gaddafi, Ibrahim, the *Mirror* or *Cook Report* – has ever suggested any such thing. The only Libyan cash Windsor or Abbasi say they ever laid their hands on was the £150,000 or £163,000. The Libyans insist they only ever sent one sum. Apart from the £163,000, the only other Libyan money ever talked about was Abbasi's $9 million, which he eventually admitted had never reached Britain, and Ibrahim's $500,000, which he said was spent by one of the People's Bureaux. On top of that, there is no record in the MACF or NUM cash-book accounts at any time of any other payment which could fit such a theory. It is simply impossible.

Nor is it conceivable that Windsor could have just got the dates wildly wrong and that the whole sequence of events he described as taking place in November, complete with cash-drops and biscuit tins, actually took place with the real Libyan money more than a month later. The idea does not bear even the most cursory consideration. Windsor, who has clung to his timetable of events through thick and thin, kept a diary during 1984, which he has used to try to pinpoint other events in discussion with the author. He is a meticulous book-keeper and collector of documents. It beggars belief that he did not record in some way the day his bridging loan was paid off, as he says, with Libyan money – and, of course, he insists he did. He also noted down the addresses of all the cash-drops, which were faithfully reproduced in the *Mirror*, and reportedly produced dates, which were not. In any case, a date for the cash delivery to Scargill in late December is no more plausible than one in early December, since the 'repayments' clearly took place several weeks before.

It is not hard to guess why Windsor might have clung to 4 December for the date of his handover of Libyan cash and the 'repayment' of his loan and the officials' repairs – even down to the absurd 9.30 a.m. timing. He knew that he did in fact give Scargill £50,000 that day; but, more importantly, he knew that it was the first date when the real Libyan money was actually available in Britain. Other evidence suggests he was already concerned about rearranging the calendar back in 1984. His own letter of receipt from Steve Hudson for the 'repayment' of his £29,500 bridging loan was forward-dated to 30 November 1984. But Windsor also got Hudson to issue two new receipts – one for £29,000, dated 4 December, another for £500, dated 10 December – seemingly because the first repayment had been £500 short. The original entries for Windsor's repayments in the NUM cash-book were Tippexed out and replaced with 4 and 10 December. The same was done with the date for the £12,000 payment to the Nottinghamshire miners, which was re-entered as 10 December – an impossible date, since Henry Richardson was at an all-day area executive meeting in Mansfield and nowhere near the NUM's Sheffield headquarters. Hudson, who was in charge of the books, has no recollection of why the entries were changed but clearly had no interest of his own in moving Windsor's repayment dates. It appears that Windsor's later version of events was being prepared even then.[45]

The former chief executive's only other possible escape from the brutal logic of the bank documentation is to hang it all on Abbasi. After all, it was the Kashmiri who channelled the Libyan money through his own accounts and delivered the cash to Windsor. Might not Abbasi have led Windsor to believe that three briefcases of cash he handed over in October and November came from Libya, and concealed the arrival of the real Libyan money from him when it actually came through in December? That get-out fares no better than the others. Among other factors, Windsor's initials on the credit slips – signed after the money had been changed into sterling on 4 December – make it impossible. The evidence that has now come to light points unavoidably to the conclusion that both Windsor and Abbasi were involved, wittingly or unwittingly, in a set-up of the miners' strike leadership: a 'sting', where quantities of cash were swapped around to cause the maximum possible political damage when the time was right.

## THE BAGMAN'S STORY

That is still, however, only the starting point for any truthful account of these events. Crucial questions remain unanswered. Who provided the £150,000 Windsor did in fact bring into the NUM? Was the real Libyan money used to refund that donor? If so, who creamed off the extra £13,701.36? If not, where did the Libyan money end up? In December 1993, the man at the centre of the NUM's Libyan connection – Salem Ibrahim Salem, to give him his full name – finally agreed to meet and talk. Meeting was to prove easier said than done. At that time, Anglo-American-sponsored UN sanctions against Libya, imposed because of its alleged involvement in the 1988 bombing of a Pan-Am airliner over Lockerbie, included a ban on flights in and out of the country. Travel for all Libyans was consequently difficult. In the case of Ibrahim, a man who had attracted *persona non grata* status in a string of countries including Britain, the difficulties were compounded. The interview was to be in Tunisia. Contact was made with Ahmad, his diminutive gofer, at a hotel bar in central Tunis. The two men had taken twelve hours to reach Tunis because of jams on the coastal road from Tripoli. A rendezvous was duly fixed at another hotel, where Ahmad reappeared with a battered Mercedes. We drove to the forecourt of a third hotel – the Abou Nuwas, named after a renowned eighth-century Arabic erotic poet – where, without explanation,

Ahmad kept the car engine running while we waited.

After a few minutes, a moustachioed figure slid onto the back seat and Ahmad drove off at some speed in the direction of the seaside resort of Marsa. Salem Ibrahim was then a broad-faced, easy-going man in his early fifties. He came from a family steeped in the politics of resistance, first to Italian colonialism and later to the corrupt neo-colonial regime of King Idris. His father, Ibrahim Salem Muhammad, founded the first trade union in Libya, the Mechanics' Union, under the Italian occupation in the 1920s. Ibrahim began working part-time for the union in the early 1950s at the age of nine. One of those employed with him at the union office in those days was Bashir Howij, who later came to head the Libyan union movement after Gaddafi came to power in 1969 and was named by Abbasi as his contact in Tripoli in 1984. During the 1960s, Ibrahim himself led a series of bitter oil-workers' strikes against Exxon, the US-based multinational which then owned and controlled the Libyan oilfields.

In the 1990s, Ibrahim acted as Gaddafi's confidant and roving envoy, constantly on the move, lobbying, organizing and wheeler-dealing as part of the effort to undermine Libya's political isolation in the wake of Lockerbie and the collapse of the Soviet Union. In many ways, Ibrahim was an archetypal radical Arab intellectual of his generation: the generation radicalized by Nasser, Qassim and the later rise of the Palestinian fedayeen. He had published two books, one on the papacy and Islam, the second on – of all subjects – political violence and terrorism. Speaking fluent English, he flitted in conversation from subject to subject: the war in Bosnia, the contradictory interests of the Western powers in relation to Libya, prospects for a new socialism, the overweening power of the Western media. Sipping mint tea in an open-air café overlooking the Mediterranean, set amidst the bougainvillaea and traditional blue- and white-washed houses of Marsa, Ibrahim finally turned to the bizarre story of Libya's contacts with the British NUM and their destructive aftermath.

'This is a subject I have discussed many, many times with the leader,' he said, as if even the Libyans themselves never knew quite what hit them. Ibrahim confirmed the account given by Scargill and Simon of their meeting in Algiers. But while he was withering about Windsor, it was clear that even then the Libyans preferred to see Abbasi more as a manipulated victim than a conscious double agent. 'I know Abbasi's psychology. He was badly treated in prison. We have an open heart for him because of his suffering. He exaggerates and he likes to inflate his own importance. But Windsor was part of the game and he used Abbasi's situation.' Ibrahim nevertheless accepts that Abbasi played the role of 'instigator' in the Libyan contacts with the NUM. His original relationship with the Libyans, Ibrahim says, was a political one. Abbasi agreed to start a 'Green Book centre' in Britain, from which Gaddafi's political ideas and texts would be disseminated. He attended a study course in Tripoli and, like all participants, was given a medal to commemorate his attendance. This was then repackaged in the *Mirror* as 'Gaddafi's highest honour' to imply Abbasi was a top-level Libyan agent. According to Ibrahim, he was nothing of the sort. The centre, needless to say, no longer existed.

As Ibrahim describes it, Abbasi approached him during the 1984–5 strike, saying the miners needed help and suggesting Ibrahim meet them. When the discussion with Scargill took place at the CGT in Paris in October 1984, they 'didn't talk money', Ibrahim says. It was agreed that Windsor would go to Libya to meet trade unionists to explain the striking miners' position. 'Maybe other people gave the impression that if you go to Libya you will get millions, but I just expressed the view that we wanted to help in the same way that the rest of the world was helping.' Ibrahim then contacted trade-union officials in Tripoli. They in turn made the arrangements for Windsor's visit. The interview with Gaddafi had been set up by the unions, as it was normal for organizations to try to get an audience with the president if they had an important visitor. But when Windsor arrived in Tripoli – Ibrahim says, echoing Abbasi – the NUM man not only 'insisted on meeting the leader', he also 'insisted that the meeting be broadcast'. Windsor's story in the

*Mirror* about going to Ibrahim's office to 'practise kissing him on both cheeks as a rehearsal for meeting the leader' was 'just rubbish' – as was his claim that he had not been told the video would be broadcast.[46]

According to Ibrahim, the NUM chief executive was, on the contrary, adamant that the meeting should be publicized.

> I said it might be misused against Scargill and the miners. My point of view was not to declare the meeting. Gaddafi asked him: Would it harm you if this meeting is made known? Windsor replied: No, we would be very proud and he embraced him. In fact, he was very eager for it to be broadcast.

Figures were not discussed with Gaddafi, but $200,000 was allocated by the unions. It was the only money Libya sent for the British miners, Ibrahim says – the $500,000 was an internal problem within the Libyan administration and had never gone anywhere near Britain. The $200,000 had been taken by a trade-union official to the Libyan Embassy in Frankfurt, after which it could be tracked through Abbasi's bank statements.

The file of documents, he explained, had only been collected five and a half years later when the scandal about the money broke in the British media in 1990. With Scargill denying that any Libyan money had ever been received, the Libyans wanted to find out where their $200,000 had gone. Once they had satisfied themselves that the Libyan union representative had indeed handed the money over to Abbasi, there was anger in Tripoli that the NUM would not acknowledge the support.

'This was normal trade-union to trade-union help, not government help, so people asked why should it not be accepted.' Resentment at what was perceived as a slight by the NUM president sparked Gaddafi's statements and interviews about the money during 1990. Three years later, however, according to Ibrahim, the Libyans were convinced that their cash support never in fact reached the NUM leaders. They were, he believes, used as pawns in a British intelligence operation.[47]

## THE STING IN THE TALE

The real story behind the NUM's Libyan connection is a very different one from that peddled during the miners' strike or the media campaign of 1990. As the evidence uncovered here shows, it was a provocation on a grand scale and, scarcely surprisingly, the NUM's enemies could not get enough of it. Not only did the threatened Libyan millions never actually turn up, but the Abbasi–Windsor link was played twice over to brilliant propaganda effect: first in October 1984 and then, even more devastatingly, as the foundation of the entire *Mirror–Cook Report* onslaught five years later. Meanwhile, real and imagined sums of money were shuffled around to provide the right mood music, staged cash-drops were held to impress the locals, and the most fantastic tales produced to earn Maxwell's shilling. In the history of the labour movement, it is a sting that must rank – if not in its results, then certainly in the cynicism of its execution – on a par with the infamous Zinoviev letter and the Cato Street conspiracy.

The Tripoli documents, the testimony of Ibrahim and the evidence available in the NUM's own archives allow a remarkable picture of events to be pieced together. At the most critical point of the miners' strike, contacts between the NUM and the state with the worst reputation in the British media of any in the world were initiated by a man convicted of a bombing conspiracy in Pakistan and taken in hand by Roger Windsor. Once in Libya, by all other accounts to visit trade unionists, Windsor enthusiastically took the opportunity to meet Gaddafi and at the very least agreed to the encounter being broadcast. The impact on the NUM was disastrous. Money was then advanced from an unknown source and used, on Windsor's advice, to make 'repayments' on the union officials' homes. If, as then seemed possible, NACODS and power cuts had tipped the dispute heavily in favour of the union, this cash could have certainly been identified as 'Libyan' and the repayments presented as corrupt – as happened five years later. The exposure proved unnecessary. But when the real Libyan money came through several weeks later, everything possible was done *at the time* to make the two sums of money appear to be one and the same. Finally, when Windsor left the union, the time bomb set during the strike was detonated in the *Mirror* and *Cook Report* and became the Scargill Affair. Whatever his motives, the Tripoli papers show that Windsor was caught up in a set-up of the NUM leadership during the 1984–5 strike itself.

Libya was, of course, a tempting bait dangled at exactly the right moment. Once the courts had seized control of the NUM and its assets through sequestration and receivership, cash began to pour in from all over the world. Trade unions in the socialist bloc were an obvious first port of call to keep the NUM afloat. So, in other circumstances, might have been oil-rich Libya. On the left, the Libyan regime was generally seen as a loose cannon, but one which had nevertheless implemented social reforms at home and challenged Western domination of the region and its resources. It had also earned opprobrium for its backing of various 'terrorist' organizations in the Middle East and beyond, among them the IRA. But the power and influence of a small North African state was obviously limited. By any objective measure, financial backing from the Soviet Union and Eastern Europe – Britain's officially designated 'enemy' of the period – was in reality far more threatening for the British authorities.

But as the *Sunday Times*'s 'book of the strike' put it: 'Seeking support from Moscow, or Peking, or Eastern Europe, or well-established Communist organizations around the world, was generally regarded as within the rules of the game.' Libya was another matter. The Libyan government had been elevated both in Britain and the United States to special diplomatic status as a unique menace to Western civilization and interests. In Britain, there was the special factor of the policewoman's killing. The NUM leaders were well aware of the sensitivity of dealing with Libya. Whatever Scargill and Heathfield knew or thought they knew about Windsor's dealings with Abbasi after his trip to Libya, everything was certainly done to keep the contacts well away from both the national officials and the union's formal structures. For the security services, wound up to fever pitch by the Thatcher government's Manichaean view of the strike, the circumstances were ideal. Here was an opportunity – fortuitous or manufactured – which could be exploited with devastating effect to smear and discredit the NUM and its leadership.[48]

As for Altaf Abbasi, his enthusiastic courting of radical groups, apparently on the Libyans' behalf, continued unabated after the miners' strike. In 1986, he helped organize delegates from black organizations in Britain to attend an anti-imperialist conference in Tripoli. Later the same year, he was off to Belfast, visiting Sinn Fein under an assumed name – though he now claims he went to the north of Ireland to buy cattle. Shortly afterwards, he was held for five days under the Prevention of Terrorism Act over an alleged Libyan-backed plot to kill an Arab ambassador, but released without charge. Salem Ibrahim told the author, somewhat regretfully, that Abbasi had 'not been in touch for a long time'. Abbasi said that he had given up working for the Libyans. He continued, however, to entertain powerful figures in Pakistani politics. Among his house guests were a retired member of the Pakistani military high command and – more than once – Murtaza Bhutto, brother of Benazir, twice Pakistani Prime Minister. Bhutto broke relations with Abbasi, however, before he went back to Pakistan in 1993 to face imprisonment for his role at the head of the al-Zulfikar movement. He had become convinced Abbasi was working for the security services.[49]

Abbasi in turn points the finger at Windsor. Looking back, he believes the NUM's chief executive may well have 'set something up' through his contacts with Libya. Abbasi says that he was told in 1984 by a senior Libyan official, who claimed to have heard it from French intelligence, that 'your man is not right'. Salem Ibrahim was also suspicious, he remembers. At the time, he says, he was sceptical, but now he has changed his mind. 'It fits in nicely with the way everything has turned out since.' Like Windsor, Abbasi says the NUM's Libyan connection caused him and his family nothing but trouble and led him to move house – in his case, from Doncaster to Nottingham. And like Windsor, he has set himself up in the property business. In the wake of his appearances on the *Cook Report* and in the *Daily Mirror*, Abbasi became joint proprietor of two old people's homes, one in Nottingham, the other in Rotherham – where in 1992 he was accused in the local press of sacking the administrator because she refused to give false evidence to an immigration tribunal.

In the summer of 1994, Abbasi was confronted with a copy of his ten-year-old LBI Geneva bank statement – showing the Libyan pit-strike donation still in his Swiss dollar account long after he was supposed to have brought it through Heathrow Airport three times in cash and handed it to Windsor at three different pick-ups. The businessman at first insisted this was not the Libyan money and then became agitated, claiming the document was a forgery. A couple of months later, Roger Windsor was also shown the Swiss bank statement, along with copies of the other Tripoli papers. He accepted that they 'could be genuine', but insisted he had not written the words 'for TINTIN' on the two credit slips. The documents were in any case, he said, 'nothing to do with me' and he was unable to explain them. Abbasi denies dealing with the security services himself. But he has no objection in principle to the idea. 'I don't think it is an unpleasant thing to be a member of an organization of a country of which I am a citizen. MI5 is there to look after the security of the country of which I am a citizen and there is no harm in working with it.'[50]

# CHAPTER FOUR

# THE STRANGE WORLD OF ROGER WINDSOR

Extreme zeal is often a cloak of treachery. *From the constitution of the London Corresponding Society, 1795*[1]

As the Conservative government's year-long confrontation with Britain's miners turned into a remorseless war of attrition, the role of the NUM's senior unelected official became ever more bizarre and destructive. The Libyan escapade would turn out to have been only the most melodramatic of a string of damaging incidents which found Roger Windsor in a pivotal position of influence. From the majority of union staff and officials, Windsor came to attract suspicion and loathing in equal measure. But with political and legal attacks multiplying in the aftermath of the 1984–5 strike, the man who had embraced Gaddafi for the cameras contrived to make himself indispensable to the NUM's embattled president. For every move by the courts or the Coal Board, Roger Windsor had his own countermove. Enthroned in his executive office on the ninth floor of the union's Sheffield headquarters, Windsor became a weaver of cunning stratagems and convoluted schemes, which both exasperated and intrigued his tireless boss.

Scargill's distrust of Windsor after the Tripoli fiasco was tempered by tolerance towards someone who seemed able to get things done. As the political and financial cost of Windsor's activities mounted, however, the miners' leader's patience for a man widely regarded as his chief fixer and bag-carrier eventually snapped. But the chief executive officer, who for a time entertained the idea of becoming the NUM's general secretary himself, was ideally placed to wreak a terrible revenge. Windsor's record of apparent bungling and his provocative role in union intrigue would finally come to a head in a face-to-face confrontation. In a suitably theatrical denouement, it was followed by the secret preparation of disciplinary action against him, Windsor's sudden flight to France and his reappearance as the leading hired witness in Robert Maxwell's multimedia assault on the leaders of Britain's longest strike. For a man who had never hewn so much as a cob of coal, Roger Windsor would leave an indelible mark on the history of the British miners and their union.

## OUTSIDER

Of all those who formed the core of the NUM national office under the Scargill regime, Roger Windsor was the undisputed odd man out. A few months after Scargill took over as president in 1982, the NUM conference had voted overwhelmingly to shift the union's headquarters from Euston Road in London into the mining heartlands. Sheffield, at the centre of the country's largest coalfield and renowned at the time as the capital of the 'socialist republic of South Yorkshire', offered by far the best deal and it was there that the NUM set up shop in the spring of 1983. The main idea was to bring the national union apparatus closer to its members and break the influence of the traditional TUC-parliament-Coal Board hobnobbing circuit. But the move had other helpful spin-offs. A large number of London-based head office employees preferred to take redundancy rather than go north and work for Scargill in Sheffield. And the new NUM president took full advantage of the opportunity provided by the clear-out to put his stamp on the organization.

The vacated jobs were filled with his political supporters from the left: people like the New Zealander Dave Feickert, who became the union's head of research, and Hilary and Trevor Cave, who were hired to run the union's education programmes and office administration. From the union's Yorkshire area

machine, the new leader brought in another left-wing supporter, Maurice Jones, to edit *The Miner*, the NUM's national
journal. Then there was Mick Clapham, a long-time Yorkshire
ally from the NUM left caucus, who followed Scargill to head
the national industrial-relations department. Almost all the new
faces came either from the mining communities or had a well-
established association with the union. Windsor was a striking
exception. As one NUM insider put it, 'he parachuted in from
nowhere'.

'Nowhere' was in fact the suburbs of West London. Born in
the final months of the Second World War, Roger Edward
Windsor was brought up and lived for most of his life on the
outer fringes of the capital. His father was a bus conductor who
ended up a Tory-voting Middlesex estate agent. Nothing in
Windsor's first thirty-odd years cut him out as someone headed
for a starring role in Britain's most dramatic postwar industrial
confrontation. At Hampton Grammar School – where his one-
time form master describes him as having been 'self-opinionated
to a degree' – he was a lance-corporal in the army cadet force
and a member of the school's Christian Society. A Scout leader
in the 1960s, he went to work for the Water Board after leaving
school, as a management trainee and then a pensions-depart-
ment administrator. But he found the job 'stultifying' and left
to become an assistant company secretary with the Hounslow-
based camping and clothing retailer, Greenfield Millets. Monitoring sales of tents and monkey boots proved more to
Windsor's taste than working in a local Water Board office. But
he eventually resigned from Millets as well, he says, after he was
asked to sack ninety members of staff in preparation for a Stock-
Exchange flotation.[2]

After ten years of paper-pushing in local business 'audit and
admin' offices, Windsor crossed over into what was then the
shadowy world of Cold War international trade unionism. In
1973, he signed up as finance officer with Public Services
International, a global umbrella organization for public-sector
unions then based in London. This was the crucial move that
would position him to join the NUM almost a decade later. The

organization Windsor went to work for had a history of manipulation by the United States and British intelligence services. In the late 1940s, the postwar effort to unite all national trade-union centres in one international – the World Federation of Trade Unions – came to grief with the onset of the East–West confrontation. Under strong American pressure and with the active connivance of the nascent CIA, noncommunist Western trade-union centres split the new WFTU and walked out to set up their own outfit: the International Confederation of Free Trade Unions. The rupture had its roots in the prewar antagonisms between communism and social democracy. But the division of the worldwide trade-union movement into hostile camps – reflecting the foreign policies of the two ideological and military blocs around the United States and the Soviet Union and competing for support in the Third World – provided especially fertile ground for intelligence manipulation.

The activities of the WFTU were effectively controlled by the Soviet and East European Communist Party international departments. In the case of the ICFTU, the CIA and a variety of intelligence front organizations were the main tools of state interference, using the respectability of a supposedly independent international organization to advance Western interests inside politically influential labour movements around the world. As embarrassing disclosures of CIA funding and interference in the ICFTU and its associated union groupings proliferated in the 1960s and 1970s, other state-funded Western outfits – like the Reaganite National Endowment for Democracy (NED) and the German Friedrich Ebert Foundation – increasingly took the lead in guiding and underwriting the more pliable international union structures.[3]

PSI, the organization Windsor went to work for in the early 1970s, was an ICFTU-linked body then representing nearly ten million public service workers. Its core outlook, despite the participation of some left-of-centre unions, was strongly anticommunist. Harry Batchelor, a former PSI assistant general secretary who worked closely with Windsor in the 1970s and early 1980s, recalls that one of PSI's main jobs at that time was to stop 'communist organizations trying to get members in developing countries'. Along with other ICFTU-linked outfits, PSI had proved to be an irresistible front for Western intelligence meddling.[4]

In one particularly notorious case, PSI played a central role in joint US–British intelligence operations to bring down successive left-wing governments led by Cheddi Jagan in British Guiana (now Guyana) in the 1950s and 1960s. The main funding for this long-running joint CIA–MI5 destabilization programme against the Guyanese Prime Minister and his People's Progressive Party was channelled through PSI. CIA cash was laundered via a foundation conduit and PSI's main United States affiliate to pay for a CIA-staffed PSI Latin American section. With such generous sources of finance, the section was able to buy off local Guyanese politicians and trade-union leaders by the score. PSI was later used as the cash cow for an even larger-scale MI5–CIA assault on Jagan's government: the provocation of interracial rioting and an eighty-day general strike directed against Jagan in the summer of 1963, underwritten by the CIA to the tune of at least one million dollars. Jagan was finally driven from office the following year. The ousting of Cheddi Jagan is one of the last known covert operations overseas involving MI5, which had a powerful 'counterintelligence' role in the British colonial system. MI5's cooperation with the CIA in British Guiana was carried out on the direct orders of the then Prime Minister, Harold Macmillan. After the Cold War, Jagan returned to office in Guyana, this time as president.[5]

In common with other Western international trade-union organizations, PSI officials insist their outfit was 'cleaned up' long ago. It is certainly true that, in later years, more left-led British unions joined PSI and helped steer it away from its traditional Cold War role. Windsor himself claims that by the early 1970s the CIA agents working at the PSI headquarters had all been cleared out and that the international was a thoroughly respectable outfit. 'By the time I got to PSI, there was no question of CIA subversion, but you just had to accept that was part of its history,' he says. Nevertheless, in the mid-1980s, long after Windsor had left the organization to join the NUM, it was still recorded – despite denials by PSI leaders – as having had projects paid for by the US government-funded NED.[6]

Windsor stayed at PSI for a full ten years, rising to become chief finance and administrative officer, responsible for the smooth functioning of the fifteen-strong secretariat and number three in the hierarchy. He was regarded by other officials as competent, if not exactly a high flier. 'His job was looking after the books and the building, making sure there were enough toilet rolls and the rates got paid', according to Colin Humphries, who worked for PSI's general secretary. Windsor was 'a bit cold' and never mixed much, he recalls. But he was also adept enough at office politics to convince his bosses to move the organization's headquarters from Central London to a Feltham industrial estate not far from his own home – courtesy of his father's estate agency.[7]

By this time, Windsor had also become active in local politics, joining the local Labour Party at the relatively late age of twenty-five. Within a year of arriving at PSI, he was elected as a local councillor – on his second attempt – for the London Borough of Hounslow, where he projected a leftish profile in a predominantly right-wing ruling Labour group. Windsor served out his four-year term, annoying the old guard with his 'verbal diarrhoea' and 'air of superiority' and failing to win advancement. Ted Pauling, a former council leader, remembers Windsor as a left-wing 'disruptionist'. Brian Price, a closer political ally at the time and still a Hounslow councillor, thought his style 'destructive'. Ever hopeful, Windsor also joined the Labour Parliamentary Association, a pressure group for would-be parliamentary candidates.[8]

By the beginning of the 1980s, Windsor was commuting back and forth between West London and the Gloucestershire market town of Stroud, where he had moved with his wife, Angie, and three young children. The family's new, larger house was almost a hundred miles from PSI's West London offices and during the week Windsor stayed at his mother-in-law's flat in Twickenham. Angie, meanwhile, threw herself into local

Labour politics, becoming secretary of the Stroud constituency party and a member of Labour's south-west women's regional council. It was the period of the high tide of the Bennite constituency left and Angie Windsor's west-country activism brought the couple into regular contact with Tony Benn himself, then still the MP for Bristol South East. Both Windsors liked to associate themselves with the fashionable left-wing causes of the time, such as the Campaign for Labour Party Democracy, the organization which master-minded Labour's internal democratic reforms of the early 1980s. Some Stroud stalwarts say they were suspicious of Roger Windsor at the time, though others appreciated Angie's hard work and May Day fêtes – which were graced by labour-movement luminaries like Benn and Rodney Bickerstaffe, the public-service workers' leader. CLPD activists, who had dealings with Windsor both before and after he went to the NUM, had the highest regard for an 'effective operator', a man unusually prepared to stick his neck out for humdrum left campaigns. In the words of Victor Shonfield, CLPD's treasurer in the 1970s and 1980s, he seemed almost 'too good to be true'.[9]

The circumstances of Roger Windsor's arrival at the NUM have, not surprisingly, become clouded with controversy in retrospect. In 1982, PSI was preparing to move its headquarters from West London to Geneva, a prospect Windsor says he did not find 'very appealing'. He first applied for a national officer's job at the hyper-factionalized Civil and Public Services Association, the civil-service union representing the lowest clerical grades. Political control of the CPSA, which was affiliated to PSI, had swung violently back and forth between left and right. But in 1982 the left had a tight grip on the executive. During that year, there was a prolonged dispute at the government's central social-security office in Newcastle. Left-wing influence in the civil-service unions was causing growing anxiety in Whitehall. The union's president was a supporter of the Trotskyist Militant Tendency, and one of its vice-presidents, Ray Alderson, was a prominent Communist Party member. Several senior officials were also active on the left.

The committee in charge of appointments, however, was more evenly balanced. In his job application, Windsor duly provided two references from opposite ends of the political spectrum: Tony Baker, former CPSA treasurer, PSI auditor and right-wing supporter of the Catholic Action Group; and Tony Benn, ex-Cabinet minister and doyen of the Labour left. Ray Alderson, who sat on the appointments committee, remembers being 'staggered' that someone could convince two such utterly contradictory political figures to act as his referees. He rang Mick Costello, the Communist Party's industrial organizer, to check Windsor out, but Costello said he knew nothing about him. 'Baker was an outrageous old right-winger,' Alderson says. 'And I couldn't find anyone on the left who had a good word to say about Windsor. Added to that, the PSI was then renowned for being to all intents and purposes a CIA front organization, and throughout the 1970s the left had been trying to get the CPSA to disaffiliate. The whole thing didn't hold water.' Alderson blocked Windsor's application.[10]

Windsor's next port of call was the NUM, then busy preparing for its move to Sheffield and a widely anticipated showdown with the Coal Board and the government. The post of finance officer fell vacant and, in November 1982, Windsor answered an advertisement for the job in the *Guardian*. This time, he gave his written referees as Tony Baker – who says now he 'didn't really know' Windsor – and Rodney Bickerstaffe, the left-wing leader of the National Union of Public Employees. Windsor had come across Bickerstaffe through PSI, to which NUPE was affiliated. His NUM application was a characteristic document, written in the bureaucratic, almost archaic, language he routinely uses, even in speech. He was, he said, a 'committed trade unionist and socialist'. He also claimed to be a member of both CLPD and the Campaign for Nuclear Disarmament – though despite his public association with CLPD in particular, neither organization has any record of his actual membership.[11]

There was no mention, as there had been in his CPSA application, of his wife's political activism in Stroud as a reason for his wanting to stay in England. And, in fact, once the couple moved to Sheffield the following year, Angie Windsor effectively dropped out of active politics – though she continued to toy with the idea of becoming a Labour MP. Windsor was interviewed at the NUM's London headquarters by Scargill, Mick McGahey and Don Loney, then the chief executive officer. Lawrence Daly, the NUM's veteran Scots general secretary, only managed a few minutes at the interview before withdrawing under the influence of drink. Scargill recalls that Windsor 'performed superbly – I only caught him out once on a question about corporation tax'. By this point, Windsor had quietly forgotten about the entirely unsuitable Tony Baker and suggested Bickerstaffe and Tony Benn as his verbal referees. The NUM president immediately contacted Bickerstaffe, who had once stayed with the PSI apparatchik after giving a talk to the Stroud Labour Party. Bickerstaffe vouched for Windsor's competence. Scargill then rang Benn – a friend and close political ally of the NUM leader – for further assurances.[12]

Tony Benn had struck up a superficial political relationship with the Windsors – more with Angie than her husband – through the left-wing Labour network in the southwest. On one occasion, Benn had stayed the night at the Windsors' Stroud home. As far as Benn was concerned, there was no reason to doubt Windsor's professed credentials. At the NUM, the PSI connection failed to ring any alarm bells. Windsor had, after all, only been an administrator, not an official. For Scargill, the joint recommendation from Benn and Bickerstaffe clinched it. Windsor got the job on the night of the interview. When Ray Alderson heard about Windsor's appointment, he was alarmed. 'I rang Arthur and told him: I think you've made a mistake. But Arthur said he'd checked him out and it all stood up.' PSI officials were equally astounded when they eventually heard Windsor was off to serve at the court of 'King Arthur'.

Derek Gladwyn, an official of the GMB general union and a member of the PSI executive at the time, is one of a select band who admits to having liked and respected Windsor. He had hoped Windsor would 'throw his hat in the ring' for the job of

PSI deputy general secretary and expected him, as chief finance man, to want to go with the organization to Geneva. However, Windsor told him his family didn't want to move. 'Then it transpired that Roger had got a job with the NUM at a time when they were moving up north, so I was even more surprised' – particularly, it seems, at the thought of Windsor becoming part of Scargill's kitchen Cabinet. 'Arthur's left-wing credentials are respected, well known and well understood, but I never had any indication that Roger Windsor had that kind of political leaning.' Gladwyn discussed his shock with others at PSI. But it was as nothing compared with their reaction to what took place later. Humphries remembers his utter amazement when he turned on his hotel television set during a trip to Tokyo in 1984 and was greeted by the sight of the PSI's former paper-clip man embracing Colonel Gaddafi.[13]

When Windsor arrived at NUM headquarters in February 1983, Scargill was immediately impressed by his administrative ability and enthusiastic loyalty. It was a time when loyalty to the newly elected leadership among the head-office staff was in relatively short supply. Once Don Loney retired, the new recruit was quickly promoted from finance to chief executive officer, the most senior unelected post at the union's national headquarters. The job gave him privileged access to the most sensitive decisions and arrangements made by the NUM's three elected national officials: the troika of Scargill, Heathfield and the NUM vice-president, Scottish communist miners' leader Mick McGahey. When the union packed its bags and moved to Sheffield, Windsor moved north with it. And when he had problems selling the family house in Stroud, the national officials stepped in with a £29,500 one-year bridging loan. It was an arrangement – offered at the time of his appointment as part of a package of staff relocation terms – which would end up being dragged through the tabloid media, a full-scale legal inquiry and the French courts.

Windsor lost no time in establishing himself as Scargill's most faithful lieutenant and before long came to be seen as the president's man. 'Roger would do everything Arthur wanted, whereas we would often argue with him,' Dave Feickert, the former head of NUM research, remembers. 'He became the Grand Vizier of the NUM. It was the role Arthur wanted him to play against the right wing in the union.' Others insist he was never the yes-man he has become in retrospect. But Windsor attracted particular criticism from the NUM's South Wales area. 'We thought he was nuts,' Kim Howells, then the area's research officer, says. 'But Scargill always defended him. He delegated to Roger Windsor infinitely more power than to anyone else.' For Howells, who became one of Scargill's most vitriolic critics, this was all of a piece with an atmosphere of foreboding that he claims flourished at the NUM headquarters under the new regime. 'There was a dreadful air of mistrust. It became a place one hated visiting, like a medieval monastery – everybody plotting, with the abbot shut away in his reinforced cell.'

For most insiders, however, there was a camaraderie at the NUM national office until much later on. And it was not only for internal manoeuvring that Scargill needed an effective and reliable operator. By the time Windsor joined the NUM, both the government and the union were preparing for what was widely understood would be the decisive industrial confrontation of the Thatcher administration. On the NUM side, the national officials kept a close watch on the fortunes of the most powerful print union, the National Graphical Association, in its battle with the union-busting free-sheet newspaper publisher, Eddie Shah. Scargill was particularly anxious to learn the lessons from the courts' sequestration of NGA property carried out under Thatcher's new anti-union laws. Well before the coal strike had begun, the new chief executive officer was entrusted with the crucial job of drawing up plans for the protection of the NUM's cash and assets in the entirely anticipated event of court action against it.[14]

## OPERATION FOROPS

Windsor was in his element. In the autumn of 1983, the NUM imposed an overtime ban over a wages dispute and the count-down to the strike began. Windsor set to work with the union's finance officer, Stephen Hudson, to devise a foolproof scheme to protect the union's money and property from sequestration. Throughout the winter, meetings were held with lawyers and bankers. There were two basic ideas. The first was to squirrel the union's cash away in foreign bank accounts, far from the clutches of the English judges. This was dubbed 'Operation Forops'. The second of Windsor's wheezes was to establish an independ-ent 'Mineworkers' Trust' to take over NUM assets, including officials' union-owned homes, with the aim of insulating them from any sequestration order. In an overlapping scheme, he also arranged for an off-the-shelf company, 'Oakedge', to be bought to protect various bits of union property, down to the office fur-niture. 'We were happy to let him get on with things,' Heathfield explained.[15]

At a secret meeting on 8 March 1984, as the strike began to spread throughout the British coalfields, Windsor's plan was given the go-ahead by the NUM executive. Later in the day, a larger gathering – including NUM area finance officers – was held at Sheffield's Royal Victoria Hotel, where advice was given as to how the union's independent area fiefdoms could adopt similar tactics to protect their own money and property. Windsor presented the main report. Roy Ottey, a right-wing member of the NUM executive who opposed the strike and resigned in October 1984 in protest against the union's defiance of the High Court, gives a graphic account of the scene:

> The meeting was held in a large room with a long table at one end and tall windows at the other, draped with closed curtains reaching to the floor. While we were having tea and sandwiches ... Roger Windsor, much to my amusement, kept peering behind the cur-tains. I don't know that he expected to find – some spies maybe – but his behaviour certainly helped to set the scene for what was to

be a mysterious meeting ... we were told that if we needed advice from Roger Windsor personal contact only should be made with him even if that meant jumping in the car over the next twenty-four hours and going to see him. It seemed we really were in the realms of James Bond: a world of spies and phone-tapping.[16]

Windsor revelled in the conspiratorial procedures which the strike and the assault by the courts imposed on the union. At one point, he circulated the NUM's area organizations with a code to use when ringing the strike headquarters to ask for picketing support. Pickets and police, he advised, should be referred to as fruit and vegetables, and requests for assistance should be couched in the language of grocery lists. So pickets should be referred to as apples, police should become potatoes, the railway should be the 'freezer', members of the National Union of Railwaymen should be 'mechanics' and seamen 'plumbers'. Windsor's code caused much merriment at picketing centres and chaos at the strike headquarters, where message-takers often had no clue as to what the code meant. As Steve Hudson puts it drily: 'Roger was very, very keen on things like this.'[17]

When the full legal maelstrom finally engulfed the union in the autumn of 1984, Windsor's taste for dramatic gestures was given full indulgence in the battle to protect the NUM's assets and keep the union functioning. Months earlier, Operation Forops had been put quietly into effect and £8.5 million of NUM cash had been spirited away from bank to bank in England, then to the Isle of Man, passing through the financial systems of seven countries before finally ending up in Dublin, Zurich and Luxembourg. Well before the High Court in London imposed its sequestration order on 25 October 1984, the union had transferred £5 million from Dublin to New York to buy Jersey currency bonds. The transactions were only completed when Roger Windsor gave the codeword 'Tuscany'. The chief executive then hired a small private aircraft and sent two other NUM employees – Steve Hudson and Trevor Cave – to Jersey to pick up £4.7 million worth of dollar bearer bonds and fly them over to an obscure Luxembourg bank, Nobis Finance. Several weeks later, towards the end of November, when the hiding place had been blown and the sequestrator was bearing down on the NUM's treasure-trove through the Luxembourg courts, Windsor chartered another private plane – again off his own bat – to make sure the union team arrived in time for the hearing. On this occasion, it was a more spacious jet, costing nearly £12,000 for the ride. Scargill was dropped off in Paris, where Alain Simon and Jeff Apter, the freelance journalist who had worked for the CGT, joined Windsor, Cave, Hudson and Nell Myers for the next leg of the flight to Luxembourg.[18]

Yet, in spite of all the elaborate planning, the drama, codewords and financial wizardry, it all came to nought. The sequestrators were tipped off and traced the hidden cash relatively quickly. 'As a way of laundering money ... it was what you would expect of a used car salesman', a City accountant was quoted as saying at the time. Windsor is happy to describe himself as having been 'instrumental' in the arrangements to protect the union's assets and he insists his strategy was 'correct'. But one after another of his wheezes to beat the courts failed or backfired spectacularly. The Mineworkers' Trust, set up in March 1984 and 'very much Mr Windsor's brainchild' in Gavin Lightman's words, proved no protection for the properties that were transferred to it. In fact, the transfers led to a breach-of-trust action by the receiver against the NUM's trustees – Scargill, Heathfield and McGahey.[19]

What is more, if the failed attempt to transfer the national officials' homes to the Mineworkers' Trust in 1984 had never been made, the NUM would have owned them outright and the sequence of events that led to Windsor's claims of corruption against Scargill and Heathfield six years later would never have taken place. Oakedge, the company which was bought at Windsor's initiative in 1983 as an alternative way of insulating union assets, turned out both to offer no protection and to involve tax disadvantages. So it was decided not to use it. Windsor's full activation of the company in 1985 – Scargill and Heathfield insisted without their authorization – subsequently became the subject of a sharp dispute between Windsor, the NUM president and other union staff members and eventually led to significant financial loss for the union.[20]

Far more important, of course, was the sequestrators' success in blowing the cover of Operation Forops and the NUM's subsequent takeover by a court-appointed receiver, partly as a result of flawed preparation for the transfer of cash abroad. The methods used to hunt down the NUM's hidden reserves are discussed later. Suffice it to say that it was only after sequestration and receivership forced the union leadership to run the day-to-day finances entirely in secret, through independent trust accounts – and mostly in cash – that the authorities appeared to lose track of what was going on. As Scargill puts it: 'They always seemed to be one step ahead of us until I decided to take things into my hands alone.' Detailed knowledge of the secret accounts, which kept the national union afloat from December 1984 until well after the strike, was restricted to a tiny core group: effectively Scargill, Heathfield and Nell Myers. Windsor was not involved.[21]

The earlier, more elaborate, effort to hide the NUM's official funds overseas was the main basis for the union's takeover by the courts on 30 November 1984. Receivership was imposed, 'in particular', because the union's trustees had 'actively sought to place trust property abroad'. It was, in the words of Sarah Burton, the NUM's solicitor at the time, 'the worst thing that happened to the NUM'. It paralysed much of the union's work in its most decisive and vulnerable period; it cost millions of pounds; and it tied the NUM leadership up in endless litigation. The export of cash overseas was also the main pretext for the receiver's breach-of-trust action against Scargill, Heathfield and McGahey, a case that was only finally settled in 1988.

The bitter irony was that if a small change to the union rule-book had been made before the strike – explicitly sanctioning the investment of union funds overseas – many of those huge extra burdens could have been avoided. The person in charge of sorting out the original legal advice had been Roger Windsor, who had a series of discussions about the issue during the winter of 1983–4 with the solicitors, Brian Thompson's. The lawyer Windsor mainly dealt with at the firm was Eddie Solomons, who gave advice to several left-wing unions about how to protect their assets from the threat of anti-union legislation at a secret meeting at the NUR headquarters in the spring of 1984. Windsor, backed up by Steve Hudson, maintained that Solomons had specifically given the go-ahead for the transfer of NUM assets abroad. But Solomons subsequently denied doing so. He had, he said, 'strongly advised against the investment of funds overseas', and the issue became the subject of litigation. It turned out there had been nothing in writing. Sarah Burton believes the case is revealing about Windsor's approach: 'What advice you get depends on what question you ask. Any lawyer would have said you couldn't do what was in fact done without changing the union's rules.'[22]

## COMEDY OF ERRORS

The Libyan episode and the unhappy fate of Operation Forops would prove to be the overture for a litany of financial and political headaches involving Windsor at the NUM. Both Scargill and Heathfield described how they repeatedly found themselves drawn into disputes through which Windsor would try to set the two leading national officials against each other. 'He was a smooth operator, always trying to play me off against Arthur,' Heathfield commented. 'He'd tell me: "The president has agreed to so-and-so." Then when I'd query it with Arthur, he would say: "Oh, Windsor told me that was what you wanted. I wasn't sure about it myself."' Windsor's habit of setting officials and staff against each other is attested to by almost everybody who worked with him at the NUM head office – though Windsor himself blames Scargill.[23]

One early example – and a taste of things to come – took place in the first couple of months of the 1984–5 strike, long before Libya, when Windsor's star was still very much in the ascendant. Peter McNestry, leader of the pit deputies' union

NACODS, had laboriously set up a three-way exchange of letters between himself, the NUM and the Coal Board with a view to kick-starting negotiations. When a phrase from the NUM letter was quoted on a radio news broadcast, neither Scargill nor Heathfield – who were driving along different motorways at the time – recognized it. Both stopped at the nearest service station and angrily rang the union's Sheffield head office to find out what was going on. Both assumed the other was responsible, only to find that the new form of words had been written, without reference to either of them, by Roger Windsor. Later, during the fateful negotiations over the NACODS dispute in October 1984, McNestry recalls Dennis Boyd, number two at the conciliation service ACAS, complaining about the 'terrible problems' they were having with Windsor's obstructive interventions.[24]

On another occasion during the strike, when the union's leaders were activating every possible international contact to raise money to keep the NUM afloat and out of the clutches of the courts, the chief executive officer went to London with Scargill to visit the Soviet Embassy. It was 15 November 1984. Both Scargill and Heathfield had had earlier meetings with Soviet diplomats and trade-union officials in an effort to raise financial support for the strike. Three weeks after the High Court had ordered the seizure of NUM assets and ten days after the Irish courts had frozen £2.75 million of miners' union funds in Dublin, the cash squeeze was beginning to bite. It was also barely a fortnight since Windsor's exposure as the NUM's man at the heart of the Libyan connection. Scargill, Windsor and the union's press officer, Nell Myers, travelled together by train to London to the meeting.

Windsor remembers a man throwing a meat pie at the NUM leader on the train. 'Scargill got up and started to act in an excited way and Nell Myers restrained him, saying: "President, president, remember where we are."' Windsor also recalls Scargill sitting in the car on the way to the embassy 'punching away on his calculator', working out how much Soviet funding for the 1926 miners' strike would be worth in 1984 prices. At the embassy, Scargill put the case for material aid to the Soviet Labour Attaché, Yuri Mazur, and a diplomatic counsellor, Lev Parshin. It was the only time Scargill went personally to the Soviet Embassy and the only time Windsor accompanied the miners' leader to any meetings with Soviet officials. It was also the only time the press was tipped off about Soviet or East European contacts. As the three NUM representatives left the embassy they were met by a gaggle of reporters and photographers, and the meeting was front-page news the following morning. Windsor has strongly denied to the author being at the embassy that day, insisting he went to a separate meeting. Neither he nor Nell Myers were in the published pictures. But reports wired back to the Foreign Ministry in Moscow and found in the Soviet Communist Party Central Committee archives in the wake of the collapse of the Soviet Union record his attendance.[25]

Peter Heathfield, who was elected NUM general secretary more than a year after Windsor was appointed, was suspicious of the union's most senior employee early on and discussed his worries with Scargill. 'I knew he was a capable bloke, but everything he was involved with caused problems.' Some were also wary of the chief executive officer's motives, and Windsor was deeply disliked by other staff. 'He was a supercilious bastard, who thought he was the gaffer,' Heathfield said. Nell Myers describes him as 'high-handed'. Mick Clapham – head of NUM industrial relations while Windsor was at the union and later a Labour MP – says the chief executive made no personal friends at the union and kept himself to himself. But having initially won the NUM president's confidence, Windsor was able to make full use of his position as 'Scargill's man'. Former employees say they never quite knew when he was acting on Scargill's behalf and when he was not. 'Windsor was a real schemer', according to Dave Feickert, the NUM's former head of research who went on to run the TUC's European office in Brussels. 'He was very manipulative and quite clever at it.'[26]

Windsor quickly developed a habit of taking decisions on his own without authority, which would later lead to huge internal ructions and cost the union tens of thousands of pounds. The issues ranged from the politically crucial to the trivial and absurd. Windsor's handling of the most humdrum tasks led to significant losses. In the summer of 1984, for example, the NUM held a strike rally in Mansfield in Nottinghamshire. Long after the strike was over, a case was brought on behalf of Mansfield Council against the NUM for damage to property at the rally and it transpired that Windsor had taken it upon himself to sign a general indemnity for any losses. The chief executive claimed authorization from the Nottinghamshire NUM officials, Ray Chadburn and Henry Richardson, who adamantly denied giving it. The union ended up with a bill for £6,000. Another £6,000 had to be paid in an out-of-court settlement with the manufacturers of the NUM's official diary as a result of Windsor's erratic interventions over the format.

Then there was the saga of the NUM Sheffield headquarters' missing front door. For the entire five years that the NUM occupied its purpose-built offices in the city centre, from 1989 until the union moved to Barnsley in 1994, the main entrance was suspended eight feet above the ground, without steps. Throughout that time, access to the building was only possible through an underground car park, because of a long-running dispute with Sheffield Council over who should pay for the pedestrianization and landscaping of the street, and the absent steps. When the dispute began, the council insisted the NUM had agreed to meet the £90,000 costs. The union's national officials both swore blind no such deal had ever been made. Council officials then triumphantly produced a letter, signed by Peter Heathfield on 30 November 1987, agreeing to foot the bill. Heathfield had no recollection of agreeing to any such thing. 'Me and Pete had a bit of a fallout about it,' Scargill says. Indeed, it was one of the few serious rows the pair had during eight years together as full-time national officials. Heathfield subsequently discovered from his diary that he had not even been in the country on the day the letter was signed. Windsor was hauled in and blithely admitted that he had sent the letter. He had used Heathfield's signature stamp to sign it.[27]

Other incidents had a direct impact on the union's industrial effectiveness. In the wake of the establishment of the Union of Democratic Mineworkers, the right-wing Nottinghamshire-based breakaway outfit, the NUM set up an accident and insurance scheme to help coax miners back to the fold. The idea was to tie it in with the 'check-off' system of automatic deduction of union subscriptions from wage packets. That way, miners could make regular, direct contributions to the scheme without the need for a special system of collections. But deduction at source required the Coal Board's agreement. The battle for members between the breakaway and the NUM was a struggle for power over Britain's energy supply. Mick Clapham and Dave Feickert – the two NUM staff members who took part in negotiations over the scheme with Windsor – say that the Coal Board's legal department eventually agreed a formula to allow the scheme to go ahead, but that Windsor subsequently changed the wording. The alteration led to a dispute with the Board, which then withdrew its cooperation. The scheme had to be abandoned.[28]

Windsor's problems were not restricted to run-ins with the two national officials. As the prospect of the denationalization of electricity, coal and rail loomed in the late 1980s, NUM staff set to work to establish a joint opposition campaign. The aim was to link up first with the rail and other mining unions against electricity privatization, which was the hors d'oeuvre on the Tory menu. Windsor suggested that the campaign be called 'FORCE', as an acronym for 'Federation of Rail, Coal and Energy Workers'. Dave Feickert told him the idea was absurd. Such an aggressive-sounding name would make it harder to win over the right-wing power unions, and the Energy Secretary, Cecil Parkinson, would make hay with it. Windsor conceded and 'UNITE' was agreed instead. But at the next meeting with the other unions, the chief executive once again proposed FORCE and the name was even given out in a press briefing, before its merciful forced abandonment. 'When I gave him a bollocking about it,' Feickert says, 'he just stood there with a stupid grin on his face. I would have thought it was childish if I wasn't already deeply suspicious of his behaviour.'[29]

Relations between Windsor and Sarah Burton, one of the NUM's ever-present legal advisers, became so bad in the aftermath of the 1984–5 strike that she effectively stopped dealing with him altogether. 'He always wanted to stick his oar in everywhere and would come up with the craziest, off-the-wall schemes.' After the High Court ordered the sequestration of the NUM's assets in October 1984, the union was prohibited from taking any action to protect its funds held in Ireland, among other countries. All contact with the Irish firm of solicitors that had been handling the NUM's affairs in the republic was suspended on legal advice. Windsor disregarded the advice and held a private meeting in Dublin with Bruce St John Blake, the NUM's main Irish lawyer.

While denying any continuing role in the Irish proceedings to the union's national officials, Windsor persisted with the contact, on one occasion having dinner with Blake in Sheffield. All the while, the NUM was spending money on an action for the protection of its funds in Dublin which it stood no chance of winning. Windsor even pressed Sarah Burton to produce the documents and affidavits necessary to keep the Irish case going. 'He was trying to do something that would put me in contempt,' Burton says. Put on the spot, Windsor accepted that he had maintained contact with Blake, but insisted he had never given any instructions about pressing ahead with legal proceedings in the Irish courts. Six years later, Blake would represent Windsor in his two unsuccessful libel actions against the NUM president.[30]

Not surprisingly in the circumstances, relations between Scargill and Windsor cooled as events took their toll in the latter part of the strike and beyond. After the Libyan episode, the NUM leaders began to keep a closer check on what their chief executive was up to. 'We thought he was getting like a jumped-up civil servant,' Scargill comments, 'trying to grab power for himself.' Once the strike was over, the pressures on the NUM grew if anything even more intense. Pit agreements were ripped up, local strikes or 'rag-outs' multiplied. The Coal

Board and the government sought to press home their advantage; opposition to Scargill's leadership from inside and outside the union solidified; and the union leaders struggled with the unprecedented takeover of their official apparatus by the courts. As the effects of the pit-closures programme began to take their toll on the NUM at all levels – with massive membership losses, staff cuts and office closures – the political infighting grew more bitter.[31]

## RESOLUTION 13

Unbeknownst to Scargill and Heathfield at the time, Windsor was in the thick of it. During 1986 and 1987, the fallout from the long-running internecine warfare in the Communist Party – between the dominant liberal 'Eurocommunist' faction and the orthodox class-orientated opposition – played havoc with the internal politics of the National Union of Mineworkers. The miners' union had the strongest communist tradition of any British trade union; and the Scottish, South Wales and Kent coalfields had a particularly deep-rooted communist presence. Even during the postwar period of right-wing control of the NUM, several of the most effective miners' leaders – people like Arthur Horner, Will Paynter and Abe Moffat – were CPGB members. Once an alliance of Labour left-wingers and communists had taken control of the pivotal Yorkshire area of the union in the late 1960s and early 1970s, the NUM was effectively at the feet of the left. Fuelled by the stunning industrial victories against Ted Heath's government, this political advance laid the ground for Scargill's eventual election as NUM president in 1981.

The Communist Party maintained its grip on the shrinking 'peripheral' coalfields of South Wales and Scotland. But while the majority of communist trade unionists opposed the Eurocommunists' drive to the right, the Scottish and South Wales NUM leaders mostly backed the new party line. As the 1984–5 strike wore on, that increasingly turned into open opposition to

Scargill's stewardship of the union. In the wake of the South-Wales-inspired return-to-work in March 1985, the gloves came off as the union machines in the historically most left-wing areas formed a common front with the right. Neil Kinnock and his 'realigned' supporters in the Labour Party made little attempt to disguise their active support for the internal opposition to Scargill. Pete Carter, the CPGB's ultra-Eurocommunist industrial organizer, who had been out-spokenly critical of the NUM leadership during the strike, played a key behind-the-scenes role. As the NUM became ever more embattled, representatives of the dissident areas began to hold secret caucus meetings, tacitly supported by disgruntled staff members at the national office.

The internal struggle in the NUM eventually crystallized over whether to compromise with the breakaway Union of Democratic Mineworkers so as to allow a return to normal national negotiations with the Coal Board. As in the aftermath of the 1926 lockout, which was also a period of splits and recriminations, the miners' union lost its right to national collective bargaining after 1985. The Board unilaterally abandoned the traditional arrangements and gave notice that from May 1986 it would only negotiate wages and conditions if the NUM agreed to accept its so-called 'majority–minority' principle. The new management position was that the majority union in a pit or area would negotiate for all miners regardless of their individual union affiliation. In Nottinghamshire – and some other Midlands pits – the scheme would have meant the breakaway UDM representing thousands of NUM members. The same majoritarian principle was not on offer, however, at national level, where it would have given the NUM – with 80 per cent of the country's miners – sole negotiating rights.[32]

The majority–minority scheme was a transparent attempt by what was now called British Coal to entrench the position of the carefully nurtured alternative 'company union' and force the NUM to come to an accommodation with it. In the absence of NUM acceptance of its formula, managers insisted on negotiating with the UDM alone and imposing its deals on all miners. The internal NUM opposition, from the 'new realists' of South Wales and Scotland to the more traditionally right-wing leaderships in Derbyshire and the Midlands, was prepared to swallow the management's medicine in the hope of getting back to what they saw as 'normality'. The Eurocommunists, in particular, were convinced that the NUM's only hope of survival in the harsh conditions of the post-strike period was to reintegrate the UDM into its ranks as quickly as possible. Scargill and Heathfield, by contrast, were unyielding in their resistance to the management's terms. So far as the national leaders were concerned, their opponents failed to understand that the corporatist relationships of the past had gone for ever – and could not be wished back to life by conceding the right to represent their own members or giving ground to the UDM.

The battle came to a head after Scargill's re-election as president in January 1988, in which rank-and-file Welsh and Scottish miners rejected their area officials' manoeuvrings and voted for the NUM leader's ticket by a greater margin than in any other part of the British coalfield. That year's NUM annual conference in Great Yarmouth was one of the most rancorous ever. The Derbyshire area submitted a cleverly worded motion – number 13 on the agenda, as luck would have it – which was calculated to maximize the largest potential coalition against Scargill's stand. While denouncing the UDM and the 'majority–minority concept', it called for a joint negotiating committee at national level, combined with a right for the NUM to represent all its own members at local level. Although not spelled out, the wording clearly implied combined NUM–UDM negotiations. The skill with which the motion had been framed was reflected in a 10–10 split on the national executive when it was debated on the eve of the conference. And a carefully argued centre-spread piece was unexpectedly inserted into the conference edition of *The Miner* under the name of Gordon Butler, the Derbyshire area secretary, pressing the case for Resolution 13. Its acceptance by delegates would have dealt Scargill's leadership a humiliating blow, cutting away a central plank of his successful re-election platform.[33]

In the event, Resolution 13 was decisively rejected on the floor of the conference in a bitter debate. The air was thick with accusations of betrayal and hypocrisy, malignancies and birth-rights. Peter Heathfield was particularly ferocious in his denunciation of those behind the motion. It was an 'exercise in academia', he charged, 'the product of people isolated from the pit point.' The isolated academics he had in mind were Mick Clapham and Dave Feickert, the NUM's heads of industrial relations and research. Both had worked in higher education for a time and their political differences with the union leadership had widened since the end of the strike.

But as the extent of the plotting around Resolution 13 gradually emerged, it became clear that Windsor had been the prime mover. His efforts had been made all the easier because several of those he approached were never entirely sure whether or not he was acting as a 'fall guy' for the leadership. Clapham, who had openly argued in favour of a joint negotiating procedure with the UDM, had played a part. Feickert – who, along with Maurice Jones, the editor of *The Miner*, was well aware of what was being cooked up – had been more sceptical. But it was the 'enigmatic' chief executive, as Clapham describes him, who actually helped draft the motion for the Derbyshire area and wrote the piece in *The Miner*. And it was Windsor who secretly met Butler to organize Scargill's defeat at the conference. The disaffected chief executive had, it turned out later, also been encouraging speculation among staff and area officials about the 'missing' Russian money.[34]

The Resolution 13 saga shattered staff relations at NUM headquarters. Immediately on their return to Sheffield, Scargill summoned Windsor, Clapham and Feickert to demand a pledge of loyalty to the union's elected leadership. Windsor seemed fearful for his job. Assurances were given, though the atmosphere remained corrosive and tense. But the full details of Windsor's failed 'coup' against his boss were not exposed until a couple of months later in an emotional confrontation in Scargill's office, with Heathfield, Clapham and Feickert all in attendance. On 16 September 1988, Windsor asked to see the union president in confidence and proceeded, according to Scargill's account, to 'purge his soul', recounting the entire story of his and other staff members' involvement with Resolution 13 and warning Scargill that Mick Clapham and Dave Feickert were in cahoots with the oppositional areas in a bid to oust him from the leadership. They had, he claimed, been holding caucus meetings with right-wing NUM officials after formal sessions at Eastwood Hall, British Coal's operational headquarters in Nottinghamshire.[35]

The national officials decided, in Scargill's words, to 'flush them out'. Heathfield went to see Feickert and told him: 'Don't tell Arthur I've told you, but Windsor has just been to see him. I want to make it clear to you and Mick that I will not be joining your plot to get rid of Arthur.' Feickert replied that the idea of a conspiracy was ridiculous: several left-wing officials, such as Henry Richardson and Sammy Thompson, had also stayed behind after meetings to have lunch at Eastwood. Feickert then buttonholed Windsor to find out what had happened in his talk with Scargill. 'Windsor said: "It was very difficult, but he has really got it in for you, comrade, and also for Mick. He says you are plotting to get rid of him."'

In the light of his conversation with Heathfield, Feickert was convinced that the plot story came from Windsor, not Scargill. So when Clapham returned from holiday on 29 September, the two of them went jointly to see the NUM president and relayed Windsor's account. 'Arthur was genuinely shocked,' Feickert says. 'You could always tell when it wasn't genuine.' Scargill then called Windsor in and told him that since he had discussed their private conversation with other members of staff, confidentiality was now broken. Windsor at first denied having made any accusations against Clapham and Feickert – as he did later. 'He was very embarrassed and tried to wriggle,' Clapham remembers. Scargill then produced his foolscap notes of Windsor's Eastwood plot allegations and proceeded to read. 'It was exactly as Peter had told me,' Feickert says. 'Windsor went bright red.' Eventually, according to Clapham and Feickert, Windsor 'reluctantly agreed' that Scargill's note was an accurate record.[36]

Mick Clapham had indeed been partly involved with Windsor's plans to defeat the union leadership over the UDM issue. He had discussed the majority–minority scheme at length with the chief executive and read through Windsor's draft article published in *The Miner*. He says that he was never certain whether Scargill had encouraged Windsor to bring the idea into the open so that he could kill it. Scargill describes Clapham as having been 'contrite' at the meeting. But Feickert had had next-to-nothing to do with the whole affair. When he heard Windsor deny their earlier conversation, Feickert went – in Scargill's words – 'berserk', threatening to throw the lanky chief executive out of the tenth-floor window. 'I called him all the names under the sun and he just sat there with that stupid smile on his face. He admitted telling Arthur the lies and I just managed to stop myself thumping him,' Feickert remembers.[37]

After the Resolution 13 confrontation, Windsor's relations with both the national officials and his fellow staff members reached their nadir. 'He has blown his cover,' Heathfield said after the meeting in Scargill's office was over. 'From then on, we treated the guy with disdain,' Clapham comments. Feickert, who refused to work with Windsor after September 1988, explains the attitude of the senior NUM staff at the time: 'All the other incidents then seemed to fall into place, not as the actions of a fixer, or merely office politics, but as something more intentionally damaging to the union.' Windsor, meanwhile, carried on as if nothing had happened. He even tried unsuccessfully to fix himself up with an individually negotiated personal contract and a better pay deal separate from the rest of the staff.

After 'catching Windsor out lying' over their role in the NUM's internal battles, Clapham and Feickert became suspicious about other goings-on involving the freewheeling chief executive. Top of their list of concerns was Windsor's use of the off-the-shelf company, Oakedge, and they took the issue up with Scargill. Oakedge had originally been bought to protect NUM assets from sequestration. It had subsequently been left dormant, though in 1986 the name was used as a 'front' for the

Derbyshire area of the union to lend money to Nottingham-shire, because area rules made a direct loan impossible. But to the NUM president's surprise, he now discovered that Windsor had fully 'activated' Oakedge, appointed Clapham and Feickert directors and used it, among other things, to buy two personal computers. The chief executive had told Feickert and Clapham that Oakedge's activation was on the instructions of the national officials but, they say, never informed them of later transactions. It also emerged that Windsor had discussed with Anne Scargill, the NUM leader's wife, the possibility of buying furniture cheaply through the company. Clapham and Feickert demanded that Windsor call a board meeting, but failed to get him to produce accounts. 'Windsor had to be put under tremendous pressure to give any information at all, which made us even more suspicious,' Feickert says. In fact, the company had already been struck off the register in the spring of 1988 – because it was not properly wound up – with the loss of more than £1,000 in its account. Windsor insists that the fault lay with NUM employees who failed to carry out his instructions.[38]

## DENOUEMENT

Roger Windsor has given a wide variety of reasons for leaving the NUM in the summer of 1989. In the meeting with Scargill at which he announced his decision to quit, he said that 'problems in the office between himself and other members of staff had made him unhappy', and that his wife, Angie, had 'had an effect on his attitude'. A few days later, he wrote a farewell note to Peter Heathfield saying that the family hadn't put down roots in Sheffield and needed a change. He was also, he said, becoming increasingly ill at ease with the rightward drift in the Labour Party. 'The dropping of the unilateral disarmament policy by Kinnock,' he added, 'was the final blow.' Windsor's letter to Heathfield ended on an ominous note. 'Goodbye, comrade, take care,' Windsor advised a man he was shortly to accuse in the mass media of personal corruption.[39]

A year later, in August 1990, Windsor said he had left because money from the Soviet Union and Libya had not been properly accounted for, because Scargill had let him down over his Libyan trip, and because of a grievance about pay – presumably the problem with the lack of a personal contract. In May 1991, he wrote that his motive for resigning and telling his story was to 'clear the path for future merger of the NUM with the TGWU' – in the belief that Scargill's departure was a necessary precondition for amalgamation. His explanation of wanting to achieve the 'removal of Scargill' has been repeated since. In the summer of 1993, he said that he had gone to the *Mirror* because of 'my deep concern relating to many financial irregularities arising from Scargill's stewardship of funds donated to the union, and particularly the Soviet money'. But perhaps Windsor came closest to the truth when he said he had decided in 1988 that he would have to leave 'because of my suspicions and my fears about what was happening within the NUM'.[40]

There is little doubt that after the Resolution 13 row, Windsor realized that Scargill and Heathfield were preparing to move against him. He may also have been aware that they were taking legal advice and building up a dossier on his activities and blunders, part of which would be presented to the NUM executive shortly after Windsor's hasty departure. 'He knew we were homing in on him on a whole range of issues,' Scargill says. Heathfield had deeply distrusted Windsor for several years. The NUM president was far more inclined to give Windsor the benefit of the doubt. But he ended up thinking his chief executive officer 'was just too much of a loose cannon, that he was completely irrational'. Windsor complains that he found himself being 'blamed for everything' and that the main problem was Scargill's intransigence. He says he tried to get a job in local government – he particularly fancied the idea of a senior post at Barnsley council – but found that Scargill and Heathfield had used their influence to block his application.[41]

Vic Allen, a long-time union adviser and member of the NUM left caucus, remembers taking part in discussions about how to get rid of Windsor at the 1988 Great Yarmouth conference, even before the full story of Resolution 13 had come out. But Windsor knew where enough bodies were buried to make his dismissal a risky venture and there was always a certain nervousness about the damage he might do. Dave Feickert blames Scargill's experiences with highly publicized staff disputes in London when he was first elected president – as well as the pulverizing pressures on the union in the late 1980s – for the failure to act against Windsor earlier. 'After what happened in London, he got very cautious. He was also under tremendous pressure. There was no let-up: court cases, receivership, sequestration, closures like a deluge. We were trebly besieged after '84–5.'[42]

Windsor finally came to Scargill's office in the late afternoon of 20 July 1989 to announce his resignation. Unusually, he had missed the NUM's annual conference and began by explaining that he needed a change and was planning to go to live in France. According to a note taken by the NUM leader immediately after he left the room, he then said he wanted to clear his conscience about a legal action which had been hanging round the NUM's neck for several years. This was over the forged letter which had circulated throughout the Nottinghamshire coalfield and the media in the immediate aftermath of the strike and was purportedly signed by David Prendergast, later financial secretary of the Nottinghamshire UDM. The letter, which was sent anonymously to the NUM Nottinghamshire leader Henry Richardson, was addressed to executive members of an obscure right-wing trade-union caucusing body, 'Mainstream'. In reality a rather anodyne document, the letter nevertheless appeared to expose the embryonic UDM as prepared to use undemocratic methods to link up with the electricians' union as part of an alternative right-wing TUC. As soon as it had been shown to be a forgery, Prendergast had begun libel proceedings against Scargill, Heathfield, two Nottinghamshire NUM leaders and the NUM itself.

Windsor now calmly said that he was responsible for the forgery. He had, according to Scargill's record of the meeting, 'transposed' Prendergast's signature from another letter. The chief executive claimed that Hilary Cave, another member of staff who had already left the union, had then taken the letter to London to post. Scargill says the admission 'blew me backwards'. He told Windsor he was confessing to a 'criminal act'. The outgoing chief executive said he 'could only express his deep regret'. When the miners' leader warned him he would have to take legal advice, Windsor 'seemed extremely nervous'. As soon as Heathfield – himself a defendant in the libel proceedings – heard that Windsor claimed to have forged the Prendergast letter, he called him to his office to express his fury. It was an icy encounter. 'Windsor's facial muscles showed a great deal of tension under strain,' Heathfield recalled. 'He developed a twitch in his cheek. But he said that in similar circumstances he would do exactly the same again.' It had been in the best interests of the union, the departing chief executive insisted.[43]

Scargill immediately gave details of Windsor's statement to the union's lawyers – contrary to what was recorded in the Lightman Report – who advised delaying any report on the alleged forgery. But in October 1989, a file of evidence was handed to the police about the Prendergast letter, the theft of documents from Scargill's office during the 1989 annual conference and the Oakedge affair. Police questioned all members of staff who could have been in any way involved. Forensic experts established that the letter from which Prendergast's signature had been transposed onto the 'Mainstream' forgery was one sent by the Nottinghamshire official to Peter Heathfield. Two pieces of evidence, in particular, tend to support the 'confession' Scargill and Heathfield claim Windsor made. An internal NUM administrative system which logged memos and letters in and out of departments and offices showed that the letter from Prendergast to Heathfield used for the forgery had never gone to the general secretary. Instead, it was booked in to Windsor's office during the crucial time, and was only much later passed on to the finance department.[44]

The second piece of evidence was that Windsor had used an

identical transposition technique about a year after the Prendergast letter first appeared. In the summer of 1986, the battle was on between the NUM and the newly established UDM for the hearts and minds of British miners. The UDM, tacitly supported by the Coal Board, was trying to break out of its Nottinghamshire stronghold into other parts of the Midlands coalfield. But there was only one other area, South Derbyshire, where the UDM was able to win over a majority of NUM members. A counteroffensive was launched in the county to win mineworkers back to the national union. The Coal Board meanwhile insisted that South Derbyshire miners who wanted their subscriptions to continue to go to the NUM would have to sign a special form. Not surprisingly, the forms were hard to come by. So Windsor was instructed to make photocopies and attach an accompanying circular so the NUM could keep its own records of South Derbyshire loyalists.

What Windsor in fact did was transpose the NCB heading onto his own altered form of words, with the NUM section photocopied onto the bottom. He then circulated bundles of these cobbled-together forms in South Derbyshire. Kevin Richards, the area secretary at the time and an NUM rightwinger, has sworn an affidavit confirming the sequence of events. 'Although one cannot define the ultimate purpose for doing this,' Richards says, 'there were two consequences: one, that what was intended as a separate sheet for our own records was no longer separate, and secondly, that the format was no longer the official British Coal document and, as such, would not be valid ... His actions had been extremely damaging to the national union.' The Coal Board complained vociferously to the NUM in Sheffield that a 'fraud appeared to be taking place' and threatened to sue Scargill, Heathfield and the union for misuse of their letterhead. 'I was present when Roger Windsor was confronted in Arthur Scargill's office,' Richards recalls. 'He admitted to Mr Scargill that he had produced the altered documents without instructions.' Both Scargill and Richards carpeted Windsor, who admitted what he had done to the national executive. When British Coal realized the responsibility was Windsor's alone, it dropped the threat to go to law.[45]

The similarity with the method used in the Prendergast forgery and the logging evidence gave Scargill and Heathfield reason for believing their chief executive's 'conscience-clearing' claims. But why Windsor should make such a damningly incriminating confession still seems baffling and he has subsequently flatly denied doing any such thing. 'I had nothing to do with it and knew nothing about it,' he says. After Windsor was interviewed by Nottinghamshire CID and South Yorkshire police about the NUM allegations, he commented:

> Mr Scargill's allegation to the police was that on the day that I left the NUM I made a confession to him that I had been responsible for this forgery. Mr Scargill suggests that, on that occasion, I decided that I needed to bare my breast and confess to something that had been worrying me for a long time. And of course, I think the police saw this as a fairly unusual thing for anybody to do.[46]

Sarah Burton, the union's former legal adviser, argues that Windsor's 'confession' had the effect of suddenly and decisively weakening the union's position in the Prendergast libel action. Once Scargill and Heathfield knew, or believed, that the forgery had been carried out by one or more of the union's employees, the NUM's case could no longer realistically be fought. Furthermore, if it had in fact come to court, Windsor could have been called as a witness and revealed that Scargill was well aware that the union was responsible for the forgery, because he had discussed it with him. The chief executive could have then claimed that he forged the letter on Scargill's instructions. In the summer of 1990, the top libel lawyer Peter Carter-Ruck took over Prendergast's case with the backing of the Goldsmith Foundation. Carter-Ruck, with whose firm Windsor says he was 'cooperating' in the same period, was anxious to get hold of Windsor's personal file at the NUM. He was keenest of all to see the note Scargill took of Windsor's 'confession' in July 1989. The document was delivered up through legal 'discovery' and tested forensically to establish whether it was indeed contemporaneous. Once it was clear that the note was genuine, Scargill and Heathfield were dropped from the action. But the Prendergast forgery still ended up costing the NUM more than £193,000 costs and damages (£372,000 at 2012 prices) in an out-of-court settlement.[47]

Before Windsor left, Scargill also asked him to settle the debt of £29,500, plus interest, that had originally been advanced as a bridging loan when he moved to Sheffield. It was this loan that had been paid off in the autumn of 1984 with the cash Windsor later claimed had come from Libya courtesy of Altaf Abbasi. He 'became agitated', according to Scargill's note of the discussion, and said he would need to 'take advice'. Formally, Windsor's debt had been paid off by the MACF 'Miners' Action Committee' cash trust fund – wherever the money originally came from – as part of the 'paper refinancing' operation to prevent the seques-trators seizing properties. In the aftermath of the strike, Scargill and Heathfield were anxious that Windsor repay the loan himself. 'A couple of years later, Scargill suddenly decided to call in that home loan,' Windsor recalls. Steve Hudson, then the NUM's finance officer, said there was 'consternation' that Windsor had still not repaid the money when he moved house in the late 1980s. 'He has been trying to get out of paying it ever since he received the money,' Hudson wrote later. Since the NUM's debt had already been settled, Windsor was asked to repay the money to the International Miners' Organization. Windsor says he refused, though the national officials submitted a letter to the Lightman Inquiry apparently signed by Windsor in 1986 agreeing to pay the money to the IMO.[48]

There was also a 1987 land-registry document assigning a £29,500 charge on the Windsors' Sheffield home to the IMO. Hudson remembers that Windsor agreed the charge. But it was in fact never registered because, despite numerous requests, Windsor failed to provide the necessary details of his house deeds. In July 1990, the *Mirror* and the *Cook Report* revealed the document to have been at least partly faked. 'New Scargill Affair sensation', the *Mirror*'s front page promised excitedly, and the rest of the media followed the story up. Neither of the two witnesses to the signatures named on the document, Meryl and Roy Hyde, had ever seen it before; their address was wrong; and Angie Windsor's signature bore little relation to the real thing. Roger Windsor was quoted as saying: 'I did not sign the document. It was a draft document only and was never formalized.' And a 'handwriting expert' was produced to confirm the Windsors had had nothing to do with the document. Scargill, it appeared, was once again in the frame.[49]

But as with so many of the other *Mirror–Cook Report* 'Scargill Affair Sensations', this one backfired horribly. Four graphologists in England and France – including two former Metropolitan Police forensic experts – have since concluded that the likely forger was Windsor himself. As early as 1989, the IMO began proceedings in the French courts for the recovery of the bridging loan, plus interest. On behalf of the IMO, evidence was produced from David Ellen, former head of Scotland Yard's document section, who found Windsor's signature on the land registry document was 'probably genuine'. He also concluded that the Hydes' signatures were probably also the work of Windsor himself. Ellen commented that it was relatively common for documents to be forged to invalidate them. Michael Ansell, ex-head of the document section at the Metropolitan Police forensic laboratory, took a much stronger line. He examined all correspondence relating to the Windsor loan, including the land registry document, and wrote: 'I therefore consider that the only reasonable possibility is that Mr Windsor signed all three disputed letters.'[50]

Windsor's own expert, Maureen Ward-Gandy – who had also been hired by the *Mirror* – backed his claim that he had had nothing to do with the forgeries. But she was in turn denounced in the most ferocious terms by Ansell, who took 'the greatest possible exception' to Ward-Gandy's 'most peculiar report'. In the light of this war of the graphologists, Windsor petitioned the court in Angoulême to appoint an independent forensic expert. But the move did not produce a happy outcome for the NUM's former chief executive. It was, concluded Madame

Marguerite Girardeau for the court, 'highly probable' that Windsor had signed his own name on the land-registry document. There were also 'strong probabilities' that Angie Windsor had modified her own signature. Finally, Roger Laufer, a handwriting expert and professor at Paris University, was appointed by the court to make a further analysis. He was the most emphatic of all. The signatures on both the 1987 land-registry document and the 1986 letter assigning the debt to the IMO 'are the original signatures from the hand of Roger Edward Windsor', his report concluded.

The Windsors continued to insist that the case would be 'Scargill's undoing'. But in November 1994, the High Court at Angoulême in south-west France delivered a crushing verdict. Roger Windsor was found to have personally signed the documents he claimed were forged by Scargill and was ordered by the court to pay the original debt, interest, costs and compensation to the IMO. By 2013, the total bill was running close to £500,000, the French courts had forced him to sell his property and the English courts imposed monthly repayment of his debt. The French judges also awarded damages against the former NUM chief executive for his 'malicious' accusations of forgery, which they described as an 'abusive defence'. His only dubious crumb of comfort was that the IMO's claim against his wife Angie was rejected because of the conflicting views of the court handwriting experts – the final assessment by the Paris University graphologist Laufer had concluded it was a possibility that Windsor himself could have forged his wife's signature on the key document. Shortly after leaving the NUM in 1989, Windsor wrote to the miners' leader acknowledging a 'moral debt' over the loan. But a quarter of a century after he promised in the *Mirror* to repay the money to the Miners' Solidarity Fund, no such payment had ever been made. Windsor's three appeals against the Angoulême judgement – including to the highest court in France, the Cour de Cassation, in 2002 – were all thrown out.[51]

The day after Windsor's dramatic resignation meeting with

the NUM president, he sent Scargill a formal letter of notice, concluding: 'May I record that it has been a tremendous privilege to serve yourself and Peter Heathfield, and hopefully to provide a service to the valiant members of the union through one of its most historic periods.' He then telephoned Terry Pattinson of the *Daily Mirror* and launched his new career as whistleblower extraordinaire and paid witness for Robert Maxwell. Within a few weeks, he had sold his Sheffield house for £135,000 and left with his family to settle in Jarnac, Southwest France. Windsor bought an imposing but dilapidated nineteenth-century farmhouse for £67,000 in the village of Gondeville, about two hours' drive from Bordeaux.

Following in his father's footsteps, Windsor set himself up in business as an estate agent, 'doing up' and selling houses to British holidaymakers and expatriates. Windsor's bolt to France was abrupt, and, in his own words, 'life hasn't been easy for us here'. Neither his wife Angie nor his children could speak French when they arrived and their two sons were held back a couple of years at school as a result. Windsor's libel actions against Scargill and two national newspapers in Ireland – handled by his old friend St John Blake – came to grief. When he failed to pay costs, as ordered by the Dublin court, that part of his pension entitlement built up with the NUM, worth £7,000, was docked to enforce the debt. Windsor's estate-agency business did not make enough for a full-time living and he had to take up extra work as a translator. One British network he was able to draw on for his business was a group of members of Democratic Left, the organization set up by the Eurocommunist faction of the old Communist Party after the CPGB was dissolved in 1991. Pete Carter, the CPGB's ex-industrial organizer who played such a key role in stoking the internal NUM opposition to Scargill's leadership during and after the 1984–5 strike, visited Windsor in France in the wake of the 1990 *Mirror–Cook Report* campaign and later put some property advice work his way.

Windsor's relations with the locals were more patchy. When the British media campaign, based on his allegations, was in full flood, neighbours helped to shield him from roaming bands of reporters. But within a couple of years, Windsor was in dispute with his French business partner, Jean Lafontaine, over an alleged breach of contract and an attempt to set up a 'company within a company'. It was 'part of a commercial difference', Windsor said. Lafontaine sued, demanding that Windsor be banned from practising as an estate agent within an eighty-kilometre radius of his home. But the case never came to court. Lafontaine remembered how when Windsor first met him, he told the French businessman he had been working for a friendly society – a 'mutuel' – in England. 'But I suppose there are many different types of friendly societies,' Lafontaine mused.[52]

## THE DALYELL LEAKS

It is possible to explain Windsor's behaviour without reference to any ulterior motive or outside agency. After all, he was far from being the only left-wing activist to come to the NUM in the early years of Scargill's presidency and end up disillusioned and determined to find a way out. Several of those who came to work in Sheffield in 1983 saw themselves as part of a labour-movement career structure, with the NUM an integral and respected part of it. But in the years following the 1984–5 strike, status and prospects for NUM employees looked increasingly uncertain as great chunks of the mining industry disappeared and the NUM became ever more politically isolated and anathematized. With his indelible association with Libya, Windsor became particularly vulnerable and he clearly nursed a grievance about the aftermath of his trip. Once it became clear that the union's leaders had finally turned against him, it is hardly surprising that he jumped ship. And the £80,000 he was paid by Maxwell (£154,000 at 2012 prices) is more than enough explanation for his headlong rush into the arms of the *Daily Mirror*.

Windsor was regarded by some of those who knew him in the NUM as a 'Walter Mitty' character, a fantasist who was forever dreaming up bizarre stratagems. Nell Myers, who worked closely with Windsor for six years, tends to believe his behaviour is better explained by personality traits, rather than by a hidden agenda. Dave Feickert describes him as a 'real schemer. He took a funny kind of pleasure in being devious. He was destructive of the way the office worked and undermined trust between the staff and Arthur. But you could say anything to him and it would run off his back like water.' In common with others who worked alongside him, Feickert maintains that Windsor – unlike all the rest who came to work for Scargill after his election as president – 'knew nothing about Marxism and left-wing politics. He didn't even know the language of socialist politics. He was just a phoney.' Sarah Burton says Windsor 'could not have screwed them up any better if that was his real job'.[53]

Roy Greenslade, the *Daily Mirror* editor who published Windsor's corruption allegations in March 1990, was struck by his oddness.

> We all thought Roger Windsor was a strange character, without exception. He let little pieces of information out, and considering he was being paid a vast amount of money, he was very unhelpful. He was clearly motivated by great personal animosity. He wouldn't come over to England because of outstanding legal action and he was very concerned about getting the money. In fact, his concern about getting the money allayed my fears about him being a stooge.[54]

In the summer of 1992, Windsor circulated a revealing proposal for a book about his time at the NUM. The synopsis, entitled 'Scargill – a Miner Dictator', betrayed not only an obsessional hatred of his former boss, but also a startling lack of any sense of proportion. 'Just like Stalin, or even Adolph Hitler and his Third Reich created to last a thousand years,' Windsor wrote, 'Scargill operates within the NUM through fear, intimidation and oppression. He has created enemies for his followers to spit upon and abuse just as Hitler identified Jews and Communists as vermin to be eliminated in order to create an Aryan society. Just like other tyrants he demands unswerving obedience, obscene flattery, unquestioned power and immunity from criticism.' Even in the case of a man like Scargill, who has been the object of more sustained public abuse than any other public figure, it is hard to find an instance of his most implacable enemies resorting to such extremes of vituperation.

And, surprisingly for someone who still described himself as a socialist and who came to the NUM as a self-proclaimed Bennite, Windsor complained that his former boss 'flouted the law of the land'. He even put the expression 'anti-trade-union laws' in inverted commas, as if he was anxious to distance himself from opposition to the Tory industrial-relations legislation of the 1980s. He damned the NUM leadership for failing to hold a 'proper ballot' during the 1984–5 strike and implied that Scargill was in fact secretly trying to hasten closures and the privatization of the coal industry. Windsor concluded that only 'a major overhaul of the trade-union movement and the legislation relating to it will prevent another Scargill in the future'. The essay exposed not only his consuming personal loathing, but also an undisguised hostility to the class politics and militant trade unionism that the miners' union had epitomized for a generation.[55]

Following the public announcement in December 1991 that Stella Rimington was to be the new director-general of the security service, MI5, Tam Dalyell and other Labour MPs and former Cabinet ministers called on the government to make a full statement on her activities during the miners' strike. In an Early Day Motion signed by the former Labour Home Secretary Merlyn Rees, Dalyell demanded in particular that her role in connection with the activities of David Hart – the property developer and confidant of Margaret Thatcher who helped organize and finance the 'back-to-work movement' – should be accounted for. A month later, on 16 January 1992, Dalyell made a direct link between Stella Rimington and Roger Windsor in questions to John MacGregor, then Leader of the House. Referring to his December motion, Dalyell said that since it had been tabled, 'statements have been made to me about the involvement of Stella Rimington and Mr Roger Windsor of the NUM. The motion raises serious issues and calls for some sort of response.' MacGregor replied that it had been a longstanding practice not to comment on MI5 operations and he did not intend to depart from that precedent.[56]

Dalyell – an old Etonian who lives in a wing of his family seat, 'The Binns', and is renowned for his wide range of high-level contacts in the civil service, police and armed forces – later told the author that his question had been based on information from two separate senior Whitehall sources. He described these informants as 'solid gold' – better placed, indeed, than those who had provided the devastatingly accurate tip-offs for his long-running campaign to expose the events surrounding Margaret Thatcher's decision to sink the Argentine cruiser *General Belgrano* during the Falklands War. By defending without question the anonymity of his 'deep throats', Dalyell became a unique conduit for dissatisfied officials – and his studied caution underpinned his reputation. As he says of himself: 'I can only point to my track record of factual accuracy, where I have not yet once slipped on the proverbial banana skin – an event which would afford delicious pleasure to a large number of great and distinguished people.'[57]

The evening Dalyell made the allegation, I rang Windsor in France, who dismissed the Labour MP's claim as 'total rubbish'. Sounding genuinely shocked and angry, Windsor said: 'I have no idea what the man's talking about. If he wants to repeat that outside the Commons, we'll deal with it in the appropriate way.' As soon as he put the phone down, Windsor called Dalyell at Westminster. Curiously, he left his message with Neil Kinnock's office, rather than with the House of Commons answering service. It was Charles Clarke, the Labour leader's *chef de cabinet*, who handed Dalyell the request to call the NUM's former chief executive – jotted down on the leader of the Opposition's office notepaper. A year earlier, in an interview with Channel Four television, Windsor had taken a more relaxed, but similar, line when asked if he had had any contact with the intelligence services.

> I've never had anything to do with intelligence. I worked for ten years for an international trade-union organization. I've been a member of the Labour Party for many years. I've served as a Labour councillor. Yes, of course, I could be a place by the CIA, perhaps even I don't know about it, but it's ridiculous. My telephone's been tapped, my family and my wife have been subjected to a tremendous amount of adverse publicity and pressure as a result of this ... I rebut it as absolute sheer nonsense.

Two days after Dalyell's statement, Windsor adopted a more whimsical tone: 'Scargill gave me the NUM job. If I had links with Stella Rimington, then so has he.'[58]

But Windsor would find it impossible to shake off the alleged Rimington connection. In the spring of 1993 – as the uproar over pit closures subsided and the rundown of the coalfields accelerated once again – Dalyell returned to his original Whitehall informants. I put written questions to one of Dalyell's sources, who replied in a laconic, but explosive, manner.

Q: At what point did Roger Windsor become 'involved' with Stella Rimington – before he joined the NUM, during the strike or later?

A: Before.

Q: What did his 'involvement' amount to – in others words, was it through a third party and was he aware of it?

A: Yes, he was aware.

Q: What services did he perform for Mrs Rimington and MI5 – was it simply passing on information or was he guided in any of his behaviour inside the NUM by MI5? If the latter, what did MI5 seek to achieve by using him?

A: To 'fuck up' the NUM.

Q: Was his role in the 1990 campaign of allegations against Scargill and Heathfield in the *Mirror* and on the *Cook Report* in any way influenced by Mrs Rimington and MI5?

A: Sure!

A third source independently approached another Scottish Labour MP, George Galloway, who had become involved in the campaign to expose dirty tricks against the miners in 1991. When Stella Rimington became the first MI5 director-general to 'go public' and had herself photographed wreathed in smiles in July 1993, it became the trigger for another parliamentary motion – this time about Windsor. The initial signatories were Galloway, Dalyell, three mining MPs – Michael Clapham, Dennis Skinner and Jimmy Hood – and Robert Litherland.[59]

The MPs noted Stella Rimington's 'central role in operations against the miners during and after the coal strike of 1984–5' and, in particular, 'her deployment of agents provocateurs within the National Union of Mineworkers'. Among them, the MPs claimed, was Roger Windsor, 'an agent of MI5 under Mrs Rimington, sent in to the NUM to destabilize and sabotage the union at its most critical juncture'. The Commons motion recalled that Windsor had made contact with Libyan officials through Altaf Abbasi and had 'staged a televised meeting with Colonel Gaddafi, causing immense damage to the striking miners'. The NUM chief executive's actions, the MPs went on, 'led to serious and expensive internal disputes, notably a £100,000 libel damages settlement as a result of a letter Windsor forged in the name of David Prendergast of the UDM'. In March 1990, Windsor had been 'the sole witness, paid £80,000 for his testimony by Robert Maxwell, behind allegations of corruption against the NUM leadership, published in the *Daily Mirror*, later proved to be entirely untrue'. Notwithstanding 'recent cosmetic changes to its image', the motion concluded, 'the security service, including Mrs Rimington, has been responsible for the subversion of democratic liberties in Britain and should be brought to account'.[60]

This was the first time an alleged MI5 agent had been named on the House of Commons order paper, and the motion was only accepted after a procedural scrap. The text was initially rejected out of hand by the Commons tabling office and was only agreed after the deletion of an allegation linking another individual who had been closely involved in the Scargill Affair to the security services. The naming of Windsor as an MI5 agent on the order paper was apparently only possible because of Dalyell's reference to links between Windsor and Rimington on the floor of the House eighteen months previously. The tabling of the motion – eventually signed by thirty-four Labour MPs – led to a flurry of responses from Windsor and other bit-part players in the saga. Kim Howells submitted an amendment blaming Scargill for having hired Windsor in the first place and subsequently defending him against the 'severe criticisms' of the NUM South Wales area and other union members, who were 'suspicious of Mr Windsor's rule both during and after the 1984–5 mining dispute and who were appalled at Mr Scargill's lack of judgement in encouraging and protecting him'. Kevin Barron put down his own amendment, raking over the ground of the Soviet money and Scargill's 1985 home loan. Windsor, he said later, was the target of a 'black propaganda campaign, a pack of lies'. But Altaf Abbasi, who had seemingly set in train the NUM's Libyan connection in 1984, was happy to encourage the accusation that his former collaborator had worked as an agent. 'All his activities lead towards that,' Abbasi said, 'whether it's MI5 or someone in MI5 who has been using him directly or indirectly.' Tory MPs dismissed the allegations against Windsor as 'paranoia in the extreme'. Further evidence would emerge in due course.[61]

Windsor once again protested his innocence to all comers from his French retreat. The accusation that he had acted for MI5 had, he insisted, been 'concocted by cowards hiding behind parliamentary privilege'. It was 'perfectly ludicrous'. He had written to John Major a month earlier, he said, claiming that 'ridiculous allegations' were going to be made against him in this book and asking the Prime Minister to confirm in writing that he had never been 'engaged by Her Majesty's security service in any capacity'. He had received a reply from Mark

Adams, Major's private secretary, referring him to a parliamentary answer given by the Prime Minister in June 1991. Asked whether the former NUM chief executive officer had 'ever been employed by Her Majesty's Government', Major had replied: 'No.' But in the light of the Galloway-Dalyell motion – which had fingered Windsor as an MI5 agent, rather than an actual employee – he wrote to the Prime Minister again, saying he was far from happy with the 'brevity and the nature' of his earlier answer. Back came a second plaintive response from Adams. Major's statement did 'represent a clear and unequivocal statement that you were not employed in any capacity by any part of the government', he wrote. This was 'an exceptional step in relation to the government's normal practice, which is not to comment on intelligence and security matters'.[62]

Windsor was thrown into a frenzy of activity over the Commons motion, ringing up journalists, friends and former NUM contacts in Britain to discuss the best response. Among those he called were some of Scargill's political opponents inside the NUM, such as George Rees, the South Wales area secretary – who refused to speak to him. Another was Johnny Burrows, a full-time official in Derbyshire who had acted with Windsor as a trustee of the Mineworkers' Trust set up at the beginning of the strike to protect NUM property. Initially introducing himself as a 'Mr Redditch of the Labour Party', Windsor was anxious to gauge the cautious Burrows' reaction to the MI5 allegation and discuss his tactical response.

His next move was to issue a bizarre open letter to Stella Rimington, which attempted to shift suspicion from himself to other NUM officers and Scargill associates. The text echoed the language and attitudes of his 'Miner Dictator' book proposal. 'I understand that your former function included subversion of the trade-union movement,' Windsor wrote to Rimington, 'and particularly the destabilization of the NUM during the miners' strike of 1984–5. As far as the NUM was concerned, your task must have been very easy. You know as well as I that Scargill never allowed stability to reign in the NUM, thus destabilization was rather like adding activator to the compost heap. It may have speeded things up, but the process of internal decay would have taken place in any case.'

Dismissing the 'great strike for jobs' of 1984–5, Windsor declared: 'Let's face it, the NUM were never more than a bunch of amateurs trying to take on the might of the state. We lacked the cohesion, discipline and organization to run any meaningful campaign, and were led by our Napoleon on to our battlefield of Waterloo.' There had been 'many examples of leaks, strange happenings and extraordinary events that one would like to attribute to you and your service', Windsor reminded the head of MI5. One example he gave was his Libyan trip. 'When Scargill instructed me to go to Tripoli, only he, I, Abbasi and Myers knew of the arrangements ... But you were there with me, your man in the fawn raincoat at Manchester keeping a friendly eye on me. Who tipped you off about this?' But this was a side issue. 'The few remaining friends of Scargill would like to believe that you and I and others all plotted and connived together to bring down the president of the NUM. Better that than to recognize that he might be responsible for his own downfall.'

'Let me make it clear,' he explained to Rimington, 'that you and I have never met, nor have I had any contact whatsoever with any member of the security services either prior to, during or after my employment with the National Union of Mineworkers.' The tone of the open letter was aggrieved, at times almost childlike. Then came a tantalizing passage: 'Perhaps you would not welcome a public inquiry into all the events surrounding the NUM activities during and since the strike, as it might reveal that you were not as effective as you would have liked to have been, or as others would credit you. But public accountability is a fundamental premise of any free society.' Citing 'gross violations of civil liberties' during the miners' strike, Windsor concluded by calling for a public inquiry into MI5's role during the dispute, including 'all those public misunderstandings about the NUM secret funds'. He would, he said, be glad to take part, adding with a final grandiloquent flourish: 'Let's restore both freedom and democracy in Britain.'[63]

*Left* Robert Maxwell's megaphone: the Scargill Affair is launched with a fanfare of false allegations in the publishing tycoon's flagship daily on 5 March 1990.

*Right* A couple of years on, Maxwell is dead and the *Mirror* has turned somersault. Alain Simon, Peter Heathfield and Arthur Scargill are fêted on the first of two huge London marches against pit closures in October 1992.

*Left* Gavin Lightman – now a High Court judge – whose 1990 report cleared Scargill of corruption. He also savaged the secret funding system used to keep the NUM afloat, but the Inland Revenue rejected the basis of his main criticisms.

*Right* Terry Pattinson, the *Mirror* journalist Roger Windsor approached to sell his story, heckles Arthur Scargill at a rally on Maxwell's pension funds theft, London, March 1992.

Robert Maxwell, acclaimed by Margaret Thatcher as 'one of us', argues with sacked miners' supporters outside the TUC congress at the Blackpool Winter Gardens, September 1985.

Neil Kinnock, then Labour leader, congratulates Frank Thorne, Ted Oliver
and Terry Pattinson on winning the British Press Awards 'Reporter of the
Year' prize for a story described by Lightman as 'entirely untrue',
June 1991.

Steve Bell, *Guardian* cartoonist, gives his own view of the BPA award – and
of the relationship between Neil Kinnock, Robert Maxwell and
his 'Mirrormen'.

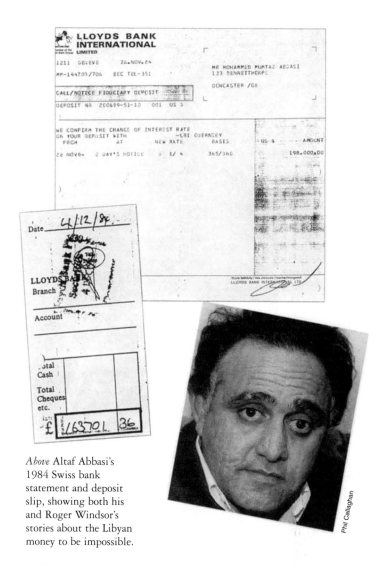

**LLOYDS BANK INTERNATIONAL**
LIMITED

1211  GB:EVE      26.NOV.84

MR-144703/706   REC TEL-351

MR MOHAMMED MUMTAZ ABBASI
133 BENNETTHORPE

DONCASTER /GB

CALL/NOTICE FIDUCIARY DEPOSIT

DEPOSIT NR  2C0689-51-10   001  US $

WE CONFIRM THE CHANGE OF INTEREST RATE
ON YOUR DEPOSIT WITH                    -LBI GUERNSEY
   FROM         AT          NEW RATE        BASIS            US $        AMOUNT

26 NOV84    2 DAY'S NOTICE    8 1/ 4      365/360                    198,000.00

Yours faithfully / Vos sincères / treuhänderergebenst
LLOYDS BANK INTERNATIONAL LTD.

Date  4/12/84

LLOYDS BANK
Branch

Account

Total
Cash

Total
Cheques
etc.

£  16370L  36

*Above* Altaf Abbasi's
1984 Swiss bank
statement and deposit
slip, showing both his
and Roger Windsor's
stories about the Libyan
money to be impossible.

Phil Callaghan

*Right* Altaf Abbasi, the Pakistani-born businessman who claimed to have
carried suitcases of Libyan cash through Heathrow airport for the NUM
during the 1984–5 strike. There is no harm in working with MI5,
he says now.

Roger Windsor, the NUM's chief executive, and Arthur Scargill leave the High Court in London in November 1985 after the union had purged its contempt of court over the miners' strike.

Windsor, named in parliament by Tam Dalyell and others as an MI5 agent, Arthur Scargill and Nell Myers, Scargill's closest political collaborator, on the floor of the TUC Congress, Blackpool, September 1987.

*Above* Scargill, the French
CGT miners' leader
Augustin 'Tin-Tin'
Dufresne and Alain Simon,
then general secretary of
the MTUI, in Paris, 1985.

*Right* Soviet Communist
Party Central Committee
document, marked
'top secret', reporting
discussions with Scargill
and Simon and
authorizing the transfer
of a million convertible
roubles, 4 February
1985. The signatures
of Mikhail Gorbachev
and Yegor Ligachev are on
the top left-hand corner.

Margaret Thatcher fresh from 'doing business' with Gorbachev, then number two in the Soviet Communist Party leadership, at Chequers, December 1984. He assured her he was not bankrolling the miners' strike.

*Left* Stella Rimington, the security service director-general who ran MI5 operations against the miners' strike, 'coming out' for the first time on the steps of the Home Office, July 1993.

*Below* Scargill being arrested during the mass picketing of the Orgreave coking plant in South Yorkshire, May 1984. On the right is Chief Superintendent John Nesbit, who eight years later declared: 'Arthur was right.'

# CHAPTER FIVE

# ALL MAXWELL'S MEN

Often the people in the left-wing press ... seemed more happy than the others to be friends of ours. *Peter Wright, ex-assistant director, MI5, 1987*[1]

Robert Maxwell was, according to Margaret Thatcher, 'one of us' – the highest token of esteem that Britain's longest-serving Prime Minister this century could bestow on any public figure. And although the Great Embezzler ritually demurred, perhaps in deference to his Labour Party friends, it is not difficult to see what she meant. The *Mirror*'s owner was a self-made man in the Thatcherite mould, a creature of essentially right-wing convictions, a proprietor who liked to wield a big stick with 'his' trade unions. And, in common with several other like-minded multimillionaires more directly associated with the Tory Party, Maxwell was found to have had his fingers in the till on an epic scale. 'I rate her as a great Prime Minister', Maxwell said of Thatcher. 'Without her, I wouldn't be where I am.'[2]

In the wake of Maxwell's mysterious death and the discovery that he stole well over £400 million from his own companies' pension funds as his bloated business empire disintegrated, the publishing magnate came to be seen as a special case, a press baron apart, a maverick whose behaviour was so extreme that he could not sensibly be compared with his fellow media proprietors. His editorial interference and the promotion of his business interests were no doubt cruder, and his cultivation of political influence less effective. On the other hand, his attacks on the unions were certainly never as extreme as Rupert Murdoch's. And if he appeared to be the living embodiment of Evelyn Waugh's Lord Copper, that caricature was invented long before the young Maxwell turned his back on his Ruthenian birthplace and began his notorious publishing career.

What really set Maxwell apart was that he controlled the only mass-circulation papers which supported the Labour Party, that he was ostensibly a Labour proprietor. This was what gave the *Mirror*'s campaign against the NUM its special force. If the Scargill stories had been run, say, in the *Daily Mail* – a paper derided by one Labour leader, Michael Foot, as the 'Forger's Gazette' for its tradition of fabricated smear stories against the labour movement – they would have been easier to dismiss. But Labour and 'its' paper, the *Daily Mirror*, were at the forefront of the onslaught. As a *Times* editorial argued triumphantly in the spring of 1990: 'It is significant that these allegations ... do not constitute an attack on Mr Scargill by the "Tory press". They ... have been deployed in particular detail by the Labour-supporting *Daily Mirror*.'[3]

This was wrongly taken by some to mean that the government and its various agencies could not have been involved in the Scargill Affair. In fact, there was no contradiction whatever. Both the Labour establishment and the government faced the same way when it came to the NUM leadership. The *Mirror* was the ideal vehicle for the attacks – as Roger Windsor shrewdly realized – and Maxwell the perfect pivot. 'Maxwell was a man of the most extreme reactionary views', the one-time *Mirror* journalist John Pilger recalls.

> He admired Thatcher enormously and he used the Labour Party really to promote himself and his own business interests. The man was clearly an outsider. The establishment of this country never allowed Maxwell in. That's why he loved Thatcher. He thought Thatcher was overturning the old establishment. But on the surface, he went along with the Labour Party because they embraced him, especially when he had the *Mirror*.[4]

The fact that it was Maxwell, since exposed as one of the world's biggest fraudsters and conmen, who accused the miners' leadership of embezzlement is one of the self-evident ironies of the whole affair. Another is that Maxwell was himself revealed after his death to have 'diverted' secret cash subsidies from the Soviet Union. As things turned out, it was money under the control of Maxwell, rather than Scargill, that went missing – and in spectacular fashion. That a businessman who was described by government inspectors as unfit to run a public company and whose whole career had been built on slush funds, shady manoeuvres, secret foreign bank accounts, mis-appropriation and autocratic megalomania was able to lead a chorus of denunciation of the leadership of the NUM for exactly such practices – and be taken seriously – must rank as one of the more ridiculous manifestations of Britain's decaying political culture.[5]

## THE SPOOKS' FRIEND

As well as being a rich and eccentric criminal, Maxwell also had wide-ranging opportunistic links with a variety of governments and their intelligence services – notably those of Britain, Israel and the Soviet Union. His entire career is littered with evidence of effective exploitation of intelligence contacts and leg-ups that came his way. That is not to say that Maxwell was an active 'spy' as such, or a double or triple agent for this or that intelligence organization. But he was a man who worshipped at the altar of raw power and readily understood the advantages he could gain from favours done for influential friends, both above and below board.

His connections with the British secret services dated back to his wartime army career. The Russian-speaking Captain Maxwell had been an army intelligence officer during the allied campaign of 1944–5 in France and Germany and naturally had contact with Special Operations Executive, the British wartime sabotage outfit. SOE grew out of the Secret Intelligence Service, MI6, and was reabsorbed by the service after the war. It was common practice for ex-military intelligence officers to main-tain links with the security services, and among Maxwell's early business backers were former members of the SOE hierarchy. These included Sir Charles Hambro, who ran SOE's London headquarters during the war and worked for MI6 for a time, and Major John Whitlock. Later, Maxwell was closely involved with Sir Robert Clark, another member of the old SOE mafia. Clark eventually became chairman of Hill Samuel, known as the 'spy bank' in the City because of its strong intelligence connections.

There is strong evidence that Maxwell, who liked to hint at his British spy links, was set up by MI6 to gather scientific intelligence from Eastern Europe, and that his early career, in particular, owed much to the sponsorship of SIS. At each stage in the establishment of his publishing company, Pergamon Press – which specialized in Soviet and East European scientific papers and journals – Maxwell was given backing by MI6 'assets'. Deals were arranged through Count Vanden Heuval, an MI6 officer who recruited businessmen to the service and acted as a 'fixer' for Hambro. Anne Dove, Maxwell's secretary in the 1950s, who had also worked for SOE, remembers being interviewed by the rival security service and asked to vouch for her boss's loyalty. This she enthusiastically did, though MI5 continued to view Maxwell with some suspicion. Shortly afterwards, Dickie Franks, head of MI6's DP4 section, in charge of recruiting British travellers to the East, approached the ambitious publisher for cooperation. Maxwell agreed and reported his observations to the spymaster. Franks, whose deputy at the time was the Soviet agent George Blake, later became head of the intelligence service.[6]

Maxwell's links with the Russians were the mirror image of those with the British secret state: ambiguous and well-rewarded. In Berlin, Maxwell is alleged by two former Soviet intelligence officers to have signed a document in the early days of the Cold War promising to assist the KGB as and when required. On a trip to Moscow in the early summer of 1968 the relationship was apparently reactivated, and Maxwell – then a Labour MP – secretly met Yuri Andropov, then KGB chairman. Later that year, he was notably conciliatory in parliament during the crisis over Soviet intervention in Czechoslovakia. In the 1970s and 1980s, Maxwell appeared to his employees to be subsidizing the sale of Soviet scientific books and his absurdly reverential biographies of Soviet and East European communist leaders. But in reality, the Soviet Union was subsidizing Maxwell with secret payments laundered through the French office of Pergamon.

Soviet Communist Party Central Committee papers published in 1991 after the failed coup and the banning of the party revealed that Pergamon was listed as a 'friendly firm' and was owed £500,000 – though Pergamon officials could find no record of the sum having been paid. This is another striking example of how those who gave the strongest impetus to the Scargill Affair, such as Maxwell and Roger Windsor, were guilty of some of the very charges they made against the miners' leaders. With the collapse of the East European regimes he had so successfully cultivated, Maxwell would claim that his business in the Soviet Union was loss-making and was carried out 'at the request of the US government'. Loss-making it was certainly not, but there is no doubt he liaised closely with Western governments over his Soviet and East European dalliances. As he liked to say, quite truthfully, of himself: 'I have always been a professed, strong anti-communist.'[7]

Maxwell's relationship with the Soviet state was, it seems, as much a matter of confusion for the KGB as it was for some servants of the British Crown. Oleg Gordievsky, the KGB defector and MI6 double agent who headed the KGB station in London, apparently believed that Maxwell was at one point being manipulated as a Soviet 'publicity agent', while admitting that most Soviet intelligence officials were convinced he was a British spy. Among the latter was the better-placed Mikhail Lyubimov, who was head of the British desk at KGB headquarters during the 1970s. Lyubimov has insisted since Maxwell's death that the Czech-born publisher was not a KGB agent of any kind. Instead, Maxwell was suspected of being an MI6 plant, and the KGB regularly warned party leaders to be wary of the corrupt businessman. A secret memorandum signed by Vladimir Kryuchkov, the KGB chief who later became one of the leaders of the ill-fated 'state of emergency' of August 1991, documented KGB fears about the exposure of Soviet links with Maxwell. But it seems likely that these worries focused on his contacts with members of the Politburo rather than Soviet intelligence. Lyubimov believes that MI6 used Maxwell to get access to officials of the powerful international department of the Communist Party Central Committee apparatus – something of an MI6 coup, as it was the international department, rather than the KGB, which was responsible for funding covert political operations in the West. The publication of speeches by Brezhnev and other senior politicians was seen by the KGB in Moscow as a ploy by the British intelligence service to get access to the top Soviet leadership.[8]

Then there is the case of Israel. Like most Maxwelliana, the original allegations about his links with the Israeli intelligence service Mossad have become hopelessly obscured by a welter of media hype, confusion, claim and counterclaim. Shortly before Maxwell's death in 1991, Seymour Hersh, a Pulitzer Prize-winning American journalist who broke the story of the US massacre at My Lai in Vietnam in the late 1960s, published a book exposing Israel's secret nuclear-weapons programme, called *The Samson Option*. In a final chapter aimed at the British market, Hersh alleged that Maxwell helped Mossad capture Mordechai Vanunu, the dissident nuclear technician who had passed information about Israel's nuclear weapons plant at Dimona to the *Sunday Times* in 1986. Vanunu had offered the same story to the *Sunday Mirror*. But instead of using the scoop, the Maxwell paper rubbished it in advance of publication by Murdoch's *Sunday Times*, calling Vanunu's revelations 'a hoax, or even something more sinister – a plot to discredit Israel'. Vanunu disappeared the same day and was lured to Rome, where he was kidnapped, taken by force to Israel and sentenced to eighteen years' imprisonment.

Hersh's claims about Maxwell and the Vanunu affair were mainly based on the evidence of an Israeli, Ari Ben-Menasche, who had worked for Israel's intelligence and military establishment. Ben-Menasche alleged that Nick Davies, the *Mirror*'s foreign editor, had betrayed Vanunu's hideaway to Mossad. And the 'Mirrorman' had also cooperated with him in secretly selling arms to Iran with the approval of the Israeli and US governments. Maxwell was up to his neck with Mossad as well, Hersh claimed, and had laundered money and facilitated the weapons sales. Former *Sunday Mirror* staff were quoted in the book describing how Maxwell had given instructions that Vanunu's photographs of Dimona were to be passed directly to the Israeli Embassy.[9]

Maxwell and Davies sued. But George Galloway, then a left-wing Scottish Labour MP, who had long had his own powerful reasons for wanting to see Maxwell humbled, short-circuited the press baron's reflex resort to litigation. Together with the Tory MP and spywriter Rupert Allason, Galloway repeated the Hersh allegations in the House of Commons under the protection of parliamentary privilege. From then on, it was open season for the rest of the press, which had hitherto hung fire in deference to Maxwell's awe-inspiring reputation for defamation writs. Maxwell ordered his loyal factotum Joe Haines to 'piss all over Allason and Galloway'. Haines obliged, and the next day's *Mirror* front page duly lacerated the MPs. Under the headline, 'Dishonourable Men and Dirty Tricks', the paper cried foul in extravagant style. The two men had 'as much honour as a pair of jackals scavenging in a rubbish heap', the *Mirror* snarled, because they had told lies about Davies and made 'absurd allegations' about Maxwell.[10]

However, the MPs' Commons pronouncements had opened the media floodgates and, for once, the rich man's libel laws could not protect the tumbling tycoon. One strand in Hersh's story was that Davies had been to Ohio in the United States in 1985 to buy arms from an American dealer. Davies denied ever having been to the state, and letters provided by Davies' ex-wife linking him to arms-sales negotiations in Ohio were denounced by the Mirror as forgeries – just as Maxwell's paper had tried the previous year to discredit evidence against Roger Windsor, its star witness in the NUM extravaganza. But two days later, the Daily Mail produced a photograph of Davies in Ohio in 1985 sipping tea with an arms dealer's wife. The *Sun* crowed: 'You Liar: Maxwell's Man is Finally Unmasked', and the *Mirror*'s foreign editor was fired for lying. Davies insists it was an innocent 'slip of the memory', but 'Mirrorgate' was born. Although some doubt was later cast on Hersh's sources – in particular, Ben-Menasche – there is little question that Maxwell 'maintained a close relationship with Mossad', as the MPs alleged, along with most other departments of the Israeli state.[11]

In fact, by the end of his life Maxwell was closely involved with the entire Israeli establishment, who turned out in force in November 1991 for what amounted to his state funeral in Jerusalem. The Israeli President, Chaim Herzog, gave an oration at the burial on the Mount of Olives, recalling Maxwell's 'significant involvement in many facets of our struggle for economic independence, for the absorption of Russian immigrants, for the security of the country'. The then Israeli Prime Minister and former intelligence boss, Yitzhak Shamir, who had personally used Maxwell's private jet, described him as a 'passionate friend of Israel' who had 'put his wide contacts on the international arena at Israel's service'.[12]

As Maxwell's former *Mirror* editor, Roy Greenslade, put it: 'To describe Maxwell as a spy for Israel was the equivalent of naming Margaret Thatcher as a spy for Britain.' But those who dismiss the suggestions of links with both Israeli and other intelligence services because of the publisher's 'uncertain grip on reality' – as did, for example, Max Hastings of the *Daily Telegraph* and Maxwell's former employee and British ambassador to Washington, Peter Jay – are unconvincing. Not only does an uncertain grip on reality often appear to be an important qualification for work with the intelligence services, but such a failing also never stopped Maxwell from being used for less covert, but politically vital, contacts. His role as an intermediary between Shamir and Gorbachev in 1990 is one example.

Peter Jay recalled that when he was considering working for Maxwell, he 'took soundings' within the Foreign Office as to whether there were any questions of 'propriety, prudence or loyalty' that should prevent a former ambassador from taking Maxwell's shilling. Apparently, there were none. That does not mean Maxwell did not have links with intelligence services. Rather, it strengthens the inference that the British government was content that he was more of an asset to them than to the Russians. He made money out of both. And Gorbachev's coinage of the term 'Maxwell Syndrome' to describe the problem of Western businessmen who promised help to the Soviet Union, but never delivered, points in the same direction. Intriguingly, at the Joint Intelligence Committee, which coordinates the British government's intelligence-gathering effort from the Cabinet office in Whitehall, Maxwell was not classed as a security risk. As Nick Davies, the sacked *Mirror* foreign editor who was regularly at Maxwell's side during his numerous overseas jaunts, comments disingenuously: 'Maxwell's connection with the KGB was known to Western, and particularly British, intelligence, but there does appear to have been a quid pro quo that Maxwell should not be touched, for some reason or another.' Why that might be scarcely stretches the imagination.[13]

Margaret Thatcher revealed after his death that Maxwell had briefed her regularly as Prime Minister on his contacts in the disintegrating socialist bloc. 'Mr Maxwell kept me informed about what was happening in Eastern European countries and what their leaders were thinking,' Thatcher recalled. John Major, her successor as Prime Minister, said Maxwell had provided the government with 'valuable insights' into the Soviet Union's power struggle at the time of the coup and countercoup in August 1991. If his only real passion in his last years was for Israel, Maxwell was nevertheless keen to do favours for the powers-that-be wherever there was any prospect that those favours could be returned – and particularly in Britain. Whether the great pensions swindler used any of his longstanding intelligence contacts in the *Mirror*'s campaign against the NUM must be open to speculation. But his record over forty years shows Maxwell was always more than simply a corrupt businessman. He was a man who delighted in being a political player in the grand style, both openly and in secret.[14]

## THE *MIRROR* AND THE MINERS

Robert Maxwell's very personal war against the miners and their leader was launched simultaneously with his first successful bid for a long-coveted prize: a mass-circulation Fleet Street newspaper he could call his own. Maxwell bought the Mirror Group and its stable of four national newspapers from Reed International for the knockdown price of £90 million on 12 July 1984. It was the fourth month of the year-long miners' strike. The drama of the dispute provided Britain's latest and largest press baron a heaven-sent instant opportunity to deploy his newly acquired political influence. The *Daily Mirror*, the group's flagship, was then selling three and a half million copies a day, with a readership of probably double that figure. The *Mirror* was the traditional paper of the core Labour-supporting working class, with a strong tradition of campaigning journalism. As surveys carried out at the time by the Coal Board showed, it was by far the most widely read daily paper among miners. It was also the only national newspaper consistently to call for a Labour vote across the country at general elections.

Even while chasing his rival Rupert Murdoch's *Sun* downmarket – and losing up to a million readers in the process – Maxwell would make ample use of such a captive audience. Among the publisher's 'solemn pledges' on taking over the *Mirror* was the following commitment: 'Under my management editors in the Group will be free to produce their newspapers without interference with their journalistic skills and judgement.' There would also, he promised, be no 'chequebook journalism' in his newspaper. When actually faced with Maxwell's chequebook, most senior *Mirror* journalists rolled over and had their tummies tickled in time-honoured Fleet Street fashion. Notable amongst them was Joe Haines, Harold Wilson's former press secretary and sharp-tongued *Mirror* leader writer. Hours before Maxwell's takeover was signed and sealed, Haines told a union meeting he would have to be 'dragged through the door to work for a crook and a monster like Robert Maxwell'. Two days later, he was promoted to assistant editor and ended up as Maxwell's trusty, with a seat on the board to match.[15]

The *Mirror*'s new Citizen Kane immediately set to work to shape the paper's coverage of the desperate industrial confrontation then engulfing the mining communities. Barely two weeks after his takeover, Maxwell's 'new line' on the miners' strike would be made unmistakably plain. On 26 July, Geoffrey Goodman, the paper's widely respected industrial editor, wrote a strongly anti-government commentary on the strike. Margaret Thatcher had opposed Ted Heath's decision to call an election in Cabinet during the miners' strike of 1974, he recalled, wanting instead to 'take on the miners, fight 'em to a finish and win'. The Prime Minister, Goodman wrote, 'has never forgotten and clearly never forgiven the miners for that [election] defeat'. The piece was entitled 'Digging into a Vendetta'. Maxwell was having none of it. He personally crossed out those lines, ordered the headline to be scrapped and replaced it with Thatcher's own catchphrase: 'The Enemy Within'. The industrial editor was only informed once the presses were already turning. Maxwell claimed he had made the changes because the piece had 'looked too grey, with too many words'. The following day, Goodman threatened to resign in protest. But the owner 'put his arms around me and said, "How can you ever forgive me for such a thing? I should never have done it."' Goodman did forgive him and agreed to submit all his articles in advance to Maxwell, who promised not to interfere. 'I fooled myself,' Goodman admitted later.[16]

This was to be the first of a stream of Maxwell-inspired attacks on the NUM and set the tone for his role of self-appointed *Mirror* editor-in-chief. But the new overlord at the *Mirror* headquarters would never be content restricting himself to the role of a propagandist. In the summer and autumn of 1984, Maxwell became personally involved in characteristically extravagant initiatives to settle the strike, and met Scargill, MacGregor and key TUC leaders on several occasions. Maxwell thought highly of his own negotiating skills. He was, after all, a veteran of some ferocious industrial disputes – including one at his printing plant at Park Royal in West London, where Maxwell arranged for the smashing up of the machinery one night in the autumn of 1983 by a group of burly men armed with 14lb sledgehammers.[17]

What quickly turned into a Maxwellian stunt began one Saturday afternoon with a telephone call from the proprietor to John Pilger, the Australian-born campaigning journalist, then working for the *Mirror*. Maxwell wanted Pilger to fix up a secret meeting with Scargill – whom the journalist had never met – preferably at a location with a convenient heliport nearby. Arrangements were made and the *Mirror* team met Scargill and Heathfield in the penthouse at the Hallam Tower Hotel in Sheffield. The owner's helicopter was in the event grounded by fog and Pilger had to endure Maxwell's thoughts about the 'lack of discipline' in the country on the train north. The meeting nevertheless kicked off well. Scargill and Heathfield took the encounter seriously, talked about police violence in the coal-fields and the reasons for their resistance to the Tory pit-closure programme, and set out the details of their various attempts to find a compromise, few of which had received an airing in the national media. Goodman, also in attendance, remembers that Maxwell was initially 'very impressed by Scargill' and that the 'two got on very well together'. But as the day wore on, Max-well started to lecture the NUM leaders on their 'responsibilities to the nation'. Maxwell told Scargill and Heathfield of his fears of a 'breakdown in law and order and civilized values'. The *Mirror* proprietor ended up 'banging the table', Pilger recalls. 'You're bringing bloody revolution to the streets of Britain, you are doing nothing less than attacking the sovereignty of the nation,' Maxwell roared at the miners' pre-sident – at which point Scargill asked if he could have a cup of tea.[18]

It was the end of a beautiful friendship. Maxwell ordered a

special issue of the *Mirror* about the strike. As it was being prepared, his animosity towards the NUM grew apace. 'Maxwell decided that Scargill had to be defeated,' Goodman recalled. He and another *Mirror* veteran, Terry Lancaster, were told to write a rubbishing feature about Scargill and the miners for Maxwell's approval. They refused to have their bylines on it, but the piece went out anyway under the headline: 'The Pigheaded Identical Twins'. The day after the return of Maxwell's retinue from Sheffield, Pilger told the proprietor they had been given substantial evidence that the Coal Board and the government were not telling the truth about their dealings with the NUM. Pilger suggested running the story. 'You mustn't be taken in,' Maxwell replied, though he agreed to a piece about police violence. David Seymour, then the *Mirror*'s number two leaderwriter, was constantly in Maxwell's antechamber negotiating for some modest degree of control over his *Mirror* 'Comment' pieces and repeatedly finding himself distorting what he believed to be the truth to suit the owner's demands. 'The whole strike became a blur for me,' Seymour recalls, 'because I was being battered the whole time by Maxwell, who was jumping up and down on my head telling me what was happening, which I knew was wrong.'[19]

Meanwhile, Maxwell held further meetings with the union and the NCB negotiating team – notably during the TUC congress in Brighton – trying to present himself as an honest broker anxious to bring the two sides together. Ian MacGregor, the Coal Board chairman, who had some 'private chats with Bob', claims he offered the tycoon a deal: 'If you stop the *Mirror* attacking the NCB, I'll work with you to try to mastermind a solution to the strike.' From then on, according to MacGregor's reckoning, 'the *Mirror*'s coverage ceased to be uniformly hostile' to the Board. Others certainly had a greater impact on Maxwell's approach. In particular, Peter Walker, Thatcher's Energy Secretary, made it his business to get 'close' to the proprietor of the paper read by most striking miners. Six years later, Walker would get even closer when he agreed to become chairmandesignate of Maxwell Communications Corporation; though after four months, the tycoon told the ex-Tory minister his services were no longer required and Walker resigned.[20]

As the 1984–5 strike wore on, the *Mirror*'s coverage became ever more poisonous towards the miners' cause. Maxwell appeared to believe that the NUM president had obtusely denied him the chance to be acclaimed as the national hero who settled the dispute. The *Mirror*'s attacks on Scargill in particular became progressively more vitriolic and personal. 'Arthur Scargill has lost the miners' strike', the paper's front page declared enthusiastically during the last phase of the dispute. 'No one else is to blame.'[21]

The conscious rewriting of history as it was being made reached its apogee on 10 September 1984, during the latest set of fruitless negotiations born out of Maxwell's much-publicized mediation efforts. 'Scargill to ballot miners on final offer', the *Mirror*'s banner headline read that day. Under the byline of Terry Pattinson, then a humble industrial correspondent, the exclusive front-page story claimed that the NUM leadership was 'now ready to recommend a vote on the Coal Board's final terms'. Inside, a second story by a 'special correspondent' described the paper's revelation as an 'astonishing development' and gave details of the 'final package'. The story was – like another, far more damaging, *Mirror* 'exclusive' Pattinson would put his name to five-and-a-half years later – entirely untrue. On this occasion, however, the hapless reporter knew nothing of the imaginary scoop that appeared under his name. Indeed, the first he heard of the story was when he was congratulated by his wife. Pattinson had indeed filed a 'holding' story, reporting accurately that 'peace talks had ended after only two hours' and that 'both sides were non-committal'. The rest had been inserted into his copy on Maxwell's orders. The night before, the *Mirror*'s wire room had received a telex message from Maxwell House, headquarters of what was then Maxwell's publishing company, Pergamon Press. There was no name on the telex, which was simply marked 'MUST'. The *Mirror* hierarchy did its duty and Joe Haines wrote a suitably enthusiastic editorial backing the nonexistent decision to ballot, entitled: 'A Vote for Sanity'.

Rupert Murdoch's *Sun* regurgitated the *Mirror*'s claims and Pattinson gave a series of interviews on radio and television on the morning of his 'scoop', staunchly defending its accuracy, before it became obvious to everyone that the story was without foundation. Pattinson had backed the 'exclusive' in his interviews because he guessed correctly that the 'miners' ballot' line had come from the *Mirror*'s proprietor and he knew that Maxwell had been in close contact with Scargill the week before. 'I thought Maxwell had pulled off a coup,' Pattinson says. When he returned to Holborn Circus, he was unable to discover who had actually written the final story. Maxwell appeared entirely unabashed that the *Mirror*'s splash exclusive was exposed as a figment of his imagination. But Pattinson, a right-wing Labour supporter, says he was 'absolutely shattered' by the incident. He complained loudly about it at a meeting of the paper's National Union of Journalists' chapel (office branch) and announced that he was compiling a dossier of Maxwell's interference. Mike Molloy, the then editor, advised him: 'If I were you, I'd forget about it.' Pattinson did. 'It was either that or be sacked.'[22]

At around the same time, Pattinson had been elected the *Mirror* journalists' 'FoC' – Father of the Chapel, the NUJ's equivalent of a shop steward. Maxwell was then in the process of cutting the *Mirror* print unions down to a size he thought appropriate. Towards the end of 1985, the maverick tycoon sacked the entire 6,500-strong Mirror Group staff – a characteristic Maxwellian tactic – and bludgeoned the unions into accepting 2,000 job losses. On the editorial floors, Maxwell demanded more than 60 redundancies. At a packed chapel meeting, Pattinson recommended acceptance, arguing it was better to get the inevitable over with as painlessly as possible. 'It was a real management lackey performance', according to the left-wing *Mirror* columnist Paul Foot, who moved an unsuccessful motion for a strike against the sackings at the same meeting.[23]

The number of compulsory job losses among the journalists was in the end whittled down somewhat. But Terry Pattinson, who was then number three on the labour desk, was not forgotten. A few months later, Maxwell told the diminutive

Geordie he wanted to give him a double promotion and make him the *Mirror*'s new industrial editor. It depended, the tycoon declared, on how he covered Murdoch's dispute then raging with the print unions at Wapping. Over the following months, Maxwell was regularly on the phone to Pattinson, and that autumn the reporter was summoned to the proprietorial presence once again. 'You've done everything I expected of you,' he declared. 'I want to congratulate you. You are now the industrial editor of the *Daily Mirror*.' Pattinson happily spread word of his rapid advancement. But later the same day, he was called back to Maxwell's ninth-floor suite to find the *Mirror*'s new editor, Richard Stott, purple-faced with rage. 'You have been blabbing,' Maxwell growled, 'this was a little secret between you and I.'

The matter was put on ice. But a few weeks later Stott, who had managed to squeeze a string of other concessions out of Maxwell in return for accepting the forced appointment, informed Pattinson that he had after all decided to give him the post. Maxwell meanwhile made it clear he was anxious for his new industrial editor to stay on as the *Mirror*'s FoC. However, after a month of trying to do both jobs at once, Pattinson decided the workload was too heavy and resigned as FoC, in the face of dire warnings from Joe Haines, at the end of 1986. 'Maxwell was a great creep detector,' Foot says of the episode. Pattinson – who later went on briefly to join a tiny right-wing breakaway journalists' union before himself being sacked by the post-Maxwell *Mirror* management – regards the claim that he was picked out by Maxwell for his role in the redundancies dispute as 'grossly unfair'. But whatever the motive, there is no argument that it was Maxwell himself who appointed Pattinson directly over the head of his editor.[24]

## SCOOP OF THE DECADE

So it was that two-and-a-half years later, Terry Pattinson was the man whose door Roger Windsor, Jim Parker and Maurice

Jones came knocking on when they decided to sell their wares to the *Daily Mirror*. And Maxwell, who was more than delighted to attract the kudos for finally finishing off the recalcitrant miners' leader, was there to hold his hand. Scarcely a month after Windsor's initial approach, Pattinson was summoned to the press baron's presence to receive Maxwell's blessing for the investigation. The media mogul's high-minded insistence when he bought the *Mirror* that there would be no chequebook journalism under his regime was quickly forgotten in the excitement over the Scargill story. It was Maxwell who personally authorized the payments of £80,000 and £50,000 to Roger Windsor and Jim Parker for their testimony against their former employer.

There were other, more public, demonstrations of Maxwell's close involvement in the Scargill Affair. On the launch day of the *Mirror*'s 'revelations' in March 1990, he would take the unusual step of giving them his personal stamp of approval by signing the accompanying editorial. This was the piece which breathtakingly damned the NUM leaders' 'shady manoeuvres' during and after the 1984–5 strike. In an interview with Hugo Young published in the *Guardian* the same day, Maxwell crowed that the *Mirror* had played a key role in the 'defeat of Arthur Scargill and the 1984 miners' strike'. Indeed, he cited the *Mirror*'s campaigns against the NUM leadership as the most important example of how he was able to use his 'megaphone' power as a newspaper proprietor. 'I take delight and some pride in having got rid of the militants out of the labour movement.'[25]

In case anyone had missed the point that this was a Maxwellian service to the kingdom, the *Mirror*'s proprietor charged around in front of the television cameras for several days, with an embarrassed editor in tow, throwing his full weight behind the allegations and demanding that the NUM president sue if he had any complaints. This was business as well as politics. For the multimedia proprietor, the joint investigation and simultaneous launch with Central Television had a special attraction, as Maxwell owned 20 per cent of Central's shares. The Scargill exposé was, the *Mirror*-Central proprietor declared to one and all, the 'story of the decade' and the most important to be run in the *Mirror* during his six-year ownership. Scargill had, after all, he liked to tell interviewers, 'tried to bring down an elected constitutional government of the country'.[26]

Roy Greenslade, who left Murdoch's *Sunday Times* to take over as *Mirror* editor at the beginning of February 1990, was loyally gung ho in defence of his new master's good faith when the Scargill story broke. 'There was no conspiracy or smear,' he told all comers during the first week of the campaign. 'It was a genuine piece of investigative journalism. I have printed this more in sorrow than anger.' Greenslade was sacked by Maxwell a year later, but in his book of reminiscences about the tyrannical tycoon he stuck to a similar line. Maxwell's decision to sign the editorial on the first day and his defence of the story on television had been 'bad tactical mistakes', Greenslade wrote, because 'it wrongly convinced Scargill and many miners that Maxwell was involved in a political plot against him'.[27]

Maxwell had gleefully informed him about the great Scargill scandal even before his arrival at Holborn Circus. Greenslade, a one-time Maoist who still held modestly leftish views, says his 'heart sank' when he was appointed editor and told that the 'biggest story in the world they'd all been talking about was about Arthur Scargill and not some captain of industry. But in the end, I believed it. It all seemed to be an amazing story of fraud and cover-up, all the witnesses seemed remote from each other and then there was the absolute assurance of Windsor that the money was for the mortgage.' Three years later, he wasn't so sure. 'I was never certain whether we weren't the victims of an MI5 dirty trick,' Greenslade said in retrospect. 'I'm not trying to run away from it. I have accepted that the central allegation was not proven. I take it on the nose that I ran it. But the MI5 issue has always troubled me.' In 1990, he regarded Scargill's failure to sue as a sure pointer to his guilt. Now he accepts that there was little prospect of the miners' leader getting a fair trial.

On day two of the great scoop, Greenslade was upbraided in the favoured *Mirror* watering hole, the Vagabonds club, by a couple of veteran Fleet Street hacks. He was an 'inexperienced sucker', they told him, who had been 'taken in' by the security services. He called in the three journalists who had carried out the investigation – Pattinson, Thorne and Oliver – to quiz them about the possibility of MI5 or Special Branch involvement. The threesome said they had thought of it, had even questioned Windsor about it, but were satisfied that their story was clean. Greenslade then gingerly discussed his anxieties with the *Mirror*'s maverick proprietor. 'Maxwell called me and said: "Do you think we could have been the victim of an MI5 plot?" And I said: "It's possible. Do you know that we have been?" He said: "I have information ..." He didn't know and he didn't say he knew, but he'd obviously had a kind of premonition maybe or a tip or a hint and so it was constantly on our minds in that first week, even while the stories were going in – could we have possibly been set up?' Maxwell, he recalls, 'loved conspiracy theories. He said we needed to be careful not to be gullible, but he clearly wasn't really bothered.' The former *Mirror* editor is himself somewhat philosophical. 'Most tabloid newspapers – or even newspapers in general – are the playthings of MI5. You're the recipients of the sting.'[28]

The *Mirror* did indeed have a particular history of close relations with the intelligence services, even by Fleet Street standards. Cecil King, *Mirror* chairman in the 1960s, was – according to Peter Wright, the whistleblowing former MI5 assistant director – 'a longtime agent of ours' who had 'made it clear that he would publish anything MI5 might care to leak in his direction'. King was the man at the centre of a bizarre plot in 1968 to oust Wilson and replace him with a national government headed by Lord Mountbatten. Wright also refers to a 'senior executive' at the *Mirror* who was controlled by an MI5 Section D4 agent runner. Cyril Morten, the *Mirror*'s managing editor, worked closely with MI6 and helpfully employed an MI6 agent as a *Mirror* photographer. Harry Wharton, at one time MI5's Fleet Street officer, had contacts with King and Hugh Cudlipp, the *Mirror* editor who succeeded King as MGN chairman. Cudlipp ended up working for Maxwell and became a

Social Democratic Party peer.[29]

However relaxed they might be about being used by the security services, Maxwell and his acolytes nevertheless remained highly sensitive about any attempt to set the record straight on the *Mirror*'s allegations against the NUM leadership. In September 1990, the Campaign for Press and Broadcasting Freedom, a trade-union-backed pressure group, made a formal complaint about the Scargill stories – along with 220 delegates to that year's TUC – to the *Mirror*'s ombudsman, the former Labour Solicitor General, Peter Archer. They accused the *Mirror* of flouting the national newspaper editors' own code of conduct and of failing to correct mistakes promptly, or offering a fair opportunity to reply, or informing its readers that its star witnesses had been paid well over £100,000 between them for their testimony. The CPBF complained that at no time during the *Mirror*'s seven-month 'investigation' were detailed allegations put to Scargill or Heathfield in a way that could be properly answered. And neither man had been given an opportunity to reply either to the *Mirror*'s own accusations or to the criticisms in the Lightman Report. They also challenged the claim by Maxwell's lawyers that the proprietor had 'played no part in the editorial content' of the stories and argued that the Scargill Affair showed that any suggestion of editorial independence at the *Mirror* was a mockery.

Peter Archer was one of a gaggle of ombudsmen who had been appointed by national newspapers to investigate readers' complaints. This was a move aimed at heading off the threat of legal controls on the press. The former Labour minister finally met the CPBF to hear a detailed submission about the Scargill complaint in January 1991. The next the campaign heard from him was a letter in March explaining that he would not be able to adjudicate after all as Robert Maxwell had 'dispensed with his services'. Maxwell made Archer redundant shortly before the latter was due to find that the *Mirror*'s central allegation in the Scargill saga had indeed been wrong. Archer was six weeks into the investigation and had taken evidence from Pattinson, as well as from Mick Gosling of the CPBF. 'I hadn't decided my final line,' Archer explained, 'but I would have certainly said the *Mirror* was wrong about the mortgage allegation.'

The publisher's excuse to Archer for the sudden sacking was that he wanted to give the new 'self-regulating' Press Complaints Commission, which had replaced the Press Council at the beginning of 1991, a chance to 'demonstrate its effectiveness'. But the former Solicitor General was sceptical. No other newspaper got rid of its ombudsman to support the PCC, and Archer himself believed it was almost certainly because of his Scargill investigation. 'I can't think of any other reason,' he said. Taking Maxwell at his word, however, the CPBF submitted its complaint to the PCC, which deliberated for six weeks before deciding that it could not consider a 'third party complaint stemming from matters which took place well before the committee was founded'. In such a way, the new system of 'self-regulation' of the press 'demonstrated its effectiveness'.[30]

Archer believed that both Maxwell and Pattinson were too involved in the story to be objective about it. In Greenslade's words, Maxwell's 'antipathy to Scargill was well known' and the *Mirror*'s then industrial editor was 'obsessed with getting Arthur'. Certainly, the *Mirror* showed not the remotest inclination under Maxwell's continued proprietorship to pull back from its discredited allegations, which Pattinson and Joe Haines continued to use every opportunity to insist were 'unanswered'. One editorial even claimed that the paper was being 'smeared' by those who questioned the reliability of its claims about the miners' union. Geoffrey Goodman described his former colleagues' treatment of the evidence in the Scargill Affair as 'extremely disturbing'.[31]

Some measure of Maxwell's personal interest in the Scargill Affair can be guessed at from reports that after the publisher's death in November 1991, stolen NUM documents were found by the Fraud Squad in a personal safe at his London flat. Jimmy Hood, the Labour mining MP, raised the discoveries – allegedly made in the course of the Serious Fraud Office's massive investigation of Mirror Group Newspapers – with the Attorney General in parliament, to no avail. Maxwell continued to the end to seize any opportunity that presented itself to publicize himself as an enemy of the outcast NUM. In the last few months of his life, the corrupt tycoon made a series of abortive attempts to set up a consortium with the participation of the NUM's non-TUC rival, the Union of Democratic Mineworkers, with the supposed aim of mounting a bid for Powergen, the larger of the two privatized electricity generators.[32]

For all that Maxwell was an outsider who was never accepted by a snobbish, anti-Semitic British establishment, his connections with City, business and legal circles were vast. Some of these involved tie-ups with key players in the Scargill campaign that would only become apparent after his death. For example, it was discovered in the wake of the multimillionaire's mysterious drowning that the accountants employed by Gavin Lightman and Frere Chomeley at vast expense to investigate the affairs of the NUM and IMO had also been working for Robert Maxwell. Cork Gully, the firm used by Lightman and Frere Chomeley, was the insolvency arm of Coopers & Lybrand – which had been Maxwell's personal accountants for twenty years. Coopers & Lybrand also worked as auditors for Mirror Group Newspapers and other Maxwell companies. The link led the NUM to make a formal complaint to the Institute of Chartered Accountants that Cork Gully had failed to declare a 'real risk of conflict of interest' when it agreed to carry out its investigation of the union's finances. Cork Gully's senior partner, Michael Jordan, who supervised the firm's work for the Lightman Inquiry and subsequent legal action, admitted the danger had been considered. But it had been decided that the company's 'objectivity and independence' could not be 'impaired', as it was 'basically obtaining facts' for Lightman. The opinions Jordan's team had expressed had only 'related to the accounting aspects'. The Institute ruled that there were no grounds for disciplinary action.[33]

Jordan was in fact a personal chum of Gavin Lightman. It later emerged – during the scandal surrounding relations between the Tory minister Michael Mates and the fugitive Turkish Cypriot tycoon Asil Nadir – that Jordan had also been a friend for twenty-five years of the intelligence-connected businessman, Lord Erskine. Jordan, who was appointed by the courts as an administrator for Nadir's bankrupt Polly Peck company, tried unsuccessfully to persuade Erskine to help him seize the firm's assets in Turkish-occupied Cyprus. Erskine, who went on a Foreign-Office-sponsored trip to meet Saddam Hussein shortly before Iraq invaded Kuwait in 1990, admitted to what he called 'peripheral links' with the intelligence services. And only a couple of months after Maxwell's death, the press baron's youngest son Kevin was seeking leave to appeal to the House of Lords against a court ruling which required him to surrender information about the Maxwell company pension funds. His worry was that he risked incriminating himself in any criminal trial. By an ironic coincidence, the younger Maxwell's brief in this particular, unsuccessful case was none other than Gavin Lightman QC.[34]

## THE LABOUR LINK

Part of Maxwell's motivation for providing such generous space and resources for a campaign transparently aimed at ousting Arthur Scargill from the presidency of the embattled miners' union was undoubtedly that he knew it would be as well appreciated by the Labour Party establishment as it would by Margaret Thatcher's Tory Cabinet. 'The motive, as far as Bob Maxwell was concerned, was to do the Labour Party a favour,' Geoffrey Goodman believed. Indeed, it was Labour leadership loyalists who most enthusiastically seized on the *Mirror* allegations and ran with them – and gave the 1990 campaign much of its political and personal venom. For Maxwell, it was clearly a good political investment.[35]

The Labour hierarchy, of course, had its own history of unhealthy entanglements with the intelligence services. Labour leaders have on the whole had a deferential attitude towards the security services – including those, like Wilson, who have been the target of their unwelcome attentions. In the postwar period, the party's Gaitskellite right wing worked closely with MI5, Special Branch and a variety of CIA front organizations to advance its cause and keep the left at bay. In the early 1960s, a group of Labour leaders – including Hugh Gaitskell, a former SOE officer, and George Brown – made a direct approach to MI5 for records of tapped telephone conversations, bank-account records of payments from Soviet-bloc organizations, or names of East European contacts which could be used to smear their left-wing opponents in the internal party factional war. Informal flows of information back and forth were more common, and over the years MI5 recruited freely in Labour's headquarters and among the parliamentary party.

And it was American dollars, rather than much-fantasized-over Moscow Gold, which helped shape the face of Labour politics in the 1950s and 1960s. Michael Stewart, Foreign Secretary in the first Wilson government during the escalation of US military action in Vietnam, and Sam Watson, the powerful Durham miners' leader and Gaitskell ally, were among those in postwar labour-movement circles who have since been identified as CIA 'agents of influence'. A section of the Gaitskellite faction would, in its later incarnation, form the basis of the Social Democratic Party breakaway in the early 1980s. CIA-inspired or US government-funded Cold War outfits, such as the Labour Committee for Transatlantic Understanding, continued to attract right-wing trade-union and Labour Party figures well into the late 1980s. Other intelligence connections with the Labour leader's office have been closer to home. Margaret 'Meta' Ramsay, for example, who advised John Smith on foreign-policy issues during his brief leadership, was previously a senior MI6 officer. The intelligence links of Tony Blair's New Labour faction, which took over the party in the 1990s, were tighter still. With friends like these, the opportunities for manipulating Labour politicians have plainly been many and varied.[36]

By the time of the Scargill Affair in 1990, Neil Kinnock had spent seven years straining to shift the labour movement to the right and was widely considered by the pundits and spin-doctors to be in with a good chance of forming the next government. Kinnock loathed Scargill. The mutual hostility between the two men dated back to before either Kinnock's election as Labour leader or Scargill's as NUM president. At Labour's watershed conference in 1981, where Kinnock and his supporters swung the vote narrowly against Tony Benn's bid for the deputy leadership of the party, he and Scargill almost came to blows in a television studio after the ballot result was announced. But it was Scargill's leadership of the strike of 1984–5 that cemented Kinnock's obsession with the miners' president. As two pro-Kinnock journalists put it in the late 1980s: 'For the Labour Party, and for its leader especially, the strike had and will continue to have for many years an effect greater than any event since the war.' To Kinnock, Scargill and the miners' rebellion represented exactly the kind of politics he had broken with so dramatically three years earlier and which he was determined to see utterly marginalized under his stewardship of the party.[37]

The importance that Neil Kinnock attached to the place of the NUM and the miners' strike in his nine years as Labour leader was bizarrely illustrated in an interview he gave shortly after stepping down. He had two great regrets, he said. One was not to have pushed for electoral reform much sooner. The other was that he had failed to speak out in favour of a national ballot in the miners' strike. 'That was my private conviction ... but I should have voiced it publicly,' Kinnock confessed. 'I said it in 1985, but I said it months too late I guess.' The remark is particularly revealing of the scar left by the whole episode, because Kinnock did in fact call publicly for a ballot in the second month of the strike. Indeed, his view could scarcely have been more public, plastered as it was all over the front page of the *Daily Mirror* on 13 April 1984. 'Kinnock calls for a ballot', the headline read, next to a quotation from the Labour leader: 'It's the only way.'[38]

While among the party membership there was strong, active support for the strike right across Labour's political spectrum, Kinnock viewed it with horror. Even before the dispute began, he had described Scargill as the 'labour movement's nearest equivalent to a First World War general'. Despite Labour's official position of unequivocal backing for the strike, the Labour leader personally saw it as a diversion from his chosen path to electability and a threat to his own authority within the labour movement. While Labour Party membership rose steadily during the dispute and the Tories' opinion-poll standing was damaged as a result of their evident determination not to settle, Kinnock took every opportunity to distance himself from the fight-to-the-finish in the coalfields, avoiding picket lines and rallies where possible, arranging private press briefings against the miners' leaders, blocking parliamentary debates.[39]

At the Durham Miners' Gala in July 1984, Kinnock was publicly humiliated when three brass bands and most of a 100,000-strong crowd voted with their feet as he delivered a lukewarm speech. At the 1984 party conference, where the NUM leadership was given a tumultuous standing ovation, Kinnock could only work up passion for a condemnation of picket-line violence and a contemptuous comparison of the strike with the Charge of the Light Brigade. For Kinnock, having to be associated with the strike at all was – in the words of Hugo Young, Thatcher's biographer – a 'cruel embarrassment', and one he never forgot or forgave. In the leader's circles, it became known as 'Labour's lost year'. In the aftermath of the strike, he blamed Scargill's continued defiance for Labour's own electoral failure in the Brecon and Radnor parliamentary by-election. At the 1985 TUC and Labour conferences, Kinnock was defeated when he tried to block demands for the reinstatement of sacked miners and reimbursement of the NUM's fines by a future Labour government. But he used the Labour conference debate to launch a comprehensive denunciation of the strike and its leadership. Such frustrated outbursts would be repeated over the subsequent years whenever the opportunity presented itself.[40]

Kinnock's post-strike verbal laceration of Scargill had eerie echoes of an earlier Labour leadership's treatment of Arthur Cook, the miners' union secretary at the time of the 1926

General Strike and Scargill's original role model. Ramsay MacDonald, the then Labour leader, told Cook at the end of that year: 'In all my experience of trade-union leadership ... I have never known one so incompetent as yourself.' Philip Snowden, another senior Labour frontbencher, wrote in the press shortly after the miners' return to work that Cook had wrecked his union and 'given to the mineowners a power they have never before possessed, given the Conservative government an excuse for lengthening hours and making a general attack on trade-union rights'. Almost sixty years later, Kinnock would make a strikingly similar attack on Cook's political successor, accusing Scargill of having 'left the management of the National Coal Board with a power, a prerogative, a force that no mining management in Britain has enjoyed for one day since 1947'.[41]

At the time of his Scargill 'revelations' in 1990, Robert Maxwell was naturally anxious to be seen as a reliable ally of the possible future Prime Minister. 'He imagined,' Greenslade says, 'that he would have a key role to play in the event of the party assuming power.' On the first day of the *Mirror*'s campaign against the NUM leadership, the corrupt press baron declared: 'I'm happy to give Kinnock first place. I'm very pleased to have been a supporter of the line.' Maxwell's links with Labour were, of course, longstanding and extensive. It was not so much a question of his personal politics, whatever the tycoon may have said about being a socialist. It was simply that, given his background and business history, 'the Tories wouldn't have had him', in the words of Anne Dove, his secretary for many years.[42]

Maxwell first stood as a Labour parliamentary candidate for North Buckinghamshire in 1959 and was subsequently elected a Labour MP in 1964. Needless to say, Maxwell made a splash in his Home Counties constituency. The young David Hart, who would later work closely with Thatcher, MacGregor and MI5 during the miners' strike, even made a film of his election campaign. Maxwell let it be known to all and sundry that he was looking to become Prime Minister in due course. But to his intense disappointment and despite the assiduous cultivation of powerful Labour politicians like Hugh Gaitskell, George Brown and Dick Crossman, the flamboyant publisher's parliamentary career was not a success. Maxwell lost Buckinghamshire in 1970, his relationship with the local party quickly degenerated, and his behaviour was censured in an internal national Labour Party report. Reselected in the teeth of local opposition, he failed to recapture the seat in the two elections of 1974. Although he continued to try unsuccessfully for other seats, Maxwell had to be content with less conventional ways of making his presence felt in the Labour Party.[43]

Kinnock initially opposed the former MP's takeover of the *Mirror*. The paper was understandably considered vital to the party's interests; its readership the bedrock of Labour support. And Maxwell was not trusted. But the Labour leader was prevailed upon to back off by his predecessor, Michael Foot, and deputy, Roy Hattersley, who had a better relationship with the multimillionaire. Hattersley was a friend of Charles Williams, a Labour peer and chairman of Ansbachers, Maxwell's first merchant bankers. But the former Labour Cabinet minister's main reasoning was more straightforward: there was nothing to be done about the buyout and it would be as well to keep Maxwell sweet. Hattersley's confidence in the media mogul would in time prove to be well placed from the Labour leadership's point of view. Under Maxwell's ownership, the *Mirror* not only never deviated from its traditional support for the Labour right, but it became progressively more sycophantic to the hierarchy as time passed. 'Maxwell saw the *Mirror* as simply a Labour Party organ that should publish smiling pictures of Neil Kinnock and laudatory articles,' Pilger comments. 'Before Maxwell, the *Mirror* never used to do that.'[44]

Maxwell also provided some financial support to a party with a notable lack of wealthy backers. On one occasion, he made a dramatic £31,000 donation from the floor of the party conference; on another, Maxwell came up with £38,000 for a High Court case against Boundary Commission recommendations which stood to deprive Labour of around thirty safe Commons seats. At the same time, the publishing tycoon gathered around him a retinue of fading Labour luminaries whose former access to government appeared to make up in some small way for his own lack of political preferment. There was Sir Tom McCaffrey, Jim Callaghan's former press secretary; Peter Jay, Callaghan's son-in-law and former Washington ambassador; Charles Williams, Labour's deputy leader in the Lords; Nick Grant, Labour's former communications director; and the ever-loyal Joe Haines.[45]

Kinnock, on the other hand, preferred to deal with Alastair Campbell, then the *Mirror*'s political editor, as his main link to the paper. The Labour leader's personal relationship with Maxwell was correct, but cool. Glenys Kinnock, his wife, could not abide the man, though both Kinnock children were briefly employed by Maxwell on his weekly paper, the *European*. Business is, nevertheless, business. Roy Greenslade recounts a grotesque scene he observed at the 1990 Labour Party conference in Blackpool, shortly after the *Mirror*'s Scargill campaign had finally run into the sand. Maxwell the Godfather was approached about the forthcoming general election by Jack Cunningham, the front-bench MP and campaign coordinator, and Larry Whitty, Labour's general secretary. 'You have my full support,' said the tycoon. 'Now what can I do to help?' There was talk of fax machines and transport. Then Cunningham blurted out: 'What about your helicopter?' An embarrassed silence descended on the gathering. The request was considered bad form. You must not ask for the helicopter – you must be given the helicopter. To be asked for his toys spoilt the rich man's pleasure in giving.[46]

The annual Maxwell Labour conference receptions had anyway by this time become something of an ordeal for members of the Labour front bench, largely because of the fallout from a small-scale but persistent industrial dispute which followed him to his death. In the spring of 1989, Maxwell sacked twenty-three members of the National Union of Journalists at Pergamon, his Oxford publishing base, for going on strike. By the autumn of the following year, the strikers had still not been reinstated and Kinnock had to be smuggled in by the back door of the thinly attended Maxwell jamboree to avoid the pickets.

The Pergamon 23 conducted a highly effective campaign of industrial guerrilla warfare, dogging Maxwell's every move with demonstrations and bad publicity. By the end of his life, the Labour Party apparatus was having to resort to ever more transparent manoeuvres to prevent the *Mirror* proprietor from being expelled from the party.[47]

Maxwell's use of the *Mirror* to wage vendettas inside the labour movement is well illustrated by the treatment meted out to George Galloway in the mid 1980s. The satirical magazine *Private Eye* published a story in the summer of 1985 alleging that Maxwell had paid for Neil Kinnock's travel expenses on a trip to Africa in the hope of acquiring a peerage. The source of the story – though it was never revealed at the time – was Galloway, then general secretary of the radical charity War on Want. Galloway says he was told about the financing of the trip by a friend working in Kinnock's office. The magazine added the twist about the peerage. Maxwell sued and won. By itself, the peerage line was plausible. It was, after all, effectively in Kinnock's gift and it seemed logical – without any suggestion of trading in honours – after the appointment to the Lords the year before of the Maxwell employees Charles Williams, Bernard Donoughue and Sam Silkin. Indeed, Hattersley had asked Maxwell directly whether he would like to join them in the unelected upper house. The Labour deputy leader later insisted this had been a joke.[48]

But the *Eye*'s informant could not appear in court. And Maxwell put on a devastating performance in the witness box over other unrelated *Private Eye* attacks on him and his wife, weeping as he spoke about the murder of his family in the Nazi Holocaust. Although he was not named in court, it became obvious to Maxwell and Kinnock that Galloway was the culprit. Both would wreak their revenge. Kinnock never spoke again to Galloway, who had previously been something of a protégé, visiting the Kinnocks at home and speaking at a meeting in the Labour leader's constituency. As a result of the *Eye* story, Galloway's rapid rise in Kinnock's Labour Party came to an abrupt end. But Maxwell – who had been the real object of the leak –

would prove to be an even more dangerous enemy.

David Seymour, a *Mirror* leader-writer at the time, was present when Joe Haines rang the then secretary of the Scottish Labour Party, Helen Liddell – who later became a Mirror Group director, an MP and then a member of the House of Lords – to ask whether she had seen the *Private Eye* story. According to Seymour, Haines told her that 'Galloway was responsible and that they wanted anything they could get on him'. Some time later, a stream of stories began to appear in the *Mirror* – whether from Liddell or other sources – about the size of Galloway's expenses claims and the internal political ructions at War on Want. Maxwell had already made clear his dislike of Galloway's support for the Palestinian cause when they both appeared on the BBC television programme *Question Time*, during the miners' strike a few months earlier. 'Ah, Mr Galway, the PLO man,' he had boomed, on being introduced. Now, Maxwell's papers – and, in particular, the Scottish *Daily Record* and *Sunday Mail* – would be mobilized to teach the upstart a lesson. Galloway was savaged as a fellow-traveller of Middle-Eastern and Irish terrorists who had dishonestly abused his position at War on Want. He was given the full tabloid treatment, culminating in the mandatory sex spinoff. Maxwell's reporters offered money to his girlfriend, posed as tax inspectors, and took photographs of the inside of his bedroom from the upper branches of an overhanging tree. Two investigations into the War on Want scandal, by the Charity Commission and independent auditors, later cleared Galloway of any dishonesty or bad faith. But by then, Maxwell had achieved his purpose.[49]

When it came to the far more ambitious assault on Scargill, Kinnock formally kept his distance, but made absolutely clear that this was a settling of accounts that had his blessing. Roy Greenslade insisted when he was still *Mirror* editor that Kinnock had been unaware of the allegations until two days before they were published. But the claim made little sense, not least because his two closest parliamentary lieutenants with coal-mining connections, Kim Howells and Kevin Barron, had both appeared on film in the two *Cook Report* programmes and been extensively quoted in the *Mirror* stories. Two other Kinnock supporters, David Blunkett and Richard Caborn, had also been interviewed on the first Cook programme. And the impending attack was the subject of widespread speculation in both Fleet Street and union circles.

Terry Pattinson says that Joe Haines told him he 'tipped off' Kinnock about the impending avalanche of 'revelations' a couple of days before the onslaught began. But Greenslade remembers that the Labour leader already knew all about them when he first arrived to take over the editorship at the beginning of February.

> Alastair Campbell told me Neil Kinnock was already fully informed and was neutral on the subject – in other words, he wanted to see it in print. He wasn't neutral in reality. The Labour hierarchy enjoyed Arthur's discomfiture. It seemed to justify their hostility to the strike.

There was certainly no question of the Labour leader warning Scargill about the allegations in advance. On the first day of the campaign, Kinnock immediately stepped in to make a carefully worded call for an inquiry. His flunkeys were despatched to brief the slavering press with the appropriate spin. 'There was no collusion', a Labour Party 'source' was quoted as saying. 'But Neil Kinnock will not have lost any sleep over what happened last week. The NUM strike was a major diversion and probably set back the Kinnock project to reform the Labour Party by a year or eighteen months. It made Neil unforgiving of Arthur Scargill.'[50]

But what really gave the Maxwell-funded campaign against Scargill and Heathfield the stamp of Kinnock's authority was the close involvement at all stages of Barron and Howells. There can be no question that they had the full backing of the Labour leader. Theirs was the role of Greek chorus in the Scargill Affair, ready to add the authentic voice of the Westminster collier whenever the campaign showed any signs of flagging or letting the main target off the hook. Barron is an ex-miner from

Yorkshire, who was a supporter of the Trotskyist Militant Tendency as a student at Ruskin College in the early 1970s. He was also Scargill's campaign manager in South Yorkshire during his presidential election campaign in 1981. Howells is a former student activist and one-time Communist Party member who cut his political teeth in the celebrated Hornsey Art College occupation of 1968 and later went to work as a research officer for the South Wales area of the NUM, where he became press spokesman during the 1984–5 strike.

Both Barron and Howells were politicians whose political advancement owed everything to Neil Kinnock's patronage. Both were one-time would-be revolutionaries who had been busy working their passage back to labour-movement respectability throughout the second half of the 1980s. Both, for example – and unusually for left-wingers of their vintage – became involved with pro-Israel lobbying efforts. Barron spent a week in Israel and the occupied territories in January 1990, sponsored by Labour Friends of Israel; Howells went the following year on an Israeli government-funded trip and later became president of Labour Friends of Israel. Both fell from political favour after Kinnock's resignation, but later clawed their way back to junior front-bench jobs. And both were enthusiastic supporters of Tony Blair's successful bid to become Labour leader after John Smith's death.[51]

Howells began the miners' strike with a reputation as a militant trade unionist – not least because of his role in supporting spontaneous industrial action by South Wales miners in 1981, which helped force Thatcher's temporary retreat on pit closures. In late 1983, Howells still felt able to write a reverential letter to the NUM president, praising Scargill's 'excellent contribution' at a rank-and-file miners' school and signing off with the words: 'remember that you always have our full support'. Such touching commitment was not to last. Howells became the first NUM employee – if a rather lowly one – to break ranks and publicly float the idea of a return to work without a settlement in the final months of the 1984–5 strike. He argued for a united, organized end to the strike, against the risk of an ignominious collapse. The move, which had been secretly planned by a small group in South Wales and backed by Kinnock and the CPGB's Euro-communist faction, created a snowball effect in the NUM and rapidly led to the narrow conference vote to call off the stoppage.

But the decision to go back to work without a settlement was strongly resented among many striking miners, not least in South Wales. They regarded it, at best, as a tactical blunder. Tyrone O'Sullivan – the NUM's South Wales area president and lodge secretary at Tower colliery, the last publicly owned mine in the valleys, and the only British coal pit to be sold to its former workforce in the 1994 privatization package – recalls: 'We didn't want to go back at the end of the strike. I think we could have got a better deal. The Board's figures on the numbers working were never right. At least we could have had a settlement for the boys who were sacked.' It is also now clear that a return to work without a settlement was exactly what the Prime Minister and her most hardline advisers were intent on achieving throughout the latter stages of the strike. David Hart, who organized and financed the National Working Miners' Committee and was named by Tam Dalyell in parliament as having worked closely with MI5 during the strike, constantly lobbied Thatcher and MacGregor not to settle and to make sure the miners went back 'without a deal'.[52]

Kim Howells' call for a return to work led to a ferocious row on the telephone with Scargill. But it also made his name and his political career. Howells had been deeply involved in organizing picketing – including some of the more clandestine operations – during the strike in South Wales. Looking back, he cites the killing of the taxi driver, who had been taking strikebreakers to work, in early 1985 as a key factor in his decision to push for an end to the dispute. Howells remembers running to the NUM area office in Pontypridd as soon as he heard the news and 'just getting every bit of picketing information that we had and shredding it' in the expectation of a visit from the police. 'It changed me, that moment,' he says. O'Sullivan, who was close to him in the early 1980s, has his own explanation of

Howells' behaviour: 'Kim Howells is a chameleon. He can be anything he wants to be. But he was hated in the pits after the strike. He was an unelected officer and had no mandate to say we were going back to work.'[53]

Hated or not, Howells prospered. He became Scargill's most outspoken and articulate critic in the NUM's ranks and established a close working relationship with Kinnock. South Wales had emerged as a key dissident area inside the union and provided the ideal vehicle for Kinnock, a Welsh MP himself, to bolster opposition to Scargill from within the organization. Howells wrote position papers for the Labour leader on the NUM and the coal industry and became Kinnock's unofficial speechwriter. It was Howells, for example, who helped draft Kinnock's most vituperative attacks on Scargill and the Militant-led Liverpool council at Labour's annual conference in the autumn of 1985. 'I also worked with Neil on reformulating Labour's industrial policy,' Howells recalls. He basked in his new-found popularity among Labour loyalist circles as a result of Kinnock's seal of approval and in 1989 was elected MP for Pontypridd with the leader's backing.[54]

Kevin Barron was a less colourful figure. He started his parliamentary career six years earlier in the left-wing Campaign Group of Labour MPs, but his 'turn to the leader' almost exactly coincided with that of his political twin from South Wales. Unlike Howells, however, Barron had never uttered a squeak of criticism of the NUM leadership during the strike. On the contrary, he appeared to be the ultimate union loyalist and even had his arm broken by police for his pains on the picket line outside Maltby, his old pit. Ironically, during the furore that followed Roger Windsor's visit to Libya during the 1984–5 strike, Barron had been one of the few to speak out publicly in support of accepting cash aid from Libya, and he sharply criticized Kinnock's condemnation of the Tripoli government as a 'vile regime'.[55]

But in the wake of the strike, Barron moved on to richer pastures. In October 1985, he abruptly resigned from the Campaign Group in a blaze of media glory, accusing his former comrades of being an 'anti-leadership group' and grumbling about their support for an amnesty for miners victimized by the Coal Board during and after the strike. Within two weeks, Neil Kinnock had rewarded him handsomely. The one-time Scargillite and NUM-sponsored MP became the leader's own parliamentary private secretary. Wiping away the dust of his former political incarnation, Barron promptly sacked his assistant – she was, apparently, too left-wing for his new patron – and was in due course promoted to be Labour's shadow coal minister. His impact in the job was slight. But when the campaign against the miners' leaders began, Barron was ideally placed to do his master's bidding. He was in the unique position of being not only Labour's coal spokesman, but also by chance that year's chair of the miners' group of MPs and therefore entitled to attend the NUM executive ex-officio. Throughout the Scargill Affair, he used this platform to the full, regularly giving television and radio interviews outside NUM headquarters after every executive meeting, egging on the media, the lawyers and the NUM opposition to go for the kill.[56]

Both he and Howells were ready whenever necessary to provide a Labour face for the media campaign, pressing for legal and police action against Scargill and Heathfield at every turn. But while Howells appeared to lose interest as the original allegation of embezzlement fell apart and the saga rumbled on through the summer of 1990, Barron became ever more persistent. He even took at one point to selling cut-price copies of the Lightman Report to MPs from his Westminster office – in defiance of union decisions – and continued to call for Scargill's resignation after the NUM had settled its dispute with the IMO and dropped its legal action over the contested Soviet and East European cash in September 1990.[57]

There would be a price to pay. Barron was censured the same month for his role in the scandal by the NUM's Yorkshire area. At the NUM special conference on the Lightman Report a month later, both he and Howells were damned by delegates for 'abusing their positions'. After the conference, Barron faxed the details of the union's decision to sue Gavin Lightman to the QC's London office and later discussed it with a member of Lightman's chambers. When the documents surfaced the following year, a complaint from the Yorkshire area led to a disciplinary hearing and Barron was expelled from the union in the summer of 1992. His insistence that he had 'merely confirmed what was in the national press' to Lightman's office the following day – in contradiction of the documentary evidence – clinched his fate. The expulsion meant the loss of the MP's NUM sponsorship, worth up to £15,000 a year. Barron said he had 'no regrets' and had anyway decided not to seek further backing from the NUM.[58]

Howells, whose NUM sponsorship had been withdrawn after he won the Pontypridd nomination against the official South Wales NUM candidate, ended up somewhat more conciliatory. In 1990, he had been the first to call for a Fraud Squad investigation, but three years later his tune had changed somewhat.

> There were no hands in the till – I would never accuse the guy [Scargill] of corruption. The issue was secrecy, the obsession with secrecy, Big Daddy knows best. That's what put our nose out of joint. The whole thing died a death. It was up to the boys whether they accepted the explanation or not – and they did.

The South Wales MP still maintained a certain loyalty, however, to the fallen press baron, even beyond the grave. Howells put down a Commons motion two weeks after Maxwell's death, for example, denouncing the Tory MP Rupert Allason for his persistent allegations about Maxwell's links with Mossad and the arms-trade contacts cultivated by Nick Davies, the *Mirror*'s former foreign editor.[59]

The Labour leader would, for his part, be unrelenting in his determination not to miss any opportunity to show his public contempt for the NUM leadership. Even after the *Mirror*'s central allegations had been widely acknowledged to be wrong – and a special conference of the NUM, a Labour affiliate, had by a large majority rejected the *Mirror*'s attacks and endorsed its leaders' actions – a grinning Kinnock nevertheless presented the British Press Awards' 'Reporter of the Year' prize to the *Mirror* team responsible for the anti-Scargill campaign. The facts, it seemed, were less important than the target, either for the Labour hierarchy or the newspaper executives who picked the BPA award winners. The Labour leader even had himself photographed in a line-up with Terry Pattinson, Frank Thorne and Ted Oliver. The picture takes pride of place on the wall of Pattinson's home in the West London suburb of Staines. Pattinson regards the award as the 'supreme accolade in journalism' – so great an accolade, in fact, that he had to be ordered to share the prize money with his two fellow reporters. 'It was my little bit of mischief,' he says. 'Those guys hijacked my story.'[60]

Kinnock's continuing unapologetic identification with the discredited *Mirror* campaign and the British Press Awards prize caused apoplexy in the NUM. The union's 1991 conference at the Blackpool Winter Gardens was the occasion for an out-pouring of rage at Kinnock's support for the previous year's onslaught. In his presidential address, Scargill – who was well aware of the continuing leaks from inside the security services – declared that the 'media hysteria against Peter Heathfield and myself sprang from an operation to destroy us'. Launching his most ferocious attack to date on Labour's leadership, Scargill then delivered a contemptuous parody of Kinnock's denunciation of the Militant-led Liverpool council – widely seen as the man's finest hour, inspired by Howells and used in Labour's 1987 general election broadcasts. 'Policies such as nationalization and unilateralism are ditched along the way, whilst the EEC and the City of London are courted,' Scargill declared, echoing Kinnock's rhetoric. 'And, finally, you end up with the grotesque spectacle of a Labour leader, a Labour leader, supporting privatization in Liverpool.'

The following day, as Kinnock addressed the Transport and General Workers' Union conference next door, the NUM delegates unanimously voted to condemn the Labour leader for presenting the BPA award to the *Daily Mirror* journalists. The resolution recorded the union's 'profound disgust' at Kinnock's association with a 'disgraceful smear campaign'. Ken Capstick, vice-president of the Yorkshire area, moving the resolution, said the Labour leader had brought 'shame on the office to which he was elected'. The Labour establishment would take its revenge for this unprecedented lashing from a Labour-affiliated union. Tom Sawyer, that year's Labour Party chair and a close Kinnock ally, made an instant, barely coded response to Scargill in his 'fraternal address' to the NUM conference later in the day, when he self-consciously used the same phrase with which Thatcher had branded the union seven years earlier. Referring to a recent by-election at Walton on Merseyside, where Labour had beaten a Militant candidate standing independently for the first time, Sawyer remarked to angry heckling: 'We didn't just defeat the enemy without, we defeated the enemy within.'[61]

Punishment was meted out swiftly to a union that was once the cornerstone of every Labour leader's power base. Longstanding NUM nominees were methodically removed from the most anodyne party committees. But the most dramatic signal that the NUM was now regarded as utterly beyond the pale came in the autumn, when a by-election was called in the safe Labour mining seat of Hemsworth in Yorkshire. Capstick, born and bred in the constituency, was the local favourite, with overwhelming support from both trade-union and local party branches. But a Labour national-executive panel led by Roy Hattersley struck Capstick off the shortlist – claiming, absurdly, that he had an insufficient record of party activity – and levered a Kinnock placeman into the seat instead. Labour's team of whispering spin-doctors quickly let it be known that the cautious Capstick's real crime was 'Scargillism'.[62]

Two weeks later, Robert Maxwell was dead. And the following spring Neil Kinnock's New Model Labour Party went down to humiliating defeat at the 1992 general election. Scargill once again tried to persuade the Mineworkers' Pension Scheme to buy the Mirror Group – as he had when he was first elected NUM president in 1982, well before Maxwell took over. The *Mirror* itself finally seemed to lose interest in its long-running campaign to oust the miners' leader. Terry Pattinson's completed full-length book on the Scargill Affair, which had been due to be published by a Maxwell-owned outfit, Macdonald Futura, was hurriedly abandoned as soon as the tycoon was safely buried on the Mount of Olives. Pattinson and Frank Thorne were later both sacked by the new *Mirror* management, and Thorne went to work for the *Cook Report*.[63]

In the wake of John Smith's election in 1992, the Labour leadership's vendetta against the miners' union was also quietly dropped. Even if there would be little enthusiasm for the NUM during the pit-closures crisis of 1992–3, protocol was at least observed. Howells temporarily returned to his preferred role of maverick dissident, with an attack on the unseemly haste and manner of the new leader's takeover. Nevertheless, he managed to secure a front-bench job as a foreign-affairs and overseas-development spokesman before Smith died. Howells later ended up as a maverick free-marketeering minister in Tony Blair's governments – on one occasion having himself photographed in Colombia with a general linked to paramilitary death squads and an army unit accused of killing and torturing trade unionists. Barron, even more closely identified with Kinnock's *ancien régime*, was unceremoniously sacked as Labour's coal spokesman, just as the rundown of Britain's coal industry was to become for a time the most important issue in British politics – though he subsequently returned as a junior member of the employment team and, along with the former Maxwell executive Helen Liddell, played an enthusiastic role in Tony Blair's 1994–5 campaign to drop Labour's 'Clause Four' commitment to common ownership. Passed over for office by Blair, he was nevertheless trusted enough to be appointed by the Prime Minister to parliament's intelligence and security committee – as was Howells, who became its chair. Both men were made privy councillors. In the wake of his earlier sacking, one prominent 'soft left' Labour MP and shadow cabinet member was heard complaining to journalists how unfairly Barron had been treated in view of 'all he had done for the party' over Scargill and the NUM.[64]

# CHAPTER SIX

# MOSCOW GOLD-DIGGERS

When we are victorious on a world scale I think we shall use gold for the purpose of building public lavatories ... meanwhile, when you live among wolves, you must howl like a wolf. *V. I. Lenin, 1921*[1]

For more than seventy years, whenever the natives grew restless and demands for political change looked like getting out of hand, establishment propagandists the world over liked to play the Russian card. Just as two hundred years ago, democrats and radicals were routinely denounced as French agents, so socialists and communists were for the greater part of the twentieth century tarred with a Russophile brush. From the MI5-forged Zinoviev letter of 1924 – which helped bring down the first Labour government – to the West European strike wave of the late 1940s, from the anti-colonial struggles of the postwar years to the 1980s peace movement, the hand of Moscow was always discovered by the powers-that-be in the nick of time if other arguments began to wear a little thin.

So it was with the Scargill Affair. When the main allegations of embezzlement had been disproved and the melodrama of the Libyan connection had run out of steam, Russian roubles were brought energetically into play. This was only to be expected. Moscow Gold was after all a party-piece which was bound to take its place of right in such a comprehensive attack on a troublesome labour-movement leader. But this was a tale of Eastern-bloc meddling with a difference. What set the Soviet dimension of the anti-Scargill campaign apart from every other piece of red-baiting since the Russian Revolution itself was that the Moscow authorities themselves – or at least some sections of them – were for the first time actually accomplices in an anti-Soviet smear. This was something altogether new. The surrealism went further. In the past, the suspected *delivery* of Moscow Gold had always been the focus of scandal for the Western media. But in this case, the exact opposite was the case. It was the *failure* to deliver the tainted cash that was the cause of all the trouble. And for many months, the British press, the Fraud Squad, pillars of the Labour establishment – and, as it appeared for a time, a significant proportion of the country's legal and accountancy profession – threw their weight behind the outraged complaint that secret Soviet funding had never materialized and that the lost treasure should be brought to Britain immediately.

## THE RUSSIANS AND THE GENERAL STRIKE

In the real world, practical solidarity between British miners and Soviet workers had a long pedigree which, unusually, survived the battering of the Cold War. Quite apart from the well-established Soviet link, the miners' union maintained for more than a century the strongest internationalist tradition of any in the British labour movement. After the First World War, when capitalist governments tottered throughout Europe in the face of a revolutionary tide, the Miners' Federation of Great Britain – forerunner of the NUM – played a central role in the 'Hands Off Russia' campaign, the movement set up to halt armed British intervention against the infant Soviet state. And the miners were a dominant voice in the Councils of Action which finally forced Lloyd George to back down from all-out war against the Bolsheviks in August 1920.[2]

Such effective solidarity was not forgotten in the East. During the nine-day General Strike of 1926 and the six-month lockout in the pits that it was called to defeat, impoverished Soviet workers collected tens of millions of roubles to keep the miners' resistance alive. Soviet trade unions and cooperatives donated a total of £1,161,459 to the Miners' Relief Fund in 1926 – more than all the money collected in Britain and the rest of the world put together. Some Soviet factories repeatedly voted to give up a day's pay for the British miners. Contemporary eyewitness accounts make nonsense of British establishment propaganda claims of the time that these were forced loans and collections. Miniature flags depicting miners and their families were sold on Soviet street corners to raise cash. Women collected clothes and set up sewing circles. One veteran Soviet activist, Valentina Yendakov, recalled at the time of the 1984–5 coal strike how, as a young girl, she had stood in the streets of Minsk nearly sixty years earlier collecting money for the British miners.[3]

George Lansbury, the future Labour Party leader, visited Russia during 1926 and declared Soviet trade-union backing for the British miners 'the finest exhibition of class solidarity the world has ever seen'. There was little need for hyperbole. A lifetime later, the Soviet solidarity campaign of 1926 still ranks on a par with the worldwide campaigns on behalf of the Spanish republic in the 1930s (when hundreds of British miners fought for the International Brigade), the international support for the Vietnamese people during the war with the United States and the global boycott movement against South African apartheid – or, in the nineteenth century, the mobilization of Lancashire cotton workers behind the struggle against slavery at the time of the American Civil War, in spite of the mass unemployment the conflict brought.

But, in a parallel with what would happen during and after the 1984–5 strike, Soviet solidarity with Britain's miners in 1926 was seized on by the Tory government of Stanley Baldwin to vilify the miners' union and its leadership. At the same time, the link-up was exploited by the right wing of the labour movement both at home and abroad to justify their lack of support for, or sabotage of, the miners' resistance. As soon as the British TUC called the General Strike on 4 May 1926 in support of the miners, the Soviet trade unions imposed an embargo on all sea freight bound for British ports. Throughout the lockout, no Soviet oil or coal was exported to Britain. Within three days, £30,000 was despatched to London. But in deference to the chorus of Moscow Gold taunts from press and politicians, the TUC returned the cheque. When the Soviet All-Union Central Council of Trade Unions (AUCCTU) then offered the rejected cash to the miners, the response was very different. A. J. Cook, the MFGB leader, wired back: 'The British miners are in desperate need of it.' Tory ministers were apoplectic, claiming the money really came from the Soviet government, and – in another forerunner of what would happen in 1984 – protested to the Soviet authorities at the financial support for the strike, which was described as 'a menace to the established order in Great Britain'. Social-democratic trade-union leaders in Weimar Germany, meanwhile, invoked Soviet cash aid as an excuse for sanctioning the export of strikebreaking coal to Britain.[4]

Nevertheless, the huge scale of Soviet support and the large number of miners who visited the Soviet Union during the period helped put down the roots of communist influence in the British coalfields. The impact was strongest in Scotland and South Wales, which came to provide a string of outstanding miners' leaders and where pit villages like Maerdy in the Rhondda Valley earned the nickname of 'Little Moscow'. But the politicization was felt throughout the union. In the long run, it would be one of the factors which laid the ground for renewed radicalization in the 1960s. That in turn led to the NUM's strike victories in 1972 and 1974 and the eventual election of a left-wing union leadership at the beginning of the following decade.

## THE NEW INTERNATIONAL

The rise of the militant left in the NUM during the 1960s and 1970s brought about a revival of the union's internationalist traditions and led inexorably to confrontation with the Cold War placemen who dominated the Miners' International Federation, the pro-Western outfit to which the NUM was then affiliated. The MIF had started life in 1890 with high hopes of directly coordinating miners' action for better pay and conditions – as well as for more far-reaching social change – on an international scale. It was a time of labour-movement advance throughout the industrial world, the founding of the Socialist International (the 'Second International'), and the dedication of May Day as a day of workers' celebration and struggle. A start was made with mutual financial backing for MIF affiliates' disputes and a wave of synchronized coal strikes in Britain, France and Germany in the spring of 1912. But the promise of all the new workers' international organizations, both political and industrial, was dashed in the chauvinism of the First World War and the anti-Bolshevik hysteria of the interwar years.

In the aftermath of the 1945 allied victory against fascism, there were high hopes that a new generation of trade-union internationals could bring together all genuine unions across the political divide. Thus was born the World Federation of Trade Unions, with the crucial and unprecedented participation of both Soviet and Western union centres. But the new-found unity was short-lived. The United States-inspired split from the WFTU in the late 1940s and the foundation of the anti-communist International Confederation of Free Trade Unions (ICFTU) ensured that what would now be two rival trade-union camps would both end up primarily as the ideological labour-movement arms of the Cold War blocs, rather than genuine coordinating centres for international trade-union action. The MIF remained technically independent of the ICFTU and never plumbed the depths reached by some of the ICFTU's satellite organizations. But it played its less-than-glorious part in fighting the growth of militant and communist-led unions in Southern Europe and the Third World, often using funds provided by Western governments.

By the late 1970s, the leftward-moving NUM leadership was arguing for a tougher stand against the increasingly aggressive mining-industry employers. The union also wanted closer links with Soviet and East European miners as a step towards greater control of the world's energy resources. Surprisingly, the idea of a united international miners' organization was backed by Joe Gormley, Scargill's right-wing predecessor as NUM president. But the British miners' approach met a wall of hostility from the anti-communist clique that controlled the MIF. The leaders of the West German miners' union, IG Bergbau, who had been content to preside over a rapid, but 'managed', pit-closure programme in Europe's most successful capitalist economy, felt particularly threatened. In Britain, once the Thatcher government was elected in 1979, no such option was any longer open to the NUM, even if it had wanted to pursue it.

A year before the 1984–5 British coal strike began, the NUM and the French CGT miners' union – excluded from the MIF on account of its communist leadership and WFTU links – called a conference to discuss the creation of a single miners' international. The aim was to unite trade unions from East and West. Like-minded mining unions from the MIF, such as the Australians, as well as East European and Latin American unions from the WFTU miners' organization, the Miners' Trade Union International (MTUI), sent delegations. The 44th congress of the MIF met the following month, May 1983, at Essen in West Germany. The NUM's proposal for the creation of one miners' international was on the table. Many of the representatives from MIF affiliates at the conference owed their positions to their anti-communist credentials. On his home turf, Adolf Schmidt, the deeply reactionary president of both the German miners' union and the MIF, denounced the new British NUM leader to the congress in the manner of a judicial indictment.

'You, Arthur Scargill, are forming an alliance with communist trade unions,' declared Schmidt – a man who in his younger days had been both a Hitler Youth activist and a wartime U-boat commander. 'You are placing yourself under the orders of other parties. You will not gain anything, but you will lose what we have guarded for many years.' In a ritual exorcism of the heretic – and a flagrant breach of the MIF's own rules and constitution – the NUM was deprived of speaking and voting rights and Scargill drowned out by table-banging when he tried to speak from the rostrum. The British and Australian delegations walked out, determined to create a new, non-sectarian organization.[5]

This was the climate in the international trade-union movement faced by the striking British miners when they set out to win material solidarity for their stoppage in 1984–5. The foundation of the new body – the International Miners' Organization – would be delayed because of the strike and the overtime ban which preceded it. When the IMO was finally established in Paris in September 1985, it was greeted with immediate calls from the US-financed Force Ouvrière for its expulsion from France. But the aggression which surrounded the new international's birth pangs would prove to be small beer compared with the obloquy that was heaped on the organization five years later.[6]

## STRIKE WITHOUT FRONTIERS

The 1984–5 miners' strike attracted international support in a way that no other industrial dispute has done anywhere in the world since the Second World War. Strikers travelled to all corners of the globe to put the miners' case, build solidarity and coordinate material support. Money, food, clothes and children's toys were collected in every continent to sustain the British miners. The greatest practical contribution to the strike effort was made by the French CGT and the Australian miners and seafarers. The CGT, which had excellent relations with the NUM leadership, threw itself into solidarity action with the British miners. The left-wing NUM Kent area – now defunct because of the closure of the Kent coalfield – had long had close links with the CGT miners of northern France. The British miners' fight struck a chord with the left in France, where the Mitterrand government had just abandoned its radical programme and was forcing through mass redundancies in coal and other traditional industries.

French solidarity was spectacular. On one occasion, CGT workers in Calais staged a 'commando action' by dumping thousands of tonnes of coal, due to be loaded for England, from train wagons at Calais. Several boats carrying coal to Britain were holed and sunk, using underwater barrages in the style of the wartime French resistance. Symbolic stoppages were staged in the surviving French coalfields. Large-scale collections for hardship relief were held throughout the country and holidays arranged for British miners' children. Two convoys of forty-odd lorries each were organized in the autumn and winter of 1984–5 to bring hardship relief and Christmas presents for the families of striking miners. With the NUM facing the seizure of its assets by the sequestrators and receiver, the CGT also became a major conduit of financial support to the besieged union. But the transfer of cash to Britain from France presented special difficulties because of French exchange-control regulations. Different methods were used to get round the problem. On one occasion in December 1984, forty CGT activists each brought around 15,000 francs (£1,500) stuffed into their clothes on the cross-channel ferry from Calais. In Dover, they took the cash to an arranged rendezvous with Jeff Apter, the English journalist who regularly acted as a translator at NUM-CGT meetings during the strike. He in turn handed the money over to Nell Myers, Scargill's assistant, and it was then taken up to York-shire by the NUM president's driver, Jim Parker.[7]

The CGT's unstinting support had a parallel in Australia. There, the Australian Miners' Federation and the seafarers' union threw themselves into enforcing a boycott of coal ship-ments to Britain, despite the difficulties in identifying ultimate destinations. Ships arriving in Brisbane to pick up cargoes of coking coal for Britain were not allowed to berth. So effective was the embargo that a British Steel director was forced to fly out to lobby the maritime unions to release the coal. Exports of steam coal to Britain from Australia's biggest coal-producing state, New South Wales, were slashed from 100,000–200,000 tonnes a month to only 3,000 tonnes in December 1984 – just as power-station demand in Britain reached its peak. At one point Bob Hawke, the then Australian Prime Minister, rang Scargill to plead with him to intercede with the Australian unions to have the embargo lifted. Thousands of Australian workers were laid off for supporting the boycott and their efforts were only matched by the action of railwaymen and seafarers in Britain itself.

Yet, despite the worldwide collections and agitation, the problem of imports of oil and coal remained intractable. Coal from West Germany, the United States and Poland – as well as trans-shipments of Australian, South African and Canadian coal through third countries such as Holland – helped to undermine the strike's effectiveness. Tiny ports all over the country were mobilized to unload coal imports away from the unwelcome attention of miners and Transport and General Workers' Union dockers. The massive use of imported oil, including from Libya, to offset reduced coal supplies to the power stations was even more damaging. But the claim by some critics of the new international, such as Kim Howells, that if the NUM had stayed in the MIF the West Germans and other Northern European mining unions might have taken action against coal exports to Britain cannot stand up to serious examination. The long-established habits and attitudes of the main European MIF unions – and the West German miners' leaders in particular – meant that there was no realistic prospect of organizations that were loath to take action for their own industry fighting for somebody else's.[8]

The stepping up of Polish coal exports to Britain, however, was another story and particularly galling for the NUM leadership. Scargill had attracted widespread condemnation in 1983 for his description of the Polish Solidarnosc union as an 'anti-socialist organization'. This was an assessment which in the light of later events seems unexceptionable. But at a time when the Western-backed opposition movement had been driven underground and renewed Cold War tensions were at their height, his remarks were treated as verging on the treasonable. The NUM leader nevertheless got small thanks in his union's hour of need from the rudderless Polish government, which took every advantage of the sharp increase in British demand for coal to boost its foreign-currency earnings. And with the exception of a handful of small left-wing groups, the Warsaw government had – in this respect at least – the support of Solidarnosc. Scargill and other NUM leaders protested furiously to the Polish Embassy.

'We have contracts to fulfil with British companies,' the ambassador explained with some embarrassment to the miners' delegation. 'You have a far more important contract with the international working class,' Scargill retorted, rejecting the lame substitute offer of holidays for striking miners. In fact, General Jaruzelski's martial-law administration – squeezed as it was between the relentless pressure of the Western banks for repayment of its foreign debt and the sullen resistance of large sections of its own population – was hardly in a position to do a great deal else. But, combined with the parallel increase in oil exports to Britain from Romania, Poland's strikebreaking export drive only served to emphasize the pass in which East-European-style socialism found itself by the mid 1980s.[9]

## MOSCOW GOLD RUSH

The Soviet Union was different – or, at least, so it appeared. As in the rest of Eastern Europe, Soviet media coverage of the British coal dispute was intensive and strongly sympathetic to the striking miners. Violent police attacks on NUM picket lines were regularly relayed in all their gory detail to tens of millions of Soviet television viewers. In the summer of 1984, one Soviet radio commentator even reported having seen a group of children playing British police and strikers in a Moscow courtyard. 'I was pleased to see the police were finding it rough going,' he added. But the Russians were prepared to go beyond propaganda. Whereas there was little effort in other parts of Eastern Europe to staunch the flow of strikebreaking fuel to Britain, all Soviet coal and oil shipments to the United Kingdom were halted in support of the strike. The decision to impose the embargo was taken in the wake of Scargill's meeting with Soviet diplomats in Paris on 8 October 1984 – the same day as the

NUM president's fateful meeting with the Libyan envoy, Salem Ibrahim. Admittedly, Soviet coal exports to Britain were on a puny scale compared with the well-established Polish trade, but oil exports – worth almost £500 million in 1983 (£1.4 billion at 2012 prices) – had been substantial.[10]

The Soviet miners' union also signed an agreement around the same time with the maritime fleet minister to suspend deliveries of fuel to Britain from third countries in Soviet ships – a move which, in view of the huge demand for oil to keep the power stations working, had a significant impact. Soviet vessels were also carrying Polish coal. For the Soviet Union, there was a potentially high political price to pay for such an embargo. This was a time when the Kremlin was becoming increasingly desperate to loosen the Western Cold War technology trade blockade against the USSR and its allies. The pressures were such that when Soviet miners' leaders publicly announced the boycott in the autumn, Nikolai Tikhonov, the Soviet Prime Minister, was wheeled out to deny 'rumours' that trade sanctions had been imposed for political purposes. In fact the embargo quietly continued. It was only relaxed, according to Soviet sources, in the final months of the strike – under direct pressure from the rising heir apparent to the party leadership: Mikhail Gorbachev.[11]

But in the summer and early autumn of 1984, the Soviet Coal Employees' Union – then getting on for two million strong – was still gung ho for the NUM. A campaign of solidarity rallies was organized throughout the Russian and Ukrainian coalfields to raise funds for the British strikers. The amount donated by each mineworker varied from area to area. In a few cases, miners worked an extra shift; in others, an agreed sum was simply deducted from wage packets. A total of 2.24 million roubles was collected, or an average of a little over one rouble per union member. These were, it should be said, modest donations and very far from Western propaganda claims of the time – later recycled during the Scargill Affair – that Soviet miners had been forced to dig deep into their pockets to finance their communist leaders' support for the miners' strike. Some

British press reports in 1990 even claimed that the Soviet miners had donated 100 million roubles – an exaggeration by a cool factor of 45. In 1984, the average Soviet wage was around 200 roubles a month. But miners were among the best-paid workers in the country, earning between 500 and 800 roubles a month for a basic six-hour shift, and the contributions would hardly have been noticed.[12]

There was no point in sending the cash to Britain, as roubles were then entirely nonconvertible and could only be spent in the USSR. So the money raised in the coalfields was channelled through a long-established solidarity agency, the 'Soviet Peace Fund', and used to provide a variety of benefits in kind for NUM strikers. Five hundred holidays in the Soviet Union, for example, were arranged for British miners and their families. NUM strikers attended all-expenses-paid courses at a Moscow trade-union training school. The forty-strong South Wales youth choir went on a Russian tour and young British miners were funded to participate in the World Youth Festival taking place in Moscow that year. A large part of the money was spent on two shiploads of food and clothing to relieve hardship in the British coalfields. The boats carrying the Soviet and East European aid, crewed by the Danish seafarers' union free of charge, arrived at Barry and Immingham on Humberside in October. But after the supplies were unloaded, they were refused entry clearance for their cargoes by British customs, supposedly because the Soviet side had failed to arrange a proper export licence. By agreement with the Soviet trade unions and the British Transport and General Workers' Union, the cargoes were reloaded and diverted to famine-blighted Ethiopia and Western-blockaded Vietnam.[13]

This sort of material aid was very welcome as far as it went. But from the early days of the strike, the NUM had been pressing the Soviet miners' union to provide cash support, insistently invoking the spirit of 1926. Scargill worked out that after allowing for inflation, the Soviet contribution of more than a million pounds to the British miners' struggle in the 1920s would be worth over £20 million in 1984 prices. Vernon Jones, the NUM's international officer, wrote to the Soviet miners' union as early as March 1984 – along with scores of other trade unions around the world – asking for donations to be paid to the Sheffield-based Miners' Solidarity Fund. This was the main hardship fund for striking miners and their families and was never touched or even threatened by the sequestrators or receiver. Money was raised for it both in Britain and all over the world, though nothing was contributed from the Soviet Union. But as the dispute wore on, the NUM leaders became increasingly anxious for financial backing for the running of the strike itself. In particular, they wanted cash to pay for the essential day-to-day expenses of the union organization, which, with the loss of all contributions income, had become a major headache. This was what they lobbied the Russians for – among others – from the summer onwards.

Soviet officials accepted relatively quickly that they had 'an obligation to help' and promised to transfer a substantial sum. Scargill, Heathfield and Mick McGahey, the 'troika' who led the strike, all met Soviet trade-unionists during 1984 to press the point, and there were regular contacts with Yuri Mazur, the Soviet labour attaché in London – who resurfaced in Dublin after the collapse of the Soviet state as a diplomat for Boris Yeltsin's Russian Federation. As the strike wore on and sequestration and receivership deprived the union of any access to its own funds whatever, the NUM officials' need for cash support to keep the national organization going – to 'sustain the fabric of the union', as they put it – became desperate. The troika were repeatedly assured that money would be forthcoming. But although the strike leaders came up with an ingenious array of different methods to disguise the transfer, money specifically earmarked for the NUM alone would never in the end be forthcoming – and the money that was sent never actually left the USSR until the strike was as good as over.[14]

Rumours and counter-rumours about Soviet financial backing for the British miners had been circulating long before the media campaign of 1990. Indeed, they became a source of excited controversy during the dispute itself. The strike leaders themselves made no attempt to hide their efforts to win financial backing from the Soviet trade-union movement. Far from it: in November 1984, shortly after the High Court ordered the seizure of the NUM's assets, Scargill personally visited the Soviet Embassy in 'Millionaires' Row' in London with Roger Windsor to press for the Soviet miners' union to send money through one or other of the specially arranged cash conduits. It was the only time the NUM leader made public contact with the Soviet authorities during the strike and the press was waiting for him as he emerged. 'We are happy with the support we're getting', Scargill was quoted as saying in the next day's *Daily Mail*, under the banner headline: 'Scargill Goes to Russians for Help'.[15]

The matter could scarcely be clearer. And if anybody had any doubts, a few days later Mick McGahey, the NUM's vice-president and former Communist Party chair, named almost exactly the sum that was finally despatched in different circumstances the following year, at a rally in Scotland. 'I see the Russian connection has now come out,' he told miners and their supporters. 'In case you don't know, I'm the guy. I had discussions with Soviet comrades. I will tell you the figure – it's $1,138,000. It's coming from Soviet trade unionists.' The story ran in the *Daily Express* under the legend: 'Red Mick Spills the Beans'. Peter Walker, then Tory Energy Secretary, issued an alarmed government health warning: 'This is a very serious situation. It's extraordinary.'[16]

Not surprisingly, although the strike ended at the beginning of March 1985, the 'extraordinary' issue of the Moscow money refused to go away, but rumbled on ominously for the next five years. It was a particular source of controversy in the NUM's South Wales area, which had swung into opposition to the Scargill-Heathfield leadership by the latter months of the dispute. Kim Howells, then the area's research officer, remembers a delegation from the Soviet miners' union coming to the NUM offices in Pontypridd six months after the strike. Emlyn Williams, who was about to retire, was determined to find out what had happened to the rumoured Soviet donation. 'We went to a café across the road from the miners' offices with them and they said they'd sent it,' Howells says. George Rees, the South Wales secretary, was told the same story and raised the matter on the NUM executive. Scargill insisted that the NUM had had no Soviet money. He even wrote to Mikhail Srebny at the end of 1985 asking him to confirm that the Soviet miners had not sent any money for the NUM. But his denials only fuelled the demand for explanations.[17]

The government had its own fanciful ideas about cash from the 'Evil Empire'. In their 1986 book on the strike – warmly endorsed by the former chancellor Nigel Lawson as the 'standard' book on the dispute – Martin Adeney and John Lloyd wrote: 'The Soviet Union was the main contributor from overseas ... British secret-service estimates supplied to the government put the contributions as high as £7 million. The reports said that the money was routed via the Confédération Générale du Travail.' The reports were wildly wrong. Not for the first or last time, it seems, the government's spies failed to cut the mustard.[18]

The mystery of the 'missing' Soviet money resurfaced at the 1988 NUM conference in Great Yarmouth, where visiting miners' union officials from the Soviet Union – now in the full flood of perestroika – encouraged the growing rumours. George Bolton, who had replaced McGahey as the Scottish miners' president and himself become chair of the slowly expiring Communist Party, was by now also convinced that Soviet cash earmarked for the NUM had been 'diverted' by Scargill. Terry Pattinson says it was the allegation made to him by a Soviet delegate at the conference that Soviet miners had donated a day's pay for the British coal strike which first set him on the trail of his grand *Daily Mirror* exposé. But when it came to it, neither Maxwell's sleuths at the *Mirror* nor those at the *Cook Report* were able to make much headway with the Moscow Gold angle. Roger Windsor's first-hand knowledge of the Soviet side of things was patchy, his visits to the embassy notwithstanding. What he did know was that the NUM had been pressing for Soviet aid, that there had been an attempt to deposit around a million dollars in the union's Swiss bank account in the autumn of 1984, and that Heathfield had told him some months later that the money had arrived in an account in Warsaw.

But the union's former chief executive had no idea whose that account actually was. Indeed, he seemed to believe it had been set up by Scargill and Heathfield under the auspices of the 'Miners' Action Committee' – which was in fact the name of the much-criticized cash trust fund. And where it had gone after Warsaw, the NUM leaders had never told him. It was left to the *Cook Report* team to try and sort out the tangled tale. They hired a relative of Gorbachev in Moscow who managed to convince Mikhail Srebny, the outgoing Soviet miners' president, to tell them that a million pounds had been sent 'via European banks'. But beyond that, they drew a blank. It was only when Scargill and Heathfield made their first full report to the NUM executive on the *Mirror-Cook Report* allegations and later gave evidence to the Lightman Inquiry that the details of what had actually taken place started to emerge: which East European countries had sent money, the amounts, the routes that had been used, and the final destination of the contested cash. Much of that information had in turn been supplied by Alain Simon, who was general secretary of the MTUI at the time of the 1984–5 strike and subsequently took on the same job in the successor organization, the IMO. But even Scargill and Simon were in the dark about the ructions and changes of heart in Moscow that had shaped Soviet policy towards the British miners during and after the 1984–5 strike. The full story only emerged in the aftermath of the Soviet Union's final collapse in 1991.[19]

Gavin Lightman, however, was convinced he knew better. The sections of the Lightman Report dealing with the Soviet cash are among the most sweeping in the whole document. Lightman pronounced himself 'quite satisfied' about the matter. Around £1 million had been raised through a levy of Soviet miners, he declared, and this money had then been paid into the MTUI's 'Mireds' solidarity fund in Dublin (later taken over by the IMO) for the NUM's benefit, between February and December 1985. Lightman was adamant that this was done to protect the cash from being seized by the receiver and that the 'diversion' of the Soviet money – along with parallel donations from East Germany and Hungary – was a serious breach of duty and 'misapplication of funds'. Lightman's insistence that Simon and Scargill, the IMO's general secretary and president, had secretly diverted Soviet cash without Soviet agreement from Scargill's own union to build up their fledgling miners' international – in which they had a 'vested interest' – proved to be a dangerous accusation. It was a charge which led to the most serious litigation in the whole saga and posed a direct threat to the future of the IMO itself.[20]

## THE GORBY FACTOR

Evidence emerged after the NUM dropped the case in the autumn of 1990 that Lightman not only got the Soviet money comprehensively wrong, but that he entirely misunderstood what had in fact taken place. It is now beyond question that it was the Soviet leadership at the highest level – rather than Scargill and Simon, or even the Soviet Coal Employees' Union – which took the decision to 'divert' the cash via the MTUI to an international trust fund in Dublin. There can also be no question that the Soviet miners' leaders were well aware of – and agreed with – their money being used for wider international miners' solidarity, rather than the NUM alone. Both the East German and Hungarian miners' leaders later confirmed that their parallel donations were intended for 'international purposes'. And the hard currency which was sent had no direct connection with the Soviet miners' union or the 2.2 million roubles it raised in the summer of 1984.

Throughout the 1984–5 dispute, the British miners' leadership and its emissaries offered Soviet trade unions and diplomats a bewildering array of different methods to donate money secretly and safely to the NUM or NUM-controlled accounts or funds. Once the union was subject to sequestration and receivership, the pleas became ever more insistent and the suggested methods of transfer ever more ingenious. But, although several East European unions coughed up cash in hard currency, and despite repeated promises and much dithering, the nervous 'second superpower' never in fact delivered on its promises.

Regular contacts with Yuri Mazur during the summer of 1984 – in the County Hotel and the London office of the NUM's solicitor, Mike Seifert – produced nothing concrete. But a secret meeting between Scargill and two well-placed Soviet trade-union officials at the TUC conference in Brighton in September seemed more promising. These were Vsyevelod Mojayev and Boris Avryamov. The breathless and heavily built Avryamov had acquired a faintly comical reputation as a sort of music-hall Russian on the British trade-union circuit and was regularly described as a KGB colonel in the Tory press. He was in reality nothing of the sort. But Avryamov was well connected in Moscow and exercised some influence as the main representative of the Soviet Communist Party's powerful international department at the World Federation of Trade Unions in Prague.[21]

Both Avryamov and Mojayev, who was in charge of international work at the central Soviet trade-union council, were sympathetic to the NUM's plight – the union was by then losing £106,000 a week in subscriptions income from its striking members. Scargill told them that the best way to transfer money would be in cash; alternatively, they could send it to the NUM's bank account at EBC (Schweiz) in Zurich. But Mojayev and Avryamov explained that there were problems raising hard currency to back the strike. By the end of the month, it was becoming clear that the union was likely to be sequestrated and its need for cash support was becoming more serious. A meeting was hurriedly arranged in Paris. On the morning of 8 October 1984 at the CGT headquarters in Montreuil, before adjourning to a separate room to meet Ibrahim and Abbasi, Scargill had extensive talks with Soviet – and Hungarian – diplomats. Augustin 'Tin-Tin' Dufresne and Alain Simon, the French communist leaders of the CGT miners' union and the MTUI, were also both present. Asked for his requirements by the most senior Soviet official, the NUM president demanded action on coal and oil exports and pressed the union's growing need for financial backing to keep the strike afloat. Simon gave the diplomat the number of the MTUI's main Warsaw account, from which funds could be transferred to the NUM. Scargill suggested that if the Russians found it impossible to provide cash, the British miners would be quite happy to have the money in gold bars.[22]

Dufresne and Simon had prepared the ground with heavy lobbying of the Soviet Embassy in Paris about the need to step up support for the British strike. Dufresne was particularly well-connected in Moscow and had a longstanding personal friendship with Andrei Gromyko, the veteran Foreign Minister and *éminence grise* of the Soviet establishment. The Paris meeting appears to have clinched a Soviet commitment. On 12 October 1984, four days after the CGT talks, the Soviet Communist Party Central Committee took a secret decision to allocate one million roubles in hard currency from the funds of the All Union Central Council of Trade Unions – the Soviet equivalent of the British TUC – to back the British miners' strike. There is no doubt that this was intended to meet Scargill's appeals for the NUM itself, rather than hardship relief in the pit villages. Soviet Communist Party archives show that on 2 November 1984, Mikhail Gorbachev, then number two in the Soviet hierarchy, personally signed the authorization of the transfer.[23]

Alexander Belausov, the Soviet miners' union secretary, was visiting Dufresne's office in the CGT complex at Montreuil in Paris a couple of days later and remembers the excitement when the news came through. 'Sitnikov, the secretary of our embassy in Paris, came in. He told Dufresne a coded message had been received, signed by Gromyko, that there would be a million roubles in hard currency for the striking English miners – about $1.4 million.' On the other side of the Channel, Mazur told Scargill that the money would now be forthcoming. But the first attempt to transfer Moscow's treasure-trove to the NUM ended in farce. It was during the period when the sequestrators were moving in on the besieged union, and the Soviet authorities were apparently unaware that all NUM bank accounts had been frozen. Some time in November 1984, around one million dollars was despatched to an NUM account at EBC Schweiz in Zurich. The money was returned by the bank and no records of the deposit recorded.[24]

Both the *Cook Report* and Roger Windsor made great play of this incident, the Central Television programme claiming: 'Arthur Scargill chose to send it back to the Eastern bloc, officially to keep it out of the hands of the sequestrators.' The clear implication was that the miners' leader had the money returned because he wanted it diverted elsewhere for his own megalomaniacal designs. Windsor insisted that the NUM president had told Stephen Hudson, the union's finance officer during the strike, to arrange for the Soviet cash to be returned. But Scargill vociferously denied he had ordered the money to be sent back. 'It's a lie, it's a lie,' he told the *Guardian* in 1990. And so it turned out to be. In his unpublished, confidential evidence to the Lightman Inquiry, Hudson remembered being told by EBC that the bank 'couldn't accept it for some reason and it was returned to the bank from which it came'. Rainer Kahrmann, the senior executive at EBC Schweiz in charge of the NUM's account, has said that the dollar transfer was rejected because the Soviet instruction making the deposit was not in the form of a 'texted telex' and was therefore technically invalid. Whether Kahrmann, who helped alert the sequestrators to the Zurich account, had other reasons for sending back the money is unclear.[25]

In the wake of the bungled Swiss deposit, the Soviet leadership began to get increasingly cold feet about direct cash aid to the British miners' union. They understandably baulked at the prospect of having their money fall into the hands of the pin-striped policemen appointed by the British courts to seize the miners' carefully husbanded assets. But there were other problems. According to both GCHQ and ex-Soviet Communist Party sources, the KGB had become aware that Western intelligence services had broken the secrecy of their East–West international financial networks and were well informed about Soviet attempts to help fund the miners' strike.

In her autobiography, Margaret Thatcher records that the British government's first 'confirmation' of Soviet financial aid to the NUM came in November, presumably as a result of the attempt to send money to Zurich. Rightly assuming that such trade-union support had to have backing from the Soviet government to get access to convertible currency, 'our displeasure at this was made very clear to the Soviet ambassador'. Intriguingly, details of the abortive Swiss deposit were leaked to the pro-government *Sunday Times* in early December 1984. Bernard Ingham, Thatcher's press secretary, recalls being contacted by the paper about 'the Soviets ... laundering money through a Swiss bank to the National Union of Mineworkers' on the eve of Mikhail Gorbachev's first visit to Britain. To what he describes as the government's relief, Rupert Murdoch's Sunday flagship spiked the story.[26]

Painfully aware of the gaping holes in the security of their cash-transfer arrangements, the Soviet authorities were anxious to cover their tracks. But there was also growing alarm in Moscow about the political price the Soviet Union might have to pay for the NUM connection. In 1984–5, Oleg Gordievsky was the KGB's second most senior officer in Britain, working undercover at the Soviet Embassy in London. He was also a double agent working for MI6. Gordievsky recalls that a rancorous controversy raged throughout the summer and autumn of 1984 in the various branches of the Soviet foreign-policy establishment over whether there should be hard currency support for the British miners' strike. Both the London KGB and the embassy advised Moscow against providing financial backing for the strike. As the officer in charge of the KGB's political work in London, Gordievsky personally formulated the station's assessment of the risks. Writing to his superiors at the Lubyanka on Dzerzhinsky Square, he argued that it would be 'undesirable and counter-productive for the Soviet Union to help the striking miners'. Coyly, Gordievsky – who by 1984 had been working secretly for MI6 for ten years – likes to suggest that in the case of his recommendation against backing the NUM, the interests of his apparent and real masters coincided. 'As a British citizen, I felt the strike was unnecessary, politically wrong and disruptive for the society and the British economy ... as a KGB officer, having the objective not to damage Soviet interests in Great Britain ... I felt it was also correct to make the recommendation to Moscow not to send money.'[27]

Yuri Mazur, the labour attaché in charge of relations with the British Communist Party and labour movement, came to the same conclusion. It was 'dangerous for the interest of the Soviet Union, for the future relationship of Moscow and Great Britain', Mazur told his embassy colleagues, 'to help the miners with money'. Both the London KGB and the 'straight, clean diplomats' feared that news of the cash support would leak out. They argued that not only could such funding damage developing state-to-state relations with the Thatcher government, but it also risked undermining the electoral prospects of the Labour Party – which the Soviet Union wanted to see return to office. Belausov remembers the controversy from the Moscow end. 'There were people who said that Moscow shouldn't interfere with the internal affairs of Britain. They didn't want to ruin relations with Thatcher's government ... It was very difficult to get this million. It was only under dreadful pressure from the trade union that the Central Committee headquarters finally decided to allocate our money.'

But there were other pressures within the Soviet power structures. Gordievsky gives the example of Boris Avryamov, the senior Soviet official at the Prague-based WFTU, who had met Scargill at the TUC conference and pressed strongly behind-the-scenes for financial support for the miners. 'In my presence he was very critical of the position of the embassy, believing it was cowardly and undignified.' The argument, the retired double agent says, was between those who still attached importance to the traditions of international working-class and communist solidarity and those who gave absolute priority to Soviet national state interests and bilateral relations with other countries. It was a tension that had existed in Soviet policy from the 1920s. Normally, the Foreign Ministry was associated with promoting Soviet 'national interests', while the powerful Central Committee international department was more ideological – or, as one of its ex-staff members puts it, 'possessed of a Messianic idea'. But the dispute over aid to the British miners also reflected the embryonic struggle between supporters and opponents of what would come to be called perestroika. Other well-placed sources from the former Soviet *apparat* say that in late 1984 Andrei Gromyko championed the miners' cause at Politburo level, while the rising Mikhail Gorbachev resisted giving anything more than rhetorical support.[28]

Without membership income or access to the union's own resources – indeed, without the right to act legally on behalf of the union at all – the NUM leaders' need for ready funds to keep its organization going was becoming ever more pressing. Through the unflagging good offices of the French CGT miners' leadership and the MTUI, two East European miners' unions – the Czechoslovak and Bulgarian – opted immediately for the common-sense solution and delivered their support in used greenbacks. So did the Greeks. The Bulgarians came up with $36,000. The cash was picked up from the Bulgarian Embassy by a veteran communist Fleet Street electrician named Len Dawson. In view of the Bulgarian diplomats' less-than-complete confidence in some of their own staff, the handover took place in the embassy gardens. Dawson, who ran a trade-union Bulgarian solidarity outfit in the 1970s and 1980s, took the money with him in a state of high anxiety on the train to Sheffield and delivered it to Heathfield in person. About a year after the end of the strike, Dawson was 'revealed', rather absurdly, in a television programme as a Bulgarian 'spy'. A *Morning Star* journalist who helped entrap Dawson for the programme maker, and was subsequently sacked, had also worked for the NUM. Both Special Branch and MI5 were reported to have been 'involved' in the exposé.[29]

The Czech handover was carried out in the true spirit of a Cold War spy thriller. Peter Heathfield – who had himself carried cash over the Pyrenees to striking Asturian miners in the days of General Franco's dictatorship – was staying overnight at the County Hotel in the Bloomsbury area of London. As he left the lobby, he was hustled into a doorway of the New Brunswick shopping centre by a woman from the Czechoslovak Embassy. Waiting in the shadows was Vladimir Polednik, then leader of the Czech miners' union, who swapped Heathfield's empty plastic carrier bag for one stuffed with banknotes. Heathfield dumped it in the boot of his car without examining its contents and drove off to a series of speaking engagements in the coalfield areas. The bag was forgotten and left in the car boot for two days, before Heathfield finally delivered it to Steve Hudson at the NUM's Sheffield headquarters. It was found to contain $96,000 in cash.[30]

But in the wake of the attempted Zurich transfer, there was still nothing forthcoming from Moscow. Scargill asked for a meeting at the Soviet Embassy and was immediately given one. Gordievsky – who, as the Secret Intelligence Service's top man in the KGB, naturally puts his own spin on these events – comments: 'For many people of the Soviet establishment ... Arthur Scargill was regarded as an important ally of the Soviet Union in Great Britain ... that's why his requests to the Soviet leadership were taken very seriously indeed.' The two diplomats who met the NUM delegation that day, Yuri Mazur and Lev Parshin, explained that there was great concern in Moscow that any Soviet donation could be seized by the British courts. The report they sent off that night to the Soviet Foreign Ministry, now held in the Russian archives, records Scargill asking that the money which had been sent to Switzerland and returned should be transferred to an account at the First National Bank of Chicago in Dublin. The account was in the name of Nell Hyett – the NUM press officer's married name – who had signed an undertaking only to use any funds sent to the account for the NUM. 'Scargill said that his request was motivated by the need to secure the NUM funds in case British courts attempted to confiscate them', the telegram explained. Still the Russians dithered.[31]

In the dying days of 1984, Mikhail Gorbachev paid what would turn out to be a fateful visit to London as heir apparent to the sick Soviet leader, Konstantin Chernenko. On a wet mid-December morning, the Soviet Communist Party's ideology supremo was driven from the London embassy to Chequers, the Prime Minister's official country residence, for lunch with Thatcher and a gaggle of Tory ministers. After coffee, Thatcher and Gorbachev retired to the Hawtrey Room for a personal talk by the fire. The British Tory leader was determined to 'cultivate and sustain' a Soviet apparatchik she was convinced she could 'do business with'. Business was opened forthwith, with a judiciously targeted protest from Thatcher that the USSR was meddling in British affairs by funding and 'helping to prolong' the miners' strike. Gorbachev replied that the strike was entirely a matter for Britain and that, as far as he was aware, 'no money has been transferred from the Soviet Union'.[32]

After both leaders were later unceremoniously bundled out of office, Thatcher grumbled that her former protégé had deceived her about his backing for what she called 'Scargill's insurrection'. 'I have since seen documentary evidence,' she wrote in her memoirs, 'suggesting that he knew full well and was among those who authorized payment.' Gorbachev was undoubtedly guilty of being – in the formulation of the British mandarinate – 'economical with the truth'. Certainly, he knew of the October decision to fund the strike and the abortive transfer to Switzerland. But at the time of his London visit, no money had in fact been successfully transferred, either to the NUM or the solidarity fund, and the British government was well aware that the strike aid was a continuing source of dispute in the Soviet power structures. Back in Moscow, Thatcher's complaint hit home where it was intended, with unwelcome consequences for the NUM's cause. Gorbachev was delighted with his new friend in London and wanted nothing to undermine the fragile new relationship with Thatcher's Britain as the power struggle over the succession to the dying Chernenko came to a head.[33]

Gordievsky remembers how 'in the weeks after Gorbachev's visit ... the operation to help the miners became nearly secret

... the people from the embassy stopped talking about it.' In Moscow, the bureaucratic wheels were immediately put into reverse. Oleg Berkutov, who at that time worked for the central Soviet trade-union apparatus, the AUCCTU, was in Mojayev's office when a call came through from Gromyko giving instructions that no money should go to the NUM after all. Neither Scargill nor Simon were told of the decision. But at the funeral of Will Paynter, the NUM's former general secretary, on 17 December 1984, Yuri Mazur told Scargill about Gorbachev's and Thatcher's discussion. The unfortunate Soviet miners' union general secretary, Alexander Belausov, who had gone on the main Soviet television news programme at the end of October to announce the fuel embargo and 'material aid' to the NUM, was also made starkly aware of the change of policy. In the second half of December, he was called in to the Central Committee to explain his behaviour and subsequently transferred to other work because of his 'excessive frankness'.[34]

## THE MOSCOW PAPERS

During the course of the strike, the NUM had offered the Russians innumerable secret conduits to help fund its battle royal with the Thatcher government. These included a direct handover in cash or gold bars; transfer through the MTUI's main account in Warsaw; payment into non-NUM accounts in the names of close associates; transfer of the cash through the left-wing Finnish trade unions (an option favoured by the Soviet Embassy in London); and funnelling the money through an account controlled by Tom Sibley, the British representative of the WFTU. An account at First Chicago Bank in Dublin in the name of Nell Hyett was opened specifically to take the expected Soviet donation. The Russians were also given the account number for the Sheffield Women's Action Group as another possible conduit. When these were turned down, Scargill suggested that they might prefer to pay the money into the account Dom Mintoff, the Maltese Prime Minister, had offered to open for the NUM in Valletta. All these schemes were explicitly intended to help fund the national strike operation, but the Soviet authorities rejected them all.[35]

Meanwhile, the union's financial situation was becoming critical. A confidential appeal to the Soviet trade unions drafted by Scargill at the turn of the year recorded that the NUM had already spent £30 million on the strike, once the costs of picketing and hardship were taken into account. £300,000 a week was needed to maintain pickets and day-to-day organization. More was required for legal bills. The NUM was looking for £10–20 million, he said. The appeal – which made a new suggestion, that money could be transferred to an NUM trust fund in the names of Alain Simon, Norman West or Nell Myers – was handed to Yuri Mazur on 28 December 1984. Around the same time, Scargill was approached by the left-wing QC and former MP, John Platts-Mills, a man with a wealth of contacts in the socialist bloc and Third World. The miners' leader gave him the number of the MTUI's longstanding Warsaw account to pass to potential donors: Narodowy Bank Polski, account number 111–126–973–151–6796. And Professor Vic Allen, who had worked closely with the NUM left caucus for many years, travelled to Moscow, Budapest and East Berlin armed with the same account number. Miners' and trade-union leaders in all three capitals – including Mikhail Srebny, Vsevolod Mojayev and Stepan Shalayev – promised to stump up. In Berlin, Allen pressed the miners' case with a member of Erich Honecker's Politburo.[36]

But the key negotiations over how to release the money were, as before, conducted by Tin-Tin Dufresne. At the turn of the year, barely two weeks after Gorbachev had returned in triumph to Moscow from his British foray, Dufresne and Simon were told by Soviet union leaders that the party leadership could not now risk direct cash support for the NUM or the strike. But it was prepared to allow the money to be paid into an MTUI international miners' solidarity fund, from which the NUM among others could benefit. From the Soviet point of view, the idea killed two birds with one stone. Donations to the NUM from a general solidarity fund under the control of the MTUI, whose largest affiliate was the Soviet miners' union, both covered Gorbachev's tracks with Thatcher and at the same time allowed them to meet requests from other unions.[37]

The Soviet miners' leaders had in fact first floated the idea of an international solidarity fund two months earlier at an MTUI conference in Prague. Heathfield, who had gone to lobby for Soviet and East European cash support and an end to Polish coal exports to Britain, was taken aside after the day's proceedings for a talk with Mikhail Srebny, the MTUI president and Soviet miners' leader. Srebny told him that the Soviet miners' union was anxious to help, but there were other organizations pressing for solidarity – such as the South African and Namibian miners' unions – and only a limited pot of hard-currency funds for labour-movement aid. Perhaps a fund should be established. He advised Heathfield to write to Konstantin Chernenko to press the British miners' case, which the NUM general secretary duly did.[38]

In the first week of January 1985, Alain Simon passed on the gist of the new Soviet position to Scargill – who was given a similar line by Yuri Mazur – in Sheffield and asked him to make the necessary arrangements for the creation of an MTUI solidarity fund. Mike Seifert, the NUM's solicitor, suggested he consult Professor Kader Asmal, Dean of Humanities at Trinity College, Dublin. Establishing the fund in Ireland had the special advantage that, unlike in Britain, multipurpose trusts are legally valid. Nell Myers flew to Dublin where Asmal – who later helped draft the new South African constitution for the African National Congress and became South Africa's education minister – recommended that the trust should be modelled on the ANC's successful International Defence and Aid Fund (IDAF) for anti-apartheid prisoners. After consultations with Simon, representing the MTUI, and the solicitors, the MTUI's own 'Miners' Defence and Aid Fund' (MIDAF) – later renamed 'Mireds' – was established by trust deed and an account opened at the Irish Intercontinental Bank in Dublin. The trustees were Alain Simon and Norman West, the NUM-sponsored MEP.[39]

Former Soviet Communist Party files, held by the Russian government in Moscow, show that two days after the opening of the Dublin account, the Central Committee secretariat finally agreed to press ahead with the decision of the previous October to send cash aid. Four days later, on 4 February 1985, a memo from three top party and foreign-ministry officials was sent to Politburo members requesting consent to the final transfer arrangements. Framed in a fog of buck-passing waffle, the final authorization, stamped 'Central Committee of the CPSU: Top Secret', records that Stepan Shalayev, then head of the entire Soviet trade-union apparatus, had passed on a report of discussions between Alain Simon and unnamed Soviet officials:

On the proposal of the AUCCTU, in accordance with the assignment (to carry out the consent given by the CPSU CC secretariat of 1 February 1985), Comrade S. A. Shalayev, AUCCTU chairman, reported the results of talks with the MTUI general secretary, Alain Simon, about the channels to transfer financial aid to British miners on strike. The aid, amounting to 1 million roubles, is being allotted to the AUCCTU from its funds.

In the course of discussions, A. Simon supported the idea of British NUM president, A. Scargill, to transfer the above-mentioned means of help to the MTUI account in the National Bank of Poland. From Warsaw, the money should be transferred in instalments of 100–150,000 convertible roubles to the account of A. Simon in a Dublin bank (Ireland). From there the money would be given to the striking miners on behalf of the MTUI.

A. Simon and A. Scargill are of the firm conviction that this channel securely covers the Soviet origin of the cash aid and guarantees the secrecy of its transfer. Comrade Shalayev shares their opinion and thinks it expedient to speed up the transfer of the financial help through this channel.

The memo goes on to ask the party leaders to give their consent to the AUCCTU proposal and is signed 'agreed' by Mikhail Gorbachev, Yegor Ligachev and Anatoly Lukyanov, then head of the Central Committee secretariat's general department.

Ligachev would later lead the ineffectual 'hardline' resistance to Gorbachev's liberal and free-market policies and Lukyanov would be arrested in the wake of the bungled 'state of emergency' of August 1991.[40]

As usual, the Soviet Union's East German allies had been rather quicker off the mark. The first deposit to be made in the MTUI's longstanding Warsaw account for the new solidarity fund was from the German Democratic Republic miners' union, which paid in an initial $100,000 on 24 January 1985. A few weeks later and eight days after the Central Committee go-ahead, the long-awaited Soviet million was finally despatched to the MTUI's Warsaw account. The mechanics were looked after by the Soviet Peace Fund. The deposit of $1,137,000, the dollar equivalent of one million roubles, was stamped 'for transfer to the solidarity fund' and dated 12 February 1985. Further deposits in Warsaw for transfer to the fund were made by the East Germans later the same month, by the Hungarian miners' union in May and by the Bulgarians in August.[41]

As things turned out, the first deposit into the Dublin trust fund, on 29 January 1985, was not from Eastern Europe at all, but was £98,568 from the NUM leaders' special cash fund, spirited away for safekeeping to Dublin through the good offices of the Transport and General Workers' Union. Only one tranche of cash from the MTUI in Warsaw actually made it to the new solidarity fund before the NUM's strike was called off. On 21 February 1985, £84,069 was deposited in the fund's Dublin account, transferred from a pool of East German and Soviet funds. The next deposit of £273,659.05 was not made until 7 March, four days after an NUM special delegate conference at the TUC headquarters in London had voted for a return to work. A further four transfers of Soviet and East European cash were made from Warsaw to the new fund between 29 March and 13 December, bringing the total to £1,404,618.11.[42]

In other words, 94 per cent of the cash arrived after the end of the dispute. The political vacillations in Moscow had deprived the NUM of the strike support Scargill and Simon had lobbied for so insistently. The Central Committee decision of 4

February 1985, agreeing to transfer one million convertible roubles to the MTUI in Warsaw and then to an account in Dublin, talked about aid for striking miners. But by the time the money was released, the strikers had gone back to work. With the MTUI's solidarity trust fund established in Dublin under Soviet pressure, the common-sense decision was taken – unquestionably with Soviet agreement – to maintain the capital and use the interest as a fighting fund to support industrial action by miners anywhere in the world. British miners could and would benefit. That the Soviet and East European miners' and party officials were well aware of what happened to their money is beyond reasonable doubt. Far from them being unhappy about it, the establishment of the Dublin trust was the direct result of the Soviet leaders' determination to quarantine themselves as far as possible from any cash link with the British NUM.

With the creation of the IMO – and the dissolution of the MTUI – in the autumn of 1985, the Midaf fund became the Mireds trust fund, but continued to operate as a permanent international fund. Before the 1990 scandal broke, British miners had received £206,000 from the Soviet and East European money – £135,000 of which had gone to the Sheffield-based hardship fund, the Miners' Solidarity Fund, between 1986 and 1989. In the late 1980s, £20,000 was paid out of the Mireds trust to support a six-month occupation by French miners of the Gardanne colliery in Provence; £10,000 was used to back industrial action by miners in the Philippines; £8,000 went to Moroccan miners on strike in Djerrada. The existence of the fund gave the IMO a power and leverage which was deeply unwelcome to the big mining corporations, governments and Western-backed trade-union internationals. And the £742,000 that was paid out when the NUM dropped its legal action in September 1990 – scarcely covering the union's own legal bills for the whole affair – had the effect of weakening the scope of the Mireds fund's impact.[43]

The confusion over the original Soviet decision to send cash to back the 1984–5 strike, the contradictory statements made by Soviet officials five years later, and the loose wording of the 1985 Central Committee minute allowed those who tied their chariot to the 1990 media campaign to insist they were right all along about the NUM's Moscow Gold. Roger Cook, for example, who glossed over the *Cook Report*'s abject failure to stand up its original allegation about the repayment of Scargill's nonexistent mortgage, insisted he had been vindicated over the Soviet cash. After the *Sunday Times* reprinted sections of the Central Committee document in 1992, he declared: 'They proved what we were saying about the Russian money was right by producing all the Kremlin documents.' His producer, Clive Entwistle, agreed. But the 'Kremlin documents' prove no such thing. Cook and the *Mirror* had alleged, it will be recalled, that Scargill had 'siphoned off' £1 million of 'hardship money' collected by the Soviet miners' union and 'diverted' it to a secret IMO bank account to further his 'political ambitions'. They also claimed that Scargill had earlier ordered the money to be sent back from an NUM account in Zurich. Taking these claims a stage further, Gavin Lightman concluded that all the Soviet, East German and Hungarian money sent to the MTUI and on to the Dublin trust fund was intended solely for the NUM. Scargill denied it and insisted that the Soviet trade unions had changed their tune at the turn of 1984–5, demanding that the money go to an MTUI fund for 'international purposes', out of which the NUM could benefit.[44]

In the light of the documentary and other evidence, the Cook–*Mirror*–Lightman tale simply does not stand up. The Zurich story was destroyed by the testimony of Steve Hudson and Rainer Kahrmann – the transfer was not accepted by the bank, apparently for technical reasons. The secret Soviet and East European donations were never solicited or sent for hardship relief. At the start of the strike, the NUM requested unions throughout the world – including the Soviet Coal Employees' Union – to send hardship donations to the Miners' Solidarity Fund (MSF) in Sheffield. This fund, which received more than £6 million (around £12.15 million at 2004 prices), was never affected by sequestration and receivership. If the Soviet trade-union movement had wanted to, it could have paid money into the MSF openly or secretly at any time without risk of seizure. It did not. All documentary evidence relating to Scargill's efforts to persuade the Soviet trade unions to transfer funds confirms that the requests were for aid to 'sustain the fabric of the union' – in other words, the NUM's national running costs – in the face of huge legal and strike expenses, dramatic loss of subscription income and takeover by the courts. The Central Committee minutes allocating the money make no reference to hardship and are transparently in direct response to this lobbying effort.

They also show that the hard currency sent to Warsaw in February 1985 had nothing directly to do with the Soviet miners' union or the pit collections in the summer of 1984. In fact, a little modest research by Lightman and the *Mirror-Cook Report* team would have revealed that the CEU had no money of its own whatsoever before perestroika – let alone £1 million in convertible currency. All union finances were centralized in the hands of the central council of trade unions – the AUCCTU. And the powerful AUCCTU would have still needed a party central committee decision to get its hands on any large-scale foreign currency reserves, even if the purpose had been less controversial than funding a bitterly-fought strike in Britain. The Soviet archives show that the AUCCTU had to provide the rouble equivalent for the $1.137 million finally sent – and well over a year later, in August 1986, Shalayev was still trying to get the Central Committee to have the expenditure repaid.[45]

As for Soviet intentions, the Central Committee minute of 4 February 1985 confirms that the Communist Party leadership at the highest level knew and explicitly approved of the 'diversion' of the £1 million through the MTUI to an MTUI-controlled account in Dublin. The memo's imprecise wording – Simon never had a bank account in Dublin, for example – makes a definitive interpretation difficult. But given the sequence of events and the cross-references in other Central Committee documents, it is clear that the remark about transferring the cash to 'the account of A. Simon in a Dublin bank' refers to one of the earlier schemes proposed by Scargill, rather than to the final international-trust formula. Almost certainly, Shalayev's recommendation in the minute was based on the NUM leader's written proposal of 28 December 1984, in which he suggested that the money could go to a trust fund in Dublin, one of whose trustees would be Alain Simon. This trust was never in fact established and was superseded by the Midaf–Mireds international fund. But Scargill's paper was given to Yuri Mazur, Alain Simon and Vic Allen, who handed it to Shalayev in Moscow.

What appears to have happened is that while the Central Committee secretariat was grinding into gear to respond to proposals made more than a month earlier, Soviet trade-union officials were already responding to growing pressures from the top and telling Simon and Dufresne that the money would need to go via the MTUI to an *international* fund. As a result, even before the 4 February Central Committee minute had formally been agreed, the Midaf–Mireds trust had been set up and the GDR trade unions had already paid over $100,000 to the MTUI for onward transmission to the new fund. Once it was realized in Moscow that the GDR had used the new international trust first requested by the Soviet trade unions themselves, the Russians were clearly happy to follow suit. The Soviet bank transfer document of 12 February 1985, allocating the $1,137,000 to 'the solidarity fund', explicitly confirms that. The minuted decision of 4 February was not the first time during this saga, of course, that the Soviet party leadership found itself discussing a proposal overtaken by events. Exactly the same thing had happened in October and November 1984, when the Central Committee agreed to an outdated earlier suggestion and sent the money to the NUM's Zurich bank, by which time the union's assets had all been frozen.[46]

Further evidence that the Soviet leadership wanted an MTUI solidarity fund for 'international purposes' – rather than any direct link with the NUM – is provided by the leaders of the Hungarian and former East German mining unions, which both donated money to the Midaf-Mireds fund through the same channel and in the same period as the Russians. The GDR trade-union movement paid over a total of $500,000 dollars during the first half of 1985. Gunther Wolf, former president of the GDR miners' union, the IGBE, confirmed in writing in 1990 that the money had been intended for 'international aims' under the control of the MTUI. More surprisingly, Antal Schalkhammer, the new pro free-market leader of the Hungarian miners' union and no friend of Scargill, confirmed to the NUM's four-man team in 1990 from union records that the just under 200,000 Swiss francs transferred from the Hungarian TUC (then called 'SZOT') in May 1985 in exactly the same way as the Soviet and East German donations had been for 'international purposes' – not for the NUM alone. Given the relationship between the Soviet Union and Eastern Europe at that time and the sensitivity of cash aid to the British miners, it is simply unthinkable that either the Hungarian or GDR trade unions would have gone out on a limb and adopted a different line from the Soviet AUCCTU.[47]

In February 1985, while the British miners' strike continued, the Russians evidently still expected most of their money to end up with the NUM strike leadership, via the MTUI and the international trust fund. But there can also be no serious doubt that they knew and approved of what happened to it once the strike was over. Valery Shestakov, the permanent Soviet representative at the MTUI in Warsaw in 1985, confirmed in writing that the Soviet donation had been for the MTUI solidarity fund and was 'not made to the British NUM. These contributions were used by the MTUI to provide assistance to miners internationally.' During the 1990 media campaign, Mikhail Srebny, CEU president until March of that year, sang a different tune, claiming on British television that he knew nothing of the Mireds international solidarity fund and that the Soviet money had been intended only for the British NUM. But he added: 'When the strike had ended and the money arrived late, maybe then the money could have wound up in a fund to help other miners.'[48]

The 'maybes' gave the game away. At the time the Midaf-Mireds fund was set up under the auspices of the MTUI, Srebny was the MTUI's president, later becoming vice-president of the IMO. In December 1985, with rumours rife in the NUM and outside about Soviet payments to the NUM of £10 million or more, Scargill wrote to Srebny asking him to confirm that 'the Soviet miners did not send any actual money to the NUM'. This is something the NUM leader would have scarcely done if he had been hoping to stash away the Moscow million without the Russians noticing. In time-honoured bureaucratic style, Srebny failed to reply, though he did give verbal assurances. The *Mirror* wrongly claimed he never received the letter. Srebny explained to the NUM's four-man team in Moscow that he had not replied to Scargill because 'the situation five years ago was different ... I was trying to help him'.[49]

In the late 1980s, several witnesses attended IMO meetings with Srebny when the Mireds fund was discussed. Among them was John Maitland, leader of the United Mineworkers of Australia, who had sharp personal and political differences with Scargill and whose union left the IMO in 1993 to join the rival MIF. Maitland remembers sitting through a meeting of the IMO's finance committee with Mikhail Srebny at the international's second congress in Cairo in 1989 when 'a report was given on the income and expenditure of all the accounts'. Vladimir Polednik – who handed over the Czechoslovak dollars to Peter Heathfield in the Bloomsbury doorway in 1984 – and Laszlo Kovacs, the Hungarian committee chair, were also in attendance.[50]

Srebny's claim not to know about the MTUI–IMO solidarity fund – which was actually earmarked on the original Soviet transfer document – is demonstrably absurd. At the 1989 IMO Cairo congress, money from the Mireds fund was even used to buy video and photocopying equipment for striking Soviet miners – some of which ended up in Srebny's office. If the Soviet miners' union had been worried about what had happened to the AUCCTU's money or unhappy about the fund, it would have had no difficulty in using its muscle as the largest affiliate of the MTUI and later of the IMO to insist that the 'missing million' was redirected to the NUM. It never did. Even after the scandal over the money had been running for more than six months, the Soviet representative at the IMO executive meeting in September 1990 – Nikolai Chebyshev, CEU secretary – abstained on the deal settling the legal action with the NUM. He then supported a motion of full confidence in Scargill and Simon, which went on to condemn the 'hateful and scandalous' campaign directed against the IMO and its leaders by 'political and media forces serving the multinational corporations'.[51]

The insistence that Scargill 'diverted' the Soviet money was always verging on Alice-in-Wonderland territory. Without the confidence that the Soviet leaders had in the miners' strike 'troika' of Scargill, McGahey and Heathfield, there would never have been any prospect of such risky financial support in the first place. That is even more true of the communist-led CGT, which was far more trusted than the NUM by the Soviet authorities. The CGT was the only significant Western union in the Eastern bloc-orientated WFTU; Alain Simon was géneral secretary of the WFTU-affiliated MTUI; Augustin Dufresne was on the Central Committee of the French Communist Party. The very idea that in 1984–5 French communist leaders would secretly trick the simple-minded Russians as to what had been done with their million-dollar NUM strike donation cannot be treated seriously.

The final arrangements depended on political and personal trust, which later broke down for reasons entirely unconnected with the British miners or their union. As Srebny himself explained to the NUM's four-man team in 1990, all agreements were verbal. He had been told by party leaders that nothing was to be written down – which was all very convenient when political circumstances changed five years later. What is perhaps more remarkable in the aftermath of the collapse of the USSR and its general denigration is that, as late as 1985, the Soviet and other East European trade unions were willing and able to provide large-scale support to the most important strike in the capitalist world for a generation. That is in retrospect just as significant as the paralysing delays and crosscurrents of the Soviet aid.

## RUNNING FOR COVER

The question remains why well-placed Soviet officials, such as Mikhail Srebny, lied about the events of 1984–5 and their dealings with Scargill and Simon, and threw their weight behind the 1990 campaign against the NUM leadership. The scandal over the 'missing' Moscow Gold was driven by three interlocking factors: political faction-fighting in the Soviet political establishment, as members of the nomenklatura sought to reinvent themselves for the post-communist era; the absolute determination of pro-Western trade-union centres and governments to discredit and destroy the IMO, the largest and most effective nonaligned union international; and the enthusiasm among Scargill's domestic opponents to use any available weapon, however outlandish, to continue their bid to smoke him out of his fast-shrinking NUM redoubt.

The underlying explanation for the Moscow apparatchiks' U-turn was to be found in the upheavals in the Soviet Union and Eastern Europe unleashed by perestroika. By 1990, the Communist Party and state apparatus had split into open factions, and the dominant reformist groups around Gorbachev, Alexander Yakovlev and Edward Shevardnadze were increasingly hostile to international policies based on working-class solidarity. Anxious for closer ties with the West, they promoted 'universal human values' as an alternative. Lower down the nomenklatura ladder, officials were busy scrambling into line with the 'new thinking' and straining every nerve to distance themselves from any past or present involvement in 'outdated practices'. The trade unions were under particular suspicion, portrayed by the party 'radicals' as inherently conservative and hopelessly tied to the interests of low-skilled industrial workers with little interest in 'market reform'. In the case of the vast Soviet mining industry, the pressure was as much from below as from above. In the summer of 1989, a wave of strikes swept the Soviet coalfields, as the ill-prepared dismantling of the old economic planning system cut into the living standards of the relatively well-paid miners. The strike committees bypassed the 'official' trade union, the CEU, and forced humiliating concessions from Gorbachev. In the backwash of the strike, at the CEU congress in March 1990, several of the old miners' union officials, including Srebny, were kicked out and new faces, including some strike leaders, voted in to replace them.[52]

Tied up with workers' demands for more independent, responsive trade unions were anti-communist pressures against 'political' trade-unionism and links with left-wing movements abroad. The IMO became a prime target. While the Prague-based WFTU was more susceptible to Soviet political cross-currents, the independent IMO refused to abandon its commitment to class politics and militant trade-unionism. Both Scargill and Simon had spoken at Soviet miners' conferences and argued against a breakaway from the CEU, for which there was growing pressure. Neither man made any secret of their lack of sympathy for the direction perestroika was taking, while by 1990 the French Communist Party was becoming ever more estranged from its Soviet counterpart. For an old Brezhnevite timeserver like Srebny, joining the chorus of Scargill's accusers must have seemed a convenient way of saving his skin. If so, the tactic failed.

In 1985, the Soviet trade unions had accepted the establishment of the IMO with some reluctance, not least because they knew they would have less control over the new East–West international than they did over the MTUI. They were also less than overjoyed about Scargill becoming IMO president, partly because he was a member of the Labour Party and thus – in the words of one WFTU official – an 'unreliable social democrat'. Five years later, they wanted Scargill out for precisely the opposite reason. In Moscow in 1990, the NUM's four-man team were shaken by the speed of the lurch to the right in the Soviet miners' union. 'They don't like Arthur's attitude', the cokemen's leader Idwal Morgan reported in a state of bewilderment, 'they say he's a Marxist.'[53]

The unhappiness with Scargill's role went further up the party apparatus. Gorbachev's allies didn't like either the NUM president's ideas about international trade unionism or his friends in Moscow and Eastern Europe. Scargill had been pressing party and union leaders at various points east of the Elbe to take more seriously the negative effects of Western largesse in buying up trade-union movements around the world. Diverting even a tiny part of the vast reserves of hard currency spent on Warsaw Pact weapons programmes to underwrite industrial struggles, he argued, would be highly effective in terms of its political impact. Using the IMO's Dublin solidarity trust as a prototype, the British miners' leader lobbied for the creation of a £30 million fund to help support international trade-union action. Some thought he had lost touch with reality. Others were highly receptive. A year before the fall of the Berlin Wall, Scargill discussed the scheme with Erich Honecker, the East German Communist leader, and Harry Tisch, head of the country's trade unions, who, he claims, agreed in principle to commit £2 million to a wider solidarity fund. He also had talks in Moscow in January 1990 with Gennadi Yanayev – the Soviet vice-president who would later achieve notoriety as the front man in the bizarre 'coup' of August 1991 – about the scheme. None of this was likely to endear the NUM leader to the Soviet reformers or their friends in the West.

With Srebny gone, the speed of political change inside the Soviet miners' union accelerated. The most powerful bureaucrat at the CEU's Moscow headquarters was its international secretary, Victor Myachin, a Lavrenti Beria lookalike who had long cultivated close relations with the West German trade unions and the Bonn government-funded Friedrich Ebert Foundation. Myachin and his allies wanted the CEU to follow the example of the Hungarian miners' union: to pull out of the IMO and join the MIF. Schalkhammer had told the NUM's four-man team the Hungarians were not prepared to go on paying subscriptions to 'finance the Scargill ideology', which he described as the dictatorship of the proletariat, the defence of the developing countries and support for what was then the South African opposition. Throughout Eastern Europe, trade unions were leaving the WFTU and signing up with the long-vilified ICFTU and its various offshoots. For the 'reformers', it was all of a piece with accepting Western 'normality' and the 'market economy'. The old demand for reunification of the international trade-union movement was abandoned in the rush to be accepted in Brussels.[54]

For Myachin and the MIF, the scandal over the Soviet money was a godsend. For the realigning Soviet apparatchiks, here was a way of discrediting the IMO and its leaders and smoothing the path to joining the MIF. For the MIF, the controversy opened up the prospect of destroying its much larger rival. The political flavour of the Soviet attacks on the IMO is illustrated by a letter sent to Alain Simon in August 1990 by Anatoly Kapustin, vice-president of the CEU and a deputy to the newly created Congress of People's Deputies. Accusing Simon and the IMO secretariat of 'hopelessly out-dated visions of the role of international activity', Kapustin complained that the organization employed 'command methods' and had a 'work style of the stagnation period' – both Soviet catchphrases used to describe the politics of the Brezhnev years.[55]

Throughout 1990 and beyond, factions in the Soviet apparatus ran their own dirty-tricks campaign against the IMO in an effort to finish off the job begun by the British media. In the aftermath of the Lightman Report, documents aimed at discrediting Scargill and Simon were sent anonymously to selected members of the NUM national executive known to be critical of the union leadership. One was Ken Hollingsworth, from the union's white-collar section, Cosa – a traditional NUM right-winger who was 'totally opposed to the IMO', believing the NUM should concentrate its international efforts on lobbying the then European Community in alliance with the West German miners' union, IG Bergbau. At an unspecified date – but which Hollingsworth believes was in the autumn of 1990 – the Cosa official received what was then a highly secret Soviet government document in a plain brown envelope: a copy of a 1984 embassy telegram sent at the time to the Foreign Ministry in Moscow, later transferred to the Communist Party Central Committee and helpfully translated into English. It was an account of Scargill's meeting at the Soviet Embassy on 15

November 1984. The telegram described him asking for the abortive Swiss deposit to be 'readdressed' to an account in Nell Myers' name in Dublin, which would be used 'only for NUM needs'. The NUM president was also quoted attacking Neil Kinnock's leadership of the Labour Party. Since 1991, the original has been lodged in the Central Committee archive under the control of the Russian government. But in 1990, copies of such a highly classified document could have only been circulated with the cooperation of senior officials in Moscow – presumably with the aim of stoking up the Soviet money scandal.

Another document sent anonymously to Hollingsworth around the same time accused Alain Simon of being a dealer in precious stones and claimed that the IMO's affiliates were mostly based in gem-producing countries. The allegation was entirely baseless, and Hollingsworth – who had never believed the *Mirror–Cook Report* stories from the beginning – dismissed these latest claims as 'incredible, malicious stuff about Arthur. I knew there were people out to get him.' Yet another rumour, circulated more openly by the IMO's enemies in Moscow, was that Alain Simon had bought marble mines in Russia and was using the IMO as a front for a lucrative marble trade.[56] This at least had some tenuous link with reality. A former Soviet miners' official elected to a Ukrainian city council had asked Simon if he could put the local state marble enterprise in touch with any potential buyers in France. Simon obliged, though nothing came of the contact. Nevertheless, this and other lurid tales were still being circulated by the CEU in October 1991, when the new Ukrainian republican miners' union brought a questionnaire to the IMO – prepared by Myachin – asking among other things: 'Has the general secretary got any other private villas apart from those in the Alps, Paris, at the Azure Beach and the Atlantic shore? Does he help the IMO with his personal fortune?' In real life, Simon had no such villas and was paid the same wage as all other French miners' officials, while the powers-that-be in the Soviet miners' union had some skeletons in the cupboard of their own. Pension arrangements, records of petty corruption in the handling of hard-currency expenses, and all the other usual instruments of bureaucratic pressure proved more than enough to keep Srebny and other current or ex-officials in line. Victor Myachin, whose wife worked in the AUCCTU accounts department, was in an unusually well-informed position to help win support for his special approach to international relations.[57]

Behind the attacks by elements of the decaying Soviet trade-union apparatus on the IMO was the desperation to distance itself from the politics of the past and to ingratiate itself with its counterparts in the West. It is hardly surprising that Western interests were just as anxious to see the destruction of the IMO, which by 1990 was six million strong and far larger than the rival MIF. The IMO was the only trade-union international prepared to give practical support and training for militant industrial action anywhere in the world. Hundreds of thousands of dollars were funnelled through the IMO – including from the Soviet trade unions – to build up the South African miners' union outside of the control of the ICFTU or the US and West European foundations. Western governments and trade-union centres wanted to see such an organization discredited in the former Soviet Union and Eastern Europe. Gavin Lightman's denunciation of the IMO and his recommendation that the NUM reconsider its affiliation played directly into the hands of these wider machinations.

From the time of the Soviet miners' strikes of 1989, British, American and West German embassy officials and representatives of a kaleidoscope of institutes and foundations kept themselves busy fishing in the politics of the Russian mining unions and communities. In the shifting Soviet political sands of 1990, the NUM–IMO Moscow Gold scandal was milked for all it was worth. The despatch to Britain of relay teams of miners from tiny Soviet breakaway unions demanding 'their' money back was all part of the show. These were the Russian visitors with the unmistakable calling cards, members of NTS, the CIA-backed Russian émigré organization once described by Yuri Andropov, the one-time KGB chief and Soviet party leader, as 'enemy number one'. Their host was the NTS's man in London, George Miller, who in the early 1980s had organized a bizarre CIA-financed demonstration in Moscow in collaboration with Brian Crozier – the freelance MI6 agent and confidant of Margaret Thatcher, Ronald Reagan and CIA director Bill Casey. Crozier arranged the cash subsidy directly with Casey. Miller provided eight days' 'training' in a London 'safe house' for the two young Tories who went to the Soviet Union to stage an anti-peace-movement stunt.[58]

In October 1990, fresh from his propaganda successes in the Scargill Affair, Miller travelled to the Ukraine with David Prendergast and Neil Greatrex of the Union of Democratic Mineworkers and Eric Hammond of the maverick right-wing electricians' union to attend what would become the founding congress of the breakaway 'independent' Soviet miners' union in the mining town of Donetsk. This event – remarkably enough, paid for by the Soviet government – was a recall of a miners' delegate congress in July, when Alain Simon among other speakers had successfully urged the rejection of a proposal to set up a new union. Simon had warned that division would be used to weaken the miners' bargaining strength. By October, however, ceaseless muckraking about the IMO and the Soviet donation of five years earlier had taken its toll. While Simon personally leafleted mines in the neighbouring town of Makeevka, delegates at the second congress voted, against boisterous protests, to exclude him from the hall. The US and German embassies, along with the ubiquitous Friedrich Ebert Foundation, were however well represented.

Miller was given the floor on several occasions and raised the issue of the 1984–5 strike donation. Both Hammond and Prendergast also spoke, the latter telling the Soviet pit representatives how his own organization had been formed to fight Scargill's 'undemocratic attitudes and communist behaviour'. At his second attempt, Miller managed to persuade the delegates, despite opposition from the chair, to vote in favour of court action by a 'committee of miners' wives' he claimed had been formed in Britain to have the Soviet cash aid of 1985 returned to the Soviet Union. If this action was not taken, he argued, Scargill and the NUM would 'absorb the money' – the opposite complaint to that unsuccessfully pressed through the British courts. At all events, nothing more was ever heard of Miller's phantom miners' wives.[59]

Since that time, the Soviet Coal Employees' Union has split into different national unions. Myachin finally succeeded in persuading the Russian union to join the MIF, though the Ukrainians stayed with the IMO. The 'independent' miners' union founded at Donetsk stagnated and was taken under the wing of the Coal Ministry. The CIA's man, George – now 'Yuri' – Miller moved to Russia in 1992 after the final collapse of the Soviet Union and became an economic adviser to the Yeltsin government. Both Sergei Massalovitch, who complained to the British Fraud Squad about Scargill's 'diversion' of Soviet aid, and Yuri Butchenko, who followed in his footsteps under Miller's tutelage, were later expelled from the Vorkuta strike committee for misappropriating the organization's equipment. Butchenko subsequently set up his own 'information agency'.[60]

Meanwhile, long after the fall of the Berlin Wall, the international trade-union movement carried on fighting the Cold War. Trade unions remained locked into structures which held back the kind of cross-border action that could match the globalization of capital. As the centrist British union leader John Edmonds predicted, the implosion of the WFTU in the wake of the collapse of the East did not reunite the international trade-union movement, but left it more fragmented than ever. In triumphalist mode, the ICFTU and its sister organizations initially hoovered up a few East European unions or paid for ideologically 'acceptable' rivals, while rejecting unity with 'tainted' organizations such as the French CGT – though that changed when the ICFTU later turned into the International Trade Union Confederation.[61]

The IMO was damaged by the political fallout from the collapse of the Soviet Union and Eastern Europe, but survived. The MIF resolutely set its face against every approach from the IMO to create one miners' international on the basis of a merger of the two organizations. The IMO was not forgiven for failing, as expected, to expire gracefully into the arms of its enemies. Nevertheless, the Paris-based organization expanded into other industrial sectors, and in 1994 merged with the old energy section of the WFTU to form an eleven-million-strong independent international, the International Energy and Miners' Organization, or IEMO, including the Russian and most of the Middle Eastern oil producers' unions. And after the financial scandal subsided, the Mireds international solidarity fund was used to provide practical support to Indian, Cuban, Moroccan and sub-Saharan African miners' unions.[62]

In the wake of the Soviet Union's demise in 1991 and the selective opening of the CPSU archives by the Yeltsin government, subsidies from the Soviet Communist Party's Central Committee to communist parties – including the British – and national liberation movements like the African National Congress were heavily publicized and became fair game for right-wing propagandists. Far less has been heard about the vast Western financing operations to anti-communist movements around the world, including sympathetic trade unions. For many years after the Second World War, money came directly from the CIA. Later, it was channelled through less embarrassing conduits, such as the US-government-financed National Endowment for Democracy. For all their apparent enthusiasm for trade-union independence and despite the end of the Cold War, ICFTU-linked unions and projects continued to receive large-scale funding from governments, the European Commission and state-funded institutes. Often, the use of that money was exceptionally crude. Daniel Ojij and Mustapha Zakari of the Nigerian Coal Miners' Union, for example, described an approach by an MIF-affiliated union leader at the International Labour Organization's four-yearly coal-mines-committee conference in Geneva in 1988. The official offered Ojij an envelope stuffed with hundreds of dollars if the two Nigerians would vote against Scargill as chair of the workers' group for the conference. They refused and joined the IMO. Scargill was elected and caused such an upheaval in the sleepy bureaucratic backwaters of the ILO that the follow-up conference, due in 1992, was postponed for three years.[63]

During the 1980s, the secret Western financing of East European 'reform' movements, such as Solidarnosc in Poland, was on a grand scale. While the Soviet party and trade-union hierarchies were fretting about whether to provide cash aid to the British miners' strike, the Reagan presidency in the United States was getting on with a highly effective destabilization programme against the Jaruzelski regime in Poland, including elaborate secret funding arrangements to the anti-communist underground. In June 1982, Reagan signed a secret National Security Decision Directive, NSDD 32, which authorized a sweeping series of economic and covert measures against the communist regimes of Eastern Europe. The most ambitious operations under the directive were carried out in Poland, coordinated by the CIA in close cooperation with the Vatican.

Vast quantities of cash and equipment – such as printing presses and CIA-supplied radio transmitters – were smuggled into Poland. Some came direct from the CIA. More often, money was funnelled through the NED, the Free Trade Union Institute or the US trade-union umbrella body, the AFL-CIO. Bill Casey, then head of the CIA, successfully mobilized his friends in the Socialist International to smooth the shipments and cash transfers. As in the NUM's case, funds were often brought in couriers' suitcases. In the dying days of the old Polish regime, $1.5 million a year was being pumped into Solidarnosc. Whether Western governments will be so generous to their trade-union friends in the future seems doubtful. But such a scale of intervention puts the relatively modest Soviet and East European trade-union aid to the miners in 1985 in some perspective.[64]

# CHAPTER SEVEN

# STELLA WARS

The whole crazy gang of fantasists, liars, double-crossers, rogues and bureaucrats that make up the intelligence community will never seem glamorous again. *Phillip Knightley, 1993*[1]

On the corner of Gower Street and the Euston Road – one of central London's most congested arteries – there stood until the late 1990s an eight-storey building of memorable ugliness. Towering over Euston Square underground station, nothing relieved the dreariness of its postwar architecture, dark-stained concrete walls, ubiquitous yellowing net curtains and forlorn-looking aspidistra plants behind its unmarked glass doors. This was 140 Gower Street, headquarters for more than two decades of the state security service, MI5: the first line of retreat for redundant colonial administrators and a fitting home for an organization where, in the words of the novelist John Le Carré – the pen-name of one its former officers, David Cornwell – 'everyone seemed to smell of failure'.

But times have changed and MI5 has come up in the world since Cornwell's day. The 2,000 strong domestic spying outfit has abandoned its eight utilitarian offices scattered around the capital and moved into far grander premises. Its headquarters are now a multimillion complex in Westminster, close to the seat of institutional and political power. The 'imperial neo-classical' Thames House on Millbank, specially converted for a trifling £238 million, is today MI5's operations centre. From there, security service mandarins are able to admire the even more opulent, neo-Ceauşescuite palace occupied by their foreign-intelligence counterpart and bureaucratic rival, MI6, on the other side of the river. Nothing, it seems, is now too good for the secret services. MI5's new thirteen-floor Edwardian head office boasts the finest walnut panelling, polished marble flooring, a gym and squash courts, two glass-roofed courtyards and a gallery staircase. A French sculptor was commissioned to design imitation rock-faces for a trophy room, worth around £25,000. But the architect thought them vulgar and they were thrown on a skip.[2]

MI5 proved itself to be a master of the Whitehall game. By switching resources in the 1970s from the thankless task of unmasking Soviet agents – success in which always tended to elude Britain's would-be spycatchers – to the more rewarding work of 'counter-subversion', fishing in troubled institutional waters, smearing and hounding political opponents, and manipulating the media and official appointments, MI5 went from being something of a seedy bureaucratic backwater to a key player in the government machine. The cosy relationship between elements of the intelligence services and the right wing of the Tory Party proved to be a vital lubricant in smoothing Margaret Thatcher's rise to power. By tacitly using its friends and influence to bolster the standard-bearer of the New Right in opposition, and by responding to her every whim in office, MI5 earned the Prime Minister's undying gratitude. Thames House is a measure of the effectiveness of MI5's strategy. Nigel Lawson, the former Chancellor of the Exchequer, remarked acidly of Thatcher's attitude:

> The security services, their establishments and their hardware, were one of the very few areas of public life virtually untouched by the rigours of the Thatcher era. Most Prime Ministers have a soft spot for the security services, for which they have a special responsibility. But Margaret, an avid reader of the works of Frederick Forsyth, was positively besotted by them.[3]

Nor did MI5 fall from favour with the ousting of its patron, the end of the Cold War, and the drastic decline in the strength of its favoured targets in the left and the labour movement.

Under John Major's administration, the privileged position of the security service was, if anything, enhanced. The new flexing of MI5 muscles achieved a first institutional casualty in 1992, when the service was awarded 'lead responsibility' over the police in the struggle against the IRA in Britain. In the wake of the 1994 IRA ceasefire, MI5 moved in on other traditional areas of police work, including drug trafficking and organised crime. While still ensconced in her plush third-floor Gower Street sanctum, Stella Rimington, MI5's first woman director-general, became a respectable public figure. She even appeared on television to give a lecture on the virtues of modern spying before a selected audience of nodding worthies. Senior police officers, who claimed that MI5 was already active in industrial espionage, warned of the emergence of a full-blown 'second, secret police force' as the security service threw its weight about in the search for a post-Cold-War role. It found that role in the aftermath of the 9/11 attacks in 2001 and the 'war on terror', more than doubling its size and attracting new levels of media deference – along with multiple allegations of complicity in torture and illegal 'rendition' of suspects.[4]

But if Thames House was a prize for faithful service, 140 Gower Street remained the monument to MI5's darkest period until then. This was the anonymous office block where, notwithstanding the sophistic denials of both ministers and Rimington herself, a gang of MI5 officers unquestionably plotted to bring down Harold Wilson's Labour government. It was from Gower Street that – in the words of MI5's most famous defector, Peter Wright – agents 'bugged and burgled [their] way across London at the state's behest'. This was the nerve centre of the massive counter-subversion operations of the 1970s and 1980s. It was also the place where a senior MI5 apparatchik masterminded the shoot-to-kill 'Operation Flavius', which ended with the gunning down of three unarmed IRA members in Gibraltar in 1988. And it was at this building – conveniently located next door to the rail-union headquarters and directly across the road from the old NUM head office – that 'Mrs R', as Stella Rimington was affectionately known by her subordinates, earned her spurs running MI5's most ambitious counter-subversion operation to date: the secret war against the miners.[5]

## THE CLEAVE LEAKS

Covert operations by the British security services against so-called subversives – effectively, those who seek to change the established social and political system – have throughout their history remained shrouded in the absolute mystery that Whitehall reserves for its guiltiest secrets. There have, of course, been dramatic revelations which have exposed MI5 to the glare of unwelcome public attention. The conspiracy by a section of MI5 against the Labour government in the 1970s was brought to light partly as a result of leaks from Wilson himself and partly because one of the plotters, the retired MI5 assistant director Peter Wright, felt he had been cheated out of a proper pension. There was also the confession of Colin Wallace, the Belfast-based army 'psychological warfare' officer, who kept documentary evidence of the anti-government Clockwork Orange dirty-tricks campaign that MI5 officers wanted him to help organize. Most telling of all was the sober testimony of Cathy Massiter, a former MI5 officer in its counter subversion section, F branch, who risked jail in the mid 1980s to expose the security service's politically directed telephone tapping, recruitment of informers, and willing manipulation by the Thatcher government in its propaganda offensive against the Campaign for Nuclear Disarmament.[6]

Sometimes, MI5 counter-subversive operations have come to light in bizarre circumstances. One such case was that of Ken Roberts, a left-wing official with the film and television technicians' union ACTT, who was 'fitted up' by the security service and tried for selling Kodak technical secrets to the East Germans in the mid 1960s. The case appears to have been tied up with internal MI5 machinations against its director-general of the time, Roger Hollis. The trial collapsed when it was shown that MI5 officers had given false evidence and another witness had been paid to lie. Another, more far-reaching, 1960s operation against the trade-union movement was actually made public by the Prime Minister of the day. Harold Wilson used MI5 bugging transcripts and informers' evidence to denounce communist influence in the 1966 seamen's strike as the work of a 'tightly knit group of politically motivated men'. Wilson brought senior MI5 officials and 'one of the operators in the field', he recorded in his memoirs, to a secret meeting with Edward Heath with the aim of winning the Tory leader's support for breaking the strike. At that time, one National Union of Seamen committee reportedly consisted entirely of Special Branch informers, and the union's right-wing officials were kept regularly informed by the security services about the tactics of NUS militants.[7]

Such glimpses of the power exerted by the secret service on the agendas of pliant politicians and trade-union leaders have been relatively rare. It was officially acknowledged for many years that MI5's main domestic target was the Communist Party and its sympathizers. But beyond the circulation of anecdotes about widespread surveillance and blacklisting, little reliable information emerged about post war MI5 and Special Branch operations against the left and labour movement. That was even more true of other parts of the intelligence establishment, such as the increasingly powerful Government Communications Headquarters, which also targets domestic government opponents. The ban on union membership at GCHQ in 1984 attracted all sorts of unwelcome attention and investigation. But the authorities remained vigilant. Three years later, the Cabinet secretary was granted an injunction preventing one senior GCHQ cryptanalyst, who left in protest against the ban, from disclosing anything about his thirty-two years at the Cheltenham complex.[8]

But the stream of detailed leaks about security-service measures against the NUM – set off by the unravelling of the 1990 media jamboree – began to expose something on an altogether different scale. Taken together with earlier evidence, the new allegations revealed the outline of the most comprehensive spying and dirty-tricks effort ever undertaken by the secret state against any domestic 'dissident' target in Britain. For anyone who cared to look, the muddy footprints of the intelligence services were clearly all over the Scargill Affair from the beginning. There was even a smattering of wry press speculation about the 'spook factor' during the early part of the 1990 campaign. In a strongly anti-Scargill editorial about the *Mirror* and *Cook Report* stories in March 1990, the *New Statesman* remarked sarcastically, but presciently: 'Let us say that the entire story of the mortgage . . . is a fabrication – it has, for the sake of argument, been planted by MI5 to distract attention from the poll tax.' The television presenter Muriel Gray, who had previously interviewed Scargill at some length, wrote in the *Sunday Correspondent* a few months later:

> I cannot be the only journalist who is suspicious of this whole series of allegations . . . Scargill has known since he started his career that his enemies, who must certainly include the intelligence service, would be forever vigilant to catch him . . . if the allegations have been orchestrated by some unseen foe, then the question is not why but who . . . I wish I had never watched A Very British Coup.[9]

It was widely assumed that the NUM in general, and Arthur Scargill in particular, must have been MI5 targets, and there had been a number of reports of longstanding surveillance of the miners' leaders. But anything other than informed speculation about security-service involvement in the media and legal campaign against the NUM and other covert operations was virtually impossible to come by. In the last few weeks of 1990, that began to change. On Tuesday, 11 December, the day after the Serious Fraud Office announced it was dropping its investigation of the NUM's affairs, the *Guardian* was contacted by a small group of discontented GCHQ employees through an intermediary.[10]

They alleged that a large-scale 'Get Scargill' operation – authorized personally by Margaret Thatcher and involving GCHQ, MI5 and police Special Branch – had been run both during and after the miners' strike. The operation had been aimed at 'destroying' the NUM leader 'both politically and socially', and was directly linked to the *Mirror* and *Cook Report* campaign. It had culminated in an abortive attempt by the intelligence services to deposit £500,000 in a Scargill-linked bank account in Dublin with the aim of framing him as an embezzler. The transaction was set up with the intention of making it appear that the miners' president had arranged for the 'disappearance' of large quantities of cash. Using the background of regular payments back and forth between various accounts belonging to the International Miners' Organization and those controlled by Scargill and his immediate associates, a man posing as a Paris-based IMO official contacted the Irish bank – which was named by our informants. Arrangements were made for the cash to be transferred from a Paris branch of the Bank of Credit and Commerce International. BCCI, which was closed down by the Bank of England in 1991 for fraudulent dealing, has since become known to have been widely used by a variety of state intelligence services. The CIA, for example, was reported to have made regular payments through BCCI to five hundred British 'contacts' in politics, commerce, the media and academia. But the Irish phoney deposit operation went awry. A man had attempted to withdraw the cash before the transfer had taken place and an employee at the Dublin bank had become suspicious. The bank-account fiasco then became the subject of a high-level official complaint to the British authorities by the Dublin government, which was primarily concerned to protect the privacy and reputation of its flourishing financial sector.[11]

Intelligence material, our informants claimed, had been fed directly into the *Mirror*'s campaign of allegations against the NUM leadership. They also reported that British and United States electronic espionage networks had systematically breached the security of banking transactions throughout Europe in an effort to track the secret movement of NUM cash and the British miners' funding links with Eastern Europe. The surveillance drive had begun during the miners' strike of 1984–5, but had continued for several years afterwards. This vast electronic eavesdropping operation – using the Cheltenham-based GCHQ and its outstations, as well as US National Security Agency facilities across Europe (its so-called 'C-group' network) – led to growing friction with the banks themselves, which rely on an increasingly fragile international confidence that all transactions are genuinely private.[12]

At the time of the miners' strike, the NSA – which is the most secretive of all the US intelligence agencies and works closely with the Central Intelligence Agency – had 'cracked' Soviet international banking networks and was able to keep track of covert transactions with the West. In November 1984, when a Soviet bank tried to lodge $1 million in an account controlled by the British miners' union in Zurich, the NSA traced the deposit as soon as it was made, tipping off British intelligence that Soviet money was being channelled to the NUM. Around the same time, the first Moscow Gold tales started to appear in the British press. The Soviet authorities were aware of their exposure and Swiss banking and government circles cooperated to seal the breach in the security of their banking system, with its potential damage to depositor confidence.[13]

The original Soviet donation was returned to Moscow and Alain Simon, then MTUI general secretary, was told by Soviet officials at the time that their international banking links were no longer secure. But the NSA tip-off led the British Prime Minister to authorize the use of GCHQ-NSA facilities for comprehensive surveillance of the European banking system in support of her war on the NUM. By the beginning of 1985, NSA listening posts across Western Europe and the Morwenstow satellite station in Cornwall – an outstation of GCHQ Cheltenham – had been mobilized to monitor all international financial transactions which could in any way be linked to the British miners. A former RAF base at Cleave, four miles north of Bude, the 'Combined Signals Organization Station' of Morwenstow (now 'GCHQ Bude') is jointly run and financed by NSA and GCHQ, using both British and American personnel. The site is dominated by huge dish aerials which can be seen for miles around. Cleave was also conveniently close to BT's satellite communications centre at Goonhilly Down, which received transatlantic and European telephone traffic until its closure in 2008.

Controversy over the abuse of these satellite spying bases for domestic political surveillance first surfaced in US congressional investigations in the early 1980s. The NSA had been using the Morwenstow station – as well as Menwith Hill, near Harrogate in Yorkshire, the biggest tapping centre in the world – to run a project called 'Minaret', aimed at recording the international telephone calls of a watch-list of anti-Vietnam war and civil-rights campaigners. Jane Fonda and Martin Luther King's successor, the Reverend Ralph Abernathy, were among those subjected to NSA bugging. An investigation by the US Senate's Church Committee led to the Federal Communications Act, outlawing NSA involvement in domestic politics. A parallel code of conduct was drawn up shortly before the miners' strike under which Downing Street had to give permission for the use of GCHQ or associated facilities in counter-subversion operations against a British domestic target. Thatcher's authorization was based on the supposition that the miners' strike and its network of international support constituted a threat to 'national security'. Without her personal go-ahead, the operation would have been illegal.

The British government was not, in fact, only concerned about financial backing from Eastern Europe and the Soviet Union. On 25 October 1984, the High Court ordered the sequestration – in other words, seizure – of the NUM's funds throughout the world, after the union refused to pay a £200,000 fine for contempt. A receiver was appointed to take control of all NUM assets five weeks later. At least initially, Roger Windsor's complex schemes to hide the union's funds were successful. Eight-and-a-half million pounds had been spirited away, even before the strike started, and routed through seven countries before ending up in banks in Luxembourg, Zurich and Dublin. In October, £4.7 million was taken from Jersey in dollar bearer bonds in a private aircraft to Luxembourg by two NUM employees and deposited in a little-known bank called Nobis Finance. On 20 November 1984, Arthur Scargill told a miners' rally: 'This firm of Price Waterhouse are going bananas. Do you know why? They can't find your money. They are going crackers.'

Scargill was wrong. Backed by a secret and unprecedented commitment by the Attorney General, Sir Michael Havers, to refund the sequestrators' costs – however large – Brian Larkins, then a partner in Price Waterhouse in charge of the sequestration effort, had already traced and frozen most of the union's money. At the time, Larkins appeared to possess almost psychic powers in tracking down NUM funds. The *Guardian*'s GCHQ informants alleged that vital pieces of the information he used to find his way through the maze of confidential bank accounts came from NSA–GCHQ surveillance. Some information was also supplied by bankers – notably Rainer Kahrmann of EBC Schweiz, who admitted in a telephone call to an enraged Scargill that he had broken banking confidence. The fact that the courts had also agreed that anyone helping the sequestrators would be reimbursed for any breach of confidentiality or loss from the union's own funds no doubt helped to loosen bankers' tongues. But Kahrmann could only provide part of the jigsaw the sequestrators needed. The Bank of England had instructed all foreign banks operating in Britain to report any accounts opened in the names of Scargill, Heathfield, McGahey, Windsor, Hudson, Myers or Trevor Cave. And the High Court ordered banks with British branches to provide details of any accounts which could be linked to the NUM. But most insist that they did not volunteer any information – the sequestrators already knew almost everything they needed by the time they arrived.

Two years later, in 1986, Larkins refused to reveal how he had 'blown the cover' of the Nobis cash, saying only that it was a 'difficult area'. German and Luxembourg banking sources insisted the tip-offs had come from Britain. The case of the NUM cash caused a small earthquake in the cosy world of continental banking, particularly secretive Switzerland, where the threats posed by the British courts to banking confidentiality had seemingly not been anticipated. In the post-strike period, continuing large-scale electronic surveillance of the European banking system – as the intelligence agencies attempted to follow the NUM leaders' ongoing financial manoeuvres – caused increasing alarm. As it became clear that electronic monitoring of bank transactions was turning into a habit, particularly with the US authorities keen to use NSA–GCHQ networks to expose drug money laundering operations, the bankers grew restive. The risk that the banks, alarmed by breaches of financial privacy, might blow the whistle on what had been going on was one reason, our GCHQ informants claimed, that the Fraud Squad suddenly dropped its Scargill investigation.[14]

Officials in Britain and Ireland stonewalled on the GCHQ allegations. In Dublin, we paid a visit to Ireland's Bernard Ingham, a garrulous bull of a man by the name of P. J. Mara, who worked as press secretary for the then Prime Minister, Charles Haughey. 'So you're saying this fellow Scargill was fitted up, then?' he asked us in his parliamentary office at the Dail, sounding genuinely intrigued. He promised to look into it, warning that sometimes the 'security boys can be a bit difficult'. Either way, he would give us a 'steer'. The next day, P.J. seemed edgy. He said he was having a spot of trouble about the inquiry, but he would sort it out and get back to us. After that, he refused to make any comment, on or off the record – either on the claim that Irish officials had protested to the British government about the phoney deposit incident or that they had demanded the surveillance of the Irish banking system be abandoned. In fact, he refused point blank even to take our calls.[15]

Senior officials at the Irish bank named by our informants as the target of the botched British secret service 'sting' against Scargill were equally nervous. In common with other Dublin banks used by the British miners' leaders and the IMO, they accepted that they were likely to be under British electronic surveillance, but threatened to sue if we named them. Continental bankers involved in the NUM's attempts to evade sequestration and receivership were more forthcoming. Several admitted privately that they were convinced they had been bugged by the British authorities and provided supporting evidence.

In May 1991, some details of the GCHQ Morwenstow leaks were published in the *Guardian* as part of an investigation of the Scargill Affair carried out in cooperation with Channel Four TV's *Dispatches* programme. The revelations led to a flurry of parliamentary activity on both sides of the Irish Sea. In Dublin, the Irish Labour leader and former deputy Prime Minister, Dick Spring called on the Haughey government to make a full disclosure. 'If British intelligence is abusing the Irish financial sector for its own ends, it would be extraordinarily reprehensible. If strong protests haven't been made, they should be,' he declared. But a series of written questions Spring submitted to the Irish Foreign, Finance and Justice ministers – including one which referred to 'allegations that the British security service attempted to make a deposit in an Irish bank as part of a dirty tricks campaign associated with the NUM in Britain and that the Irish bank allegedly refused to accept the transaction because of suspicion that the transaction was not genuine' – drew a bureaucratic blank. At Westminster, the Labour MPs Tam Dalyell and George Galloway took up the allegations. Several questions were met with the standard: 'It has been the policy of successive governments not to discuss the work of the intelligence services.'[16]

However, on 3 June 1991, Dalyell made a breakthrough. In answer to a query about the methods used to sequestrate NUM funds, John Major confirmed for the first time that the government provided information directly to Brian Larkins of Price Waterhouse to help him trace the hidden cash. 'The sequestrators requested and obtained from the government, as well as others, information relevant to the discharge of their duties to the court,' Major admitted. The apparently anodyne reply underpinned the GCHQ group's claims that details of banking transactions gleaned from surveillance intercepts had been given to Larkins. Major later refused to reveal what information had been passed on because it was 'provided to the sequestrators in confidence'. But as John Hendy QC, who acted for the NUM, commented: 'I am not aware of anything legitimate that the sequestrators would need to know from the government.' Dalyell declared: 'I cannot think of any other interpretation than that the Prime Minister has confirmed the allegations made in the *Guardian*.'[17]

With its vast technical resources, GCHQ had been increasingly drawn into tapping the telephone calls and other communications of domestic 'subversives' – something that had in the past been an MI5 prerogative. By the 1990s, satellites and monitoring equipment linked to the GCHQ network already had the capacity to 'harvest' all international telecommunications, along with domestic telephone links. As well as monitoring international diplomatic and military communications, GCHQ was used to 'hoover the airwaves' in cooperation with the United States and other NATO countries. Employing around 5,500 people, GCHQ targets came to include commercial firms, newspapers, radical groups of all kinds, as well as foreign embassies and 'suspected terrorists'. As the quantity of surveillance mushroomed, computer systems were developed to search for key words and recognize voices. A special unit called K20 was set up in the 1980s to process surveillance material about 'subversives', which was then passed to Joint Intelligence Organization officials in Whitehall. But as demonstrated by the NSA leaks to the *Guardian* in 2013 revealing mass surveillance of global internet, email and mobile phone traffic, the scale of NSA–GCHQ electronic spying has since reached another level altogether.[18]

Our 1991 GCHQ informants, who were based at Cleave camp, Morwenstow, had been directly responsible for the surveillance of the NUM leadership and its attempts to 'squirrel away', in the words of Sir Michael Havers, vast sums of money outside the reach of the British judiciary. As far as the Cleave group was concerned, their station and other former Cold War spying facilities were being routinely abused for domestic politicking. The government ban on union membership at GCHQ, imposed in January 1984, just six weeks before the start of the miners' strike, left a lingering bitterness among many of those who agreed to leave their unions – as well as those who resigned or were sacked for refusing to do so. There are also a significant number of United States citizens working at GCHQ, who lack the deferential Whitehall mentality which afflicts many British civil servants. The GCHQ Cleave group had approached a Labour MP – a man from a mining area who, they said, was known to be 'close to Kinnock' – about their concerns over the Scargill operations. To their surprise, nothing had happened. But with the airing given to some of their allegations in the *Guardian*, they felt they had made their point. In the gossip factory of Whitehall, it was said that Major had let it be known he would not cover up for his predecessors' abuses of the security services and the country's electronic eavesdropping network. But in the wake of the *Guardian*'s disclosures, an internal leak inquiry was ordered at Morwenstow. Copies of several tapes and transcripts were sent abroad for safekeeping until the excitement blew over.

## STELLA RIMINGTON AND THE MINERS

Further leaks about the security services and the miners would follow. In December 1991, the Home Office announced that Stella Rimington had been appointed the new director-general of the security service to succeed Sir Patrick Walker. It was the first time the government had ever publicly named the head of MI5, and 'Mrs R' also became the first woman to head any major security and intelligence organization anywhere in the world. Eighteen months later, a smiling Stella Rimington posed for pictures in her Gower Street office with the Home Secretary, Michael Howard, the first occasion on which an MI5 officer had ever been willingly photographed for public consumption. Her 'coming-out party' was lapped up by most of the media as a 'charm offensive' by Britain's new spymistress, the 'Queen of Spies'. But the public-relations coup had its own kickback, leading directly to the naming of Roger Windsor in parliament as Rimington's 'agent provocateur'.

A career civil servant who joined MI5 in 1969, Stella Rimington was sold in off-the-record briefings to journalists at the time as one of a new breed in the secret service who had had 'wide experience in all areas' of security work. She was 'not a hardliner' from the old guard, it was said, nor tainted by the treasonable, anti-democratic plotting of the semi-fascist MI5 gangs of the 1970s. A woman who had once unsuccessfully applied to be headmistress of Roedean, the girls' public school, she was described as a 'Shirley Williams type', who liked to walk her dog, do the weekly food shopping at Marks & Spencer and give her daughter driving lessons. She was even said to have had reassuring domestic quarrels with her neighbours over the height of her garden fence. The carefully programmed effort to rehabilitate MI5 and its deeply tarnished reputation reached a climax in the summer of 1994, when Rimington delivered the annual televised Richard Dimbleby lecture from the Banqueting Hall in Whitehall – site of Charles the First's execution 345 years earlier. She gave an accomplished performance, full of bland assertions and tongue-in-cheek asides. MI5, she told the assembled company, was modern and accountable, the accusations made against it 'ludicrous'. The invited audience of notables cheered her to the rafters.[19]

But her security career hardly bears out such a comforting picture, divided as it has mostly been between MI5's two dirtiest areas of work: running operations against the labour movement and the war against the IRA. Most of her time was spent in F branch, the domestic subversion department and the growth area of the 1970s and early 1980s. There was a period in F5, covering Ireland, when she occasionally visited Belfast, and another as head of F2, which targets the trade unions and industrial disputes. In the late 1980s, she was appointed director of counter-terrorism, covering both the IRA and Middle Eastern groups operating in Britain. It was in this capacity that she was alleged to have overseen Operation Flavius, which ended with the killing of an unarmed three-person IRA active service unit in Gibraltar (though she herself says she was put in charge of counter-terrorism shortly afterwards). Despite the fact that MI5 admitted at the inquest to having passed on seriously misleading intelligence to the SAS, which carried out the shootings, the security service considered Flavius a 'successful operation'.[20]

The announcement of Rimington's appointment was supposed to be 'in line' with MI5's new formal legal status following the passage of the 1989 Security Service Act. But there was no requirement to publish the MI5 director-general's name under the Act, and the suspicion was that John Major's administration, which started life without a single female Cabinet minister, was simply trying to win equal-opportunities acclaim. One persistent campaigner against the subterfuges of the secret state who took that view was Tam Dalyell. For Dalyell, the news that Stella Rimington would be the new MI5 director-general also came as something of a shock. Her name – as well as her maiden name, Whitehouse – was well known to him from the time of the miners' strike of 1984–5. As the dispute dragged on and picket-line confrontations became more bitter, police chiefs from the Lothians and Border Police, the force covering Dalyell's Linlithgow constituency (including the then chief inspector Donald McKinnon), had repeatedly complained to him about interference by MI5 officers in the policing of the strike.[21]

As head of MI5's F2 section and an MI5 assistant director, Stella Rimington had overall control of MI5 operations throughout the year-long coal dispute and reported directly to government. For the service, and for Rimington's career, it was a crucial test. As Dalyell puts it: 'MI5 wanted to ingratiate themselves with the PM – who looked a permanent fixture – by breaking the NUM.' One senior Lothians police officer, who remembered her from Edinburgh University as Stella Whitehouse, described the rising security-service apparatchik as 'intimately involved' in supervising the whole gamut of MI5 activity against the strike, from mass surveillance to 'fieldwork', including the running of agents. MI5-guided agent provocateur operations against striking miners in the Scottish coalfield caused enormous tensions with the local conventional force. But with the green light from Thatcher, MI5 ran amok in the mining areas throughout Britain. Its freedom of manoeuvre was vastly expanded during the strike because the division of responsibilities between the local county police forces, the police 'national reporting centre' – which coordinated police action against the miners on a countrywide basis – Special Branch and MI5 itself was never defined.[22]

As one senior police officer who repeatedly clashed with MI5 put it: 'Ground rules! You must be joking! What ground rules?' Tam Dalyell remarks drily: 'The Lothians and Border Police, many of whose sergeants and constables, and some of whose senior officers came from mining families, were not kept in the picture.' Police Special Branch – sometimes described as MI5's footsoldiers – also ran their own dirty tricks during the strike, particularly on picket lines. Policemen dressed as pickets were often reported as singling out miners for arrest or provoking violent incidents, while Special Branch informers – or 'snouts' – in pit villages earned £30–40 a week during the strike for passing on snippets of information and giving regular confidential reports to the police.[23]

But the government was not remotely satisfied with Special Branch's intelligence efforts. One chief constable of an English county force at the centre of the 1984–5 strike described a gathering of his fellow police chiefs from all over the country during the dispute at which a Home Office mandarin appeared with a 'personal message from the Prime Minister'. 'She was convinced', the official reported, 'that a secret communist cell around Scargill was orchestrating the strike in order to bring down the country. The fact that the police could not prove that this conspiracy existed was because of the weakness of our intelligence-gathering. She wanted us to set up a secret Public Order Intelligence Unit, to infiltrate and monitor groups and activities which threatened order.' The unit was to be separate from Special Branch and CID, though formed from their officers. While Special Branch 'only looks at subversive groups and activities', this was intended to concentrate on 'legitimate groups like the NUM', to gather intelligence for the control of 'public order'. To the unfortunate chief constable's 'surprise and horror, instead of telling her that it was rubbish, my senior colleagues all agreed to do it. It's been set up in London, I believe, but I've been frozen out because I showed my shock.' It does not take an enormous leap of imagination to guess which elements, inside and outside the government machine, convinced Thatcher about the 'secret communist cell' running the strike.[24]

One local agent provocateur operation reportedly run by MI5, which gives some idea of what the service got up to on the ground and which led directly to the closure of a pit, took place at Polkemmet colliery in Scotland in the summer of 1984. Polkemmet, the last coal mine in West Lothian, had a reputation as a Protestant 'Orangemen's' pit and supplied the politically sensitive Ravenscraig steelworks. Bert Wheeler, then the Coal Board's Scottish area director, was one of the hardest-line corporation managers, a man prepared to use every tactic to break the strike and force miners back to work. Efforts were concentrated on pits where men had originally voted at NUM branch level against striking, but had then accepted the majority decision of the Scottish coalfield to support the national action and had stayed out. Polkemmet was one of them. In the summer of 1984, the strike organizers at Polkemmet heard from NCB clerks working at the pit that six miners were planning to go back to work on the Monday after the Glasgow Fair holidays. A series of mass pickets were held in protest in the second half of August and twenty-seven strikers were arrested one morning in clashes with the police as the six, mostly surface workers, were bussed into the colliery. Alan Ramsay, then a face-worker and member of the NUM branch committee, was one of those detained that day. He describes how a police chief inspector – a man who had been brought up in the same village – singled him out for arrest on the picket line. Like thousands of other miners in 1984–5, he was badly beaten by police officers. 'There are things that happen to you in your life that you never forget, experiences that are ingrained in your heart,' he says, looking back.[25]

The strikebreakers were in contact with local Conservative Party figures at the time of their return to work, while security-service officers operated behind the scenes. Their job was made easier because miners at Polkemmet had moved there from closed pits all over the country. One of the six who crossed the picket line had recently arrived from the north of England to get a job in the Scottish coalfield. The first to go back was a man named Bob Marshall – nicknamed 'Silver Cabbage' by the strikers after the Nottinghamshire working miners' organizer, Silver Birch. Interviewed by the local paper a couple of weeks after he first broke the strike, Marshall had 'found it difficult to pinpoint any one reason for his return to Polkemmet colliery . . . "Enough was enough" is all he offers in explanation, shrugging his shoulders unhappily.' With emotions running high, the strikers occupied the colliery locker rooms and decided to picket out members of NACODS, the pit deputies' union – who traditionally supervise safety work in the mines – after the NCB refused to accept their demand that the six working miners be sent home.[26]

The NUM continued to allow a limited number of NACODS members through for essential safety work. But while in other areas management took over the responsibility for safety when NACODS members refused to cross picket lines, Wheeler would not allow managers to provide safety cover at Polkemmet and other Scottish pits. Wheeler's tactics were a game of brinkmanship, set against the background of the NCB's determination to close dozens of collieries. 'You sit it out,' he said. 'We were asking people to go to work . . . we must have the courage to take it to the ultimate.' At other collieries, the threat that the pit would be lost without proper safety cover drove miners to abandon the strike. This was the game-plan at Polkemmet, which was used by the Coal Board to erode the strikers' morale throughout the Scottish coalfield. As Jim Neilson, the Polkemmet NUM branch delegate in 1984, puts it: 'They were trying to scare men back to their work.' In the absence of full safety cover, Wheeler ordered Polkemmet's power supply, pumps and fans – essential to keep mines clear of gas and water – to be switched off on 21 August 1984, without giving Neilson the customary prior warning. The campaign in the local media for a return to work reached fever pitch. While emergency safety teams were stopped from taking action, Polkemmet was badly flooded and the pit was lost as a result. Neilson told the press at the time: 'Management have caused the present problem by coercing scabs to come in ... they refused to allow our safety men into the pit.' Among NUM and NACODS members, the flooding was seen as deliberate Coal Board sabotage. Polkemmet colliery was closed for good almost immediately after the strike.[27]

The Polkemmet incident was widely and effectively used in Coal Board return-to-work propaganda. But the close involvement of MI5 in the affair enraged the local constabulary. As Tam Dalyell – who regularly went to the Polkemmet picket line, at the request of both the local NUM and police – puts it: 'There was great concern among local police forces about the involvement of state authorities over which they had no control.' Dalyell says he was told by senior Scottish police sources that 'the six Polkemmet miners who crossed the picket lines, and led to the stopping of the pumps which flooded the pit, were put up to it. They did not do it off their own bat, or on their own initiative. It was foreseeable and foreseen what would happen to the safety arrangements, if any miners tried to break the strike.' Despite the police worries, one of the six joined the local force as soon as the dispute was over. Alan Ramsay was sacked during the strike but was taken back at the Longannet complex, the last British Coal colliery in Scotland. Jim Neilson was forced to take redundancy and ended up at a private mine from which he was sacked for his trade-union activities in 1993. After their experiences, neither is much taken aback to discover that there were covert forces at work during the August 1984 crisis at Polkemmet. 'It doesn't surprise me that there was state interference,' Ramsay says. 'We have the most ruthless and evil ruling class on this earth.'[28]

Dalyell had referred to Stella Rimington's role in the miners' strike in the draft of his 1987 book *Misrule*. But his publisher, Hamish Hamilton, demanded that any reference to the MI5 officer be removed to 'avoid trouble'. With the announcement that Rimington was to be the new MI5 director-general, however, he decided to try again. It was the day after the appointment was announced by the Home Office that Dalyell put down his first Commons motion calling for a statement on Stella Rimington's role in the 1984–5 coal dispute. In particular, he demanded an account of her 'connection with the activities of Mr David Hart', the eccentric millionaire who had advised the Prime Minister and the Coal Board during the strike and had played a central role in the financing and organization of the back-to-work movement. The government response – that it never comments on MI5 operations – is dismissed by Dalyell as unacceptable.

> They opened this Pandora's box to win political brownie points. If they parade the excellence of their choice, they can't be surprised if other people want to know a bit more about her. It would be quite unacceptable if the head of the security service had been party to any activities as an *agent provocateur* in an industrial dispute.[29]

Crucially, from the point of view of its political impact, Dalyell's motion was signed by Merlyn Rees, a former Labour Home Secretary, who had in the late 1970s himself been the minister responsible for MI5 during one of its wildest periods. Rees had notably deferred to the intelligence services, both as Northern Ireland Secretary and Home Secretary. In 1976, for example, he meekly accepted security-service and CIA demands and ordered the deportation of Philip Agee, an ex-CIA officer, and Mark Hosenball, an American journalist, on national-security grounds, after they had started to expose the extent of CIA operations in Britain. Rees had convinced himself that he controlled the security services 'completely' and dismissed Harold Wilson as 'absolutely paranoid' when the former Prime

Minister started to talk about the secret-service conspiracies against him in the late 1970s.[30]

As the truth of what had actually been happening in MI5 – while Rees had been confident he was in 'complete control' – started to emerge in the 1980s, he began to change his mind. MI5 had even forged a letter, it transpired, with Colin Wallace's help, insinuating that Rees was a contributor to the American pro-IRA Noraid organization. By 1990, the former Home Secretary was ready to admit: 'There has got to be much wider public discussion about the policies of the security services.' Dalyell's motion was also signed by Peter Archer QC – later Lord Archer – who had been Solicitor General in the last Labour government. Archer had changed his mind as well. 'I now think that Wilson was clearly right about the security service. There definitely was a section of MI5 that was out to overthrow him.'[31]

## HART OF DARKNESS

David Hart was a rich, freewheeling property developer and farmer, occasional novelist, film-maker and journalist, and a former bankrupt who made and lost a fortune in the early 1970s' speculative boom. He was also a deeply ideological person of pronounced right-wing 'libertarian' views, a professional anti-communist, variously described as a 'conspiratorial ... somewhat bizarre figure' and a 'man with a mission' in the more restrained accounts of his activities. Accepted in the inner sanctums of the Tory right for well over a decade, Hart's role in the secret crusade against the miners and their leaders was crucial.

The victim of vicious anti-Semitic bullying as a schoolboy at Eton, David Hart had an unusual family background. His father, from whom he inherited vast wealth, co-founded Ansbacher's merchant bank. His aunt, Jennifer Hart, was a Comintern agent, who shared the same Soviet controller in the 1930s as Kim Philby and Anthony Blunt. A man who at one time entertained both the communist trade-union leader Ken Gill and the guitarist Eric Clapton at his country-house parties, David Hart's commitment to the New Right took on a messianic flavour in the years of the Thatcherite ascendancy. From the early 1980s, he developed close links with the Prime Minister herself and became, in the phrase of the then editor of *The Times* Charles Douglas-Home, foremost among the 'Downing Street irregulars'. Some of his initial contacts with Thatcher were through Ian Gow, the Tory leader's parliamentary private secretary and a Thatcherite 'ultra' with close ties to MI6. By 1982, Hart was already providing the grateful Prime Minister with holiday reading lists. 'Thank you,' she wrote to him on 15 September of that year, 'for guiding me to the chapters which were *compulsory* reading.' And during the 1983 general election, he was a constant adviser.[32]

Early in the 1984–5 strike, Hart arranged accreditation for himself from *The Times* as a feature writer and began to tour the mining areas in a Mercedes driven by his chauffeur, a former policeman named Peter Devereux. Concentrating his efforts on the divided Midlands pit villages, the banker's son set about organizing a network of disaffected and strikebreaking miners. Overcoming with cash and force of personality the suspicion that not surprisingly greeted his efforts, this bizarre Biggles-like figure travelled more than 35,000 miles in three months, crisscrossing the coalfields, holding secret meetings in pubs and hotels. Hart encouraged a spirit of clandestinity. He adopted the alias David Lawrence. John Liptrot, one of the main working miners' organizers and litigants, took the name John Joseph. In extravagant patrician style, he entertained his coalfield protégés at his suite in Claridge's Hotel in London. Gradually, linking up with active local strikebreakers – like the former market trader, Chris Butcher, glamorized by the media as Silver Birch – Hart put together around twenty-five cells of dissident miners to rally the back-to-work movement under the auspices of the National Working Miners' Committee. Hart originally financed the committee himself. Out of his obsessive activism grew the political roots of what would later become the

Union of Democratic Mineworkers.[33]

Hart reported regularly to Thatcher by telephone and in hand-delivered notes. With her agreement, he had introduced himself to the Coal Board chairman, the elderly American Ian MacGregor, who had worked with his brother Tim at the merchant bankers Lehmann Brothers. 'He could ... circulate just as easily among the miners of Nottinghamshire as he did in the highest political circles,' MacGregor wrote later.

> As we chatted, I began to realise that he was the man I had been looking for ... His experiences confirmed my feelings that there must be numbers of men out there who would respond to any help, guidance or encouragement we could give. Someone like David could assist them in launching campaigns to go after the NUM on legal grounds.[34]

This Hart did with gusto, while deliberately avoiding using the Tories' provocative new anti-union legislation. The strategy was to bring case after case against the NUM from the working miners' groups, bog down the union leadership in time-consuming legal wrangles, and launch a direct assault on the union's funds. Hart called the tactics the 'Gulliver concept' – because 'each one of the many actions tied another tiny legal rope around the NUM until it woke up one day and couldn't move' – and the 'insect concept', because that was how he saw the union, with Scargill as the head, the national executive as the thorax and the miners the body. The actions were aimed at applying pressure on the thin connections between each part. Hart raised the cash for many of the cases from rich Conservative businessmen, among other sources. Sir Hector Laing, chairman of United Biscuits, and Lord Hanson, who were both also major Tory Party contributors, stumped up for Hart's strikebreaking miners. So did John Paul Getty II from his hospital bed in a London clinic, where Hart turned up with MacGregor after hearing that the billionaire had donated money to the striking miners. Around half a million pounds was raised for Hart to pay both legal and media advertisement costs.

One of the most devastating of the legal actions was set in train by two working Yorkshire miners, Ken Foulstone, who was later convicted of robbery and cleared on appeal, and Bob Taylor, who ended up running a small business on the South Coast. MacGregor describes the Foulstone and Taylor case as having been 'the key to the solution of the strike'. The initial funds were provided through Chris Butcher, and Hart liaised with the Conservative lawyers who handled the case. In September 1984, the High Court ruled the strike unofficial and unlawful. Arthur Scargill rejected the decision: 'There is no High Court judge going to take away the democratic right of our union to deal with its internal affairs. We are an independent democratic trade union.' The NUM national executive and a special delegate conference agreed.[35]

The solicitors immediately applied for leave to bring contempt proceedings. The order was issued on the Monday of the Labour Party conference in Blackpool, which the NUM was taking by storm. But the writ had to be served on Scargill that day or its validity would expire and proceedings would have to be postponed for weeks. Hart stepped in, chartered a helicopter from his luxurious country pile – Coldham Hall near Bury in Suffolk – flew to London heliport to collect the process server, landed him in Blackpool and then used a phoney press pass to sneak the official into the conference hall, so that he could serve the legal documentation on an outraged miners' president. All the while, Hart patrolled about 'looking like a Spitfire pilot'.[36]

The following week, the NUM was fined £200,000 and Scargill £1,000 for contempt. The union and its president ignored the fines and on 25 October Mr Justice Nicholls in the High Court ordered the sequestration of the NUM's assets. When the sequestrators ran into difficulty laying their hands on the millions of pounds the union had moved abroad, Hart convinced Colin Clarke and fifteen other members of the Working Miners' Committee to go back to court to call for the NUM trustees – Scargill, Heathfield and McGahey – to be replaced by a receiver. Hart described Clarke, who was later appointed a director of British Coal Enterprise, as a 'saint'. This

Hart initiative became the most effective legal assault on the NUM of all. The Working Miners' Committee action, based on the flaws in Roger Windsor's scheme for hiding NUM funds overseas, was successful against all legal precedent. And from the beginning of December 1984 until June 1986, the NUM and all its property was in the legal control of a court-appointed solicitor, Michael Arnold: the 'official receiver'. Arnold subsequently sued the three former trustees – and the banks which helped move the NUM's funds abroad – for breach of trust. The action against the union's officials was only finally dropped in 1988, after a settlement was reached with the banks.

The NUM had been expecting sequestration and had prepared for it. The miners' leadership was after all committed to the collective decision taken by the Trades Union Congress at Wembley in 1982 to defy anti-trade-union legislation as an attack on fundamental democratic rights. Receivership, the legal takeover of the union itself, was something else altogether. No other trade union has been the subject of such a court order, before or since. It left the real NUM, rather than the High Court's legal fiction, as an effective outlaw, living out of carrier-bagfuls of secret cash donations – much of it from abroad – These were exactly the circumstances which would be used in 1990 as the basis for the *Mirror* and *Cook Report*'s allegations of financial misappropriation and chicanery.

As the strike wore on, Hart became the Coal Board chairman's closest adviser. In Tam Dalyell's words, Hart 'developed a weird hold over MacGregor'. During the latter months of the strike, the balding, mustachioed conspirator was to be found in the chairman's office at Hobart House as often as the chairman himself. At one point when MacGregor was abroad, Hart actually issued orders in MacGregor's name. MacGregor himself admits that it was Hart who convinced him to see the fight with the NUM as a crusade for democracy against Marxist tyranny, and the working miners as its 'freedom fighters'. Hart also brought in Tim Bell of the Saatchi and Saatchi advertising agency, who had helped run the Tories' propaganda campaigns in the general elections of 1979 and 1983. The aim was to harden up the Coal Board's less-than-scintillating public-relations effort. Hobart House traditionalists, such as the industrial-relations director Ned Smith and PR director Geoff Kirk, were enraged by the role played by Hart and Bell. They were convinced that Hart sabotaged possible settlements, and both retired from the Board before the end of the dispute. Kirk died a few months later in a freak boating accident off the Isle of Skye, where he was writing a book about his experiences.[37]

During the NACODS dispute in the autumn of 1984 – when, by Margaret Thatcher's own admission, her government came closest to defeat – Hart was intimately involved in the frantic efforts to prevent the pit deputies from joining the NUM strike. Eric Hunt, a right-wing member of the NACODS executive at the time, remembers a visit from Hart during October 1984 at the Metropole Hotel in London. 'He called up saying he was a Times feature writer and myself and Joe Benham, the union's treasurer, met him that night. He was full of promises and offered to arrange a personal meeting with either Maggie Thatcher or MacGregor independently of the executive. He conned us.' The following morning, Kevan Hunt – MacGregor's head of industrial relations, who played an important intelligence-gathering role during the strike – phoned the two officials at 8 a.m., saying that Peter Walker, the Energy Secretary, already knew about Hart's discussions with them. The Coal Board man came straight over to the hotel with a secretary, who took detailed notes of their version of the encounter.

During the same period, Ned Smith was summoned by MacGregor to his Belgravia flat in London to talk over the NACODS crisis with Hart and Tim Bell. 'Both Hart and Bell referred to the NACODS leadership in emotional terms. A number of them were accused of being communist sympathisers, which was ridiculous. I was asked if it was possible to cooperate with them on stirring things up, but I refused.' The day before the deputies' strike was due to close down Thatcher's lifeline – the working Midlands collieries – the NACODS executive voted to call off the action and accept the Coal Board's offer of a nonbinding independent review procedure for pit-clo-sure decisions. Ten years later, that procedure had not saved a single colliery, NACODS had been all but wiped out as a union and Thatcher said she remained 'unclear' why the deputies had settled and saved her skin. NACODS leaders from the strike period say that some of the union's more pliant officials were offered 'backhanders', jobs and special pension deals in return for their cooperation over the dispute. Eric Hunt, who admitted he kept Coal Board managers fully briefed during September and October 1984, came to believe, like the majority of the surviv-ing 1984 NACODS executive, that he 'ought to have voted for a strike'.[38]

Whatever might be conceded to buy off the deputies, David Hart was utterly determined that there should be no deal of any kind with the NUM, and by the autumn of 1984 had appar-ently convinced the Prime Minister. In a note to MacGregor on 10 October 1984, Hart wrote that the strike was clearly political and it was 'not in the national interest' to reach any kind of compromise with Scargill. In the last stages of the dispute, he began to fear wrongly that his efforts to 'frustrate all attempts by Peter Walker and Ian MacGregor to negotiate a settlement' were foundering. Any negotiated agreement with the NUM would be 'politically undesirable', Hart warned the Prime Minister. It was essential, Hart believed, that the miners should be forced to return to work without a settlement – which, at the initiative of Kim Howells and others in the NUM's South Wales area, is what eventually happened. 'I couldn't have done without him,' Thatcher said privately of Hart in the late 1980s.[39]

Among the claims Hart himself later made about the miners' strike was that Scargill and the NUM were trapped into con-centrating mass picketing on the British Steel coking plant at Orgreave near Sheffield – scene of the most violent con-frontation in postwar industrial relations. Action against Orgreave began after the state-owned steel corporation broke a written agreement with the union regulating deliveries to the plant. Running battles between police and pickets rose in intensity throughout May and the first half of June 1984 and reached a crescendo on 18 June, when Scargill was knocked unconscious at the site. In the NUM president's absence, the Yorkshire and other area union leaderships rapidly scaled down the picketing. Orgreave had been canvassed, not least by Scargill, as a potential rerun of the miners' victory at Saltley in 1972 and a way of galvanizing the labour movement. So the outcome was seized on as a historic failure of the tactic of mass picketing. But ironically, on 18 June, Robert Haslam, British Steel's chairman, had in fact ordered Orgreave to be closed to prevent further scenes of mayhem and the plant was temporarily shut down – not unlike the initial closure of Saltley coke depot twelve years earlier.

According to Hart, however, Orgreave was a 'set-up by us'. The coke was not needed. 'It was a battle ground of our choosing on grounds of our choosing . . . the fact is that it was a set-up and it worked brilliantly.' His words echoed those of the police commander at Orgreave, Assistant Chief Constable Anthony Clement, who told the 1985 trial of ninety-five Orgreave pickets charged with riot before its ignominious collapse that if there was to be a battle he had wanted it to be 'on my own ground and on my own terms'. The allegation also chimed with some pickets' memories of being directed towards the plant on the day. Both NUM officials and British Coal managers, however, were more sceptical. And in view of the pickets' success in temporarily forcing the plant's closure, it seems likely to be at best only part of the story. The chief constable of South Yorkshire later conceded that if mass picketing had continued after 18 June, the police would have had difficulty keeping the plant open.[40]

Both during the strike and afterwards, Hart kept in regular touch with the Prime Minister and acted as her unofficial adviser and speechwriter. MacGregor confirms Hart's role as an intermediary: 'I never knew the extent to which either Tim [Bell] or David Hart were privy to the Prime Minister's thinking, but on the few occasions when messages were passed on, they were never in the form of orders.' His influence with

Thatcher riled the less hawkish Energy Secretary, Peter Walker, who had told Hart that he did not believe the coal dispute could be usefully run from Claridge's. 'I seem to be doing all right so far', was Hart's supremely arrogant reply. Later, Hart took a close interest in the breakaway Union of Democratic Mine-workers, which partly grew out of the Working Miners' Committees and which he regarded as a 'bulwark against Marxism'.[41]

According to highly placed police and Whitehall sources, Hart also maintained close links with Stella Rimington and MI5's operations against the striking miners as he roamed the country plotting and organizing strikebreakers in 1984–5. Both his legal and practical initiatives in the coalfields were coordinated informally with Gower Street. Brian Crozier, the Cold Warrior who worked for both the CIA and MI6, records that Hart had 'indirect but reliable access to two members of the [NUM] executive' throughout the strike. With the imprimatur of the Prime Minister and his wide network of contacts, he was an ideal and highly effective MI5 fellow-traveller and unofficial agent. As Ian MacGregor described Hart's role on the tenth anniversary of the strike: 'His job was to find intelligence on which we could base our campaign. It was just like in wartime.'[42]

In the years after the coal strike, the multimillionaire actively nurtured his links with the intelligence world, which were extensive on both sides of the Atlantic. Hart was a friend of the late CIA director William Casey and was fêted in Reaganite Washington. Fred Ickle, who had been number two at the Pentagon, was a guest at Hart's country mansion. Herb Meyer, a former senior CIA officer, helped to edit a hard-line Cold War monthly bulletin, *World Briefing*, for Hart in the late 1980s and early 1990s. Hart also paid for a visit to Britain in 1988 by Adolfo Calero, the Nicaraguan Contra leader, and ran a samizdat agency for Russian and East European dissidents in the dying days of the Soviet Union.[43]

Around the same time, Hart took over from Brian Crozier – himself an assiduous intelligence 'asset' – the publication of a monthly political smear-sheet, *British Briefing*, which attempted to pin communist sympathies on a host of unlikely Labour MPs, writers, lawyers and charities. Among its targets in the late 1980s were the then Labour frontbencher Bryan Gould, the playwright Howard Brenton, the QC Lord Gifford, and the National Council for Civil Liberties (NCCL). *British Briefing*, previously called *Background Briefing on Subversion*, was described by Hart as a 'monthly intelligence analysis of the activities of the extreme left' and distributed free to selected journalists, politicians and industrialists. Until 1990, Hart's monthly was edited by Charles Elwell, a former assistant director of the security service and head of 'FI', the section of MI5's domestic 'subversion' branch which dealt with the Communist Party.

Elwell has been linked with the MI5 gang who plotted against Wilson in the early 1970s. He was also the security-service officer who ordered the targeting of left-wingers in the media and classified the NCCL – now renamed Liberty – as a subversive organization. The branding led, as Cathy Massiter revealed, to a large-scale surveillance operation against the pressure group. Neither *British Briefing* nor Elwell's earlier research efforts give cause for much confidence in the quality of MI5's intelligence about 'subversion'. Shortly after retiring from the security service, Elwell published a survey of the left press which was notable for its factual inaccuracies – including, in passing, about the author of this book. Colin Wallace, the former army information officer, remarked of Hart's monthly freesheet: 'Many of the smears in *British Briefing* are exactly the same sort of thing I was being asked by MI5 to spread in the 1970s. Some of the politicians … are the very same people I was being asked to smear.' Hart was also a long-time associate of Rupert Allason, one of the then Tory MPs considered closest to MI5. He was campaign organizer for Allason, alias the spy writer Nigel West, when he fought Kettering and Corby in 1979.[44]

Hart continued to move in elevated government and intelligence circles in the late 1980s and early 1990s, despite Thatcher's decline and fall. He was in regular contact with Sir Percy Craddock, the chairman of the Joint Intelligence Committee, the powerful Whitehall outfit which processes material from MI5, MI6, GCHQ and military intelligence. Despite his failed attempts to become a Tory MP, he carried on visiting Downing Street after Major took over, and guests at his country estate included Cabinet ministers such as Norman Lamont, when he was the Chancellor of the Exchequer, and two long-standing friends, Malcolm Rifkind and Michael Portillo. Between 1989 and 1992, Rupert Murdoch, the English-speaking world's most powerful media tycoon, saw fit to finance Hart's activities to the tune of £270,000.

In the wake of the 1992 general election, Hart re-emerged from the political shadows to position himself once again at the heart of policy-making. His house guests became his patrons. The following year, Hart was appointed as a consultant to Malcolm Rifkind at the Ministry of Defence, where he advised on the privatization of service property and infuriated the military establishment with unflattering comparisons between the cost-effectiveness of the RAF and that of the Israeli air force. Hart's companies had, it turned out, made well over a million pounds from property deals for British Coal's pension funds in the five years after the end of the miners' strike. By 1994, Hart was also working as a political adviser to the then darling of the Tory right, Michael Portillo. Indeed, when Portillo was Chief Secretary to the Treasury, Hart laid on a free office for his 'special adviser', Alison Broome. As for the coal strikebreakers Hart once championed, their admiration for him had long since evaporated as formerly protected UDM collieries were ruthlessly shut down with the rest. In the words of Chris Butcher, who ten years after the pit strike admitted he believed Scargill had been right after all: 'David Hart is an entrepreneur who basically couldn't give a damn about the miners.'[45]

## SPASM OF CLASS PANIC

The scale of the involvement by the intelligence services in covert operations against the NUM and its leadership has its origins in the spasm of class panic that gripped the establishment in the early 1970s. Every few generations, sections of the British ruling class have lost their nerve in the face of a rising tide of social unrest. And every time that has happened, the authorities have turned to time-honoured techniques of infiltration, espionage, disinformation and surveillance against domestic dissenters – alongside propaganda and the open use of force – as part of their armoury of self-defence.

In the early nineteenth century, when large areas of the North of England were in open insurrection at the time of the Luddite revolt, the infected regions were successfully flooded with spies as well as troops. Hundreds of informers and agents provocateurs were sent into the radical and reform movements. Others supplied information, real or imagined, on an ad hoc basis for 'payment by results'. There was 'Citizen Groves', for example, an executive member of the influential pro-Jacobin London Corresponding Society in the 1790s, who was accused of being a government informer, tried by the society's general committee and triumphantly acquitted. But he was, in fact, a spy. In the years after Waterloo, 'Oliver the Spy', the legendary agent provocateur who worked for the Home Office and was dramatically exposed by the *Leeds Mercury*, helped to incite the 'Pentridge uprising' so that the government could stage a few exemplary treason trials. Then there were the pitiful Cato Street conspirators of 1820, who plotted the assassination of the Cabinet under the guidance of a provocateur, were arrested, hanged and thus helped the government through a tricky election.[46]

After the First World War, when industrial militancy was sweeping the country and the 'Bolshevik plague' threatened every government in Europe, terrified industrialists set up a private political vetting service, the infamous Economic League – which continued to blacklist thousands of political and industrial activists into the 1990s – and MI5 forged the Zinoviev letter which helped bring down the first Labour government. The letter, purportedly sent to the Communist Party by the president of the Comintern in Moscow and calling for 'agitation-propaganda' in the armed forces, was almost certainly passed to Conservative Central Office by an MI5 officer named Joseph Ball. It was then leaked to the *Daily Mail*, which published it four days before the general election of October 1924.[47]

It was in the aftermath of the Russian Revolution that MI5 first switched attention from spycatching to fighting the threat from its own people. As the security service's own self-serving history of itself, published in 1993, put it: 'After the Bolshevik coup d'état of October 1917, MI5 began to counter the threat of Communist subversion.' Arthur Cook, leader of the miners' union during the General Strike and the six-month coalowners' lockout, was the target of almost continuous surveillance by police and Home Office agents from the second half of the First World War onwards. The intelligence operations against Cook were never on the scale deployed half a century later against Scargill, but the endless stream of informers' reports on his syndicalist and anti-war militancy in the South Wales coalfields sent the authorities into apoplexy. He was a 'sedition-monger' and an 'agitator of the worst type' who should be prosecuted and jailed, the Chief Constable of Glamorgan, Captain Lionel Lindsay, repeatedly warned the Home Office. Cook was, in the event, twice sent to prison for his political and trade-union activities.[48]

The early 1970s were another such time of class panic. Two successful miners' strikes in two years, a rising tide of industrial action, the electoral defeat of a Tory government on a 'Who runs the country?' ticket, a government climbdown in the face of a threatened general strike over the jailing of five dockers, and the growing radicalization of the Labour Party and the trade unions sent the country's business and political elites into a tailspin. Throughout the capitalist world, the postwar boom was giving way to an upsurge in working-class militancy and successful challenges to American global power. In Portugal, Spain and Greece, Western-backed fascist regimes were overthrown. In Southeast Asia and southern Africa, anti-imperialist movements were coming to power. The oil-producing states were flexing their muscles. As the United States faced defeat in Vietnam, it unleashed a murderous coup d'état on the Chilean people to rescue them from the left-wing government they had elected. Everywhere, the governing classes were getting nervous.

In Britain, they were getting positively hysterical. There was widespread talk of coups, national governments and private armies. 'It was a time of paranoia', the journalist Godfrey Hodgson recalled more than a decade later. 'Rich men made plans to shift their money abroad ... Industrialists met secretly to discuss what was to be done, paid private armies to train in the West Country. Establishment cabals muttered that what we needed was a strong man.' The Heath government repeatedly declared national emergencies and used troops in industrial disputes. Factions in the security services plotted to forestall and then bring down a Labour government. Some elements in MI5 had even managed to convince themselves that Harold Wilson was a Soviet agent. Brian Crozier, the MI6 and CIA 'alongsider', gave regular talks to groups of army officers warning of the possible need for military intervention. On one occasion, he recalls the audience 'rose as one man, cheering and clapping for fully five minutes'.[49]

The second miners' strike, the three-day week and the defeat of the Heath government ratcheted up the rising panic. As Tony Benn puts it: 'Capital was utterly demoralized at that time. Their reading of the [1974] miners' strike was that it had been a sort of rerun of the General Strike and that they had lost.' Rumours and smear stories of the most lurid kind were spread through 'helpful' journalists and politicians. In a case which bears more than passing similarities to the abortive Scargill bank-account operation described by the GCHQ whistle-blowers, a forged Swiss bank account was leaked to the press after Labour's return to office in 1974. It appeared to show that Ted Short, then Labour's deputy leader, was breaking exchange-control legislation and illegally investing abroad. A Scotland Yard investigation was suddenly and inexplicably abandoned. Short, now Lord Glenamara, is convinced that the forgery was a security-service dirty-tricks job – a suspicion confirmed by Peter Wright. In an even dirtier operation the same year, sections of MI5 reportedly helped foment the 1974 Ulster loyalist strike against 'power sharing'. Links between the intelligence services and the right wing of the Tory Party were close. Together they regarded Heath as a traitor and worked for Margaret Thatcher's election as Tory leader. There is a very real sense in which 'Thatcherism' grew out of a right-wing faction in the defence and security establishment.[50]

This was the background to the huge increase in activity by the security services against the left and the trade-union movement in the 1970s and early 1980s. Peter Wright claims that it was Edward Heath himself who encouraged the switch of MI5 resources from counterespionage to countersubversion, particularly in the trade unions – though any such 'encouragement' was filtered through Victor Rothschild, the head of Heath's think-tank, who undoubtedly had his own agenda. The 1972 miners' strike was the turning point. Power cuts were followed by a state of emergency and the dramatic closure by mass picketing of the strategically vital coke depot at Saltley. The miners' flying pickets, joined by thousands of striking Birmingham engineering and building workers, were led by Scargill, then a little-known Yorkshire NUM activist. The Battle of Saltley Gate clinched the strike victory and came to obsess the Tory leadership and the state-security machine for the next twenty years. As a direct result, the entire Whitehall national-emergencies apparatus was reconstituted under the Civil Contingencies Unit, and the national 'war plan' was redrafted with a new emphasis on coping with an 'internal enemy'.[51]

Within a few weeks, Sir Michael Hanley, then MI5 director-general, called a day-long seminar at 140 Gower Street to explain what was to be the new focus on 'domestic subversion'. The centre of MI5's concern should now be what he called the 'far and wide left', and a rapid expansion of F branch was needed to cope with it. 'The Prime Minister and the Home Office ... had left him in no doubt that they wanted a major increase in effort on this target.' The old guard, who were more concerned with the anti-Soviet crusade, were resistant to the new line and the downgrading of their pet projects. In Peter Wright's words: 'Big Brother loomed'. When he retired from MI5 in 1976, Wright thought that F branch, the growth area in the service, 'was something I didn't like the look of at all. It seemed more and more like a Gestapo.'[52]

Special Branch recruitment within the trade-union movement had already been stepped up by the time of the first miners' strike of 1972. More than a dozen SB officers were working full time on the unions in London alone. But the discovery by MI5 that Special Branch bodyguards were feeding information on trade-union leaders directly into the Prime Minister's office led to a Whitehall row. The SB was brought to heel and MI5 took a far more active lead in industrial operations. In 1970, there was one man and an assistant in charge of monitoring the trade unions at Gower Street. By the early 1980s, MI5's industrial unit had twelve desk officers – backed up by a small army of handlers, agents and informers, technical and secretarial staff – guiding Special Branch and overseeing the service's own trade-union work. According to one former security-service officer, 'literally hundreds' of trade-union officials and activists were signed up in the 1970s as informers – or 'sources', as they are known in MI5. Among those the security services tried to recruit was Alan Jinkinson, who took over in 1993 as leader of Britain's biggest union, the newly merged Unison – reported at the time to be a target for increased surveillance because of its potential industrial strength. Jinkinson was approached by an MI5 agent active in the Labour Party.[53]

MI5 also targeted labour correspondents in both newspapers and broadcasting during the 1970s and early 1980s, who were recruited in droves for their contacts with a wide range of trade-union officials – and with each other. The operation was apparently a 'great success'. According to Peter Wright, MI5 had always had about twenty senior journalists working for it in the national press. 'They were not employed directly by us,' he explained, 'but we regarded them as agents because they were happy to be associated with us.' The labour correspondents' operation was something extra. As well as using the reporters to get close to left-wing union leaders, MI5 was particularly keen to feed into a small coterie of journalists around Mick Costello – industrial editor of the *Morning Star* and later the Communist Party's industrial organizer – who was then a prominent member of the labour and industrial correspondents' group. According to one former officer, as many as three-quarters of the labour correspondents at that time became informants of one type or another for the security service or Special Branch. MI5's success in press penetration puts a whole new perspective on the remark by Nell Myers, the NUM's press officer – which scandalized some journalists at the time – that the labour correspondents were 'basically our enemies' frontline troops' during the 1984–5 miners' strike.[54]

Among those labour reporters to have spoken publicly about being approached by the security service to work as an informer is Tim Jones of *The Times*. In 1975, he was invited to lunch at Simpson's-in-the-Strand in Central London by an MI5 officer who said the security service was worried about 'Soviet penetration' of industrial correspondents' circles. Jones told the agent that he was being transferred to Wales and would therefore not be of much use. Terry Pattinson, principal author of the *Daily Mirror*'s 1990 campaign against the NUM leadership, says he was also asked to work for MI5. Pattinson remembers being taken out to lunch when he worked at the *Daily Express* by a man who said he was a 'retired consultant' from an employers' organization with 'friends in high places'. He was a 'charming old fellow. He asked what my politics were and whether, if in the course of my job I could be of use to my country, I would be prepared to do so. What he meant was that he wanted information about the left. They thought there were too many reds in the Industrial Correspondents' Group and too many journalists being suborned by the Communist Party. I wasn't and never would be.' Pattinson says that he told his host he didn't see how he could help. The MI5 man gave him a number to ring if there was anything he felt he could pass on.

Pattinson called some time later 'to see if he was genuine', but the number was unobtainable. MI5 and Special Branch recruits among industrial and other correspondents would prove invaluable when the showdown with the miners finally took place several years later.[55]

During the 1970s and into the early 1980s, telephone tapping, mail interception, infiltration and break-ins against the left and the trade unions in particular were all sharply increased. Routine security reports on the trade unions had been passed to employment ministers for many years, as Barbara Castle discovered in the 1960s. After 1972, as extra resources were channelled into the F2 trade-union branch, surveillance became frenetic. Disinformation, smear campaigns and psychological operations were stepped up in what was already a tense political atmosphere. The train drivers' union leader Ray Buckton was the target of death threats, and the white-collar workers' leader Clive Jenkins had a bullet shot through his living-room window. Armed Special Branch guards were provided for leading trade unionists, though Buckton was convinced that his death threats had been engineered to provide an excuse for round-the-clock surveillance. Forty volumes of material were collected by MI5 on the two most powerful trade-union leaders of the 1970s, Jack Jones and Hugh Scanlon, in an attempt to link them with the Communist Party and East European intelligence services. The files were then used to bar them from government appointments. As with the files that MI5 keeps on hundreds of thousands of other people, their dossiers were at that time stored in the vast hall on the first floor of its Curzon Street offices in Mayfair.[56]

Every significant strike was the focus of concentrated MI5 and Special Branch activity. 'Whenever a major dispute came up . . . it would immediately become a major area for investigation', according to Cathy Massiter, who resigned in 1984 after fourteen years in MI5 because she believed that counter-subversion operations were 'getting out of control' and that the service was breaking its own rules in the political interests of the Tory government. When Ken Gill, the communist leader of the draughtsmen's union TASS, was planning a merger with the engineering workers' union, MI5 broke into his South London house to bug the room where crucial discussions about the amalgamation were taking place. Details of internal union debates and tactics were often passed to ministers and officials. As one civil servant told a Fire Brigades' Union negotiator who complained about phone-tapping during the firefighters' strike of 1977: 'We've got to know what you're going to do.'[57]

## BRIXTON TIP-OFF

By the time of the 1984–5 miners' strike, the counter-subversion machine was primed and at peak strength. Whitehall preparations for the confrontation, based on the Tory right-winger Nicholas Ridley's report drawn up in opposition, were comprehensive. After Thatcher temporarily backed down over the threat of a national pit-closures strike in 1981, the process of building up power-station coal stocks, mobilizing the police 'national reporting centre', boosting oil-firing at power stations, and increasing the exorbitantly expensive input from nuclear power were all intensified. Preparations by the security services were just as thorough. The analogy offered a decade later by Nigel Lawson, Chancellor of the Exchequer in 1984–5, gives a flavour of the government's approach: 'It was just like arming to face the threat of Hitler in the late 1930s,' he said. 'One had to prepare.'[58]

The phone-tapping operation in 1984–5 was the most ambitious ever mounted. Arthur Scargill and Mick McGahey, two of the three NUM national officials during the strike, had been under comprehensive surveillance for many years. Anyone considered close to the NUM president was also fair game. During the 1980s, for example, Professor Vic Allen, an associate of Scargill and now the NUM's official historian, was put on the immigration service's Suspects Index, with the instruction that MI5 should be informed of his movements as a matter of routine. One former MI5 clerk who transcribed bugging tapes told

Channel Four television in a signed affidavit that Scargill's phone had been tapped continuously from the 1970s. Massiter put the surveillance down to 'his particular history and his known political views'. The MI5 clerk recalled that:

Scargill himself would occasionally shout abuse into the phone at the people who were tapping him. Mick McGahey was subjected to intensive surveillance, including the tapping of his home telephone. This gave rise to an office joke about the girls who had to listen to Mrs McGahey's interminable telephone conversations with friends and relations. But we were able to get information from her chatting about his movements, which he himself was careful to conceal.

McGahey's regular London hotel, the County in Bloomsbury, was bugged by MI5. So was the North Sea Fish Restaurant in Leigh Street, the fish-and-chip shop near the old NUM headquarters in London where Scargill, McGahey and other left-wing members of the executive used to meet to discuss tactics.[59]

Throughout the year-long dispute itself, the security services leased the building directly opposite the NUM's headquarters at St James's House in Sheffield. Every NUM branch and lodge secretary had his phone monitored. So did the entire national and area union leaderships, as well as sympathetic trade unionists and support-group activists all over the country. 'Tinkerbell', as the national British Telecom tapping centre was known, was the heart of the operation, though GCHQ also played an important role. At that time, thirty thousand individual lines were estimated to be tapped every year in Britain. By 2008, hundreds of thousands of phone and private communication intercepts were being authorised. In the 1980s, GCHQ's domestic tapping effort was using voice- and word-recognition equipment to ratchet up the tappers' reach. A generation later, its vastly increased capacity allows blanket surveillance of internet, email and mobile phone traffic. The scale of surveillance during the miners' strike was already so great that it created an unmanageable 'information mountain' as words like 'picket' were used to trigger the system. On one occasion, the entire Tinkerbell operation simply ground to a halt when all the tapes ran out.[60]

Surveillance apart, Scargill was personally the target of several violent attacks during the dispute – a couple of which in particular would be difficult to dismiss as the spontaneous actions of enraged members of the public. On one occasion in the summer of 1984, the NUM leader was driving home from Chesterfield on an empty road when another car repeatedly tried to force him off the road towards a steep incline. Scargill was able to accelerate away. At a rally in Derby, in front of a crowd of around ten thousand people, a man charged across the platform and hit him with an iron bar. Scargill was only stopped from being knocked off the ten-foot platform by Tony Benn and Jim Parker, the NUM driver. Miraculously, none of the massed ranks of television crews and photographers present caught the incident on film, and Scargill's assailant was given a nominal fine.

A few months later, the miners' leader was shot at as he got out of the car in front of his Worsborough home. Police were called and found a bullet hole in the house wall, though no progress was made in tracing the assailant. These and other unexplained incidents were hushed up by the union for fear of encouraging copycat assaults. Whether they were intended to intimidate, cause injury or kill – and who was responsible – can only be a matter for speculation. But the gun attack on Scargill bore some similarity to that on Clive Jenkins's house a few years earlier. Jenkins was later told by Special Branch that there was a plot afoot to assassinate him, Jack Jones and Hugh Scanlon, and all three were provided – as Ray Buckton had been before them – with round-the-clock police 'protection'. In Scargill's case, striking miners formed their own 24-hour-a-day guard on his home.[61]

The end of the strike did not, of course, bring an end to surveillance and provocation by the security services. Nor were operations against the miners' leader run only by MI5 and GCHQ. Just as the *Daily Mirror* and *Cook Report* stories were breaking in March 1990, Scargill received a letter from a woman who had been working for British Coal as a secretary.

She asked for a 'confidential chat' with the NUM leader, saying she wanted to pass on 'some information with which to fight back'. When Scargill made contact, the woman explained that she had had a longstanding affair – which was now finished – with a police Special Branch officer named Dave Kelly. The SB man was well known to the NUM leader, as Kelly had at one time worked at Scargill's old pit, Woolley colliery. Indeed, Scargill had helped get specialist medical attention as an NUM official for one of Kelly's children. He later left the coal industry, joined the police and became the bodyguard to Roy Mason, the right-wing NUM-sponsored MP who ended up as a hard-line Northern Ireland secretary in the Callaghan government. The woman then described how Kelly's car had been broken into while she and the Special Branch officer had been away together for the weekend. A Filofax-style book, containing details of SB surveillance and covert operations against Scargill and a number of other people, had been stolen from the car and Kelly had been moved to the uniformed branch shortly afterwards. She then advised the NUM president to be extremely careful in any dealings he had with a particular MP – not Mason – whom she identified and whose name is known to the author. He was, she warned, 'very close' to Special Branch – and her former lover in particular. She told the NUM president that he was being set up and that preparations for a smear campaign against him had been going on for several years. The woman refused to elaborate further, but warned Scargill to be 'very careful and watch your back'.[62]

At the time of the 1984–5 strike, MI5's director-general was John Jones, and F branch was headed by David Ransom, who had just returned from a stint in Washington as a security liaison officer. Both men had been heavily involved in operations against the two miners' strikes of the early 1970s. But it was Stella Rimington, then an assistant director and head of the politically sensitive F2 section, who made the running in the great domestic confrontation of the Thatcher years. Her job gave her overall responsibility for the trade-union movement (F2n), but also for the media, education and members of parliament (F2r). During the strike, she was in charge of the 'Box 500' reports to government – MI5's traditional Whitehall alias – giving regular briefings to the Civil Contingencies Unit on the NUM leaders' tactics and morale and the progress of the dispute. The material was then fed through to the Joint Intelligence Committee, of which Bryan Cartledge, head of the CCU, was a member. Margaret Thatcher regularly sat in on the JIC sessions, the only Prime Minister to have done so.

Robin Robison, a JIC administrative officer during the 1980s, remembers Rimington's visits to the Cabinet Office in Whitehall for JIC subcommittee meetings as a regular feature of the bureaucratic routine. But details of MI5 agents operating inside the NUM were known only to 'very small cabals, mostly by word of mouth'. Such highly secret domestic intelligence was discussed not at the JIC, but at the Cabinet Office Defence Committee, run by Christopher Mallaby, later the British ambassador to Paris. 'There are two defence committees at the Cabinet Office,' Robison says, 'one that deals with Ministry of Defence material and the other in the sealed-off area on the second floor that deals with very sensitive domestic material of that nature.'[63]

Technically, there was no need for even senior Home Office or Cabinet Office officials to know the identity of sources and agents inside the NUM, even if their intelligence was vital to the government's tactics during the strike. But one former security-service officer remarks: 'You have to allow for human nature.' Even Stella Rimington did not have to have direct contact with her agents and sources in the union. In most cases, this was the job of the agent handlers from F4 or an F2 desk officer. Usually, MI5 only takes over the running of an agent after Special Branch has done the talent-spotting and cultivation. As MI5's first public account of its work, published in 1993, explained:

> Agent operations are highly specialized and are often conducted over the long term. The work involves the ... careful direction of an individual ... within a target organization ... Substantial

resources are devoted to providing support both for the agent and the security service case officer ... close attention is also paid to the welfare of the service's agents both during and after their agent career.

Rimington herself, in her 1994 television lecture, remarked:

> Those who wish to damage the state will naturally organize themselves, and make plans, in secret ... we may have to ... recruit members of those organizations as agents to tell us from the inside what is being planned. Then we have to analyse and assess the information, and use our findings to counter the harm which is intended.[64]

In the run-up to the miners' strike, MI5 was anxious to place an agent as close as possible to Scargill in the NUM's new Sheffield headquarters. The security service already had, in the words of one former officer, 'very good information about what Scargill was doing during this period, as he had been a target for years'. A good deal of this intelligence was being delivered by police Special Branch. But the union was a 'major priority', 'perceived to be a threat to the country', and MI5 needed extra 'coverage' of its activities at the highest level. In the winter of 1982–3, Cathy Massiter, then a desk officer in F branch, was present at a meeting with a long-time MI5 agent, his handler and another F-branch officer at a security-service safe house in London. The agent was Harry Newton, a Yorkshireman and a well-respected left-wing academic active in the northern labour and peace movements. In his other persona, he was a paranoid anti-communist who had worked undercover for MI5 for nearly thirty years.

Newton had been a vice-chair of the Institute of Workers' Control and a leading figure in the Campaign for Nuclear Disarmament in Yorkshire. He also had a longstanding connection with the Yorkshire miners and Arthur Scargill, who was astounded to discover Newton's secret life. 'Harry Newton often used to come round to my house for a cup of tea, saying: "How're you going on, Arthur?",' Scargill recalls, mimicking

Newton's soft-spoken Leeds accent. 'I first met him back in the mid 1950s in the Young Communist League, when he used to teach young miners. I had a very reasonable relationship with him, very friendly. I regarded him as a very dedicated and loyal member of the movement.' Newton had played an active role advising the NUM left caucus in Yorkshire during the 1969–70 unofficial strikes and often used to visit Scargill at his Barnsley office when he was president of the Yorkshire NUM.

In the early 1980s, MI5 brought Newton down to London to work at CND's national headquarters. It was a time when CND was attracting crowds a quarter of a million strong to its demonstrations and the government was anxious to prove communist and Soviet manipulation of the peace movement. But by the winter of 1982, Newton was not in the best of health and it was agreed that he would move back to Yorkshire. At the London meeting with his handler and the two MI5 officers, there was a discussion about whether it might be possible to get Newton a job in the NUM national office when the union moved to Sheffield the following April. MI5 was anxious to 'park him alongside Scargill', to get someone in close to the NUM president in preparation for the coming confrontation with the miners. Newton was 'not averse' to the idea, though Massiter never heard any more about it. Newton never in fact applied to work at the NUM, but Scargill says he 'would have been viewed very sympathetically' if he had done. The veteran infiltrator died in July 1983 and was exposed as an agent two years later in Massiter's whistleblowing television critique of her experiences at MI5.[65]

Nevertheless, between the winter of 1982 and the summer of 1983 – the period when Roger Windsor, among others, joined the NUM – the security service apparently found another candidate for the job that had been lined up for Harry Newton. Shortly before the 1984–5 strike began, Michael Bettaney, an MI5 officer who had been arrested in September 1983 for passing information to the Soviet Embassy, told his solicitor – Sarah Burton of Seifert Sedley Williams, the legal firm representing the miners' union – that MI5 had succeeded in planting a male undercover agent 'high up' in the NUM's national office in Sheffield. Bettaney was sentenced in April 1984 to twenty-three years in prison and released on parole in the late 1990s. A member of MI5 since 1975, he had been transferred the year before his arrest to counterespionage work. But he had also worked in counter-subversion and was well connected in MI5's F branch. Bettaney gave Burton the information in a written note – to avoid their conversation being picked up by bugging devices – in an interview room in the high-security wing of Brixton gaol, where he was being held on remand. He did not know the MI5 mole's name, but asked Burton to warn Scargill. During the strike, in the summer of 1984, she privately passed on the tip-off to the NUM president – and a decade later, Bettaney confirmed his original statement from prison to another lawyer.[66]

According to the jailed MI5 man, who also knew of a well-placed agent in the communist-led draughtsmen's union TASS, the atmosphere inside the security service about such operations was relatively loose. 'There was a sort of kudos in the agency about how well they spied on the unions,' Sarah Burton says. One former MI5 employee has described a training session where a woman lecturer told recruits 'rather boastfully, that MI5 had long-term moles inside certain trade unions, so deep that even their families didn't know their true purpose'. The NUM was, not surprisingly, awash with rumours of infiltration and dirty tricks both during and after the 1984–5 strike. Augustin Dufresne, the French CGT miners' leader, also warned Scargill in 1984 that a high-ranking Soviet official had told him MI5 had an agent in a senior position at the NUM's national office. As Sarah Burton remembers: 'Lots of people were pointing fingers at each other.' As the internal post-strike struggle became more bitter, the suggestion that someone was an agent became a useful weapon in the fight. From the security services' point of view, such an atmosphere of paranoia and suspicion is a useful by-product of infiltration operations.[67]

Spying by governments on their own people is, as already touched on, a deep-rooted British tradition – an unacknowledged facet of the country's heritage, it could be said. But despite its well-established national pedigree, it has been an equally longstanding British practice to pretend that such things only happen abroad. As the historian Edward Thompson described attitudes in the early nineteenth century, when there was a positive infestation of spies from one end of the country to the other: 'It was the fond belief of the English people that the employment of spies in domestic affairs was un-British, and belonged to the "continental spy system". In fact it was an ancient part of British statecraft as well as of police practice.' Certainly, it long predated the Elizabethan playwright Christopher Marlowe's work as a government spy, or the sweeping espionage and counterespionage operations against the Catholics and Jacobites.[68]

In the modern capitalist world – at least until the 21st century 'war on terror' – the main targets of agents provocateurs, informers and plants have been the labour movement and the left. One of the most notorious cases in twentieth-century revolutionary history was that of Roman Malinovsky, Lenin's main deputy inside Russia in the years before the First World War and leader of the Bolshevik group in the Duma, the Russian parliament. Malinovsky was an undercover agent of the Tsarist secret police, the Okhrana. Strong evidence that he had been responsible for the arrest of leading Bolsheviks, including Bukharin, Sverdlov and Stalin, led to repeated public accusations that Malinovsky was a spy – despite the fact that exposing a police agent was a penal offence. Lenin roundly denounced Malinovsky's accusers and defended him fiercely. But when the Okhrana files were opened in 1917, the truth was revealed and Malinovsky was tried and shot the following year.[69]

The Malinovsky case – having had no appreciable effect on the course of the Russian Revolution – is sometimes cited as evidence that informers and agents provocateurs cause less harm than is supposed, since to be effective to their masters, they have to be of even more use to the movements they infiltrate. The NUM's experience, where corrosive damage was done at the heart of the union over a long and crucial period, shows that this is by no means necessarily the case. A distinction can be made

between passive informers, who simply pass on inside information, and agents provocateurs, who seek to manipulate and
disrupt the organizations they infiltrate. In reality, the separa-
tion between the two is far less sharp – accurate intelligence is
in itself a source of power. It is sometimes said that MI5 is not
in the provocation game. The spywriter and one-time Tory MP
Rupert Allason, for example, has insisted that MI5's F-branch
officers only had a 'reporting brief' and were 'not authorised to
conduct counter-subversive operations'. One former MI5 officer
says that Special Branch finds it easier than the security service
to bend the rules over provocation. But the NUM's experience
– let alone that of MI5's Irish targets – leaves little doubt that,
when necessary, the formalities are only a part of the game. As
Dame Daphne Park, a retired senior MI6 officer, disarmingly
describes the secret service's approach: 'You set people very dis-
creetly against one another. They destroy each other – you don't
destroy them.'[70]

Bernard Ingham, who was as close to Thatcher as anyone
during her years in office and attended with her the regular
meetings of the Cabinet committee monitoring the miners'
strike, gave an inkling during the 1992–3 pit-closures crisis of
the mentality behind the secret campaign to break the NUM.
During a television panel debate with Ingham and others on the
security services, Arthur Scargill referred to the attempt to
make a phoney cash deposit in an account under his control and
complained about having been under surveillance for more than
twenty years. His views and actions were in no way secret,
Scargill said, while the security services were a law unto
themselves. Far from challenging the NUM leader's account,
Ingham ridiculed any suggestion that there was anything sinister or untoward about such operations. Scargill had, he
declared, just restored his faith in the security services 'because
since 1972, to my certain knowledge, he's been trying to
overthrow the elected government of this country and he's no
doubt still at it. It is therefore very important for the security
services to keep him under close surveillance.'[71]

The scale and character of the security services' anti-subversion operations directed against the miners and their leaders – from mobilization of military spy satellites to the use of agents to destabilize the union from within, to the encouragement of a mendacious campaign of corruption allegations – have been unique. MI5 claims that, with the end of the Cold War and the declining 'capabilities of subversive groups', it 'no longer undertakes counter-subversion work'. In fact, a good part of that 'work' has been transferred to police outfits such as the 'national domestic extremism unit'. But from the time Sir Anthony Duff took over MI5 in 1985 there was a steady shift of money and personnel away from chasing the increasingly enfeebled domestic left. Resources were channelled first into the war against the IRA, and then, from the late 1990s – and even more dramatically after 2001 – into targeting Islamist and jihadist groups and the wider Muslim community. MI5 funding doubled and its staffing increased two and a half times in a decade. Even so, security-service enthusiasts still grumble that the organization is hamstrung by bureaucratic caution, 'rectitude and memo-writing', born of years of politically motivated criticism.

But the fact that Stella Rimington, who ran and supposedly modernized MI5 in the mid 1990s, was in charge of the NUM operations – described by thirty-four MPs on the House of Commons order paper as a 'subversion of democratic liberties' – by itself means that that record cannot simply be consigned to the history books of the Thatcher years. John Major distanced himself from the most dubious intelligence activity promoted by his predecessor, but also enthusiastically backed Rimington's empire-building expansion, which continued at a frenetic pace under her successors. As Peter Archer, former Solicitor General and the *Mirror* ombudsman sacked by Maxwell as he was preparing his report on the Scargill campaign, said of the stream of allegations and evidence about MI5 and the NUM: 'Ten years ago I wouldn't have thought it was true, but now I can believe it. The Thatcher administration was wild.'[72]

## CONCLUSION

# WHO FRAMED ARTHUR
# SCARGILL?

*This is a sustained attack upon the mining industry because the previous Prime Minister regarded the NUM as the Enemy Within. Tony Benn, former Energy Secretary, October 1992, House of Commons*

The sacrifice of the greater part of the safest and most advanced coal industry in the world in the single-minded pursuit of private interest and class revenge will continue to reverberate through Britain's political and industrial culture for years to come. It was only in the wake of the 1992–3 pit-closures crisis, well after Margaret Thatcher's political demise, that the full extent and significance of the assault on the nationalized mining industry became apparent. In the final run-up to privatization, with deep-mine production reduced to a third of its pre-strike level and the number of miners employed in the public sector slashed by 95 per cent, collieries cutting coal at less than two-thirds of import prices were still being closed in the rush to create a profitable rump industry for the rigged energy market. As the bill to sell off what remained of the industry made its way through parliament in the spring of 1994, the larger of the two privatized electricity generators quietly acknowledged that the cost of power from new gas stations was – as the NUM had been insisting, to widespread scepticism – almost 30 per cent higher than that generated by the coal-fired plants they were replacing. Meanwhile, Tim Eggar, the Tory Energy Minister confirmed that, despite earlier protestations, the £1.3 billion annual nuclear power subsidy continued to be regarded by the government as a price worth paying to reduce still further the country's fast-eroding dependence on coal.[1]

But by then, few still bothered to argue that the cold-eyed destruction of the mining industry was simply a matter of the market at work, a modern rerun of the fate of the hand-loom weaver or an aspect of the inexorable shift of nineteenth-century industries to the Third World. Even some non-Thatcherite ministers from the time of the 1984–5 strike began to be alarmed. Lord Whitelaw, Deputy Prime Minister during the year-long stoppage, complained ten years later: 'If the government had imagined that the industry might have been reduced to the state it is in today, it would have acted differently.' Lord Walker, Energy Secretary during the strike and another hand-wringing accomplice to the strangulation of King Coal, agreed that what was being shut down was in fact an 'extremely competitive industry'. The continuing attack on the miners, the *Guardian* commented as British Coal managers bribed and bullied men out of the pits in preparation for the 'ultimate privatization', was 'indisputably a national scandal ... politically, not economically, driven'. There is simply no parallel, in the industrial history of Britain or of any other country for that matter, for the breakneck rundown of such a productive sector.[2]

It was precisely to resist the earlier phases of this remorseless attack that the vast majority of Britain's miners struck in 1984–5. There is no question in retrospect, if it was not self-evident at the time, that this was the most important industrial dispute since 1926 and a defining moment of postwar British history. Indeed, there has been nothing quite like it – in its size, its duration and its national and international impact – anywhere else in the world. It is scarcely surprising, therefore, that the return to work without a settlement in March 1985 was not going to prove enough for the British government. Not only would the Coal Board be licensed to use every form of industrial and financial intimidation to change the balance of power in the country's most industrially strategic sector. It was also necessary to discredit the strike itself, to rubbish its leadership, to paint it as the work of a clique of violent, unrepresentative and undemocratic extremists. This the bulk of the media toiled loyally to do in the years after 1985, assisted by those in the labour movement who were desperate, for their own reasons, to draw a line under the dispute and fix it in the collective memory as an insurrectionary throwback which had demonstrated once and for all that militancy doesn't pay.

## THE RECKONING

But however assiduously the story of the strike and its outcome was rewritten, the strikers and their leaders continued to be regarded by large sections of the population as people of principle who had dared to resist when others had bent the knee. How better to seal the image of this epic confrontation and close an entire chapter of working-class history than to reveal its leaders to be men of straw, grubbing around with the rest for the perks of office, shuffling vast sums of money between foreign bank accounts for personal advancement and pocketing strike funds to pay off their home loans? It is small wonder that the tales peddled by the *Mirror, Cook Report* and later Gavin Lightman QC were devoured with such an insatiable political appetite. But as time passed, the Scargill Affair turned out to be the very opposite of the drama that was originally played out through the British media in the spring and summer of 1990. And the inversions of fact and fantasy it entailed became a cruelly illuminating commentary on our public life and times.

What was billed as the ultimate exposé of the last dinosaurs of militant trade unionism ended up exposing those who led the chorus of denunciation. The newspaper baron who falsely accused Arthur Scargill and Peter Heathfield of theft and embezzlement was revealed eighteen months later to be one of the greatest thieves and embezzlers of the twentieth century. The eminent QC and judge-to-be who savaged Scargill in 1990 for assorted breaches of duty and misapplications of funds – later shown to be unfounded – was four years later facing, with his publisher, a six-figure bill in costs and damages after the NUM sued him for breach of confidence and fiduciary duty. The former NUM chief executive who charged the two miners' leaders with having used strike funds to pay off their home loans had, it transpired, been the only one of the three who was guilty of the allegation. This same hired witness has since been found four times by the French courts to have himself signed documents he claimed were forged by Scargill and been shown to have been wrong in every detail about the 'Libyan money' he claimed had been used for the repayments. Of the other whistleblowers, one had been imprisoned in Pakistan for allegedly plotting to blow up a mosque, another jailed in Britain for fraud. Two of the dissident Russian miners' 'representatives' flown over to accuse Scargill of misappropriating Soviet cash donations were soon afterwards expelled from their own Western-funded organization for taking equipment.[3]

In the event, every single one of the original claims proved to be untrue, unfounded, wildly misrepresented or so partial as to be virtually unrecognizable from any factual foundation. Neither Scargill nor Heathfield paid off – or ever could have paid off – mortgages with Libyan or any other strike funds, as the *Daily Mirror* and the *Cook Report* insisted to fifteen-million-odd readers and viewers, because neither had a mortgage. Absurdly, the claim was never put in any recognizable way to either man in advance. It was just 'too sensitive', the *Cook Report* producer explained at the time. Nor, as the evidence now makes clear, could what in fact were simply 'paper refinancings' have ever been made with Libyan cash – because the fabled 'Gaddafi money' never even arrived in Britain until long after the transactions were carried out. The central allegation was a paper-thin lie, the by-product of a deliberate set-up, but also the vital hook on which the whole campaign depended.[4]

The fall-back stories fared little better. As original Soviet documentation has confirmed, it was Mikhail Gorbachev and Yegor Ligachev – not Arthur Scargill and Alain Simon, as alleged by the *Daily Mirror*, the *Cook Report* and Gavin Lightman – who took the decision to 'divert' Soviet strike support cash to the Miners' Trade Union International, from where it was transferred – again on Soviet instructions – to a specially created MTUI solidarity fund in Dublin. Once the money arrived late, almost all of it after the strike was over, the operation of the Dublin trust account – including the donation of hundreds of thousands of pounds to the British miners' hardship fund long before the *Mirror* and *Cook Report* ran their stories – was incontestably known of and approved by the Soviet miners' union leadership. Then there was the matter of the 'secret accounts' used to beat sequestration and receivership. The Inland Revenue's acceptance that they were either valid independent trusts or 'constructive trusts' for the donors – in other words, that they were legally independent and that none of the cash that passed through them belonged to the NUM – demolished the entire basis of the Lightman Report's repeated claims that the union leadership was guilty of financial impropriety, breaches of duty and misapplications of union funds.

At every stage and in every aspect of the affair, the fingerprints of the intelligence services could be found like an unmistakable calling card. From the openly advertised intelligence contacts used in the original *Sunday Times* scoop on Roger Windsor's 1984 Libyan trip, to the CIA's tame Russian miners who helpfully called in the Fraud Squad, to the explicit intelligence sources of the lawyers' surveillance report on Alain Simon, through Robert Maxwell's own longstanding links with the security services, to the CIA's funding of Windsor's former employers at PSI, to the GCHQ leaks on secret-service manipulation of the *Mirror-Cook Report* stories, to Miles Copeland's warning to Scargill and Heathfield about an intelligence set-up, to Tam Dalyell's Whitehall and police tip-offs about Windsor and Stella Rimington, to the Libyan leadership's pained recognition of Altaf Abbasi as a double agent: the intelligence connection ran like a poisoned thread throughout the 1990 campaign, the last great propaganda thrash against the NUM and its recalcitrant leadership.

But rather than simply the illegitimate offspring of an intelligence sting or a grand coordinated conspiracy to finish off the miners' president, the 1990 campaign gained momentum from a powerful coincidence of interest between different forces, all of whom wanted for different reasons to see the back of Scargill and the IMO: the Thatcher government, which was determined to smooth the rundown and privatization of coal and complete its unfinished business with the NUM; the Labour Party and TUC leaders, who were anxious to see Scargill silenced within the labour movement and to forestall the risk of a merger between the NUM and the Transport and General Workers' Union; the pro-Gorbachev wing of the Soviet nomenklatura, which was happy to use the affair as a stick to beat its domestic 'hardline' opponents and undermine their friends in the French Communist Party and the IMO; the pro-Western ICFTU-linked trade-union internationals and their state-funded foundation backers, which had long wanted to see the liquidation of the IMO; and Maxwell, who was only too happy to do favours for all of them. It was that tacit alliance of convenience that gave the scandal its special force and savagery.

Without the determination of the Thatcher administration to destroy the miners' union – a policy her successors continued to prosecute, even if in a less overtly aggressive form – the allegation and litigation campaign could never have got as far as it did. The claim often made by hostile union leaders, politicians and journalists during the 1980s and early 1990s that Scargill was the Tories' stalking horse, their secret weapon to frighten voters off Labour and damage the trade unions, was an absurdity. The true picture had been monotonously exposed by repeated pieces of customized legislation designed to close off this or that legal loophole exploited by the NUM leader, the government's huge expenditure and mobilization of every conceivable legal and administrative power to crush the miners' industrial strength, and the skewing of its entire energy policy from 1979 towards the neutralization or destruction of the coal industry as a base for the NUM. Without the Prime Minister's explicit approval, there would never have been such far-reaching covert operations against the union and its leadership. And it is inconceivable that without at least tacit support from above in 1990–1, there could ever have been such enthusiastic participation by every conceivable quango and state agency – from the Fraud Squad to the Trade Union Certification Office – in the campaign against the miners' union.[5]

## YEARS OF CORRUPTION

The attempt to 'stitch up' the NUM leadership exemplified the cynicism and corruption that spread so deeply into political and public life in the 1980s and 1990s: the tacit complicity between government and opposition; the breathtaking double standards of the courts and the press; the pliancy of supposedly independent public-office-holders; the hounding of anyone who demonstrated political independence by the political establishment and its cheerleaders, busily lining their pockets at the public expense. As the 1980s wore on, financial scandals multiplied among the Conservative government's closest allies and supporters in the City of London. Tory corporate financiers were routinely discovered up to their necks in fraud and misappropriation on a gargantuan scale. While the media pursued the mirage of embezzlement and misappropriation in the miners' union throughout 1990, real financial scandals were erupting on an almost weekly basis in City and corporate boardrooms: at Polly Peck, Rover, Lloyd's, Ferranti, Barlow Clowes, House of Fraser, Guinness, British & Commonwealth, Dunsdale Securities. Such standards, set by Thatcher's administration, became the norm under her successor.

The late 1980s and the early 1990s were the years of high sleaze. The four Conservative election victories between 1979 and 1992 were underwritten with millions of pounds donated by five foreign businessmen implicated in criminal tax evasion, insider dealing and fraud. At least two of the party's largest donors – Asil Nadir, the Turkish Cypriot tycoon, and Octav Botnar, the ex-chairman of Nissan UK, who between them gave £1.5 million – fled the country to avoid criminal prosecution. Another couple of Hong Kong businessmen who gave the Tory Party several hundred thousand pounds hedged their bets as part-time advisers to the Chinese government. The largest single Conservative Party donor was an alleged Nazi collaborator and enthusiastic supporter of the Greek colonels' dictatorship in the early 1970s, John Latsis. He paid over £2 million to John Major's party in 1991. The system of Tory funding was underpinned for many years by a network of secret companies to secure covert donations. Latterly, Conservative Party treasurers set up a special offshore account in Jersey for donors who preferred to avoid the attentions of the tax authorities. Quite independently of its Maxwell connection, the Labour Party was also found to have taken money – though on a far more modest scale than the governing party – from a fraudulent runaway businessman in the early 1990s.[6]

At the same time, these masters of political corruption were the very people who excoriated the miners' leadership and bayed for the Fraud Squad over the use of foreign bank accounts and communist-bloc cash donations to protect the NUM. But the financing of the 1984–5 coal strike and the maintenance of an independent miners' union in the face of the most far-reaching judicial action against organized labour for more than a century was the very opposite of corruption. Those who had money gave to those who did not and the City of London and the courts were for the most part simply bypassed. The strikers and their families, the picketing operations, the national and area organizations were all funded by individual supporters and sympathetic unions, in Britain and abroad, on the basis of trust, without reference to the official legal and financial system. As the legal vice tightened, almost the entire operation came to be carried out in cash. The realization that militant trade unionists were handling millions of pounds, mostly in plastic bags and cardboard boxes, without reference to the high priests of finance came as a great shock to the powers-that-be. The control of such large sums of money was, after all, their preserve. The interlopers had to be brought to heel.[7]

The web of legislation and litigation woven around the trade unions in the 1980s achieved its greatest effect in the case of the miners. While the government made enormous efforts to ensure that contract and common law – rather than its own anti-trade-union statutes – were used against the NUM during the year-long strike, it encouraged David Hart's Gulliver strategy to tie up the union leadership in unending, energy-sapping legal battles. Throughout the post-strike period, the ability of Scargill and other NUM leaders to concentrate on the industrial and political war being waged by the Coal Board and the government was hampered by the litigious aftermath of sequestration, receivership, the receiver's breach-of-trust action and other legal disputes. Time and again – most notably in the case of receivership – the judiciary jettisoned received legal wisdom and precedent with cheerful abandon in its enthusiasm to deliver the Enemy Within bound and gagged. Trust and injunction law was rewritten on the hoof by the judges during the strike, and a whole raft of decisions had to be overturned by the Appeal Court after receivership was lifted in 1986 to clear up the damage to the legal system. The avalanche of cases unleashed in 1990 was, in effect, an extension of the Gulliver tactic. By dragging the miners' leaders into another legal maze, the opportunity to rebuild NUM members' confidence and resist the oncoming threat of privatization and sweeping pit closures was drastically undermined.[8]

At crucial stages of the 1990 campaign, lawyers formally employed by the NUM played decisive roles in driving this process forward. Gavin Lightman's decision to demand an extension of his terms of reference led directly to the legal action for 'recovery' of the Soviet money and to the prosecution of the national officials by the Certification Office. Even as the central arguments in his report began to look increasingly shaky, Lightman took the manuscript to Penguin to rush it out as an instant paperback book – a decision he would regret at his leisure. And it was Lightman's friend Bruce Brodie who took the NUM's four-man team in hand after the executive had been 'advised' to sue its own leadership, who commissioned a private security firm to spy on Alain Simon and who proved so strikingly reluctant to hand over vital case papers to his own client, the NUM, once the action had been abandoned.

For the new model Labour Party and the 'me-too', 'one of us' philosophy that flourished within its leadership during the Thatcher years, the *Mirror*-Cook campaign was manna from heaven. From the point of view of the labour-movement hierarchy, this was an ideal opportunity to bury the spectre of class politics and trade-union militancy which haunted its efforts to construct a post-social-democratic electoral machine. As Hugo Young puts it in his biography of Thatcher:

> In the miners' strike ... the Conservatives could have been said to be doing Kinnock's work for him. By eliminating Scargill from the board, they removed not only an enemy of the state but a major embarrassment for the middle-of-the-road brand of socialism which Kinnock was seeking to advance. But that is not the way the public saw it, or the way Kinnock was able to exploit it. He was left with ... a party in which significant numbers continued to see Scargill as he saw himself: the only one in all that multitude who dared to stand and fight against the evil of Thatcherism.[9]

Neil Kinnock's courtiers lost no opportunity to tighten Scargill's rack in the service of their much-vaunted – but little-availing – 'new realism'. The speed and enthusiasm with which Kevin Barron and Kim Howells, the Labour leader's two closest allies in and around the miners' union, seized on the *Mirror-Cook Report* allegations was an unmistakable signal that this was an operation which had the unstinting blessing of the Labour Party *apparat*. Even after the central allegations in the campaign had been comprehensively discredited, Kinnock was there personally to hand out the 'Reporter of the Year' prizes to the *Mirror* journalists responsible for peddling them. And in case anyone missed the point, the ill-fated Labour leader had himself photographed with the three reporters in an extravagant showbusiness pose.

Most bizarre and confusing of all for those who tried to follow the twists and turns of the campaign was the Soviet dimension. The Soviet leadership originally considered Scargill an important ally, even if he was never entirely trusted. But by

1984, the Soviet political elite was seriously split about how to respond to the British miners' strike and whether to risk the developing relations with the Thatcher government. Gorbachev was privately opposed to both the Soviet trade-union coal and fuel embargo and to providing cash support, particularly once he had made a private commitment to Thatcher at their Chequers meeting in December 1984. The Kremlin dispute over aid to the British miners was an early taste of the emerging divisions at the heart of the Soviet Communist Party. By the end of the decade, the USSR was in rapid and terminal disintegration and large sections of the party and state apparatus were looking for ways to reinvent themselves in a post-communist world. The 1985 compromise of siphoning the British miners' strike support money off into an international solidarity fund would be seized on by pro-Gorbachev reformers as the sort of arrangement that could profitably be used to rubbish their political enemies. Scargill's discussions at the beginning of 1990 with Gennadi Yanayev, Soviet vice-president and Gorbachev opponent, about building up the fund can have only intensified their hostility.

## WATCHDOG AS LAPDOG

The multimedia onslaught unleashed by Maxwell's *Mirror* and Central Television on the miners' leaders was in reality a classic smear campaign. Indeed, the treatment of the whole farrago of allegations and legal cases was a particularly revealing example of how the British media – and particularly the press – routinely operates against designated enemies. Facts were not checked, inconvenient angles not investigated. They didn't need to be. For the most part, even the broadsheet press and television news programmes simply repeated the sensational claims, without any serious attempt to investigate allegations or sources. The story casually changed from one day to the next. As each allegation was shown to be false or misleading, another took its place. Against all the supposed rules of journalism, the story continued to run regardless of the accumulating mass of counterevidence. It is inconceivable that such serious accusations – fraud, falsification, theft and corruption – would ever have been made in a national newspaper against almost any other public figure without a watertight case of compendious detail.

At the height of the 1990 campaign, Paul Foot, then the *Daily Mirror*'s top columnist, suggested an analogy. Imagine, he said, that he had run a story on the front page of the *Mirror* about two Tory MPs who had paid off their mortgages out of funds they had raised for charity. 'I'm sure you'd agree that's a very good story,' he said. Suppose, he went on, that an official inquiry had then found that one of the MPs had never had a mortgage at all and the other MP had paid his mortgage off long before the charity money had even been raised. And say it was also revealed that the paper's main source – and this was, he said, the 'most extraordinary thing about a source that I have ever come across in a lifetime of investigative journalism' – had been shown to be the 'only person on earth' who was guilty of the allegation he had made against the two MPs in the *Mirror* and was still paid handsomely for his testimony. And imagine that his other main source was a man convicted of plotting to blow up mosques in Pakistan. 'First of all,' he said, 'I would never have been able to get such a story published. But if I had had such a story published and all these facts had then come out, my feet wouldn't have touched the ground. I'd have been fired and nobody would ever have believed a word I'd have written ever again about Tory MPs or anything else.' But in the case of the Scargill story, instead of the journalists being called to account or the Press Council protesting at such an abuse, the allegations were repeated again and again even though they had been proved to be false. And each time one allegation was discredited, another took its place, like the multiheaded Hydra of ancient Greek legend. 'Since these allegations have nothing to do with facts or investigative journalism,' Foot queried, 'how and why is it that the story continues to run?' It ran, he concluded, because the most powerful vested interests in society wanted it to run.[10]

The author was passed information supporting the miners' leaders' case by another national newspaper journalist during the 1990 media campaign because the reporter's own 'quality' paper was not interested in publishing stories that contradicted the general line of attack. Such things are utterly unexceptional in the media. They are the mostly unspoken daily norm. In a highly concentrated communications industry, where 93 per cent of the daily and Sunday newspaper market is 'serviced' by five media conglomerates and their multimillionaire proprietors, the control and manipulation of information constitutes a permanent negation of free debate. Without the monopoly ownership grip by multinational companies on great swathes of the media, the Scargill Affair could never have taken off. It would have been quickly exposed as a malevolent and fraudulent set-up. While those promoting the smears constantly pointed to Scargill's failure to sue Maxwell as evidence of guilt, his inability in practice to do so when the accusations against him were so demonstrably false constituted an indictment of the libel laws rather than the miners' leader. As a rule, libel action is a practical and effective option only for the very wealthy or for those on whom they bestow their favours.[11]

The 1990 media attacks were in any case only the most extreme of a string of propaganda campaigns over the previous decade against the NUM leadership. As the journalist Hunter Davies remarked of Scargill in the wake of the pit-closures controversy of 1992–3: 'No living person in the land has had a worse press.' Only the treatment meted out to Tony Benn has come near to the anti-Scargill savagery, and even Benn arguably never quite matched the sustained level of vilification that Scargill was subjected to from the early 1980s. Both have been 'abused by the media to the point of harassment and beyond', in the words of the BBC Television and *Financial Times* industrial editors who covered the 1984–5 miners' strike. In the case of the NUM president, a pitch was reached during the dispute which only really subsided with the public outcry over colliery closures in 1992. Nicholas Jones, the BBC political correspondent who covered the 1984–5 strike, believes journalists were 'caught up in an anti-Scargill feeding frenzy'. Simon Jenkins, the former *Times* editor, described press coverage of the miners' strike while the dispute was still raging as 'ludicrously biased ... Fleet Street's loathing for [Scargill] is almost palpable ... a public kept in ignorance of the nature of his support, and told merely of his idiocy, grows ever more mystified at his survival. It is the tale of duff propaganda down the ages.'[12]

To leaf through newspaper cuttings from the strike period a decade later is to be transported back to an Alice-in-Wonderland world of long-suffering policemen and saintly strikebreakers fighting the good fight against swaggering picket-line thugs with money to blow, of impossible return-to-work figures and fantastic power-supply projections. Take, more or less at random, the banner front-page headline run by the *Sunday Express* on 25 November 1984: 'Suitcases of Cash Pay for Terror'. The story was about the cash loans and donations then keeping the NUM afloat at a time when its own funds had been frozen by the sequestrators. 'Suitcases packed with thousands of pounds in £1 and £5 notes are being ferried to NUM leaders in Yorkshire', the piece began, accurately enough. But by the second paragraph, the reporter was already away with the fairies. 'Moderates in the NUM are convinced the cash is being used to finance terror squads of militant youths,' he fantasized, 'and a group of intimidators selected to "persuade" working pitmen to rejoin the strike ... free-spending intimidators leading the campaign to stop the flood of miners returning to work have been nicknamed "Fat Cats" in Yorkshire.'

A report more remote from reality would be hard to imagine. Or at least it would have been hard had it not been for the multiplicity of other similar episodes during the dispute, such as the *Sun*'s attempt to publish a front-page picture of Scargill appearing to give a Nazi salute – which Fleet Street print-workers refused to typeset – under the legend: 'Mine Führer'. Then there was the case of the BBC coverage of the most violent confrontation of the strike, at Orgreave on 18 June 1984, when footage broadcast on television was reversed to show the mounted police charge as a response to missile-throwing from pickets. The real, diametrically opposite, sequence of events was only later demonstrated when the police's own video was produced at the insistence of the defence in the subsequent riot trial.[13]

But press and, to a lesser extent, broadcasting coverage of the strike and its protracted aftermath was not simply distinguished by bias and vitriol. It was also marked by a level of government, police and secret-service manipulation unmatched in the reporting of any other running domestic story. Security-service media guidance was insistently offered, at all levels. Sir John Jones, then MI5 director-general, for example, called in editors and senior broadcasting executives in the autumn of 1984 to 'reveal' Soviet backing for Scargill and the danger the intelligence services believed this posed to the state. Press, radio and television should, he told them, reflect an appreciation of this in its coverage of the strike. Lower down the media hierarchy, the intervention was far cruder. As Nicholas Jones puts it:

> [Thatcher] was using agencies at the side which we'd not actually come across before – people who were capable of manipulating the newspapers in a way that we hadn't seen before. And we know that sections of the news media were closely involved, the security services were involved, a lot of information was being passed about. We saw the conduct of journalists changing, because a closer relationship developed between journalists and some police officers handling the dispute. The flow of information ... from the police and the security forces ... to the news media was, I think, quite a significant factor in that dispute.[14]

This cosy trade continued long after the end of the strike. 'Offside' steers and leaks abounded. At the beginning of June 1985, for example, with the NUM in the hands of the court-appointed receiver, Scargill was in Paris discussing with Alain Simon and other French CGT officials the union's plight and the forthcoming foundation of the new International Miners' Organization. With no prior warning, Simon asked him to travel the same day to Czechoslovakia to meet the leadership of the communist-led World Federation of Trade Unions in Prague. Scargill joined a Czechoslovak airline flight in Paris that night at the last minute, after all the other passengers were already on board. Throughout the flight he sat alone at the back of the aircraft. At Prague airport, he waited until the plane was empty before crossing to the terminal building, where visa formalities were waived and he was whisked, apparently unseen, behind the sliding-door entrance reserved for VIP guests. There he was greeted by the Sudanese WFTU general secretary, Ibrahim Zakaria, and other WFTU and Czechoslovak trade-union officials. After two days in Prague, he flew back to Britain, via Paris. At the NUM, only Roger Windsor and Nell Myers were told about Scargill's trip.

But four days later, a well-briefed front-page story in, once again, the *Sunday Express* regaled readers with details of the WFTU visit. 'Arthur Scargill has sparked off a new wave of alarm in the NUM', the piece began, 'over his links with the Communist bloc with a hush-hush trip behind the Iron Curtain ... When the Executive meets on Thursday Mr Scargill will be asked why he goes to Communist countries in secret, who pays for the trips and what he discusses. And he will be asked in particular to explain reports that on arrival in Prague he was met by four "Afghan looking types" waiting for the Prague–Kabul connection.' Clearly, someone had been monitoring Scargill's travelling arrangements very closely, even if they did have trouble distinguishing Afghans – a connection which would have been politically more suggestive at a time when there were 100,000 Soviet troops in Afghanistan – from Sudanese. When the *Sunday Express* reporter rang Nell Myers at the NUM to check the details, he apologized in advance for running such a story.[15]

The incestuous relationship between the intelligence services and sections of the media is, of course, nothing new. The connection is notoriously close in the case of some foreign correspondents. Kim Philby was, after all, offered a job as Middle East correspondent for both *The Economist* and the *Observer* – at a time when the security services had yet to uncover his real allegiances – after a couple of discreet telephone calls from the Foreign Office. More recently, Sandy Gall, the ITN reporter and newsreader, boasted of his work for MI6 in Afghanistan during the 1980s and his liaison meetings with MI6 officers at Stone's Chop House in Piccadilly. 'Soon after I returned to London,' Gall wrote in his memoirs, 'I received an invitation to have lunch with the head of MI6 … I was flattered, of course, and … resolved to be completely frank and as informative as possible, and not try to prise any information out of him in return. This is not normally how a journalist's mind works.' Indeed not.

But Gall was far from being alone. David Cornwell, the former intelligence officer turned bestselling spywriter John Le Carré, has remarked that in his time 'the British secret service controlled large sections of the press, just as they may do today'. After US Senate hearings in 1975 revealed the extent of CIA recruitment of both American and British journalists, 'sources' let it be known that half the foreign staff of a British daily were on the MI6 payroll. There are several recent cases known to the author of well-known reporters in both television and print journalism – and these are doubtless a handful among many – who became entangled with MI6, sometimes to their cost as well as benefit. Needless to say, those journalists who double up as part-time spies do no favours for their colleagues, who can come under dangerous and unjustified suspicion as a result. But far less appreciated is the extent of MI5 manipulation of the press at home, which intensified in the years of industrial unrest in the 1970s and 1980s and reached a peak during the miners' strike and its pulverizing aftermath. This was the period when the security services are said to have recruited three-quarters of national labour and industrial correspondents as informants of one kind or another, along with a small army of agents inside the trade unions themselves.[16]

The 1990 smear campaign against the NUM was, it is now clear, in part the poisoned fruit of this corrosive relationship. The accumulation of evidence now uncovered about the events surrounding Roger Windsor's disastrous visit to Tripoli in the autumn of 1984 shows that there was unquestionably a deliberate and meticulously constructed attempt to 'set up' the miners' leadership during the most finely balanced weeks of the dispute. The broadcast meeting with Gaddafi, the convict middleman, the staged banknote drops, the officials' home 'repayments' carried out on advice, the timely cash advance on the real Libyan money, the phoney laundering of funds through the CGT: all were primed to cause maximum propaganda damage if and when required. The first phase of the sting was activated with the detailed revelations of Windsor's Libyan connection and the 'scoop of the year' in the *Sunday Times*. The second – and far more damaging – phase was held in reserve, as the looming threat of defeat for the government receded in the final weeks of 1984. Just over five years later, it would be brought into play with devastating effect in the *Daily Mirror* and *Cook Report*.

Behind this operation stood the most secretive and unaccountable arms of a secretive state. Britain's intelligence and security services remain a profoundly anti-democratic force. As the account by Peter Wright and others of the conspiracy against the Wilson government has shown, it is the security services – rather than the left and the trade unions – who have been the real subversives, operating through fear and an effective veto on political and public appointments, undermining democratic government and accountability. When Michael Hanley, then director-general of MI5, confirmed to Harold Wilson in August 1975 that 'only a small number' of 'disaffected right-wing' security-service officers had been plotting against him, the intimidated Labour Prime Minister was reduced to swearing at his chief spycatcher, rather than sacking him. When Jim Callaghan succeeded Wilson, he politely asked the intelligence services to confirm that they had done nothing wrong and they duly obliged.

Ten years later, at the height of the publicity about the Spycatcher allegations, Callaghan accepted that he had been misled, while his successor Margaret Thatcher repeated the whole charade of allowing MI5 to investigate its own treachery and give itself a clean bill of health. If no action was taken over an attempt to destabilize an elected government, it can hardly be surprising that the Tory beneficiary of that destabilization should be prepared to countenance comprehensive covert operations – infiltration, provocation, fraud, forgery, bugging and frame-ups – against a trade union which had faced down two Conservative governments three times in a decade.

Clive Ponting, the former Ministry of Defence official, remembered senior MI5 officers he dealt with as 'utterly reactionary'. Edward Heath, the former Prime Minister, described the secret force supposedly under his control as follows:

> I met people in the security services who talked the most ridiculous nonsense and whose whole philosophy was ridiculous nonsense. If one of them were on a tube and saw someone reading the *Daily Mirror* they would say: 'Get after him, that is dangerous. We must find out where he bought it.'

The whole apparatus would simply be the butt of ridicule and contempt if it were not also a powerful and poisonous influence in political and industrial life. At the same time, there is not the slightest reason to suppose that if the extent of the covert action taken against the NUM had become known during or after the miners' strike it would have commanded public support. The security services thrive in secrecy not least because they would not survive the glare of accountability.[17]

And thrive they continue to do. Despite the end of the Cold War, the disappearance of large sections of the left and the manifest weakness of the trade unions, MI5 carried on expanding its apparatus, power and influence – a process highlighted by its widely publicized turf-war victory against police Special Branch in 1992 over control of 'mainland' intelligence operations against the IRA. Later the IRA ceasefire encouraged MI5 to launch other hostile takeover bids for police work – such as drug trafficking, money laundering and organized crime – to keep itself in business. The talk was of 'integrating secret intelligence into the judicial process' and turning the security service into a British FBI – until radical Islamism and takfiri terror groups provided a more suitable new enemy. There were even signs that – despite, or perhaps because of, its supposed overriding allegiance to the crown – the security service had taken to intervening in the affairs of the royal family, apparently with the aim of protecting the House of Windsor from itself. Naturally, Stella Rimington dismissed the latter allegation out of hand. But, then – as she obliquely admitted – who was ever to know, when under the 1989 Official Secrets Act MI5 officers commit a criminal offence if they disclose any evidence of MI5 activity, illegal or otherwise, even to their MP? Meanwhile, the threat of smear and whispering campaigns continued to hang over anyone in public life – or indeed outside it – who failed to play the part allotted to them. Britain's secret state remains a dangerous political and bureaucratic cesspit, uniquely undisturbed by any meaningful form of political accountability.[18]

## THE LEGACY

In a sense, the smear campaign against the NUM leadership was successful. The planned merger with the TGWU – concern about which in both government and the Labour hierarchy was one reason for the virulence of the onslaught – failed to come off, partly because of the time and confidence that was lost while Scargill and Heathfield fought to clear their names. The position of the IMO, under heavy attack in the wake of the collapse of the communist regimes in the East, was significantly weakened. Scargill's reputation among his own membership, the left and labour movement, and the British public at large was damaged. Despite the collapse of the main charges – itself largely unreported in the press and broadcast media – there continued to be a widespread sense that something dodgy had been going on at the heart of the miners' union. Some of the mud had stuck. And the NUM national officials were tied up in litigation and internal argument for well over a year, when the union was already demoralized and needed a determined mobilization to fight privatization and pit closures. The revival of Scargill's popularity in 1992 owed more to the government's incompetence and a widespread public sense that he had been dramatically vindicated than to his dogged success in fighting off the earlier media and legal attacks.

No doubt those who lent their support, tacitly or overtly, to the orchestrated scandal felt it had all been worthwhile, even if the ultimate prize of the NUM president's head on a platter finally eluded them. But the Scargill Affair also had less welcome spin-offs for its sponsors. For one thing, it revealed for the first time the NUM leaders' remarkable success in short-circuiting the attempt to outlaw their organization. It laid bare the extraordinary lengths the strike leadership went to during, but more especially after, the 1984–5 dispute to evade the judicial takeover of the union and maintain its resistance to the Thatcher government. In doing so, the campaign exposed to other trade unionists options its sponsors would have preferred to remain hidden. The secret funding of the NUM after the autumn of 1984, in defiance of the courts, using both millions of pounds in cash and a hidden and parallel system of trust-fund accounts, was an operation unprecedented in the history of the British labour movement. Most alarmingly for the government – as Tory ministers admitted in private when Scargill disclosed details of the arrangements in 1990 to clear his name of the corruption charges – it worked.

And unlike the ill-fated transfer of NUM funds overseas in 1984, the system of independent accounts and funds Scargill and Heathfield used to keep the NUM afloat was never cracked by the sequestrators and the receiver – nor, indeed, by the security services. Significantly, although Scargill's friend Jean McCrindle and his secretary Yvonne Fenn were involved in part of the funding arrangements, the system was known in its entirety only to Scargill, Heathfield and Nell Myers. The NUM president was strongly criticized, when the details of the secret accounts were finally revealed, for having failed to 'come clean' with his executive before. Running such an operation until receivership was lifted in 1986 – or even until the receiver

dropped his breach-of-trust action against the union leadership
in 1988 – was one thing, the argument went. But continuing to
keep the details secret once the legal threat had gone was
intolerable, it was said, even if the unions which had lent money
to the various trusts and accounts wanted their involvement
kept confidential.

But the criticism missed the essential point. Only if all the
funds and accounts were kept scrupulously independent and had
no formal link with the union whatever could they be protected
from seizure or, later on, from other forms of retrospective
action. To have declared them to the executive at any time
would have been to accept that they were in reality NUM
accounts. The proof of the pudding was in the eating. As soon as
the seventeen accounts were in fact disclosed, in 1990, a string
of investigations and legal actions was sparked off. They hinged
crucially on Gavin Lightman's claim that all the trusts and
accounts were shams, and that all the money which had passed
through them in fact belonged to the union. The claim was put
to the test in law and found wanting. As a result of the Inland
Revenue investigation, which ruled in 1992 that the money
used to maintain the NUM had either belonged to the donors or
to genuine trusts, three of the unions that gave or lent money
during the NUM's receivership found themselves facing tax
bills for tens of thousands of pounds. Clearly, anything that had
undermined the independent status of the accounts at any stage
would have attracted a still greater flood of claims and litigation
against Scargill and the NUM.

The secret funding operation showed a willingness to take
the fight for independent trade unionism to its logical conclusion. It incidentally put into practice the Trades Union
Congress's own 1982 decision to defy the government's legal
attack on the labour movement. Most importantly, it demonstrated that unions can face down such anti-democratic
legislation and continue to function. The experience of the
NUM and other unions that came up against the Tory anti-
union laws – such as the print and seafarers' unions – convinced
many British trade unionists that defiance and noncooperation

were a dead end. It fuelled the so-called 'new realism' that came to dominate trade-union thinking in the late 1980s and early 1990s. If you embark on an unlawful strike, workers were told, your union will be subject to crippling fines and may be destroyed altogether. Given that nine pieces of anti-union legislation had made almost any kind of effective industrial action potentially illegal, the threat of union fines and sequestration – let alone receivership – combined, along with mass unemployment and job insecurity, to bring organized labour to its knees.

But the NUM's experience showed that it was possible both to defy anti-union laws and for the official full-time union organization to survive. In August 1990, Scargill declared: 'With hindsight I now know exactly how to beat sequestration without getting into a breach-of-trust action or a receiver being appointed.' And he teasingly offered a foolproof package to any union prepared to fight the Tory legislation. In the political conditions of the early 1990s, there were few takers for such an approach. Full-time officials were especially threatened by the government's legal battery, which was quite deliberately aimed at formal union structures and assets and designed to drive a wedge between union full-timers and ordinary members. The legislation was intended to force union officials to police their own membership. The NUM's independent funding system revealed how to short-circuit that divide-and-rule tactic. The full existing panoply of anti-trade-union laws – and most crucially, the statutes outlawing solidarity or 'secondary' action – will ultimately only be repealed if trade unionists are prepared to fight it. No Labour government would have the political will to go beyond some modest loosening of the legal straitjacket without relentless pressure on the ground to assert trade-union independence. As workers inevitably come into conflict with the legislation once again, the NUM's little-understood success in defeating sequestration and receivership in the 1980s has the potential to become a significant industrial and political weapon.[19]

From 1972, the NUM posed the single most powerful challenge to the increasingly determined attempts to reorder

British capitalism and shift the balance of power sharply in favour of the employers and the freedom of capital. The 1984–5 coal dispute was the most serious frontal assault on organized labour and the sharpest political and industrial confrontation with the state in Britain since the General Strike of 1926. The war against the miners was not a political aberration, but the inevitable response to a political and industrial force that could not be accommodated within the existing order. As David Lloyd George, Prime Minister of the day, told a delegation from the Triple Alliance of miners, railway and transport workers on the point of a united strike in 1919: 'If a force arises in the state which is stronger than the state itself, then it must be ready to take on the functions of the state, or it must withdraw and accept the authority of the state.'[20]

From the mid 1970s, the Conservative Party and its allies in the security services and the wider governmental machine set themselves the strategic objective of breaking the NUM. That overriding goal refashioned the country's energy sector, under-lay the privatization of electricity and coal, and brought about fundamental changes in both the law and methods of polic-ing. Arthur Scargill and his supporters became the focus and core of resistance to that process, as the disintegration of the Communist Party corroded the traditional centres of left-wing miners' leadership in South Wales and Scotland. Quarantined by the labour-movement hierarchy throughout the late 1980s and 1990s, Scargill and his uncompromising syndicalist-influenced politics endured, a symbol of a militant class and trade-union tradition that stubbornly refused to give way to the politics of the self-proclaimed 'new realists'. The conventional wisdom that Scargill's intransigence and refusal to play by the estab-lished rules of the trade-union game hastened – or even brought about – the destruction of the mining industry is an inversion of what actually took place. There is no evidence that a more pliant and flexible leadership during the 1980s – such as that offered by the government-sponsored breakaway Union of Democratic Mineworkers – would have saved the miners or their collieries.

The lead given by Scargill and the NUM in 1984 offered the miners and the trade-union movement as a whole the chance to stop the Tory government's offensive in its tracks against the alternative of certain further retreat and defeat. In a different context, the same could be said about the opportunity handed to the labour movement in 1992, when the Major government's ill-prepared attempt to force through the closure of more than half the surviving coal industry led to a national political crisis. By then, Scargill and his dramatically diminished union were ripe for rehabilitation. It became customary, even in the press, to marvel at how the NUM president's predictions about Conservative intentions towards the miners and their industry – derided as scare-mongering a decade earlier – had been proved right after all. Memories of the months of smear and character assassination in 1990 and the years of hatred and ridicule momentarily melted away.

But once the government had temporarily backed down, the political momentum to halt the destruction of the coal industry became bogged down in court cases, reviews, consultants' reports and select-committee inquiries. While the Industry Secretary Michael Heseltine regained his political balance and his minions traded pits for parliamentary votes with Conservative MPs, the deep longstanding distrust of the NUM and its leaders resurfaced in the Labour and TUC hierarchies. There was little appetite for harnessing the overwhelming public support for the miners to a mass campaign to defeat the government. As the reality of the Cabinet's manoeuvring became apparent, Norman Willis, the TUC general secretary, wrote to John Major to complain that his efforts to persuade the NUM to 'pursue legal means of redress' were going unrewarded.[21]

By the time the miners' leaders began to agitate for industrial action as the only weapon left to them in defence of mining jobs and communities, the eleventh-hour reconciliation was well and truly over. With massive coal stocks, increasing imports and a rapidly shrinking market, the NUM's capacity to make an industrial impact by itself was severely limited. But the miners voted for a campaign of national strikes – the first such ballot result for twenty years. And throughout the early months of 1993, Scargill coaxed and cajoled the reluctant railway workers' leaders to back a joint campaign of industrial action against job losses and the threat of privatization in both industries. The outcome was a successful rail ballot and two days of synchronized strikes which simultaneously closed down the NUM-controlled mines and the entire rail network, keeping millions of employees from work throughout the country. Bloodied and massively weakened though his organization was, the NUM president demonstrated he was not quite the 'broken man' his opponents claimed. The assault on the miners and their union would continue unabated.

The NUM and its leadership were the object of attack not for their weaknesses, but for their strengths. In the aftermath of the last wave of pre-privatization pit closures, that came to be more widely understood. The NUM was seen to have stuck by its principles and paid for them. No other union could have inspired the sort of direct-action campaigns run by Women Against Pit Closures. No other group of workers could bring a quarter of a million people out onto the streets of London twice in one week to defend their industry. Few other trade unionists had been prepared to make the sacrifices the miners had made in the fight to defend their industry. Isolated and shrunken, the wreckage of its industry sold off to the new coalowners of the 1990s, the miners' union remained the conscience of the labour movement.[22]

# POSTSCRIPT TO THE
# FOURTH EDITION

Two decades after *The Enemy Within* was first published, Britain's coal industry and miners' union have been all but destroyed; the country's power supply is in the grip of a profiteering private cartel; job and workplace insecurity has mushroomed; the security services are booming on the back of a 'war on terror' without end; blacklisting of trade unionists and police infiltration of protest movements has flourished, while NSA and GCHQ global electronic surveillance has reached dizzying dimensions; New Labour has risen and fallen; the Thatcherite economic model has crashed, slashing the living standards of the majority; and sections of the media have been shown to have been running their own phone tapping and police-bribing operations on an industrial scale.

More has been uncovered during those twenty years about government and secret state operations against the miners' union and wider labour movement – as well as against anti-corporate and environmental groups. But throughout that time there has barely been the slightest official acknowledgement that there might be anything problematic about such an anti-democratic campaign. Within a couple of weeks of *The Enemy Within*'s original appearance in November 1994, fifty MPs had put their names to a House of Commons motion declaring that Stella Rimington was 'not a fit person to run the security service and should be dismissed' if the book's 'disturbing allegations' were shown to be well founded. Accounting for almost a fifth of the parliamentary Labour Party at the time, the MPs called for an independent public inquiry into 'the systematic abuse of security service powers against the miners' union and its leadership' and pointed to 'further evidence ... that Roger Windsor, former NUM chief executive, was an MI5 agent sent into the union to destabilize it'.

The same demands were made by the civil-rights organization Liberty. The former home secretary Lord Merlyn-Rees called for the evidence of GCHQ surveillance of domestic targets to be 'cleared up' by a future Labour government. The writer Christopher Hitchens widened the field, arguing that the exposure of the dirty-tricks campaign against Arthur Scargill and the NUM was 'the first serious test of the calibre' of the then new Labour leader Tony Blair. 'Can he demand less than a parliamentary select committee, along the lines of Senator Frank Church's hearings on the CIA', Hitchens wrote optimistically, 'to investigate the abuse of power by the intelligence services?' The response to all this, as the *Sunday Times* put it, was mostly 'embarrassed silence'.

Under persistent questioning, John Major retreated to his carefully worded three-year-old official statement that Roger Windsor had never been 'employed' by the government. But the Tory prime minister refused to confirm that the former NUM chief executive had had no contact with MI5 during or after the miners' strike, relying instead on the traditional stonewalling of questions about the 'operations of the security and intelligence services'. In a letter to George Galloway, then a Labour MP, Major added the classic civil servant's rider that there was 'little new in the allegations contained in Mr Milne's book or the associated *Dispatches* television programme' – as though the reports I and others had published in the *Guardian* about the secret war against the miners had already been rebutted or even responded to in some way. Plainly, they had not.

Security service sources privately expressed their 'concern' about the book and Stella Rimington's successor as head of MI5, Stephen Lander, let it be known that, far from being alarmed by MI5 operations against the NUM during and after the 1984–5 miners' strike, senior police officers had in fact pressed for greater involvement. There was, meanwhile, little prospect of the new Tory-dominated Parliamentary Intelligence and Security Committee – packed then, as now, with Downing Street–approved trusties – investigating these or other recent episodes of secret service malpractice. In case there was any doubt, Major's Foreign Secretary Douglas Hurd soothingly reassured the intelligence world that 'the past is another country' and Lord Howe, his predecessor and a committee member, promised it would not be delving into 'political archaeology'. Nor did Hitchens's hopes of an inquiry into the abuse of power by the intelligence services stand any more chance after the election of Tony Blair and New Labour, who made every effort to ingratiate themselves with the security establishment from an early stage.[1]

Nevertheless, November 1994 did not prove to be a happy month for Roger Windsor, the man paid by Robert Maxwell for his false testimony against the leaders of Britain's most important postwar strike. The judgement delivered on 3 November by a French court in favour of the miners' union and IEMO – finding that the former NUM employee had lied and was himself the author of documents he claimed had been forged by Scargill and Alain Simon – could scarcely have come at a worse time. Windsor, who had assured all comers that the then five-year-old case would vindicate him, claimed the decision was 'flawed' and dismissed the Angoulême High Court – perhaps unwisely, in view of French legal pride in the Napoleonic Code – as only a 'little country court in the middle of France'. The judges' ruling might also have embarrassed the *Daily Mirror*, the *Cook Report* and other newspapers which had pointed the finger at Scargill over the forgeries four years earlier, if they had actually bothered to report it. True to form, they did nothing of the kind. And on the day *The Enemy Within* was published and the accompanying *Dispatches* film broadcast, Windsor still felt able to threaten libel writs against Channel Four, the *Guardian*, the publishers Verso, and the author. He even speculated that Stella Rimington might be called to the High Court to testify on his behalf.[2]

As things turned out, the 'little country court' did not prove to be the end of the matter. Windsor appealed against the Angoulême court judgement three times. But on each occasion his case was rejected: twice by the Bordeaux court of appeal, in 1998 and 1999, and finally by the highest court in France, the Cour de Cassation, which in March 2002 upheld all three previous judgements against Windsor and ordered him to pay his original debt of £29,500, plus interest, damages, compensation and costs, by now running into hundreds of thousands of pounds. Three decades after what Windsor called his 'moral debt' was first incurred and getting on for twenty-five years after he promised the *Daily Mirror* to repay it to the miners' hardship fund, no such payment had been made.

Instead, in 2009 Windsor was ordered by the French courts to sell his property in France and pay his share of the proceeds to the IEMO – which amounted to just under £105,000 and was duly handed over in 2012. But that was just the start of it. In 2010, the central London County Court ordered £50 a month to be deducted from Windsor's NUM pension. That figure was increased to £350 a month by Worcester County Court in 2013, to be paid until the remaining debt of what still totalled over £389,000 had been settled. Windsor had by this point returned to England to live near Hereford – where he and Scargill came face-to-face at the county court in 2011 for the first time since he left the NUM to make a string of false allegations against the miners' leader twenty-two years earlier. Perhaps unsurprisingly, not a word was exchanged.[3]

In the month after *The Enemy Within*'s appearance, the welter of new evidence about the Scargill Affair and what lay behind triggered renewed investigations by the Nottinghamshire and South Yorkshire police, first called in by NUM leaders in the autumn of 1989 after Windsor's sudden departure to France. The South Yorkshire force returned to the case of the theft of NUM documents and Nottinghamshire CID reopened its investigation into the damaging 1985 letter forged in the name of the UDM official David Prendergast. That had cost the NUM close to £200,000 in an out-of-court libel settlement. At a meeting to discuss the Prendergast forgery with Scargill and the NUM's solicitor Gareth Peirce, in December 1994, the senior Nottinghamshire detective handling the investigation, Acting Chief Superintendent

Michael Cox, revealed that the case had originally been referred to the director of public prosecutions – who had taken a year to decide not to pursue it. The new evidence generated from the French court action and *The Enemy Within* pointed to a pattern in Windsor's behaviour and made him 'very uneasy', Cox told Scargill. 'This could go deeper than even you think.'[4]

One of the striking features of the mainstream media response to the book and *Dispatches* documentary was the effortless ease with which even the most implacable critics now admitted that the original *Mirror–Cook Report* accusations against Scargill and Peter Heathfield had been nonsense – something none had ever seen fit to mention before. No effort was made to explain why the press had got it all so spectacularly wrong during the ferocious six-month campaign of 1990. Instead, there was an instant and orderly retreat to a new line of defence. This was that the allegations of MI5 operations against the NUM and involvement in the smear campaign were 'unproven' – as if long-serving GCHQ and Whitehall officials were seriously expected to risk their jobs, pensions and lengthy gaol sentences in order to go on the record for the sake of civil liberties and the reputation of the National Union of Mineworkers. In the wake of Stella Rimington's own memoirs, and disclosures by former MI5 officers such as David Shayler, even that fallback position began to melt away.[5]

Most gratifying at the time was the first-ever acknowledgement from the *Daily Mirror* that the prize-winning story it had launched nearly five years earlier had been a fairy tale. The security service, the paper reported in November 1994, was 'said to have inspired newspaper investigations four years ago – first printed by the *Daily Mirror* – which accused Mr Scargill of using Libyan cash to repay a home loan. That allegation has since been discredited.' The then Tory loyalist *Daily Express* used the same formulation. The free-market *Economist* accepted that Scargill had been 'subjected to a succession of smears and that these culminated in an entirely false allegation … that he used money donated to strikers to pay off his mortgage'. The *Independent* described the *Mirror* and *Cook Report* allegations as having been simply 'untrue'.[6]

But in view of the fact that Roy Greenslade, the *Mirror* editor who first ran the stories, was by then already publicly berating himself for not having been 'sceptical enough' and speculating whether he had been the 'victim of an MI5 sting', perhaps they had little choice. Even those most closely involved at last began to back away from their central accusations. Terry Pattinson, the former *Mirror* industrial editor who won the Reporter of the Year award for his part in the Scargill Affair, acknowledged that the cash he had claimed was brought from Libya in suitcases to pay off the NUM leader's nonexistent mortgage might not have been Libyan after all. 'It does not matter whether the cash came from Russia, Libya, MI5 or elsewhere,' he explained testily. Roger Windsor took a similar line. 'I've no idea', he said, 'where Mr Abbasi got the money from – he told me it had come from Libya.' And as he floundered in the face of documentary evidence showing his original allegations to be impossible, Windsor let slip another extraordinary admission. 'I can't tell the truth of how Scargill paid off his mortgage,' he exclaimed. 'Whether he ended up with personal gain or not, I don't know.' Since the charge of embezzlement had been at the core of his 1990 testimony, there was little ground for him left to defend. Roger Cook refused even to discuss his Scargill programmes. It was left to Greenslade to write an epitaph for the whole miserable saga: 'I've followed the story ever since I was involved with it and, God, I wish I'd never been involved with it.'[7]

In 2002, following the forgery judgement against Windsor by the highest court in France, Greenslade went further and wrote a comprehensive apology to Scargill and Peter Heathfield in the *Guardian* for his decision to publish the 1990 *Mirror* smear stories. 'I am now convinced that Scargill didn't misuse strike funds', Greenslade declared, 'and the union didn't get money from Libya. I also concede that … it was understandable that Scargill didn't sue … We were all taken in.' Neither the final French court judgement nor Greenslade's apology was reported elsewhere in the mainstream press. But the *Daily Mirror* did later publish an unsigned article, in the course of which the paper commented that, during his time as the *Mirror's* editor, Greenslade had been involved in 'falsely smearing Arthur Scargill's reputation with a despicable link to Libyan dictator Colonel Gaddafi'.[8]

Also within a couple of weeks of the original publication of *The Enemy Within*, Richard Gott, the *Guardian*'s leftist literary editor, was accused by the *Spectator* of having been a KGB 'agent of influence'. The charge, levelled with a fanfare of high moral outrage by two journalists with 'extensive connections to the conservative "security" milieu' – as they were characterized in the *London Review of Books* – was made on the basis of a tip-off from Oleg Gordievsky, the KGB double agent and defector now living on an MI6 pension. To anyone who had read his assorted anti-Soviet outbursts over the years, the idea that Gott was a Soviet agent of influence seemed absurd. Gott had nevertheless had contacts with KGB officials, who had paid for him to travel to meetings on the Continent. He resigned because he had not told the *Guardian*'s editor about the trips. But MI5 had known about them for years, it transpired, as the service had summoned Gott to discuss his KGB contacts in the late 1980s after Gordievsky's defection.

Inevitably, there was widespread speculation about both the timing of the Gott 'revelations' and the involvement of the intelligence services. The *Observer* reported 'highly placed sources' claiming the leak had been engineered in revenge for the *Guardian*'s pursuit of Jonathan Aitken, the then Tory treasury secretary, over sleaze allegations. Elsewhere, Christopher Hitchens linked it with official annoyance over both the Aitken scandal and the *Guardian*'s publication of an extract from *The Enemy Within*.

Whether there was any basis to either connection, the witch-hunting Gott affair at least had the advantage of allowing a rare public airing of the far more significant domestic and US intelligence interference in British press and broadcasting. 'Many British journalists benefited from CIA or MI6 largesse during the Cold War', the *Times* coolly informed the British public for the first time. The same point was made by two former ministers from Margaret Thatcher's government, Lord Gilmour and Alan Clark, in a letter to the *Guardian* defending Gott. Peregrine

Worsthorne described his own chummy, cash-lubricated relationship with the CIA in the *Sunday Telegraph*. Jon Snow, the Channel Four news presenter, revealed that he had been offered the chance to double his salary, 'with no trouble from the taxman', to spy on fellow journalists for the British security services. Naturally, newspapers like *The Times* denounced any comparison between the large number of journalists doing favours for 'our side' and those, evidently far fewer, in contact with the KGB. No journalist who worked for the CIA and MI6, the Murdoch-owned paper claimed, was supporting a 'totalitarian regime' – a particularly difficult point to defend, since most of the bloodiest dictatorships of the postwar period were installed and sustained with the help of Western intelligence.[9]

Not surprisingly, there were those in the media who were equally outraged at the allegations in *The Enemy Within* about the heavy MI5 and Special Branch targeting and recruitment of labour and industrial correspondents in the 1970s. Some sought to ridicule the idea that anything of the kind could have taken place – even advancing the bizarre argument that labour correspondents were too pro-union to get into bed with MI5 – while others tried to justify the collusion. In a letter to the *Spectator*, Terry Pattinson, who had admitted being asked to inform for MI5 during the same period, painted a lurid picture of the supposed influence of the Communist Party and Soviet Embassy officials among industrial correspondents. 'Is it any wonder that the British security services tried to redress the balance by recruiting agents of their own? … I can guess at two volunteers – one used to be in military intelligence – but both were too right-wing, drunk and stupid to be of any real use to MI5 chief Stella Rimington.'

As in Richard Gott's case, some of those regarded as agents or 'contacts' by MI5 or Special Branch officers doubtless had a quite different view of the relationship or were even unaware they were dealing with the security services at all. And, of course, allegations by former employees of the security and intelligence apparatus, schooled in a world of disinformation and self-aggrandizement, have to be treated with particular care. But there are now enough independent sources and separate pieces of supporting evidence to leave no room for reasonable doubt that industrial journalists were singled out for special attention in the years of industrial militancy. And unlike Gott, who could only offer his Soviet contacts gossip and observation, they were in a position to give the security services the direct access to left-wing union leaders and activists that was otherwise only available through bugging, surveillance and infiltration.[10]

The credibility of Gordievsky's long-heralded list of British 'confidential contacts' in any case received a body blow after he identified the former Labour leader Michael Foot as the KGB's 'Agent Boot' in the *Sunday Times* – a charge so widely derided it had to be rapidly scaled down to that of 'Target Boot', particularly after Foot sued. One of Gordievsky's real contacts when he worked at the Soviet Embassy as the undercover acting KGB station chief was the left-wing Scottish Labour MP Ron Brown, who was also a regular visitor to Libya. Gordievsky, Brown says, was forever pumping him for 'juicy titbits' about Labour MPs' private lives. He also pressed for information about the NUM's Libyan connection during the miners' strike. In retrospect, Brown – who, without the knowledge of the NUM leadership, had approached the Libyans about the possibility of financial support for the miners in 1984 – was convinced Gordievsky was acting not for the KGB, but for his real masters in MI6. 'The information he was seeking was far more valuable to the Tories than it would ever have been to the KGB.'[11]

New evidence emerged after the publication of *The Enemy Within* to highlight how covert state-sponsored action against the left in the NUM and other trade unions went far beyond the operations of the official security services themselves. Cabinet papers released in 1995 revealed that in the early 1960s the Conservative government authorized a secret payment of £40,000 – around £710,000 in 2012 prices – to a semi-clandestine anti-communist trade-union organization known as the Industrial Research and Information Service (IRIS). The money was allocated from the 'secret vote', the intelligence services budget, on the orders of the then Prime Minister Harold Macmillan, with the aim of stemming the advance of the left in the labour movement and 'inspiring' media stories culled from 'secret sources'. The government funding, agreed after an approach from a former Labour minister, Lord Shawcross, was matched by large private companies like Ford and Shell. It was used to hire full-time 'undercover' IRIS organizers in the NUM, the Amalgamated Engineering Union (AEU) and elsewhere to defeat left-wing candidates for union positions and build 'anti-communist cells'. The government also agreed to a secret committee, made up of industrialists, civil servants and intelligence officials, whose task was to 'enlist the help' of the BBC, *Daily Mirror* and various suitable newspapers in the propaganda war against 'communism' and industrial militancy on the shop floor.

More than twenty years later, several right-wing trade-union leaders involved with IRIS would play key roles in the 1984–5 miners' strike. Among them was Bill Sirs, then general secretary of the steelworkers' union, the ISTC, who joined the IRIS board in January 1984 and went on to chair the organization. Maintaining coal supplies to the country's steelworks was a high priority for the Tory government during the dispute, and Sirs was instrumental in a series of behind-the-scenes local deals struck with NUM area officials in the teeth of opposition from Scargill and Heathfield. Sirs was a member of the TUC general council at the time, while Ken Cure of the AEU, another IRIS director, sat on the Labour Party national executive throughout the year-long stoppage. Through the two of them, IRIS had direct access to both the labour movement's ruling bodies – essential intelligence in the strikebreaking effort. Another IRIS director from 1988 was Sir Jack Smart, former local NUM official and Labour leader of Wakefield council and the Association of Metropolitan Authorities.

By this time, most of the money for IRIS came from a glittering array of British-owned multinational companies – including ICI, Unilever, Hanson Trust, Glaxo, United Newspapers, Boots and BP – which bankrolled political interference in their employees' unions through tax-deductible donations. These were made via a charity fund-raising front, the Industrial Trust, whose trustees included the former Coal Board chairman Lord Robens, the Tory peer Lord McAlpine and Lord Boyd-Carpenter, then chairman of the Tory backbenchers in the House of Lords. After the Charity Commission launched an investigation into the trust's political role, most of the IRIS money was diverted instead through the Kennington Industrial Company. The same conduit also helped pay for the McCarthyite smear-sheet *British Briefing*, published in the late 1980s by Margaret Thatcher's coal-strike confidant and MI5 collaborator David Hart.

IRIS and similar groups, such as Common Cause, continued to operate into the 1990s, but they had long since become discredited as transparent Cold War front organizations outside the narrowest of hard-right labour-movement circles. In later years, the more respectable Jim Conway Foundation, which acted as an educational outfit, took over part of IRIS's role as a focus for right-wing networks in the trade-union movement. The foundation's accounts from the 1990s showed that it was being financed by the Dulverton Trust, which was established by a Conservative peer and industrialist and whose trustees included the former Tory ministers Lord Carrington and Lord Gowrie. The same trust also funded IRIS and the Institute for the Study of Conflict, the propaganda outfit run by the CIA and MI6 'alongsider' Brian Crozier.[12]

In time, it seems, the vanity of those employed by the state to spy on its citizens becomes increasingly hard to contain. And in 2002, the Metropolitan Police and other forces' chief constables gave the go-ahead to former Special Branch officers and agents to talk for the first time in public – for a three-part BBC television documentary, *True Spies* – about their efforts to infiltrate and undermine the left and the unions in the 1970s and 1980s. Among twenty-three senior trade-union officials said to have been secret police informers at the time were Joe Gormley, the right-wing NUM president during the victorious miners' strikes of the early 1970s, and Ray Buckton, former left-leaning general secretary of the train drivers' union ASLEF. That Gormley, ennobled by Margaret Thatcher, turns out to have been a Special Branch nark who tipped off his handlers about NUM strike plans, is mostly a surprise because he might instead have been expected to pick up the phone and talk to government ministers directly. 'He was a patriot,' his former Special Branch handler offered by way of explanation. The claim that the well-liked Buckton was a Special Branch contact came as more of a shock, even if some in his old union had privately harboured suspicions about his loyalties.[13]

A generation later, neither the trade unions nor the left have anything like the same clout. But the pattern of covert collaboration between the security service, police and private corporations against union and political activists has nevertheless continued and spread since the days of IRIS and the miners' strike. Just as in the depths of the Cold War, when the business-funded and MI5-linked Economic League blacklisted left-wingers and trade unionists, its successor outfit, the anodyne-sounding Consulting Association, was revealed in 2013 to have been colluding with Special Branch across the country to run a corporate espionage operation, blacklisting thousands of building workers for the country's largest construction companies. Undercover police intelligence on environmental and anti-corporate activists is routinely passed to private corporations – a practice exposed in 2009, when covert information about Climate Camp protesters was shown to have been handed to the German-owned private energy giant E.ON by government officials.[14]

In the 1990s and thereafter, MI5 made much of its downgrading of the 'counter-subversion' effort it had run against the left and trade-union movement since the First World War. In practice, the job was largely taken over by a string of secret police outfits, from the traditional Special Branch to newer organizations such as the National Public Order Intelligence Unit. Subversion was rebranded as extremism and the focus widened to environmental, animal rights and anti-racist groups. A taste of what these units were up to was revealed in a series of undercover policing scandals in 2011: long-term infiltration of police spies and agents provocateurs into political organizations and protest groups; disinformation and dirty tricks operations against anti-racist and police corruption campaigns – including the family of Stephen Lawrence, the black London teenager murdered by a racist gang in 1993 – and the use of sexual relationships with activists to strengthen the spies' cover. One undercover officer was even exposed as having helped draft a famously libellous leaflet for environmental campaigners about the fast food chain McDonalds that drew them into the longest-running civil trial in English history. Any idea that the habits of surveillance, infiltration and provocation, which have been the stock-in-trade of Britain's secret state for hundreds of years, died with the end of the Cold War is clearly fantasy.[15]

The mobilization of that covert state against the miners – along with the full panoply of coercive government and judicial powers – was, however, certainly unparalleled in modern peacetime Britain. Formerly secret government papers released since 2010 confirm both the extent of NUM surveillance and penetration and the enthusiasm with which ministers, including Margaret Thatcher, lapped up that intelligence to pursue their campaign against the union. They include a report to the prime minister from the then cabinet secretary, Robert Armstrong, in the runup to the 1984–5 strike on the political affiliations, relationships and drinking habits of NUM leaders, based on MI5 briefings. Scargill and Heathfield, among others, are identified as 'communist sympathisers' (and so legitimate targets for surveillance in MI5 logic), while around 1,000 miners are reported to be Communist Party members (along with a couple of dozen in smaller leftist groups). Recommendations are made – after consultations with an MI5 officer, John Deverell – about what sort of 'publicity could be helpful' while 'keeping our sources of information open': in other words, what stories gleaned from spying could be leaked to the press without compromising agents or informants. According to the authorized, and therefore sanitized, history of MI5, Deverell (who was killed in a helicopter crash in Scotland in 1994) had been seconded to the cabinet office to come up with 'ploys' against the left in the trade unions. These included using MI5 surveillance material to engineer the sacking of the British Leyland Longbridge plant convenor Derek Robinson, branded 'Red Robbo' in the press.[16]

Other declassified state papers underline both the scale of Thatcher's preparations for a confrontation with the miners and her ambition to drive the whole trade union movement to the margins of industrial and political life: including plans to 'erode trade union membership', keep unions out of the new industries and end the union link with the Labour party. They reveal detailed discussions about using troops to move coal during the expected strike – an option Thatcher left open and revived as she feared the government faced defeat in October 1984. Nor did she believe the NUM was finished after the end of the strike – as government support for the campaign to discredit Scargill and Heathfield five years later made clear. Within months of the miners' return to work, ministers secretly made preparations to see off further industrial action and seal the fate of the coal industry: by creating huge permanent coal stockpiles; boosting imports, opencast mining, nuclear and gas-fired power stations; and tightening the legal vice on strikers and their families.[17]

What remains of the British coal industry has now been in private hands for two decades. Most was originally sold by John Major's government to Richard Budge, a man identified in a confidential 1994 report for the Trade and Industry Department by the accountants Coopers & Lybrand as 'unfit to be concerned in the management of a company'. The phrase echoed the words used by DTI inspectors in 1971 about Robert Maxwell, whose entanglement with the NUM proved so disastrous. Critical of the funding of Budge's motor-racing hobby from company funds, the Coopers & Lybrand report also considered that loans had been made to the businessman which breached the Companies Act. To achieve its 'ultimate privatization', the government nevertheless wrote off £1.6 billion-worth of British Coal debts in a sweetener to the new private owners, far outstripping the £960 million raised in the sell-off. As the deal was pushed through in the final months of 1994, Labour leaders quietly abandoned the commitment they had made to renationalize coal barely six months earlier.

Budge's company, RJB Mining, went on to employ most of the few thousand miners still working in the industry, and together with other private operators initially reopened more than a dozen pits closed by the Tory government. Ten years later, Budge had been ousted from what had become UK Coal and – despite some limited aid from the Blair government – the surviving industry struggled with the legacy of a rigged electricity privatization and failure to invest in the necessary power-station technology to meet emission controls. Twenty years after privatization, Budge was bankrupt; UK Coal (now Coalfield Resources) had had to be saved from collapse by a Tory-led government; deep mining had been reduced to three collieries; coal imports were surging; carbon dioxide emissions were rising; under-investment threatened power shortages; David Cameron's coalition had signed a nuclear reactor deal guaranteeing prices at double their existing level for thirty-five years; and the privatized energy sector was in the grip of six mainly foreign-owned companies that between them controlled 98 percent of electricity supply and were able to drive up prices at will. The destruction of the coal industry had finally broken the power of the miners' union, but done nothing to create a sustainable clean energy sector that could deliver for the public and the wider economy.[18]

Arthur Scargill, meanwhile, retired as NUM president in 2002, but carried on as the union's honorary president until 2011 (despite a series of legal disputes with current NUM officials), as president of the IEMO and leader of the Socialist Labour Party he established in the mid-1990s. The union's new leaders were left with fewer than 2,000 members – but trusts with cash and assets worth getting on for £20m. As for those who had been drawn into Thatcher's secret war against the miners, Salem Ibrahim, Colonel Gaddafi's confidant who took Windsor to Libya in the middle of the 1984–5 strike, was imprisoned after US, British and French military intervention in the country's civil war led to the fall of the Tripoli regime and the lynching of its former leader. David Hart, Thatcher's 'Blue Pimpernel' during the 1984–5 strike whose intelligence links were confirmed by the former Conservative minister Jonathan Aitken, died in 2011 – but not before a warrant for his arrest had been issued by Equatorial Guinea for his alleged involvement in a coup attempt against its government. Neil Greatrex, president of the breakaway Union of Democratic Mineworkers – formed out of the strikebreaking coalfield networks that had been championed and financed by Hart – was jailed in 2012 for stealing nearly £150,000 from a miners' charity.[19]

Stella Rimington continued to take a special interest in the coal and energy industries long after the 1984–5 strike. In the wake of the pit-closures crisis of the early 1990s, the then MI5 director general collared the leaders of both the power industry and coal managers' unions – Tony Cooper of the EMA (father of the front-bench Labour politician Yvette Cooper) and Doug Bulmer of BACM – who were planning to join forces, and grilled Cooper in particular about the proposed merger. The aim had been to link up with the gas industry managers to form a grouping across the entire energy sector, but the amalgamation collapsed in recriminations and legal action the following year. After her retirement from MI5 in 1996, Rimington went to work as a non-executive director for Marks & Spencer and other private corporations – though she still privately warned New Labour leaders in the run-up to the 1997 election that they would need to keep a close eye on what was by then a comprehensively marginalized left inside the party.

But controversy about her former MI5 role, particularly against the miners' union, would again flare up around the publication of her memoirs in 2001. The initial draft – including Rimington's first public acknowledgement of her part in 'counter-subversion' operations against the 1984–5 strike – had been leaked to the *Sun* the previous year, apparently by Whitehall securocrats determined to punish her for breaking the intelligence agencies' code of *omertà*. References to the strike were further watered down, at the urging of her MI5 successor, to a bland insistence that everything MI5 had done had been entirely proper and reasonable. The security service, she wrote, had only targeted 'the activities of those who were using the strike for subversive purposes'. These included the NUM's three national leaders (Scargill, Heathfield and Mick McGahey) because they had supposedly 'declared that they were using the strike to try to bring down the elected government of Mrs Thatcher'. Picket lines had not been MI5's concern, she insisted, 'though they were of great concern to the police'.

It was part of the theology of MI5 and other branches of the security services that they did not target trade unions, peace movement or other protest groups as such, but only the elastically defined 'subversives' operating within them. Given that MI5 regarded the NUM's leadership at all levels to be subversive (in common with, for example, that of the Campaign for Nuclear Disarmament), the distinction was one of supreme sophistry. But it does help to explain some of Rimington's more bizarre pronouncements, such as her claim that MI5 had no agents in the NUM. As one senior MI5 official put it to me: 'That doesn't mean we didn't have agents among the subversives in the NUM.'

In an interview with the *Guardian* to mark the publication of her memoirs, Rimington finally went on the record about Roger Windsor, choosing her words with the greatest care. Asked whether Windsor had been an MI5 informer or had any contact with the security service, she replied: 'It would be correct to say that he, Roger Windsor, was never an agent in any sense of the word that you can possibly imagine and that MI5 did not run agents in the National Union of Mineworkers.' Pressed as to whether she meant the security service had no NUM informers at all, Rimington then added: 'That's not to say that the police or Special Branch ... might not have been doing some of those things.' The studied ambiguity of her response inevitably only whetted the appetites of her critics. As Labour's then chair of the House of Commons Home Affairs Select Committee Chris Mullin (later a Foreign Office minister) wrote shortly after Rimington's *Guardian* interview: 'One would still like to know the relationship between ... Roger Windsor and the security services.' Quoting her comment about Windsor, he went on: 'What was he then? Whose idea was it to send him to Libya and then leak news of the trip to the *Sunday Times*? What part did MI5 play in the attempts to frame Arthur Scargill by pretending that he had used money donated to the strike fund to pay off his mortgage? These are all areas in which Rimington could assist with inquiries, but she does not.'

Windsor himself had by then finally launched a libel action against the *Sunday Express* after it ran an article by the former Tory MP and spy writer Rupert Allason (writing under the pseudonym Nigel West) categorically stating that Windsor had worked as an

MI5 agent for Rimington and wrongly claiming that this had been confirmed by the MI5 whistleblower David Shayler. After the *Express* titles were sold to Richard Desmond, the newspaper eventually reached an out-of-court settlement with Windsor and published a retraction. The former NUM chief executive was backed in the *Sunday Express* action by Carter-Ruck. This was the same legal firm which in 1990 had unexpectedly taken over the Prendergast case against the NUM, with the support of the Goldsmith Foundation, while at the same time 'cooperating' with Windsor. The confirmation of that cooperation in 1994 led to a complaint by Scargill and the NUM to the Solicitors' Complaints Bureau. The complaint was initially upheld by the Bureau's investigating officer, but finally rejected in 1999 after Carter-Ruck provided information which was not disclosed to the union because the firm insisted it was 'privileged'.

What David Shayler had in fact reported about the NUM, when he broke cover in 1997, was that he had seen parts of Scargill's forty-volume MI5 file while working for the security service. The file confirmed, he said, that at least one highly placed source in the NUM national office had during the 1984–5 strike been feeding Rimington everything from picketing tactics to details of the NUM leader's private life. 'MI5 was obsessed with Scargill,' Shayler commented. 'He even had his own classification – "Unaffiliated Subversive"'. This term, MI5's authorized history has since disclosed, was personally dreamed up by Rimington (after 'agonising' about it) to justify the continued tapping of Scargill's phone, which had begun in November 1973. Her reasoning was again that the miners' leader wanted to bring down the Conservative government. Which of course he did – 'legitimately', as Scargill puts it, by bringing about a general election, as had happened as a result of the coal strike of 1974.[20]

The attempt by Rimington and her successors to deflect criticism of MI5's role in the miners' strike on to Special Branch is specious. But the political police have traditionally acted as MI5's boots on the ground, and there's no doubt they were far more directly involved in the pit villages and efforts to undermine picketing – running their own large-scale surveillance and agent operations, as well as working in tandem with the security service. In the run-up to the miners' strike, MI5 gave Special Branch officers advanced training in agent handling at the Fort Monckton spy school outside Portsmouth. Not to be outdone by the leaks about MI5 infiltration, police commanders boasted in the *True Spies* BBC documentary about a Special Branch agent within Scargill's 'inner circle', codenamed Silver Fox. Tony Clement, the assistant chief constable in South Yorkshire who ran the police operation at Orgreave, says the agent was 'at the level where he would sit round the table with the NUM leadership'. John Nesbit, the chief superintendent who arrested Scargill at the coking plant confrontation (and eight years later declared 'Arthur was right') describes the informant as providing 'very specific and precise information' about picketing which, he claims, was 'correct every time' and 'beat the strike'. If the allegations about picketing tipoffs are correct, Silver Fox is unlikely to have been based at NUM headquarters (as Windsor was) because, with the exception of Orgreave, picketing was organized at area level. But the intelligence would certainly have been passed to Rimington and MI5.[21]

More about the covert methods and dirty tricks used against the miners' union and others on the left and in the trade union movement will doubtless come to light in future – as has already happened over more recent targeting of Muslim, anti-war and environmental activists. It's a measure of the lengths to which the establishment is prepared to go when faced with a serious challenge to its authority. But it would be a mistake to overestimate the power of the security services and their collaborators, or to accept the claim that they played a decisive role in the outcome of the 1984–5 strike and the mining communities' subsequent fate. MI5, Special Branch and GCHQ were just one part – albeit an important and previously hidden part – of a much wider state mobilization aimed at breaking the miners' extraordinary resistance. That in turn depended on the collaboration of sections of the labour movement and the exploitation of internal divisions and weaknesses.

As the real story of what took place has emerged – and as those, such as the power managers, who played a central role in maintaining electricity supply have felt free to reveal how close the strike came to success – the events of 1984–5 and its aftermath have come to be reassessed. Far from being remote from our time, the miners' opposition to Thatcher's market and privatization juggernaut makes even clearer sense in the wake of the 2008 crash than it did at the time – as does the anti-democratic danger of the secret state after the exposure of untrammelled NSA and GCHQ surveillance and undercover police operations against political activists and protesters. Mick McGahey, the Scottish miners' leader and NUM vice-president during the 1984–5 stoppage – who made little secret of disagreements with Scargill in later years – gave his own view at a meeting to mark the tenth anniversary of the strike at Dalkeith in Midlothian. 'I've often been asked the question: had the miners any alternative in 1984? Yes, they had. The miners could have capitulated. Scargill, Heathfield and McGahey could have said: "There you are, walk over the top of us." You had an alternative in 1984 – I'm proud you did not take it. Be proud that you defended the interests of the British people.'[22]

# NOTES

## INTRODUCTION: THE SECRET WAR
## AGAINST THE MINERS

1. *Guardian*, 29 November 1993.

2. *Financial Times*, 21 June 1991.

3. Copeland telephoned the NUM in Sheffield on 6 March 1990 while Scargill was in London visiting lawyers, and a message was then left with the NUM's counsel, John Hendy QC. Scargill called Copeland back the following day on the office conference phone and Heathfield took part in the exchange. Scargill kept a note of the conversation, and Heathfield and Hendy confirm the account. Copeland's CIA background is summarized in Miles Copeland, *The Real Spy World*, London 1975. On his later CIA links, see *Guardian*, 6 May 1987.

4. See the account of the 'Libyan connection' in Chapter 3; the allegations about the use of Soviet money are examined in detail in Chapter 6. The other principal *Mirror–Cook Report* claims are described in Chapter 1 and analysed in Chapters 2 and 3.

5. *Guardian*, 17 January 1992 and 18 December 1991.

6. Andrew Murray in the *Morning Star*, 19 March 1984; Émile Zola, *Germinal*, Paris 1885, and Harmondsworth 1954, p. 499.

7. Peter Walker, *Staying Power*, London 1991, p. 166; Geoffrey Goodman, *The Miners' Strike*, London 1985, p. 19; Peter Wilsher, Donald Macintyre and Michael Jones, *Strike*, London 1985, p. 25; Hugo Young, *One of Us*, London 1991, p. 366.

8. Wilfred Miron, report to NCB chairman, 6 December 1973, quoted in Jonathan Winterton and Ruth Winterton, *Coal, Crisis and Conflict*, Manchester 1989, pp. 9–11.

9. *Yorkshire Post*, 10 March 1994; *Sunday Times*, 7 March 1993; *The Economist*, 27 May 1978; Nicholas Ridley, *My Style of Government*, London 1991, p. 67; Margaret Thatcher, *The Downing Street Years*, London 1993, p. 346.

10. The evidence is laid out in detail in Mike Parker and John Surrey, *Unequal Treatment – British Policies for Coal and Nuclear Power, 1979–92*,

SPRU, Sussex University 1992; see also Martin Adeney and John Lloyd, *The Miners' Strike*, London 1986 and 1988, p. 15; Cecil Parkinson, *Right at the Centre*, London 1992, p. 119.

11. Nigel Lawson, The View From No. 11, London 1992, pp. 168 and 680; House of Commons Energy Committee, *The Government's Statements on the New Nuclear Power Programme*, HMSO 1981, para. 20.

12. Parkinson, *Right at the Centre*, pp. 119 and 280–81.

13. *Independent on Sunday and Sunday Times*, 18 October 1992.

14. Parker and Surrey, *Unequal Treatment*, p. 58.

15. British Coal Annual Report 1993 (colliery industrial manpower figures pre-1986 adjusted for comparability by BC); *New Statesman & Society*, 2 July 1993; Nicholas Jones, BBC Radio 4, *Special Assignment*, 'The Final Payout', 2 July 1993.

16. *Guardian*, 7 March 1994.

17. Adeney and Lloyd, *The Miners' Strike*, p. 28.

18. See V. L. Allen, *The Militancy of British Miners*, Shipley 1981, pp. 181–220; Michael Crick, *Scargill and the Miners*, Harmondsworth 1985, pp. 52–63; Frank Watters, *Being Frank*, Doncaster 1992, pp. 61–72.

19. Wilsher et al., *Strike*, p. x.

20. Young, *One of Us*, p. 366; Wilsher et al., *Strike*, p. 31.

21. Frank Ledger and Howard Sallis, *Crisis Management in the Power Industry*, London 1995, pp. 108–9; Frank Ledger, former operations director, CEGB, interviewed in 'The Men Who Kept the Lights On', BBC2 Television, broadcast 23 April 1994; Goodman, *The Miners' Strike*, pp. 26–41; Wilsher et al., *Strike*, pp. 38–51; John McCormack, *Polmaise: The Fight for a Pit*, London 1989, pp. 17–44.

22. Wilsher et al., *Strike*, p. 81; Watters, *Being Frank*, p. 140; Vic Allen, *Morning Star*, 22 November 1993.

23. British Coal Annual Report 1993. The exceptional year, 1985–86, when thirty-six pits closed, was effectively a catch-up on the suspension of closures the previous year. The economic irrationality of pit closures at the social level was set out in a paper by Andrew Glyn, an Oxford University economist, and published by the NUM during the strike in *The Economic Case against Pit Closures*, Sheffield 1984.

24. See House of Lords European Communities Committee, *Restructuring the EC Steel Industry*, 24th Report, 1992–3 Session, 27 July 1993. By the spring of 1994, all deep-mine British Coal collieries in South Wales had been closed and only one, Longannet, remained open in Scotland.

25. *Sunday Telegraph*, 26 September 1993; Ledger and Sallis, *Crisis Management in the Power Industry*, p. 159.

26. Walter Marshall, former CEGB chairman, and Frank Ledger, former CEGB operations director, interviewed in 'The Men Who Kept the Lights On'; Ledger and Sallis, *Crisis Management in the Power Industry*, p. 142 and pp. 157–68. In 1982–3 Thatcher had privately pressed cabinet officials to prepare for the use of troops to move coal in the event of a national strike: see *Guardian*, 1/8/13.

27  Margaret Thatcher, interview in 'The Thatcher Years', Part 2, BBC Television, broadcast on 15 October 1993; Thatcher, *The Downing Street Years*, pp. 363–8.

28  NUM 1992 Annual Conference, Scarborough. A crude, but typical, example of the standard view of the history of the 1984–5 miners' strike can be found in Alan Sked and Chris Cook, *Post-War Britain*, London 1990, pp. 444–53; another, from a right-wing labour-movement perspective, can be found in Robert Taylor, *The Trade Union Question in British Politics*, Oxford 1993, pp. 292–8.

29  Adeney and Lloyd, *The Miners' Strike*, p. 7. A similar point was made by Kim Howells in BBC Radio Wales, 'The Longest Strike', broadcast 12 March 1994.

30  *Guardian*, 20 June 1991; despite the overwhelming weight of propaganda about violence and 'extremism', public-opinion polls (MORI, for example, conducted three general polls about the dispute while it was running) registered between 30 and 40 per cent support for the strike at the time.

31  *Guardian*, 1 August 1992.

32  Goodman, *The Miners' Strike*, p. 204.

33  *Guardian*, 27 November 1984; Young, *One of Us*, pp. 371–2.

34  Robert Reiner, *Chief Constables*, Oxford 1991, p. 191.

35  Wilsher et al., *Strike*, p. 257. The training of 'storm troopers' was a reference to twenty NUM activists who had attended a course at a Moscow trade-union school.

36  NUM Annual Conference Presidential Address, 1 July 1985.

37  Wilsher et al., *Strike*, p. 259. Cabinet papers released in 2010 confirm the scale of the government's post-strike preparations for another miners' stoppage and its determination to run down the coal industry: see *Guardian*, 29/8/10.

38  Thatcher, *The Downing Street Years*, p. 359. During Scargill's re-election campaign in November 1987-January 1988, it was sometimes claimed that the Tories wanted him to win. See, for example, *Guardian*, 24 November and 22 December 1987. In reality, ministers anxiously avoided getting involved for fear of encouraging a Scargill victory: *Guardian*, 22 January 1988. Under the government-funded redundancy scheme which operated until 1987, the £80,000 figure applied to miners in their early fifties with thirty years' service, and included weekly payments until the age of sixty-five as well as lump sums.

39  *The Times*, 8 July 1991; Parkinson, Right at the Centre, p. 257.

40  Thatcher, *The Downing Street Years*, p. 686.

41  *Guardian*, 9 March and 10 July 1990.

42  Phil Bassett, *The Times*, 8 July 1991; *New Statesman & Society*, 2 July 1993; *The Miner*, February 1992. Mandela's remark was made at a farewell dinner in Johannesburg on 24 January 1992 for the South African miners' leader, Cyril Ramaphosa, who was moving over to become secretary-general of the African National Congress. See also Paul Routledge, *Scargill*, London 1993, p. 268.

43  *Mail on Sunday*, 12 December 1993; *Guardian*, 17 October 1992.

44. *Daily Mirror*, 22 October 1992; Routledge, *Scargill*, pp. 237–8.

45. House of Commons, Hansard, 5 July 1993; *Guardian*, 7 June 1993.

46. *The Times*, 8 July 1991; Kinnock's view of his handling of the 1984–5 strike was given in 'The Enemies Within', the second episode of *Kinnock – The Inside Story*, broadcast on 25 July 1993 on the ITV network.

47. See, for example, the *Independent*, 22 May 1991, on the Channel Four *Dispatches* film about the Scargill Affair, and the responses in the *Daily Mirror*, 22 and 23 May 1991, to the *Guardian-Dispatches* investigation.

48. Routledge, *Scargill*, pp. 199–231.

49. For example, *Private Eye*, 26 March 1993, and *Independent on Sunday*, 1 August 1993.

50. *Daily Mirror*, 23 and 27 May 1991; *Daily Mirror*, 1 May 1987.

51. Stephen Dorril and Robin Ramsay, *Smear!*, London 1991, p. ix; A. J. P. Taylor, *The First World War*, Harmondsworth 1963, pp. 16–20.

52. Peter Dale Scott, *The War Conspiracy – The Secret Road to the Second Indochina War*, New York 1972, p. 171.

53. *Central Live*, Central Television, 22 January 1993.

54. Crick, *Scargill and the Miners*, p. 93; *Guardian*, 25 January 1988.


# 1:  OPERATION CYCLOPS

1. William Cobbett, *Political Register*, August 1830.

2. *Sun*, 3 March 1990; *Sunday Correspondent*, 11 March 1990.

3. Roy Greenslade, interview with the author, 19 March 1993; *Sunday Mirror*, 4 March 1990.

4. *Sunday Mirror*, 4 March 1990.

5. Arthur Scargill, interview with the author, 28 August 1990; *Guardian*, 31 August 1990.

6. *Daily Mirror*, 5, 6 and 7 March 1990.

7. Central Television, *Cook Report*, 'Where Did the Money Go?', 5 March 1990.

8. *Daily Express*, 6 March 1990; Roy Greenslade, interview with the author, 19 March 1993.

9. Clive Entwistle, producer/director, *Cook Report*, letters to Scargill, 28 February 1990.

10. Nell Myers' diary, February–March 1990; Anne Scargill, interview with the author, 28 March 1993; Gavin Lightman, *The Lightman Report*, London 1990, p. 146.

11. *Daily Mirror*, 5, 6, 7, 8 and 9 March 1990.

12. *The Times*, 6 March 1990; *Sun*, 5, 6 and 8 March 1990.

13. *New Statesman & Society*, 9 March 1990; *The Times, Independent, Today, Express*, 6 March 1990.

14. *Guardian*, 7 and 9 March 1990; *Cook Report*, 5 March 1990; *Daily Mirror*, 6, 7 and 9 March 1990; *The Times*, 7 March 1990.

15. See Frank Watters, *Being Frank*, Doncaster 1992, pp. 151–5 and 177–81; also Martin Adeney and John Lloyd, *The Miners' Strike*, London 1986 and 1988, pp. 296–9.

16. *Guardian*, 18, 24, 25 July and 29 September 1977; Michael Crick, *Scargill and the Miners*, Harmondsworth 1985, pp. 78–9.

17. Jim Parker, interview with the author, 2 April 1993; Frank Watters, note of meeting with Jim Parker, 11 July 1989; Terry Pattinson and Dave Feickert, interviews with the author, 15 March and 5 June 1993; Paul Routledge, *Scargill*, London 1993, pp. 200–201.

18. Sarah Burton, interview with the author, 27 April 1993; *New Statesman & Society*, 9 March 1990; Roy Greenslade, interview with the author, 19 March 1990; Nell Myers' diary, March 1990; Watters, *Being Frank*, p. 182; Apex NUM branch letter to Arthur Scargill and Peter Heathfield, 15 April 1985. The whole NUM national office staff sent a letter to Scargill and Heathfield backing their leadership after the end of the strike in 1985. Although the 1988 NUM presidential election was by secret ballot, all but one of the fifteen NUM members at the head office are recorded as having voted for Scargill. The identity of the single member who abstained is known to the author.

19. *Daily Mirror*, 3 July 1989; Frank Watters, note of meetings with Parker, 11 July and 22 November 1989; Jim Parker, interview with the author, 2 April 1993; Mick Clapham, interview with the author, 15 June 1993.

20. Jim Parker, interview with the author, 2 April 1993.

21. Hilary Cave, interview with the author, 30 October 1992.

22. *Sheffield Star*, 1 September 1992; Terry Pattinson, interviews with the author, 15 March and 2 April 1993; Roy Greenslade, interview with the author, 19 March 1993.

23. The time of writing: October 1994. Terry Pattinson and Jim Parker, interviews with the author, 15 March and 2 April 1993; Roy Greenslade, interview with the author, 19 March 1993; Windsor's pledge was reported in the *Daily Mirror*, 6 March 1990.

24. *Nottingham Evening Post*, 11 October 1989; *The Miner*, October 1989; *Daily Express*, 12 October 1989; *Sunday Times*, 15 October 1989; *Mail on Sunday*, 16 July 1989; Routledge, *Scargill*, p. 201.

25. Terry Pattinson, interview with the author, 15 March 1993.

26. Mark Hollingsworth, interview with the author, 14 March 1993. Magnum went into liquidation in early 1993.

27. Roy Greenslade, interview with the author, 19 March 1993; Terry Pattinson, interview with the author, 15 March 1993.

28. Terry Pattinson, letter to the author, 25 November 1994, and interview with the author, 15 March 1993; *Sunday Times*, 11 March 1990.

29. *Guardian*, 9 March 1990.

30. Clive Entwistle, interview with the author, 25 August 1993; Terry Pattinson, interview with the author, 2 April 1993; Thorne later went to work for the *Cook Report*.

31. Roy Greenslade, *Maxwell's Fall*, London 1992, p. 397.

32. Clive Entwistle, interview with the author, 25 August 1993; Terry Pattinson, interview with the author, 15 March 1993; Roy Greenslade, interview with the author, 19 March 1993.

33. Roy Greenslade, interview with Oliver Wilson, 6 October 1994; Greenslade, *Maxwell's Fall*, p. 111; and interview with the author, 19 March 1993.

34. Roy Greenslade, interview with the author, 19 March 1993.

35. Lightman, *The Lightman Report*, pp. 74–5.

36. Stephen Hudson, note to Arthur Scargill, 17 July 1984, confirming the sale of his house to the NUM for tax purposes.

37. This account is based on Lightman, *The Lightman Report*, pp. 68–90; transcript of evidence given to the Lightman Inquiry by Stephen Hudson, Ian White and Hazel Riley, 24 May 1990; unpublished written evidence to the Lightman Inquiry by Arthur Scargill and Peter Heathfield; MACF records 1984–5; Scargill's commentary on the Lightman Report for the 1991 Certification Office prosecution; and Roger Windsor, interview with Lorraine Heggessey, Channel Four *Dispatches*, 1991.

38. Stephen Hudson, unpublished transcript of evidence to Lightman Inquiry, 24 May 1990; Lightman, *The Lightman Report*, pp. 123 and 242; Windsor's own loan was £29,500, but only £29,000 was repaid on the disputed day. The correct figure was given in the *Cook Report*, 5 March 1990.

39. Stephen Hudson, interview with the author, 18 February 1994; Stephen Hudson, Ian White and Hazel Riley, unpublished transcript of evidence to Lightman Inquiry, 24 May 1990; Stephen Hudson, letter to Arthur Scargill, 26 March 1992; *Independent on Sunday*, 5 September 1993; Roy Greenslade, interview with Oliver Wilson, 6 October 1994.

40. *Daily Mirror*, 5 July 1984 and 6 July 1990; Nell Myers, note to the author, 25 July 1994.

41. Roger Windsor, interview with Lorraine Heggessey, Channel Four *Dispatches*, 1991.

42. Henry Richardson, letter to Gavin Lightman, 20 June 1990; Lightman, *The Lightman Report*, p. 86; *Daily Mirror*, 6 March 1990; the MACF cash records have been examined by the author.

43. *Daily Mirror*, 9 March 1990.

44. *Morning Star* and *Guardian*, 9 March 1990. Among those papers that challenged the media attacks at the time were the *Morning Star, Tribune* and *Socialist Worker* – the latter ran a particularly unstinting countercampaign throughout the year and its role in 1990 was singled out for praise by Scargill after the publication of this book: *Socialist Worker*, 10 December 1994.

45. Sarah Burton, interview with the author, 27 April 1993; *Daily Mirror*, 7 March 1990.

46. The NEC report is reprinted in Lightman, *The Lightman Report*, pp. 148–62; *Sunday Times*, 11 March 1990.

47. *Daily Mirror*, 10 March and 3 April 1990; *Guardian*, 23 March 1990.

48. Lightman, *The Lightman Report*, p. 3.

## 2:  A HIDDEN HAND

1. Adam Smith, *Wealth of Nations* [1776], Chicago 1976, p. 477.

2. The Anti-Defamation League, which aims to fight anti-Semitism and campaign for minority rights, was revealed in the United States as running a massive political espionage network in collaboration with the US police, FBI and Israeli government, whose targets include a variety of left-wing groups. But there is no evidence that the ADL in Britain has run any kind of parallel operation. See *San Francisco Examiner*, 1 and 4 April 1993; *New York Times*, 25 April 1993; *Covert Action Quarterly*, Summer 1993.

3. Gavin Lightman, *A Trade Union in Chains: Scargill Unbound*, January 1987; Sarah Burton, interview with the author, 27 April 1993; *Sunday Times*, 15 July 1990.

4. Gavin Lightman, the Lightman Report, London 1990, pp. 51–67, 75, 83, 122–4 and 131.

5. Lightman, *The Lightman Report*, pp. 17–18, 20 and 125–9.

6. Stephen Hudson, memo to Arthur Scargill, 17 July 1984; Scargill's commentary on *The Lightman Report* for the Certification Office prosecution, 1991; Lightman, *The Lightman Report*, pp. 66, 85 and 89. Abbasi confirmed the evidence of Yvonne Fenn's log in an interview with the author, 14 May 1993.

7. Alain Simon's letters to Lightman explaining the IMO's position are reprinted in Arthur Scargill, *Response to the Lightman Inquiry*, Barnsley 1990; Lightman, *The Lightman Report*, pp. 120–21.

8. *Daily Express*, 6 July 1990; *Independent*, 5 July 1990; *Daily Mail*, 7 July 1990; *Guardian*, 6 and 10 July 1990; *Daily Telegraph*, 5 July 1990; *Sunday Times*, 8 July 1990.

9. Roy Greenslade, interview with the author, 19 March 1993; Terry Pattinson, interview with the author, 15 March 1993; *Independent on Sunday*, 5 September 1993.

10. Central Television, *Cook Report*, 'The Lightman Report', broadcast 9 July 1990.

11. *Cook Report*, 9 July 1990; *Daily Mirror*, 9 July 1990.

12. *Guardian*, 24 July 1990; Lightman, *The Lightman Report*, pp. 91–5 and 129; Scargill, *Response to the Lightman Inquiry*, p. 8; Arthur Scargill, note to the author, 7 April 1994; *Cook Report*, 9 July 1990; *Independent on Sunday*, 15 July

1990.

13. *Guardian*, 10 July 1990; *Cook Report*, 9 July 1990; *Sunday Times*, 15 July 1990.

14. *Guardian*, 10, 11 and 12 July 1990; *Daily Mirror*, 10 July 1990.

15. *Independent*, 11 July 1990; *Guardian*, 14 and 18 July 1990.

16. Gill Rowlands, interview with the author, 17 August 1993; *Guardian*, 10 July 1990; *Daily Express*, 12 October 1989; *Sunday Times*, 15 October 1989.

17. Brian Crozier, *Free Agent*, London 1993, pp. 231 and 222–8.

18. Gavin Lightman's 'Opinion' for the NUM executive, 19 July 1990; *Guardian*, 24 July 1990; *Sunday Correspondent*, 22 July 1990; record of NUM Special Delegate Conference, 10 October 1990, pp. 38 and 58.

19. Gavin Lightman's 'Opinion' and 'Further Opinion' to the NUM executive, 19 July 1990.

20. Letter from Bruce Brodie to Dr Helmut Preyer of Messrs Schonherr Barfuss Torggler and Partner, 19 July 1990; exchange of correspondence between David Brookland of Cork Gully and Arthur Scargill, 17 August and 24 August 1990; exchange of correspondence between Gavin Lightman and Arthur Scargill, 23 and 29 August 1990. Lightman wrote to Scargill on Friday, 20 July 1990, giving him until the following Tuesday at 4 p.m. to object to the correspondence handover. Michael Jordan of Cork Gully wrote on Monday, 23 July 1990, giving until noon on Wednesday. On 2 August, Brookland informed Scargill the papers had not been released because of the lack of time allowed for his consent. But on 17 August he wrote again to say the documentation had now been given to Frere Chomeley.

21. *Guardian*, 20 and 21 July 1990; *Independent*, 20 July 1990; NUM Special Delegate Conference, 10 October 1990, p. 53.

22. *The Times*, 12 July 1990; *Sunday Times*, 15 July 1990; ITN interview with Vladimir Louniov, 11 July 1990.

23. *Guardian, Independent* and *Daily Mirror*, 20 July 1990; ITN, transcript of interview with Mikhail Srebny, 19 July 1990.

24. *Daily Telegraph* and *Independent*, 6 July 1990.

25. National Endowment for Democracy and Free Trade Union Institute, annual reports; Kim Philby, *My Silent War*, London 1968, p. 140. Miller offered to arrange £100,000 of funding, through 'trade-union and business connections', for another dissident Soviet miners' organizer, Viktor Yakovlev, who originally came to Britain under the auspices of a Trotskyist solidarity campaign. See *Militant*, 27 April 1990.

26. Crozier, *Free Agent*, pp. 259–61; *Guardian*, 27 July 1990; *Tribune*, 22 June and 3 August 1990; George Miller, unpublished letter to the *Guardian*, 27 July 1990; *Cook Report*, 9 July 1990.

27. *Guardian*, 25 July 1990. Scargill was represented at the Sofitel meeting by Jonathan Crystal, a London barrister suggested by Sarah Burton. Neither she, Michael Seifert nor John Hendy were able to act for the NUM

leader because they were considered to be 'NUM' lawyers.

28. Record of NUM Special Delegate Conference on the Lightman Report, 10 October 1990, p. 34; *Guardian*, 27 July 1990.

29. *Daily Mirror*, 26 July 1990.

30. Arthur Scargill, note to the author, 22 March 1994; *Daily Telegraph* and *Guardian*, 27 July 1990; *Sunday Telegraph*, 29 July 1990; *Daily Telegraph*, 11 December 1990.

31. *Daily Telegraph*, 23 July 1990.

32. *Observer*, 8 July and 26 August 1990; *Spectator*, 28 July 1990; *New Statesman & Society*, 27 July 1990; *Guardian*, 18 July 1990; *Independent*, 25 August 1990.

33. *Guardian*, 11 July and 20 August 1990.

34. *Sunday Times*, 5 August 1990; *Guardian*, 6 August 1990.

35. *Daily Mirror*, 6 August 1990; Terry Pattinson, interview with the author, 2 April 1993; Peter Thompson and Anthony Delano, *Maxwell*, London 1988, p. 184.

36. *Guardian*, 13 August 1990.

37. Ken Hollingsworth, interview with the author, 3 November 1993; *Guardian*, 6, 7 and 23 August 1990; Geoffrey Goodman, interview with Lorraine Heggessey, Channel Four *Dispatches*, 1991; Scargill, *Response to the Lightman Inquiry*; 'Defend Scargill – Defend the NUM' advertisement, *Guardian*, 1 October 1990.

38. Paul Foot, interview with the author, 15 March 1993; Graham Hind, recording of Sheffield rally, 24 August 1990; *Observer*, 26 August 1990.

39. Bruce Brodie's notes and reports on the NUM four-man team's meeting with the Soviet and Hungarian miners' union leaderships, Moscow and Budapest, 18 and 20 August 1990; *Guardian*, 4 September 1990; record of NUM Special Delegate Conference, 10 October 1990.

40. *Guardian*, 5 September 1990.

41. *The Times*, 6 September 1990; Nicholas Jones, interview with Arthur Scargill, 4 September 1990, *BBC News; Daily Telegraph*, 14 November 1990.

42. Bruce Brodie, letter to Henry Richardson, 1 October 1990.

43. *Guardian*, 8 September 1990.

44. Record of NUM Special Delegate Conference, 10 October 1990; NUM NEC minutes, 13 September 1990; *Guardian*, 10, 11 and 12 September 1990.

45. IMO Executive Bureau resolution, 19 September 1990; *Guardian*, 14 and 21 September 1990.

46. Verbatim record of the NUM Special Delegate Conference on the Lightman Report, Sheffield, 10 October 1990.

47. *Financial Times*, 11 December 1990; *Guardian*, 24 October and 11 December 1990.

48. Mark Stephens, interview with the author, 22 January 1993; correspondence between Stephens Innocent, NUM and Frere Chomeley, 11 February–7 March 1991; correspondence between Cork Gully, NUM and

Stephens Innocent, 28 February–21 March 1991; correspondence between Gavin Lightman, Herbert Smith, Stephens Innocent and NUM Yorkshire area, 22 February-3 April 1991.

49. Bruce Brodie, letter to Peter Heathfield, 17 May 1991.

50. Network Security Management, 'Alain Simon – Initial Report', July 1990; *Guardian*, April 1991; Stephen Dorril, *The Silent Conspiracy*, London 1993, p. 306; NUM–Frere Chomeley correspondence on Network, 17 December 1990–30 August 1991; NUM Finance and General Purposes Committee minutes, April 1991. Network was later reportedly used by Lord Archer, the former Conservative Party deputy chairman and novelist, to try to trace the source of leaks about his proxy Anglia TV share-dealing: *Observer*, 11 September 1994.

51. Channel Four *Dispatches*, 'The Arthur Legend', broadcast 22 May 1991; *Sunday Telegraph*, 2 June 1991; *Independent*, 22 May 1991; *Guardian*, 23 May and 24 June 1991; *Financial Times*, 21 June 1991. Lorraine Heggessey later became a senior BBC and production company executive.

52. Gavin Lightman, letter to Peter Heathfield, 12 October 1990; *Financial Times*, 21 June 1991; *Guardian*, 18, 19 and 20 June 1991; *Daily Telegraph*, 20 June 1991.

53. *Guardian*, 15 July 1991. Under the 1993 Trade Union Reform and Employment Rights Act, the Certification Officer was given new powers to set up investigations into unions' financial affairs, and anyone convicted of an offence in connection with such investigations is disqualified from union office.

54. See Chapter 4 and Postscript on the outcome of the French litigation; Writ of Summons, *NUM v. Gavin Lightman and Penguin Books*, 21 June 1991; *Yorkshire Post*, 24 and 25 April 1991; *Guardian*, 24 June 1991.

55. *Guardian*, 3 August 1992; KPMG Peat Marwick, Offer in Settlement, 11 May 1992; Inland Revenue Special Office (Bristol), letter of agreement, 14 May 1992; NUM Report to Inland Revenue Special Office, Bristol, and Review by KPMG, 15 August 1991; Lightman, *The Lightman Report*, pp. 17–18, 111–19 and 125–7. The assessment of the ownership of the MACF money was also applied to one other of the independent accounts used during and after the 1984–5 strike: that in the name of the Sheffield Women's Action Group (SWAG).

56. Arthur Scargill, note to the author, 22 March 1994; Sarah Burton, interview with the author, 27 April 1993; *Financial Times*, 8 October 1990; Record of NUM 1992 Annual Conference.

57. High Court Chancery Division, CH. 1991-T-No. 7199, Order, 23 December 1993, entered 11 January 1994, and Writ of Summons, 21 June 1991; *Guardian*, 20 May 1994; Sarah Burton, interview with the author, 27 April 1993.

58. NUM Annual Conference, Scarborough, 2 July 1992. Peter Heathfield died in 2010.

## 3: DANGEROUS LIAISONS

1. Victor Serge, *What Everyone Should Know About State Repression* [1926], London 1979. Serge was a Belgian socialist who worked for the Comintern after the Bolshevik Revolution; his booklet was based on an analysis of the files of the Tsarist political police, the Okhrana.

2. *Sunday Telegraph*, 24 October 1993.

3. Roger Windsor, interview with the author, 22 August 1990; *Guardian*, 23 August 1990; Roger Windsor, interview with Lorraine Heggessey, Channel Four *Dispatches*, 1991; *Daily Mirror*, 6 March 1990.

4. Altaf Abbasi, interview with the author, 14 May 1993; *Guardian*, 6 January 1994.

5. *Sunday Times*, 28 October and 4 November 1984; *Independent on Sunday*, 5 September 1993; Peter Wilsher, Donald Macintyre and Michael Jones, *Strike*, London 1985, p. 191.

6. Altaf Abbasi, interview with the author, 14 May 1993, and interview with Oliver Wilson, 11 June 1994; *Independent on Sunday*, 5 September 1993; *Daily Mirror*, 5 March 1990; Central Television, *Cook Report*, 'Where Did the Money Go?', broadcast 5 March 1990. In an interview with Callum Macrae on 20 October 1994, Windsor said he believed Abbasi had made his initial approach to the NUM through a Labour MP, after which Abbasi wrote to Scargill.

7. *Sunday Correspondent*, 11 March 1990; *Sunday Times*, 28 and 4 November 1984; *Sunday Times*, 7 April 1985.

8. Roger Windsor, interview with Lorraine Heggessey, Channel Four *Dispatches*, 1991; *Independent on Sunday*, 5 September 1993; Arthur Scargill, confidential submission to the Lightman Inquiry, pp. 22–3; *Sunday Times*, 28 October 1984 and 5 August 1990; *Daily Mirror*, 5 March 1990; *Sunday Correspondent*, 11 March 1990.

9. Alain Simon, interview with the author, 2 April 1991; Altaf Abbasi, interview with the author, 14 May 1993; Gavin Lightman, *The Lightman Report*, London 1990, p. 67.

10. *Daily Mirror*, 5 March 1990; Roger Windsor, interview with Lorraine Heggessey, Channel Four *Dispatches*, 1991; Altaf Abbasi, interview with the author, 14 May 1993.

11. Altaf Abbasi, interview with Oliver Wilson, 11 June 1994.

12. Lightman, *The Lightman Report*, pp. 64–5; Peter McNestry, interview with Lorraine Heggessey, Channel Four *Dispatches*, 1991.

13. Sarah Burton, interview with the author, 27 April 1993.

14. Wilsher et al., *Strike*, p. x.

15. *Independent on Sunday*, 5 September 1993; Roger Windsor, interview with Richard Norton-Taylor, 22 July 1993; Wilsher et al., *Strike*, p. 190.

16. *Daily Mail*, 29 October and 2 November 1984; *Guardian*, 29 October 1984; *Daily Express*, 29 October 1984; *Yorkshire Post*, 29 October 1984; *Daily*

*Mirror*, 5 March 1990; Wilsher et al., *Strike*, p. 189.

17. 'The Men Who Kept the Lights On', BBC2 Television, broadcast 23 April 1994.

18. *Guardian and Daily Mail*, 29 October 1984; *Sunday Times*, 4 November 1984; Wilsher et al., *Strike*, p. 193; Channel Four *Dispatches*, 'The Arthur Legend', broadcast 22 May 1991.

19. Arthur Scargill, interview with the author, 28 August 1990; *Daily Mirror*, 5 March 1990.

20. Nicholas Jones, *Strikes and the Media*, Oxford 1986, pp. 156–9.

21. *Daily Express* and *Daily Mail*, 19 November 1984.

22. *Observer*, 13 January 1985; Altaf Abbasi, interview with the author, 14 May 1993; the Gill–Abbasi meeting was referred to in Gill's trial at the Old Bailey, *Daily Telegraph*, 21 March 1986.

23. Altaf Abbasi, interview with the author, 14 May 1993; *City Limits*, 12 July 1990; *Daily Mirror*, 7 March 1990; *Sunday Times*, 4 November 1984.

24. *Rotherham Advertiser*, 7 August 1987; Dave Feickert, interview with the author, 5 June 1993, and letter to the author, 19 September 1993; *Daily Mirror*, 7 March 1990.

25. Film of Scargill at Goldthorpe on the morning of 4 December 1984 was shown on the Channel Four *Dispatches* programme, 'Spy in the Camp', broadcast 23 November 1994; Roger Windsor, interview with Lorraine Heggessey, Channel Four *Dispatches*, 1991; *Daily Mirror*, 7 March 1990; *The Times*, *Yorkshire Post* and *Sheffield Star*, 5 December 1984; *Free Press* (Journal of the Campaign for Press and Broadcasting Freedom), June 1991. In an interview with Callum Macrae for Channel Four *Dispatches* on 20 October 1994, Windsor conceded that the story about storing money in biscuit tins was '*Daily Mail* talk, if you like'.

26. Stephen Hudson, Ian White, Hazel Riley and Nell Myers, unpublished transcript of oral evidence to the Lightman Inquiry, 24 May 1990; Peter Heathfield, oral evidence to the Lightman Inquiry, 11 June 1990; unpublished written evidence to the Lightman Inquiry by Arthur Scargill and Peter Heathfield; Roger Windsor, interview with Lorraine Heggessey, Channel Four *Dispatches*, 1991; Stephen Hudson, record of telephone conversation with Roger Windsor, 9 August 1989, reproduced in Lightman, *The Lightman Report*, pp. 154–5; *Daily Mirror*, 6 March 1990.

27. *Daily Mirror*, 30 October 1984; *Sunday Times*, 5 August 1990.

28. Tom Sibley, interview with the author, 9 February 1994; Peter Heathfield and Jeff Apter, interviews with the author, 11 February 1994.

29. Roger Windsor, interview with Ian Pollard, 26 March 1991; Arthur Scargill, confidential submission to the Lightman Inquiry, pp. 25–8.

30. Altaf Abbasi, interview with the author, 15 May 1993; Peter Heathfield, interview with Callum Macrae, 1994; *Cook Report* and *Daily Mirror*, 5 March 1990.

31. Dave Feickert, letter to the author, 19 September 1993; Roger

Windsor, interview with Ian Pollard, 26 March 1991; Roger Windsor, interviews with the author, 1990 and 1991; Arthur Scargill, note to the author, 22 March 1994.

32. Altaf Abbasi, interviews with the author, 14 May 1993, and Oliver Wilson, 11 June 1994; Roger Windsor, interview with Callum Macrae, 20 October 1994; Martin Adeney and John Lloyd, *The Miners' Strike*, London 1986, p. 175; *Cook Report*, 5 March 1990; Central Television, *Cook Report*, 'The Lightman Report', broadcast 9 July 1990.

33. Arthur Scargill, confidential written submission to the Lightman Inquiry, 1990; Lightman, *The Lightman Report*, p. 89.

34. Arthur Scargill, notes to the author, 13 May and 6 December 1993; Alain Simon, interview with the author, 10 December 1993.

35. The Libyan cash was held in LBI Geneva in a US dollar call notice fiduciary deposit account, number 200689–51–10 001, in the name of 'Mohammed Mumtaz Abbasi' – Mumtaz being another name sometimes used by Abbasi. The account was closed in 1990.

36. Abbasi's UK Lloyds dollar account into which the money was transferred from Geneva was in the name of M. Abbasi, number 11935100. According to Lloyds, it is standard for transfers from overseas branches to take two days to clear.

37. December 1984 exchange rates, Datastream, *Financial Times*. The exchange could not have been carried out any later than the morning of 4 December, as the dollar strengthened during the day, ending at 1.2095 to the pound. That would have produced only £162,877 from $197,000 – not enough to account for the £163,701.36 deposit. The first four digits on the deposit slip are 30–92; the full sort code for Lloyds' Doncaster High Street branch is 30–92–68.

38. Roger Windsor, interview with Lorraine Heggessey, Channel Four *Dispatches*, April 1991.

39. NUM cash-book accounts October–December 1984; Lightman, *The Lightman Report*, p. 151.

40. Arthur Scargill, interview with the author, 12 February 1994; Gavin Lightman, letter to Henry Richardson, 18 June 1990, and Henry Richardson's reply, 20 June 1990. Lightman pressed Richardson because of his belief that the 'paper refinancing transactions' had been intended more to protect the officials from receivership rather than sequestration, but accepted in his report that they were 'probably' carried out in late November.

41. The author has examined Scargill's and Heathfield's engagements diaries and the relevant expense records for the October–December 1984 period.

42. Heathfield's two building-works receipts are detailed in Lightman, *The Lightman Report*, p. 77; see also pp. 82–3. Lightman assumed that the bills had first been paid with NUM money and then refunded out of Windsor's cash hoard – and therefore thought the 'repayments' must have happened after 12

November. But there is no evidence to support that. Scargill's receipt is signed by Hudson and – unlike the specially prepared cosmetic receipts for the refinancing operation – was also filed in the NUM receipt book, no. 12147.

43. Alain Simon, interview with the author, 10 December 1993, and interview with Callum Macrae, 19 October 1994.

44. Margaret Thatcher, interviewed in 'The Thatcher Years', Part 2, BBC Television, 15 October 1993; 'The Men Who Kept the Lights On', BBC2 Television, broadcast 23 April 1994.

45. Steve Hudson, interview with the author, 18 February 1994; NUM cash-book account, October–December 1984. It seems likely that the rewriting was done after the appointment of a receiver at the beginning of December, which meant accounts and receipts would be under direct scrutiny.

46. Salem Ibrahim, interview with the author, 11 December 1993; *Daily Mirror*, 5 and 7 March 1990.

47. Salem Ibrahim, interview with the author, 11 December 1993; Arthur Scargill, notes to the author, 13 May and 6 December 1993.

48. Wilsher et al., *Strike*, p. 194.

49. George Galloway, interview with the author, 9 March 1993. Murtaza Bhutto was killed in 1996, his sister Benazir in 2007.

50. Roger Windsor, interview with Callum Macrae for Channel Four *Dispatches*, 20 October 1994; Altaf Abbasi, interview with Oliver Wilson, 16 August 1994; Altaf Abbasi, interview with the author, 14 May 1993; *Independent on Sunday*, 5 September 1993; *Sheffield Star*, 21 May and 30 December 1992; *Guardian* 31 March and 28 May 1986.

## 4: THE STRANGE WORLD OF ROGER WINDSOR

1. E. P. Thompson, *The Making of the English Working Class*, Harmondsworth 1963 and 1980, p. 539.

2. Roger Windsor, interview with Lorraine Heggessey, Channel Four *Dispatches*, 1991; *Independent on Sunday*, 5 September 1993; Roger Windsor, application for the post of NUM finance officer, 13 November 1982.

3. *Washington Post*, 9 July 1984; Don Thomson and Rodney Larson, *Where Were You, Brother?*, London 1978, pp. 5–16; Philip Agee, *Inside the Company – CIA Diary*, Harmondsworth 1975, pp. 74–7; *Tribune*, 2 and 30 September 1988; *International Labour Reports*, no. 33, May–June 1989; *Time* magazine, 24 February 1992.

4. Harry Batchelor, interview with Ian Pollard, 14 August 1993; Agee, *Inside the Company – CIA Diary*, p. 76.

5. *Guardian*, 1 January 1994; William Blum, *The CIA: A Forgotten History*, London 1986, pp. 117–23; Jonathan Bloch and Patrick Fitzgerald, *British*

*Intelligence and Covert Action*, London 1983, p. 31; Stephen Dorril, *The Silent Conspiracy*, London 1993, p. 38.

6. *International Labour Reports*, no. 33, May/June 1989; according to the 1985 NED report, its funds were used for programmes run jointly by the PSI and the US public service union AFSCME; *Independent on Sunday*, 5 September 1993.

7. Colin Humphries and Harry Batchelor, interviews with Ian Pollard, 14 and 16 August 1993.

8. Alf King and Ted Pauling, interviews with Ian Pollard, August 1993; Victor Shonfield, interview with the author, January 1992.

9. Victor Shonfield, interview with the author, January 1992; Pete Willsman, interview with the author, 16 June 1993; *Independent on Sunday*, 5 September 1993.

10. Ray Alderson, interview with the author, 11 June 1993.

11. In the case of national CND, some records from that period have been lost; there is also the possibility that Windsor may have been a member of a local CND group. Tony Baker, interview with Ian Pollard, August 1993.

12. Rodney Bickerstaffe, interview with the author, 1 July 1993; Arthur Scargill, interview with the author, 23 June 1993.

13. Derek Gladwyn, interview with Ian Pollard, 15 January 1991; Colin Humphries, interview with Ian Pollard, 14 August 1993; Ray Alderson, interview with the author, 11 June 1993.

14. Dave Feickert, interview with the author, 5 June 1993; Kim Howells, interviews with the author, 22 June and 22 July 1993; Yorkshire Television, 22 July 1993.

15. Peter Heathfield, interview with the author, 27 March 1993; Roger Windsor, 'Scargill's Wondrous Web', unpublished article, submitted to the *Guardian* 27 May 1991.

16. Roy Ottey, *The Strike*, London 1985, pp. 71–73.

17. Steve Hudson, unpublished evidence to the Lightman Inquiry, 24 May 1990; Kim Howells, interview with the author, 22 June 1993; Martin Adeney and John Lloyd, *The Miners' Strike*, London 1986 and 1988, p. 111.

18. Nicholas Jones, BBC Radio 4 *International Assignment*, 'Code Word Tuscany', broadcast 21 March 1986.

19. Roger Windsor, interview with Lorraine Heggessey, Channel Four *Dispatches*, 1991; *Sunday Times*, 2 December 1984; Gavin Lightman, *The Lightman Report*, London 1990, pp. 21–2 and pp. 72–3.

20. Lightman, *The Lightman Report*, pp. 72–3 and 108–9. Windsor had said he believed he had the go-ahead to activate the company.

21. Arthur Scargill, interview with the author, 17 January 1992; see Chapter 7 for a discussion of how the NUM's funds were traced.

22. Sarah Burton, interview with the author, 27 April 1993; statement by Brian Thompson, 25 October 1986; statements by Roger Windsor and Steve Hudson in preparation for the breach-of-trust case, 13 and 15 December

1985; Gavin Lightman, *A Trade Union in Chains: Scargill Unbound*, London 1987, p. 3.

23. Peter Heathfield, interview with the author, 27 March 1993; *Independent on Sunday*, 5 September 1993.

24. Peter McNestry, interview with the author, 4 March 1994; Peter Wilsher, Donald Macintyre and Michael Jones, *Strike*, London 1985, p. 128.

25. Roger Windsor, interview with the author, 4 February 1992; telegram to 2nd European Department, Soviet Foreign Ministry, 15 November 1984, now held in the CPSU Central Committee Archives, Moscow.

26. Mick Clapham, interview with the author, 15 June 1993; Dave Feickert, interview with the author, 5 June 1993; Peter Heathfield, interview with the author, 27 March 1993.

27. Arthur Scargill, interview with the author, 28 March 1993; Peter Heathfield, interview with the author, 27 March 1993; a series of Windsor blunders were listed in a confidential report made to the NUM national executive, 17 October 1989.

28. Arthur Scargill, interview with the author, 28 March 1993; Dave Feickert, interview with the author, 5 June 1993; Mick Clapham, interview with the author, 15 June 1993.

29. Dave Feickert, interview with the author, 5 June 1993.

30. Sarah Burton, interview with the author, 27 April 1993; Arthur Scargill, interview with the author, 28 March 1993; written statement by Roger Windsor in preparation for the breach-of-trust case, 13 December 1985; *Yorkshire Post*, 24 and 25 April 1991.

31. Arthur Scargill, interview with the author, 10 August 1993.

32. Frank Watters, *Being Frank*, Doncaster 1992, p. 151–5; Tony Hall, *King Coal*, Harmondsworth 1981, pp. 57–8.

33. Verbatim record of NUM Annual Conference, Great Yarmouth, 1988; *Guardian*, 25 June 1988.

34. Dave Feickert, letter to the author, 19 September 1993.

35. Scargill's first meeting with Windsor, Clapham and Feickert about Resolution 13 was on 4 July 1988.

36. Memo by Mick Clapham and Dave Feickert, 18 December 1990; Mick Clapham, interview with the author, 15 June 1993; Dave Feickert, interview with the author, 5 June 1993; Dave Feickert, letter to the author, 19 September 1993; Arthur Scargill and Peter Heathfield, interviews with the author, 18 October 1993; *Independent on Sunday*, 5 September 1993.

37. Mick Clapham, interview with the author, 15 June 1993; Arthur Scargill, interviews with the author, 28 March and 18 October 1993; Dave Feickert, interview with the author, 5 June 1993; Dave Feickert, letter to the author, 19 September 1993.

38. Roger Windsor, interview with the *Sheffield Star*, August 1992; Dave Feickert, letter to the author, 19 September 1993, and interview with the author, 5 June 1993; Lightman, *The Lightman Report*, pp. 106–9.

39. Scargill's note of the meeting with Windsor was typed up by Nell Myers the same evening, 20 July 1989; Roger Windsor, letter to Peter Heathfield, 28 July 1989; *Guardian*, 23 August 1990.

40. Roger Windsor, interview with the author, 22 August 1990; *Guardian*, 23 August 1990; Roger Windsor, 'Scargill's Wondrous Web', 27 May 1991; Roger Windsor, interview with Lorraine Heggessey, Channel Four *Dispatches*, 1991; Roger Windsor, letter to the *Guardian*, July 1993; *Independent on Sunday*, 19 September 1993.

41. Arthur Scargill, interview with the author, 28 March 1993; Roger Windsor, interview with Lorraine Heggessey, Channel Four *Dispatches*, 1991; *Independent on Sunday*, 5 September 1993.

42. Vic Allen, interview with the author, 27 March 1993; Dave Feickert, interview with the author, 5 June 1993.

43. Peter Heathfield, interview with the author, 27 March 1993; Scargill's note of the Windsor resignation meeting, 20 July 1993.

44. Arthur Scargill and Margaret Fellows, head of NUM administration, interviews with the author, 28 March 1993; Kevin Richards, affidavit sworn 7 September 1993. Contrary to what is claimed in *The Lightman Report*, Sarah Burton confirms that Scargill contacted her about the Prendergast letter, Oakedge and thefts from his office immediately after his interview with Windsor. It was the lawyers who advised a delay in going to the police. Sarah Burton, interview with the author, 27 April 1993; Arthur Scargill, interview with the author, 28 March 1993; Lightman, *The Lightman Report*, p. 110.

45. Kevin Richards' affidavit, 7 September 1993; Arthur Scargill, interview with the author, 28 March 1993.

46. *Sheffield Star*, 1 September 1992; *Independent on Sunday*, 5 September 1993.

47. Roger Windsor, interview with Callum Macrae for Channel Four *Dispatches*, 20 October 1994; Sarah Burton, interview with the author, 27 April 1993; Peter Carter-Ruck, letter to Seifert Sedley Williams, 3 October 1990. Total costs and damages paid by the NUM in the Prendergast case were £193,295. £50,000 was paid into court and Prendergast's costs were £90,000.

48. Roger Windsor, interview with Lorraine Heggessey, Channel Four *Dispatches*, 1991; Lightman, *The Lightman Report*, pp. 96–7 and 154–7; Scargill's note of the Windsor meeting, 20 July 1989.

49. *Daily Mirror*, 9 July 1990; Lightman, *The Lightman Report*, p. 155.

50. Michael Ansell, submission to the French court, 2 October 1990; David Ellen, interview with Lorraine Heggessey, Channel Four *Dispatches*, 1991.

51. Judgement given by the Angoulême High Court, no. 232/94, *IMO* v. *Windsor*, 3 November 1994; *Guardian*, 23 November 1994; Marguerite Girardeau, handwriting expert to GGCF in Angoulême county court, Bordeaux, 12 November 1991; Michael Ansell, submission to the court and letter to Stephens Innocent, 21 and 28 September 1992; Roger Laufer, expert

submission to Angoulême county court, 23 October 1993; Roger Windsor, letter to Arthur Scargill, 2 September 1989; *Independent on Sunday*, 5 September 1993; *Daily Mirror*, 5 March and 9 July 1990. Windsor has also said he would consider 'repaying' Libya. Windsor's property in France was sold by court order in 2010 and his share of £104,863 paid to the IEMO in 2012. In 2013, Worcester County Court calculated his outstanding debt at £389,099 and made an attachment of earnings order of £350 a month against his NUM pension.

52. Pete Carter, interview with the author, 11 January 1995; Nina Temple, letter to the author, 1 December 1994; Jean Lafontaine, interview with the author, September 1991; *Guardian*, 28 September 1991; Roger Windsor, interview with Lorraine Heggessey, Channel Four *Dispatches*, 1991; Channel Four TV *Dispatches*, 'The Arthur Legend', broadcast 22 May 1991; Windsor, 'Scargill's Wondrous Web', 27 May 1991; *Private Eye*, 11 September 1992; *Independent on Sunday*, 5 September 1993. Others around Democratic Left who have been in touch with Windsor about properties in France include Hugh Tisdale and Bert Munro – though Windsor has no link with the organization itself.

53. Sarah Burton, interview with the author, 27 April 1993; Dave Feickert, interview with the author, 5 June 1993.

54. Roy Greenslade, interview with the author, 19 March 1993.

55. Roger Windsor, book proposal submitted to Verso, 18 June 1992.

56. *Guardian*, 17 January 1992; House of Commons Early Day Motion, *Guardian*, 18 December 1991.

57. Tam Dalyell, interview with the author and Richard Norton-Taylor, January 1992; Tam Dalyell, *Misrule*, London 1987, pp. 1–28.

58. Tam Dalyell, interview with the author, 2 March 1993; Tam Dalyell, interview with the author and Richard Norton-Taylor, January 1992; *Daily Mirror*, 18 January 1992; Roger Windsor, interview with Lorraine Heggessey, Channel Four *Dispatches*, 1991.

59. Tam Dalyell, letter to the author, 13 March 1993; *Guardian*, 19 November 1994.

60. House of Commons, Early Day Motion 2352, 'Mrs Stella Rimington and the Miners' Union', 20 July 1993; *Guardian*, 22 July 1993.

61. See Chapter 7. Altaf Abbasi, interview with Oliver Wilson, 11 June 1994; *Daily Express*, 22 July 1993; House of Commons, amendments to EDM 2352, 21 and 22 July 1993; *Independent on Sunday*, 5 September 1993.

62. *Guardian*, 23 and 26 July 1993; Hansard, Prime Minister's written answers, reply to George Galloway, 12 June 1991.

63. Roger Windsor, open letter to Stella Rimington, *Observer*, 25 July 1993; *Independent on Sunday*, 5 September 1993.

## 5: ALL MAXWELL'S MEN

1. *Independent*, 22 October 1987.

2. *Guardian*, 5 March 1990.

3. *Times*, 6 March 1990.

4. John Pilger, interview with the author, 11 March 1993.

5. The key passage from the damning 1971 DTI report on Maxwell is reprinted in Tom Bower, *Maxwell*, London 1992, p. 287.

6. Stephen Dorril, *The Silent Conspiracy*, London 1993, p. 276; Bower, *Maxwell*, pp. 57, 59 and 91–2; *Private Eye*, 3 July 1992; *Central Intelligence Machinery*, HMSO, London 1993.

7. *Guardian*, 5 March 1990; Bower, *Maxwell*, pp. 143–8, 331 and 501.

8. Oleg Gordievsky, *Next Stop Execution*, London 1995, pp. 293–5; Dorril, *The Silent Conspiracy*, pp. 277–8; *Sunday Times*, 15 December 1991; *Independent*, 3 January 1992; *Sunday Express*, 15 March 1992.

9. Seymour Hersh, *The Samson Option*, London 1991, pp. 308–15.

10. Roy Greenslade, *Maxwell's Fall*, London 1992, p. 333.

11. Nicholas Davies, *The Unknown Maxwell*, London 1992, p. 307; Bower, *Maxwell*, pp. 552–4.

12. Greenslade, *Maxwell's Fall*, pp. 359 and 365.

13. Nicholas Davies, *The Unknown Maxwell*, London 1992, pp. 329 and 340; Dorril, *The Silent Conspiracy*, p. 278; Bower, *Maxwell*, p. 568; Greenslade, *Maxwell's Fall*, pp. 208–9 and 338–9.

14. Greenslade, *Maxwell's Fall*, p. 358.

15. John Pilger, *Heroes*, London 1986, p. 551; Bower, *Maxwell*, pp. 382 and 388.

16. Bower, *Maxwell*, pp. 385–6; Pilger, *Heroes*, p. 552.

17. Bower, *Maxwell*, p. 351.

18. John Pilger, interview with the author, 11 March 1993; Bower, *Maxwell*, p. 386; *New Statesman & Society*, 17 December 1993; Pilger, *Heroes*, p. 555.

19. Bower, *Maxwell*, p. 387; Pilger, *Heroes*, p. 555; Bower, *Maxwell*, p. 386.

20. Martin Adeney and John Lloyd, *The Miners' Strike*, London 1986, pp. 244 and 252; Ian MacGregor, *The Enemies Within*, London 1986, pp. 270–71; Greenslade, *Maxwell's Fall*, pp. 307–9; *Evening Standard*, 14 January 1992.

21. *Daily Mirror*, 28 January 1985.

22. Nicholas Jones, *Strikes and the Media*, Oxford 1986, pp. 129–30; Pilger, *Heroes*, pp. 555–6; Terry Pattinson, interview with the author, 2 April 1993.

23. Paul Foot, interview with the author, 15 March 1993.

24. Terry Pattinson, letter to the author, 25 November 1994, and interview with the author, 2 April 1993; Paul Foot, interview with the author, 15 March 1993.

25. *Guardian*, 5 March 1990.

26. *Times*, 6 March 1990.

27. Greenslade, *Maxwell's Fall*, p. 111; *Sunday Times*, 11 March 1990.

28. Roy Greenslade, interview with Oliver Wilson, 6 October 1994, and interview with the author, 19 March 1993; Channel Four *Dispatches*, 'Spy in

the Camp', broadcast 23 November 1994.

29. David Leigh, *The Wilson Plot*, London 1988 and 1989, pp. 114 and 157; Peter Wright, *Spycatcher*, London 1987, p. 369; Stephen Dorril and Robin Ramsay, *Smear!*, London 1991, pp. 173–84; Peter Thompson and Anthony Delano, *Maxwell*, London 1988, pp. 185 and 218.

30. Peter Archer, interview with the author, 23 January 1992; *Guardian*, 24 June 1991; *Free Press*, journal of the Campaign for Press and Broadcasting Freedom, June 1991.

31. *Daily Mirror* 22, 23 and 27 May 1991; Roy Greenslade, interview with the author, 19 March 1993; Greenslade, *Maxwell's Fall*, p. 111; Geoffrey Goodman, interview with Lorraine Heggessey, Channel Four *Dispatches*, 1991.

32. See House of Commons Early Day Motion, no. 244, 1991–2 session; the *Mirror* was anxious to let it be known that no stolen documents had been found on the premises of MGN itself, *Daily Mirror*, 18 January 1992; Greenslade, *Maxwell's Fall*, p. 189.

33. Arthur Scargill, interview with the author, 16 January 1992; letter from Michael Jordan to Stephens Innocent (NUM solicitors), 4 February 1992; complaint to Institute of Chartered Accountants, 14 May 1992 – the Institute ruled on 6 October 1992. Cork Gully and Coopers & Lybrand both later became part of PricewaterhouseCoopers.

34. *Independent*, 30 January 1992; *Guardian*, 23 June 1993; Gavin Lightman, *The Lightman Report*, London 1990, p. 4.

35. Geoffrey Goodman, interview with Lorraine Heggessey, Channel Four *Dispatches*, 1991.

36. Dorril, *The Silent Conspiracy*, pp. vii–ix; Richard Heffernan and Mike Marqusee, *Defeat from the Jaws of Victory*, London 1992, p. 111; Dorril and Ramsay, *Smear!*, pp. 14–17, 24–33, 62 and 165–6; Labour Committee for Transatlantic Understanding and United States Youth Council (Labor Desk) records, 1984–86, released under US Freedom of Information Act; *Tribune*, 2 and 30 September 1988; *Observer*, 3 May 1987; Brian Crozier, Free Agent, London 1993, pp. 147–50.

37. Adeney and Lloyd, *The Miners' Strike*, p. 291.

38. *Daily Mirror*, 13 April 1984; *Daily Mail*, 29 June 1992.

39. Robert Harris, *The Making of Neil Kinnock*, London 1984, p. 164.

40. Heffernan and Marqusee, *Defeat from the Jaws of Victory*, pp. 48–61; Peter Wilsher, Donald Macintyre and Michael Jones, *Strike*, London 1985, p. 259; Hugo Young, *One of Us*, London 1993, p. 620. Kinnock came to believe that without Scargill and the miners' strike he would have become prime minister: see Francis Beckett and David Hencke, *Marching to the Fault Line*, London 2009, p. 249.

41. Paul Davies, *A. J. Cook*, Manchester 1987, pp. 137–8; *Reynold's Illustrated News*, 2 January 1927; Adeney and Lloyd, *The Miners' Strike*, p. 295.

42. Greenslade, *Maxwell's Fall*, p. 233; Bower, *Maxwell*, p. 116; *Guardian*, 5 March 1990.

43. Wilsher et al., *Strike*, p. 183; Bower, *Maxwell*, pp. 116–49, 263–8, 297–303 and 312–15.

44. John Pilger, interview with the author, 11 March 1993.

45. Bower, *Maxwell*, pp. 372 and 406.

46. Greenslade, *Maxwell's Fall*, pp. 187–8.

47. *Sunday Telegraph*, 8 December 1991.

48. Bower, *Maxwell*, pp. 427–31; *Private Eye*, 12 July 1985.

49. George Galloway, interview with the author, 9 March 1993; David Seymour, affidavit held with Biddle & Co.; David Seymour, interview with the author, 21 October 1994; Sheena Smith, assistant commissioner, Charity Commission, letter to Dr K. G. H. Ritchie, 2 September 1987.

50. *Sunday Times*, 11 March 1990; Roy Greenslade, interview with the author, 19 March 1993; Terry Pattinson, interview with the author, 15 March and 2 April 1993.

51. *Observer*, 14 October 1990.

52. Tyrone O'Sullivan, interview with the author, 26 January 1994; *Yorkshire Post*, 10 March 1994; 'Strike – The Big Picture', BBC2 Television, broadcast 10 March 1994; Crozier, *Free Agent*, p. 254; Kim Howells, letter to Arthur Scargill, 26 September 1983; Paul Routledge, *Scargill*, London 1993, pp. 181–2.

53. Kim Howells, interview with the author, 22 June 1993; BBC Radio Wales, 'The Longest Strike', broadcast 12 March 1994.

54. Kim Howells, interview with the author, 22 June 1993; Tyrone O'Sullivan, interview with the author, 26 January 1994; Adeney and Lloyd, *The Miners' Strike*, p. 296.

55. *Yorkshire Post*, 29 October 1984.

56. Heffernan and Marqusee, *Defeat from the Jaws of Victory*, pp. 124–5; *Labour Briefing*, February 1994.

57. *Daily Mirror*, 14 September 1990; *Guardian*, 1 November 1990.

58. *Guardian*, 12 June 1992 and 18 September 1990; Report of the NUM National Disciplinary Committee, 10 June 1992; Kevin Barron, press statement 11 June 1992.

59. Kim Howells, interview with the author, 22 June 1993; House of Commons Early Day Motion, no. 230, 21 November 1991.

60. Terry Pattinson, interviews with the author, 15 March and 2 April 1993; Paul Foot, interview with the author, 15 March 1993.

61. *Guardian*, 9 and 11 July 1991.

62. Heffernan and Marqusee, *Defeat from the Jaws of Victory*, pp. 106–7.

63. Terry Pattinson, interview with the author, 15 March 1993.

64. *Guardian*, 30 December 1994; *Guardian*, 11 February 2008.

## 6: MOSCOW GOLD-DIGGERS

1. V. I. Lenin, 'The Importance of Gold Now and After the Complete Victory of Socialism', *Pravda*, 6 November 1921.

2. In the first part of this chapter, I have drawn on the record of international support for the miners' strike in Jonathan Saunders, *Across Frontiers*,

London 1989. For the history of the British miners' international solidarity, see Robin Page Arnot's two-volume history of the MFGB, London 1949 and 1953.

3. Saunders, *Across Frontiers*, p. 27.

4. Ernie Trory, *Soviet Trade Unions and the General Strike*, Brighton 1975, pp. 9–12 and 21.

5. NUM National Executive Committee minutes, 16 May 1983; Saunders, *Across Frontiers*, p. 38.

6. *The Times*, 23 September 1985.

7. Jeff Apter, interview with the author, 6 September 1993; Nell Myers, evidence to the Lightman Inquiry, 24 May 1990.

8. Saunders, *Across Frontiers*, pp. 36–9, 104–8 and 113–22.

9. Arthur Scargill, note to the author, 7 April 1994; *Sunday Telegraph*, 4 September 1983; *Daily Mail*, 8 September 1983.

10. Moscow World Service, 29 June 1984; *Guardian*, 31 October 1984. In 1983, the USSR exported to Britain around 20,000-odd tonnes of anthracite and 2.7 million tonnes of oil, of which around 150,000 tonnes was heavy fuel oil.

11. Frank Ledger and Howard Sallis, *Crisis Management in the Power Industry*, London 1995, p. 203; Alexander Belausov, ex-general secretary of the Soviet Coal Employees' Union, interview with Lorraine Heggessey, Channel Four *Dispatches*, 1991; *Guardian*, 31 October and 3 November 1984; Peter Wilsher, Donald Macintyre and Michael Jones, *Strike*, London 1985, pp. 222–3.

12. *Independent and Daily Telegraph*, 6 July 1990; *The Times*, 15 September 1984. Shortly after the 1984–5 strike, the CIA-funded Radio Liberty broadcast claims that the government had been deducting several roubles a month for the NUM. See also Saunders, *Across Frontiers*, p. 131.

13. Mikhail Srebny, statement to NUM four-man team, Moscow, 18 August 1990; Vladimir Louniov, interview with ITN, 11 July 1990; Arthur Scargill, written submission to the Lightman Inquiry, 1990.

14. Arthur Scargill, written evidence to the Lightman Inquiry, pp. 32–40; Peter Heathfield, interview with the author, 27 March 1993; Arthur Scargill, 'Miners' Strike – Urgent Need for Financial Aid', note for Soviet officials, drafted 28 December 1984, and handed to Yuri Mazur.

15. *Daily Mail*, 16 November 1984.

16. *Daily Express*, 18 November 1984.

17. Kim Howells, interview with the author, 22 June 1993; Central Television, *Cook Report*, 'Where Did the Money Go?', broadcast 5 March 1990; NUM Special Delegate Conference on *The Lightman Report*, 10 October 1990, pp. 33–4.

18. Martin Adeney and John Lloyd, *The Miners' Strike*, London 1986, pp. 174–5.

19. Roger Windsor, 'Scargill's Wondrous Web', unpublished article

submitted to the *Guardian*, 27 May 1991; Terry Pattinson, interview with the author, 15 March 1993; *Cook Report*, 5 March 1990; *Sunday Mirror*, 4 March 1990.

20. Gavin Lightman, *The Lightman Report*, London 1990, pp. 24–9, 44–5, 51–62 and 122–3.

21. Oleg Gordievsky, interview with Lorraine Heggessey, Channel Four *Dispatches*, 1991.

22. Arthur Scargill, interview with the author, 31 March 1993.

23. The decision and date (reference number IV 80/22) are referred to in the CPSU Central Committee minute of 4 February 1985: reference numbers, F4/O22/G206, documents 106–8. The papers are held in the archive of the former Soviet Communist Party, under the control of the Russian government.

24. Alexander Belausov, interview with Lorraine Heggessey, Channel Four *Dispatches*, 1991; Lightman, *The Lightman Report*, p. 55.

25. Roger Windsor, interview with the author, 22 August 1990; Rainer Kahrmann, interview with Lorraine Heggessey, Channel Four *Dispatches*, 1991; Steve Hudson, unpublished evidence to the Lightman Inquiry, 24 May 1990, pp. 10–11; Arthur Scargill, unpublished evidence to the Lightman Inquiry, 6 June 1990, p. 24; *Guardian*, 31 August 1990; *Cook Report*, 5 March 1990.

26. Margaret Thatcher, *The Downing Street Years*, London 1993, p. 369; Bernard Ingham, *Kill the Messenger*, London 1991, p. 269; Alain Simon, interview with the author, 2 April 1991.

27. Oleg Gordievsky, interview with Lorraine Heggessey, Channel Four *Dispatches*, 1991.

28. Oleg Gordievsky, *Next Stop Execution*, London 1995, p. 308; Alexei Vassiliev, *Russian Policy in the Middle East*, Reading 1993, pp. 217–21; Alexander Belausov and Oleg Gordievsky, interviews with Lorraine Heggessey, Channel Four *Dispatches*, 1991.

29. Peter Heathfield, transcript of unpublished oral evidence to the Lightman Inquiry, 11 June 1990, p. 17; *Sunday Times*, 21 September 1986.

30. Peter Heathfield, interviews with the author, 27 March and 30 November 1993; Peter Heathfield, oral evidence to the Lightman Inquiry, pp. 16–17; Lightman, *The Lightman Report*, pp. 43–4.

31. Telegram to 2nd European Department, Soviet Foreign Ministry, 15 November 1984, now held in CPSU Central Committee Archives, Moscow; Arthur Scargill, written submission to the Lightman Inquiry, p. 35; Oleg Gordievsky, interview with Lorraine Heggessey, Channel Four *Dispatches*, 1991.

32. Thatcher, *The Downing Street Years*, pp. 452–3; Ingham, *Kill the Messenger*, pp. 269–70; Hugo Young, *One of Us*, London 1993, pp. 392–3; *Sunday Mirror*, 4 March 1990.

33. Thatcher, *The Downing Street Years*, p. 369.

34. Alexander Belausov, interview with Lorraine Heggessey, Channel Four *Dispatches*, 1991; Alain Simon, interview with the author, 10 December 1993.

35. Oleg Gordievsky, interview with Lorraine Heggessey, Channel Four *Dispatches*, 1991; Dave Feickert, interview with the author, 5 June 1993; Arthur Scargill, written submission to the Lightman Inquiry, 1990.

36. Vic Allen, interviews with the author, 27 March 1993 and 3 July 1994; Arthur Scargill, letter to John Platts-Mills, 4 January 1985; 'Miners' Strike – Urgent Need for Financial Aid', December and January 1985 drafts, submitted to the Lightman Inquiry.

37. Alexander Belausov, interview with Lorraine Heggessey, Channel Four *Dispatches*, 1991; Alain Simon, interview with the author, 2 April 1991; Arthur Scargill, interview with the author, 28 March 1994; notes of the meeting between NUM 'four-man team' and Soviet AUCCTU and miners' union officials, 18 August 1990.

38. Peter Heathfield, verbal evidence to the Lightman Inquiry, 11 June 1990, pp. 20 and 32; Peter Heathfield, interview with the author, 27 March 1993.

39. Alain Simon, interview with the author, 2 April 1991; Nell Myers, verbal evidence to the Lightman Inquiry, 24 May 1990, pp. 34–41; Arthur Scargill, interview with the author, 18 October 1993; Arthur Scargill, unpublished written submission to the Lightman Inquiry; Lightman, *The Lightman Report*, pp. 24–5.

40. CPSU central committee archive, Moscow, document 106, reference number F4/O22/G206, 4 February 1985. Parts of this document were quoted for the first time in the *Sunday Times*, 2 February 1992, in a controversial pre-election selection of Central Committee papers about Soviet relations with the British labour movement. Some crucial phrases, such as 'on behalf of the MTUI' in the second paragraph, were left out of the *Sunday Times* quotations.

41. A copy of the transfer document from the Soviet Union to the Narodowy Bank, Warsaw, is held at the Paris headquarters of the International Miners' Organization and was examined by the author, 2 April 1991.

42. Unpublished accounts of the MTUI account at the Narodowy Bank, Warsaw, and of the Mireds account in the Irish Intercontinental Bank, Dublin.

43. *Guardian*, 31 August 1990; Lightman, *The Lightman Report*, Annexe W, p. 273; Alain Simon, letter to Gavin Lightman, 18 May 1990, reprinted in Arthur Scargill, *Response to the Lightman Inquiry*, Barnsley 1990; £85,000 was paid out of the Mireds fund to the Miners' Solidarity Fund via Steve Hudson in May 1986.

44. Clive Entwistle, interview with the author, 25 August 1993; Central Television, *Cook Report*, 'The Lightman Report', broadcast 9 July 1990. More recently, Cook has refused to discuss the claims made in his Scargill programmes at all – see *Independent on Sunday*, 21 May 1995.

45. Stepan Shalayev, memo to the CPSU Central Committee secretariat, 6

August 1986, Central Committee archives; Alexander Belausov, interview with Lorraine Heggessey, Channel Four *Dispatches*, 1991; *Sunday Times*, 2 February 1992; Vladimir Louniov, interview with ITN, 11 July 1990.

46. Alain Simon, interview with the author, 2 April 1991; *Guardian*, 22 May 1991; Arthur Scargill, unpublished written submission to the Lightman Inquiry, appendices 23 and 24; Arthur Scargill, note to the author, 7 April 1994.

47. Bruce Brodie's record of the four-man team meeting with Antal Schalkhammer, general secretary of the Hungarian miners' union, 20 August 1990; Gunther Wolf, letter to Alain Simon, 20 June 1990.

48. Mikhail Srebny, interview with ITN, 19 July 1990; note by Valery Shestakov, 11 May 1990, reproduced in Scargill, *Response to the Lightman Inquiry*.

49. Bruce Brodie's notes of the meeting between the NUM four-man team and Soviet trade-union and miners' officials, Moscow, 18 August 1990; *Daily Mirror*, 25 July 1990; Scargill's 1985 letter to Srebny is reproduced in Scargill, *Response to the Lightman Inquiry*.

50. John Maitland, interview with the author, 28 April 1993.

51. Minutes of the meeting of the IMO executive bureau, Paris, 19 September 1990.

52. *Guardian*, 27 August and 7 December 1990. The Soviet miners' union effectively set its seal on the legitimacy of the Mireds solidarity fund by subsequently applying for aid from it.

53. *Guardian*, 4 September 1990.

54. Bruce Brodie's notes of the NUM four-man team's meeting with the Hungarian miners' union leadership, 20 August 1990.

55. Anatoly Kapustin, letter to Alain Simon, 14 August 1990; *Guardian*, 6 September 1990.

56. Ken Hollingsworth, interview with the author, 3 November 1993.

57. Alain Simon, interview with the author, 10 December 1993; questionnaire prepared for the Ukrainian mining union republican council delegation to Paris, October 1991.

58. Brian Crozier, *Free Agent*, London 1993, pp. 247–8 and 261.

59. *Guardian*, 7 December 1990; notes of five-day Donetsk miners' congress by Cliff Slaughter; *Workers Press*, 22–28 October 1990.

60. Crozier, *Free Agent*, p. 271; Sergei Massalovitch and Yuri Dashko, interviews with Lorraine Heggessey, Channel Four *Dispatches*, 1991.

61. *Guardian*, 28 December 1990, 24 May and 9 August 1991 and 19 May 1992. The ICFTU became the International Trade Union Confederation (ITUC) after a merger in 2006, when the CGT joined the new organisation.

62. *Lloyd's List*, 28 July 1994; *Guardian*, 15 May 1993.

63. Daniel Ojij and Mustapha Zakari, interview with the author, 28 June 1993; *International Labour Reports*, No. 33, May/June 1989; see also Don Thomson and Rodney Larson, *Where Were You, Brother?*, London 1978.

64. See Carl Bernstein's report on 1980s covert US action against Poland

in *Time* magazine, 24 February 1992; *The Times*, 20 February 1992; *International Labour Reports*, no. 33, May/June 1989.

## 7: STELLA WARS

1. *Sunday Times*, 26 September 1993.

2. *Daily Mirror*, 3 January 1994; Stephen Dorril, *The Silent Conspiracy*, London 1993, pp. 142 and 429; *The Security Service*, HMSO, London 1993.

3. Nigel Lawson, *The View From No. 11*, London 1992, p. 314. The political machinations of MI5 and other branches of the 'secret state' during the 1960s and 1970s are painstakingly chronicled in Stephen Dorril and Robin Ramsay, *Smear!*, London 1991. See, in particular, pp. 282–8.

4. *Guardian*, 28 February and 20 January 1995; *Observer*, 18 September 1994; *Guardian*, 20 June 1994; Stella Rimington, 1994 Richard Dimbleby Lecture, 'Security and Democracy – Is There a Conflict?', BBC Television, broadcast 12 June 1994; *Independent*, 25 January and 4 February 1993; *Sunday Times*, 22 December 1991; *Guardian*, 25 October 1995. Stella Rimington first spelled out her determination to expand MI5's brief into new areas of work in a lecture to the City of London Police: see *Guardian*, 4 November 1994.

5. Dorril, *The Silent Conspiracy*, p. 103; *Daily Telegraph*, 13 June 1994; the official MI5 'handbook', *The Security Service*, HMSO, 1993, dismisses the evidence of an anti-Labour plot in a masterful piece of Whitehall drafting. See *Guardian*, 14 October 1988. In her memoirs, Stella Rimington says she was based during her period in counter-subversion at Curzon Street House, while reporting to MI5 headquarters in Gower Street. See Stella Rimington, *Open Secret*, London 2002, p. 160.

6 Wright said he was 'tempted' to join the MI5 conspirators in 1974, but thought better of it. See Peter Wright, *Spycatcher*, London 1987, pp. 369–70. Others are sceptical of his supposed reluctance: see Dorril and Ramsay, *Smear!*, p. 247 and 256–9; Chapman Pincher, *Inside Story*, London 1978, p. 19; Paul Foot, *Who Framed Colin Wallace?*, London 1989; David Leigh, *The Wilson Plot*, London 1988.

7. Harold Wilson, *The Labour Government 1964–70*, London 1971, pp. 307–12; and Pincher, *Inside Story*, p. 137; Tony Benn, *Conflicts of Interest, Diaries 1977–80*, London 1990, pp. 509–10; *Guardian*, 5 February 1994.

8. MI5's focus on the Communist Party in its 'counter-subversion' operations was first acknowledged in the 1962 Radcliffe Report on security procedures, and emphasized to a lesser extent by the 1982 Security Commission Report. See Richard Norton-Taylor, *In Defence of the Realm?*, London 1990, pp. 35 and 53–4.

9. *Sunday Correspondent*, 29 July 1990; *New Statesman & Society*, 9 March 1990.

10. The original contact was made with Paul Brown at the *Guardian*, who

worked on the story with the author and Richard Norton-Taylor, the paper's intelligence specialist.

11. The name of the Dublin bank has been omitted for legal reasons. See *Guardian* 22, 25 and 26 July 1991; Dorril, *The Silent Conspiracy*, p. 300.

12. *Guardian*, 22 May 1991.

13. The claim by the GCHQ sources about the breach in Soviet security has been confirmed by a prominent European banker. Alain Simon, interview with the author, 2 April 1991.

14. Nicholas Jones, BBC Radio 4 *International Assignment*, 'Code Word Tuscany', 21 March 1986.

15. P. J. Mara, interviews with Paul Brown and the author, 7 and 8 February 1991.

16. Written parliamentary answers, Dublin, 29 May 1991; Prime Minister's Written Answers, Hansard, 7 June 1991; *Guardian*, 23 May 1991.

17. Prime Minister's Written Answers, Hansard, 3 and 10 June 1991; *Guardian*, 5 June 1991.

18. Norton-Taylor, *In Defence of the Realm?*, pp. 51–3; *Guardian*, 6, 7, 8, 12, 17 and 22 June 2013.

19. Stella Rimington, 1994 Richard Dimbleby Lecture, broadcast 12 June 1994; *Guardian*, 13 June 1994; Daily Mirror, 4 January 1994; *Guardian*, 19 January 1993; *Sunday Times*, 7 March 1993; *Independent*, 1 February 1993; *Evening Standard*, 16 July 1993.

20. *Independent on Sunday*, 24 January 1993; Dorril *The Silent Conspiracy*, pp. 102–8 and 128; Stella Rimington, *Open Secret*, London 2001, p. 210; Christopher Andrew, *The Defence of the Realm*, London 2009, pp. 745–6.

21. Tam Dalyell, interview with author, 2 March 1993; *The Times*, 17 December 1993; *Guardian*, 3 October 2000.

22. Tam Dalyell, letter to the author, 13 March 1993.

23. Tam Dalyell, letter to the author, 13 March, 1993; Jim Coulter, Susan Miller and Martin Walker, *A State of Siege*, London 1984, pp. 39–40 and 103–4.

24. Robert Reiner, *Chief Constables*, Oxford 1991, p. 191.

25. Alan Ramsay, interview with the author, 24 April 1993; Joe Owens, interview with the author, 1 June 1994; *West Lothian Courier*, 24 August 1984.

26. *West Lothian Courier*, 31 August 1984.

27. Jim Neilson, interview with the author, 23 April 1993; *West Lothian Courier*, 31 August 1984. See also John McCormack, P*olmaise – The Fight for a Pit*, London 1989, p. 56; *Public Inquiry into the Proposed Closure of Polkemmet Colliery*, Whitburn, 1985; Peter Wilsher, Donald Macintyre and Michael Jones, *Strike*, London 1985, pp. 165–6; and Martin Adeney and John Lloyd, *The Miners' Strike*, London 1986, p. 184, The latter claims that 'the NUM prevented management going in', but an independent report in the wake of the strike broadly accepted the union's version of events.

28. Joe Owens, interview with the author, 1 June 1994; Jim Neilson, interview with the author, 23 April 1993; Alan Ramsay, interview with the author, 24 April 1993; Tam Dalyell, letter to the author, 13 March 1993; *Guardian*, 22 July 1993.

29. Tam Dalyell, interview with the author and Richard Norton-Taylor, 24 January 1992.

30. Benn, *Conflicts of Interest, Diaries 1977–80*, pp. 202–3 and 403; Tam Dalyell, interview with the author, 2 March 1993; *Guardian*, 18 December 1991.

31. Peter Archer, interview with the author, 23 January 1992; *Guardian*, 27 April 1990.

32. Michael Seifert, interview with the author, 12 August 1994; Wright, *Spycatcher*, pp. 264–6 and 227; *Observer*, 9 December 1990; Dorril, *The Silent Conspiracy*, p. 39; Wilsher et al., *Strike*, pp. 119 and 183; and Adeney and Lloyd, *The Miners' Strike*, p. 161.

33. Geoffrey Goodman, *The Miners' Strike*, London 1985, p. 122; Adeney and Lloyd, *The Miners' Strike*, pp. 168, 173 and 266.

34. Ian MacGregor, *The Enemies Within*, London 1986, p. 220; Brian Crozier, *Free Agent*, London 1993, p. 253.

35. MacGregor, *The Enemies Within*, pp. 224, 229 and 231.

36. Adeney and Lloyd, *The Miners' Strike*, p. 171.

37. Goodman, *The Miners' Strike*, pp. 99–100; McGregor, *The Enemies Within*, p. 231; Tam Dalyell, *Misrule*, London 1987, pp. 86–7; Adeney and Lloyd, *The Miners' Strike*, pp. 161 and 197–200.

38. Eric Hunt, interview with the author, 6 March 1994; Peter McNestry, interview with the author, 6 March 1994; Frank Redman, interview with the author, 4 March 1994; *Guardian*, 7 March 1994; Margaret Thatcher, *The Downing Street Years*, London 1993, p. 368.

39. Crozier, *Free Agent*, p. 254; Channel Four broadcast, 17 July 1986, cited in Dalyell, *Misrule*, p. 89.

40. Paul Routledge, *Scargill*, London 1993, pp. 155–6; *Guardian*, 20 June 1991.

41. *Spectator*, 24 October 1992; MacGregor, *The Enemies Within*, p. 257; *Independent on Sunday*, 11 March 1990; Wilsher et al., *Strike*, p. 184.

42. *Yorkshire Post*, 10 March 1994; BBC2 Television, 'Strike – the Big Picture', 10 March 1994; Crozier, *Free Agent*, p. 253; Tam Dalyell, letter to the author, 13 March 1993; Dalyell, *Misrule*, pp. 82–9.

43. *Observer*, 9 December 1990; *Guardian*, 10 December 1990; *Daily Mirror*, 14 December 1990; *Independent on Sunday*, 11 March 1990.

44. *Daily Mirror*, 14 December 1990; Charles Elwell, *Tracts Beyond The Times*, Social Affairs Unit 'Research Report 3', London 1983; *Guardian*, 14 December 1989 and 10 December 1990; Norton-Taylor, *In Defence of the Realm?* p. 85; Dorril and Ramsay, *Smear!*, pp. 246 and 372.

45. *Guardian*, 13 October 1994; *Scotland on Sunday*, 11 September 1994;

*Sunday Telegraph*, 21 August 1994; *Guardian*, 26 July 1994; *Daily Telegraph*, 30 July 1994 and 29 October 1993; *Financial Times*, 10 May 1994; *Independent*, 9 May 1994; *Evening Standard*, 11 November 1993; *Independent Magazine*, 7 November 1992; *Observer*, 9 December 1990; *Guardian*, 15 December 1989; *Daily Mirror*, 14 December 1990. David Hart died in 2011.

46. Robert Reid, *Land of Lost Content*, London 1986, pp. 69–70, 92–3, 100–101 and 192–3; E. P. Thompson, *The Making of the English Working Class*, London 1963 and 1968, pp. 146–7, 532–40, 711–34 and 769–80.

47. Norton-Taylor, *In Defence of the Realm?*, p. 18; Mark Hollingsworth and Richard Norton-Taylor, *Blacklist*, London 1988, pp. 147–8.

48. Paul Davies, *A. J. Cook*, Manchester 1987, pp. 26–42 and 56–7; *The Security Service*, HMSO, London 1993.

49. Geoffrey Hodgson, quoted in Dorril and Ramsay, *Smear!*, p. 282; Crozier, *Free Agent*, pp. 121–2; *Guardian*, 4 August 1993.

50. *Guardian*, 28 April 1995; Ben Pimlott, *Harold Wilson*, London 1992, p. 712; *Observer*, 3 May 1987; Nicholas Costello, Jonathan Michie and Seumas Milne, *Beyond the Casino Economy*, London 1989, p. 277; Norton-Taylor, *In Defence of the Realm?*, p. 98; Dorril and Ramsay, *Smear!*, pp. 256–63; see also David Leigh, *The Wilson Plot*, London 1988; and Chapman Pincher, *Inside Story*, London 1978, which gives a strong flavour of the security-service mentality of the time.

51. *The Times*, 24 July 1984; Dorril and Ramsay, *Smear!*, pp. 212–13; Wright, *Spycatcher*, pp. 365–6; New Left Review 92, July–August 1975; Frank Watters, *Being Frank*, Doncaster 1992, pp. 61–72; Routledge, *Scargill*, pp. 70–79.

52. Peter Wright, *The Spycatcher's Encyclopaedia of Espionage*, Melbourne 1991, p. 86.

53. *Independent* 21 March 1993.

54. *Independent*, 22 October 1987; Stephen Dorril, interview with the author, 17 March 1993; Dorril, *The Silent Conspiracy*, pp. 37–8; the success of the industrial correspondents' recruitment drive was confirmed by, among others, the former MI5 F-branch officer, Cathy Massiter; *Guardian*, 3 June 1985; Channel Four *20/20 Vision*, 'MI5's Official Secrets', 8 March 1985.

55. Terry Pattinson, interview with the author, 15 March 1993; *Independent*, 29 September 1987.

56. Hollingsworth and Norton-Taylor, *Blacklist*, pp. 122–8; Clive Jenkins, *All Against the Collar*, London 1990, pp. 160–68; Dorril and Ramsay, *Smear!*, p. 232.

57. Channel Four, 'MI5's Official Secrets'; *Guardian*, 1 March 1985; *Mail on Sunday*, 9 July 2006.

58. *Yorkshire Post*, 10 March 1994; *The Economist*, 27 May 1978; Wilsher et al., *Strike*, pp. 15–18; Lawson, *The View From No. 11*, pp. 149–51; Jim Coulter, Susan Miller and Martin Walker, *A State of Siege*, London 1984, pp. 17–18; *Guardian*, 1 August 2013.

59. Channel Four, 'MI5's Official Secrets'; *Observer*, 3 January 1988; *Guardian*, 28 December 2007.

60. *New Statesman & Society*, 29 July 1994; Patrick Fitzgerald and Mark Leopold, *Stranger on the Line*, London 1987, p. 111; Norton-Taylor, *Defence of the Realm?*, p. 77. The security services' leasing of the building overlooking St James's House was arranged by the estate agent Eadon, Lockwood and Riddle. *Daily Telegraph*, 29 January 2008; *Guardian*, 10 October 2013.

61. Arthur Scargill, note to the author, 22 March 1994; Jenkins, *All Against the Collar*, p. 160.

62. Kelly also discussed SB activities against the NUM with other people. Annette Pyrah, letter to Arthur Scargill, 6 March 1990; Arthur Scargill, note to the author, 22 March 1994, and interview with Callum Macrae, 15 October 1994; Mick Clapham, interview with the author, 19 October 1994.

63. Robin Robison, interview with the author, 26 March 1993.

64. *Guardian*, 13 June 1994; The Security Service, p. 21.

65. Geoff Seed, interview with the author, 27 September 1993; Arthur Scargill, interview with the author, 28 September 1993; Channel Four, 'MI5's Official Secrets'.

66. Sarah Burton, interview with Oliver Wilson, 6 October 1994, and with the author, 27 April 1993.

67. Channel Four *Dispatches*, 'Spy in the Camp', broadcast 23 November 1994; Sarah Burton, interview with Oliver Wilson, 6 October 1994, and with the author, 27 April 1993; Arthur Scargill, note to the author, 22 March 1994. See John Torode in the *Guardian*, 16 July 1985, for speculation about – and attempted justification of – the existence of an agent provocateur in the NUM national office.

68. Thompson, *The Making of the English Working Class*, p. 532.

69. See the account of the Malinovsky affair in David Shub, *Lenin*, Harmondsworth 1948 and 1966.

70. *Observer*, 21 November 1993; BBC Television, *Panorama*, 'On Her Majesty's Secret Service', 22 November 1993; *Guardian*, 6 March 1985; Nigel West, *A Matter of Trust*, London 1982, p. 239. One revealing example of the provocative role of MI5 agents was that of Patrick Daly, the INLA infiltrator, whose role in a thwarted bombing campaign based in the West Country led to two Old Bailey convictions and a £400,000 'resettlement' for the retired spy. See *Guardian* and *Independent*, 17 December 1993.

71. Central Television, *Central Live*, 22 January 1993. See also Bernard Ingham, *Kill the Messenger*, London 1991, p. 239. Rupert Allason, who also appeared on the programme, only queried whether it was MI5 – or some other agency, domestic or foreign – that tried to make the phoney deposit.

72. Peter Archer, interview with the author, 23 January 1992; Tam Dalyell, letter to the author, 13 March 1993; Dorril, *The Silent Conspiracy*, p. 239; *The Security Service*, pp. 12 and 17; *Sunday Times*, 13 March 1994; House of Commons Early Day Motion 2352, 'Mrs Stella Rimington and the Miners' Union', 20 July 1993. *Guardian*, 16 February and 25 October 2009; *Guardian*, 8 September 2011.

## CONCLUSION:
## WHO FRAMED ARTHUR SCARGILL?

1. *Financial Times*, 14 January 1994; *Guardian*, 27 October, 12 November, 20 November and 22 November 1993; *Guardian*, 31 January 1994.

2. *Guardian*, 13 November 1993 and 7 March 1994. Even during the 1992–3 pit-closures programme, some still insisted that the rundown was simply the 'economic logic for a declining industry': see, for example, Robert Taylor, *The Trade Union Question in British Politics*, Oxford 1993, p. 298.

3. *Guardian*, 23 November 1994 and 20 May 1994.

4. Clive Entwistle, letter to Arthur Scargill, 28 February 1990.

5. For the NUM as secret Tory weapon argument, see for example John Torode in the *Guardian*, 16 July 1985; Marion Chambers of the CPSA, *Guardian*, 4 September 1991; or Howard Davies, CBI director-general, *Guardian*, 9 September 1992.

6. Martin Linton, *Money and Votes*, London 1994, pp. 67–71; *Sunday Times and Observer*, 27 June 1993.

7. Paul Foot, speech at 'Campaign to Defend Scargill and Heathfield' rally, Sheffield, 24 August 1990.

8. Michael Seifert, interview with the author, 23 August 1994.

9. Hugo Young, *One of Us*, London 1989 and 1993, p. 377.

10. Paul Foot, speech at 'Campaign to Defend Scargill and Heathfield' rally, Sheffield, 24 August 1990.

11. Granville Williams, *Britain's Media*, London 1994, pp. 27–39; *UK Press Gazette*, 20 December 1993; House of Lords Select Committee on Communications, 1st Report, chapter 4, June 2008.

12. BBC Radio Wales, 'The Longest Strike', 12 March 1994; Martin Adeney and John Lloyd, *The Miners' Strike*, London 1986, p. 299; *Independent*, 13 April 1993; *The Times*, 5 November 1984.

13. *Guardian*, 20 June 1991; *Sunday Express*, 25 November 1984; *Media and the Pits*, Campaign for Press and Broadcasting Freedom pamphlet, 1985.

14. BBC Radio Wales, 'The Longest Strike', 12 March 1994.

15. Arthur Scargill, interview with the author, 18 October 1993; *Sunday Express*, 9 June 1985.

16. Sandy Gall, *News from the Front*, London 1994, pp. 116–18 and 158; Stephen Dorril, *The Silent Conspiracy*, London 1993, p. 281.

17. Stephen Dorril and Robin Ramsay, Smear!, London 1991, pp. 296–7; Ben Pimlott, *Harold Wilson*, London 1992, pp. 719–20; Richard Norton-Taylor, *In Defence of the Realm?*, London 1990, pp. 96–7.

18. Stella Rimington, 1994 Richard Dimbleby Lecture, BBC Television, broadcast 12 June 1994, transcript p. 26; *Observer*, 18 September 1994; *Guardian*, 13 June 1994; Hansard, 15 January 1988; *New Statesman*, 5 December 1986; *Guardian*, 18 February 1993.

19. *Guardian*, 31 August 1990.

20. Ken Coates and Tony Topham, *The Making of the Transport and General*

*Workers' Union*, Oxford 1991, p. 716.

21. Norman Willis, letter to John Major, 23 December 1992.

22. *New Statesman & Society*, 2 July 1993.

## POSTSCRIPT

1. John Major, letter to George Galloway, 11 January 1995; House of Commons Early Day Motion no. 190, 'Conduct of Stella Rimington, Head of MI5', 5 December 1994; *Sunday Times*, 29 January 1995; *London Review of Books*, 8 December 1994; *Guardian*, 27 March 1995, and 6 December and 29 November 1994; *Tribune*, 23 December 1994; Liberty – formerly the National Council for Civil Liberties – AGM, 29–30 April 1995.

2. *Independent*, 23 November 1994; *Barnsley Star*, 21 November 1994; *Daily Mirror*, 9 and 10 July 1990; Central Television's *Cook Report*, 'The Lightman Report', broadcast 9 July 1990. Windsor first threatened legal action while this book was still being written: Roger Windsor, letter to the author, 16 July 1993.

3. Tribunal de Grand Instance, Angoulême, 29 October 2009; Central London County court, attachment of earnings order, 8 October 2010; Worcester County Court, attachment of earnings order, 23 May 2013.

4. The meeting between Acting Detective Superintendent Michael Cox and Acting Chief Inspector Carr of Nottinghamshire CID, Scargill, Nell Myers, Gareth Peirce and Margaret Fellows took place in London on 9 December 1994. A note of the discussion was taken by Nell Myers. Gareth Peirce, interview with the author, 11 May 1995. For details of the Prendergast forgery, see Chapter 4.

5. See, for example, *Times Literary Supplement*, 10 February 1995; *Economist*, 10 December 1994; *Yorkshire Post*, 22 December 1994; *Guardian*, 29 November 1994.

6. *Independent*, 21 May 1995; *Economist*, 10 December 1994; *Daily Mirror*, 23 November 1994; *Daily Express*, 26 December 1994; *Evening Standard*, 19 December 1994.

7. *New Statesman & Society*, 16 December 1994; Roger Windsor, interview with Callum Macrae for Channel Four *Dispatches*, 20 October 1994; Roy Greenslade, interview with Oliver Wilson for Channel Four *Dispatches*, 6 October 1994.

8. *Guardian*, 27 May 2002; *Daily Mirror*, 31 July 2003.

9. *London Review of Books*, 12 January 1995; *New Statesman & Society*, 6 January 1995; *The Times*, 16 December 1994; *Guardian*, 12, 17 and 30 December 1994; *Observer*, 11 December 1994; *Sunday Telegraph*, 10 and 18 December 1994.

10. *Spectator*, 21 January 1995 and 17 December 1994; *Economist*, 10 December 1994.

11. *Daily Express*, 26 December 1994; *Sunday Times*, 19 February 1995; *Guardian*, 20 February 1995; Oleg Gordievsky, *Next Stop Execution*, London 1995, pp. 243 and 288.

12. *New Statesman & Society*, 10 February 1995; *Guardian*, 2 January 1995; Public Record Office, 1963–4 cabinet papers, PREM 11/4684, released under the 'thirty-year rule', which allows the inspection of 'weeded' government documents after thirty years. The Dulverton Trust accounts for 1993–4 show a donation of £58,000 to the Jim Conway Foundation – thanks to Dave Osler for his research. See also Brian Crozier, Free Agent, London 1993, pp. 157 and 174. On the history of IRIS, see *Observer*, 15 December 1990, and Stephen Dorril and Robin Ramsay, *Smear!*, London 1991, pp. 27–8, 34–5 and 213. Bill Sirs, former ISTC general secretary, says IRIS was not involved with the government or Tory Party when he was a director, but worked with industrialists and union officials to see that trade unions were run 'in a moderate way': interview with the author, 2 June 1995. The Charity Commission report into the Industrial Trust found it had 'on balance' used its funds for carrying out its stated objectives.

13. *True Spies*, broadcast BBC2, October/November 2002; *Guardian*, 24 October 2002; *Daily Telegraph*, 24 October 2002.

14. *Guardian*, 20 April 2009; *Observer*, 4 March 2012; *Guardian*, 5 December 2012; *Guardian*, 18 August 2013; *Observer*, 13 October 2013.

15. Rob Evans and Paul Lewis, *Undercover*, London 2013, pp 145–7; *Guardian*, 13 January 2011; *Observer*, 23 January 2011; *Guardian*, 22, 24 and 26 June 2013.

16. Memo to the prime minister from Sir Robert Armstrong, 20 October 1981, and 'note by officials', 24 September 1981, declassified 2011, PREM19/494 f5 and Margaret Thatcher Foundation website; Christopher Andrew, *The Defence of the Realm*, London 2009, pp. 671-2.

17. *Guardian*, 1 August 2013; *Financial Times*, 1 August 2013; *Guardian*, 30 August 2010.

18. *Guardian*, 9 July 2013; *Guardian*, 26 July 2013; *Financial Times*, 7 August 2013; *Guardian*, 29 October, 2013; Francis Beckett and David Hencke, *Marching to the Faultline*, London 2009, p. 255.

19. Jonathan Aitken, *Margaret Thatcher: Power and Personality*, London 2013, pp. 448-452; *Daily Telegraph*, 6 January 2011; *Independent*, 27 April 2012.

20. Tony Cooper, interview with the author, 26 May 1995; Doug Bulmer, interview with the author, 1 March 1995; Stella Rimington, *Open Secret*, London 2002, pp. 163–5; *Guardian*, 8 September 2001; *Guardian*, 29 September 2001; Mark Hollingsworth and Nick Fielding, *Defending the Realm*, London 1999, p. 77; *Mail on Sunday*, 24 August 1997; *Sunday Express*, 21 May 2000; *Sunday Express*, 7 July 2002; Christopher Andrew, *The Defence of the Realm*, London 2009, p. 677; *True Spies*, programme 2, 'Something Better Change', broadcast BBC2, 3 November 2002; Arthur Scargill, interview with the author, 10 November 2013.

21. *Guardian*, 1 November 2002; *True Spies*, programme 2, 'Something Better Change'.

22. Mick McGahey, speech at Mayfield Labour Club, Dalkeith, Midlothian, 11 March 1994; *Guardian*, 7 March 2009; *Guardian*, 12 March 2009.

# LIST OF ABBREVIATIONS

| | |
|---|---|
| AUCCTU | All-Union Central Council of Trade Unions (of the USSR) |
| BC | British Coal (formerly NCB) |
| CEGB | Central Electricity Generating Board |
| CEU | USSR Coal Employees' Union |
| CGT | Confédération Generale du Travail (General Confederation of Labour) |
| CIA | US Central Intelligence Agency |
| CPBF | Campaign for Press and Broadcasting Freedom |
| CPGB | Communist Party of Great Britain |
| CLPD | Campaign for Labour Party Democracy |
| CPSU | Communist Party of the Soviet Union |
| DST | Direction de la Surveillance du Territoire (French counter-intelligence) |
| EMA | Engineers' and Managers' Association (now part of Prospect) |
| FBU | Fire Brigades' Union |
| GCHQ | British Government Communications Headquarters |
| ICFTU | International Confederation of Free Trade Unions (now the International Trade Union Confederation) |
| IEMO | International Energy and Miners' Organization (IMO successor) |
| IMO | International Miners' Organization |
| IRIS | Industrial Research and Information Service |
| JIC | Joint Intelligence Committee |
| KGB | Komitet Gosudarstvennoi Bezopasnosti (Committee of State Security) |
| MI5 | British Security Service |

| | |
|---|---|
| MI6 | British Overseas Secret Intelligence Service |
| MFGB | Miners' Federation of Great Britain |
| MIF | Miners' International Federation |
| MTUI | Miners' Trade Union International |
| NACODS | National Association of Colliery Overseers, Deputies and Shotfirers |
| NCB | National Coal Board (later BC) |
| NED | US National Endowment for Democracy |
| NGA | National Graphical Association (now part of Unite) |
| NSA | US National Security Agency |
| NUJ | National Union of Journalists |
| NUM | National Union of Mineworkers |
| NUPE | National Union of Public Employees (now part of Unison) |
| NUR | National Union of Railwaymen (now part of the RMT) |
| PCC | Press Complaints Commission |
| PPP | Pakistan People's Party |
| PPP | People's Progressive Party (of Guyana) |
| PSI | Public Services International |
| SIS | Secret Intelligence Service, another name for MI6 |
| TGWU | Transport and General Workers' Union (now part of Unite) |
| TUC | Trades Union Congress |
| UDM | Union of Democratic Mineworkers |
| WFTU | World Federation of Trade Unions |
| YCL | Young Communist League |

# INDEX